Richard Witts first met Nico when she appeared in a TV programme he co-presented for BBC2. She later visited his London apartment to watch a series of films starring her ex-lover Alain Delon, and just before her death she invited him to write her biography.

Formerly Director of Manchester's New Music Exchange, London's Camden Festival, and South Hill Park in Berkshire, he now works on new opera projects in Paris. His background is music, and as a percussionist he played regularly with the Hallé Orchestra, the contemporary music ensemble Dreamtiger, and the group The Passage.

Richard Witts has written many polemical articles on new music and modern dance, and he can be heard on arts programmes such as BBC Radio 4's *Kaleidoscope*. Of Witts, Nico said: 'I like to go over to his place because his TV has a good colour, and he has records I've never heard of.' He lives in Brighton.

NICO

The Life and Lies of an Icon

RICHARD WITTS

This edition first published in Great Britain in 1993 by
Virgin Books
an imprint of Virgin Publishing Ltd
332 Ladbroke Grove
London W10 5AH

First published in 1993 by Virgin Books

ISBN 0 86369 655 4

A catalogue record for this title is available from the British Library

Typeset by TW Typesetting, Plymouth, Devon
Printed and bound in Great Britain by
Cox & Wyman Ltd, Reading, Berks

Nico ne semblait si belle que parce que d'une féminité
absolument jouée. Quelque chose de plus que la beauté,
de plus sublime, en émanait, une séduction différente. Et
il y avait une déception à apprendre qu'elle était un faux
travelo, une vrai femme jouant au travelo.

La séduction est toujours plus singulière et plus
sublime que le sexe, et c'est à quelle que nous attachons le
plus de prix.

(*L'Éternelle ironie de la communauté:* De la séduction –
Jean Baudrillard, 1979)

Nico seemed so beautiful only because her femininity
appeared so completely put on. She emanated something
more than beauty, something more sublime, a different
seduction. And there was deception: she was a false drag
queen, a real woman, in fact, playing the queen.

Seduction is always more singular and sublime than
sex, and it commands the higher price.

(The Ecliptic of Sex, from *Seduction* –
Jean Baudrillard, 1979, translated by Brian Singer)

Contents

Illustrations

Introduction

History is a truth that in the long run becomes a lie,
whereas myth is a lie that in the long run becomes a
truth.

JEAN COCTEAU

'WHY IS THAT miserable old junkie on the show?' The comedian
Ben Elton was pointing at Nico. I had to tell him that it was
my doing, and that at least she was cheap. She lodged just
three miles away from our TV studio in Manchester; she needed only
her little Indian organ – no backing band. Ben had not heard of her
reborn cult status, of the 'Nico-teens' who formed her new young
following, nor that her fifth solo LP, *Drama of Exile*, was now out
after two years of infamous litigation. He knew her as the Chelsea
Girl, the High Priestess of Weird, the Sixties Warhol Superstar who
'turned fat and became a junkie', as Warhol bitchily noted in his
diary.

In November 1983 Ben Elton and I were presenting a creaky youth
TV series for the BBC (though it was less creaky than many). *The
Oxford Road Show* was relayed live to the nation every Friday night,
produced by 40-year-olds, researched by 30-year-olds, aimed at
20-year-olds and watched by 10-year-olds. Rock groups performed
'live', sometimes really live but mostly to a tape. Nico sang really live
and I noticed a remarkable thing. She sang her rhapsodic 'Janitor of
Lunacy' without drums or guiding pulse of any kind. Yet the accuracy
and discipline she displayed was that of a classical musician.

Nico's voice had been described in Andy Warhol's *Popism* as 'an
IBM computer with a Garbo accent' and more romantically as 'a
fragile lifeline through an inexpressible plague ridden past'. Yet here
was a deep, clear contralto tone, free of vibrato and exact in pitch.
She was a professional. Nico had by then been singing for twenty
years, succeeding her career as a fashion model. Her self-penned
songs may have been the work of a nihilist, as she often claimed;
she was certainly a heroin addict. However, her precision and dignity
belied Ben's image of her as 'that miserable old junkie'.

In 1985 I met Nico more often. She stayed in a shared London
flat near Brixton Library. I was living farther up Brixton Hill, and

she would occasionally walk or cycle over to watch my TV because 'it has a good colour'. One night she wanted to watch a dubbed French *crimi* film, 'because it stars my husband'. Until I sat with her and watched the film, I did not know she meant Alain Delon. 'He's dubbing his own voice, I recognise his tone – he always must be in charge. He looks good for his age, doesn't he? I'm glad we both have kept our image. He's fifty and I'm three years younger. I'm glad you can't tell that.' I had said no such thing, but I had noticed how much this film was stepping into real life. Delon was playing a police chief whose son was accused of murder. In actuality Delon had a son called Anthony who was, at that very time, arraigned for attempted murder. I asked Nico if she knew this. 'Oh, yes; he has destroyed my son.' I was too shy to ask further. 'Isn't it funny to see this film, no? It's like a blueprint. Of course, Alain must always have some scandal to keep his picture in the papers. You remember his wife was caught up in a murder and then it was all hushed up?' 'You mean you, Nico?' 'No, his other wife, Nathalie. That was a bad year, when Brian Jones died in a swimming pool.' In this way she would drift through her history and tell me stories, many of which contradicted others.

One day she asked me to write her autobiography. I replied that she must write it herself for it to be autobiographical. 'No, I don't want it to be a straight thing. I want it to be more like a novel, half things true, half not.' I told her that I knew a young American novelist of some controversy and acclaim. Maybe she could help Nico. So, on Friday, 9 August 1985, Nico gave a concert at the Chelsea Town Hall, and I invited Kathy Acker to meet her after the show. This was a disaster. It was like two cats in a backyard. Kathy was friendly and businesslike. Nico sat behind a table, ice cold. She told me later, 'I don't like women.' I saw Nico again, by chance, in 1988, and she asked, 'How is my autobiography? Have you thought about it? I have made some notes. They may be helpful.' I never saw them until 1992, after she had died.

At the time I last met her, I was Director of the Camden Festival in London, an annual arts fixture. I had considered a Nico concert of some kind at the Scala cinema in King's Cross. It would show consecutively with the Warhol films in which she featured, accompanying songs sung by Nico and scored by John Cale for the Kronos String Quartet from San Francisco. This came to nothing, but the research I undertook revealed that Nico was far more revered than I had presumed. Firstly, as a *chanteuse* she had influenced Leonard

Cohen, Patti Smith and Siouxsie Sioux amongst others. Secondly, her image was seminal. Nico was the link between the psychedelic Sixties scene and the 'decadent' gothic world of the Eighties. Thirdly, her style of singing, her formidable appearance and her introspective lyrical imagery were 'unique' in the sense that their heritage could not so easily be assigned. As Warhol said, 'Nico was a new kind of Superstar – weird and untalkative.'

Fourthly, I saw that the impression thrown to the public by the rock press was dishonest. It seemed as though there was an attempt to write her out of history. She was a female composer who did not match the generic categories of rock or folk; she sang her own creations not with a staged passion but with clarity and eloquence. They wrote only about a junkie who once fucked a bunch of stars. I have long witnessed the loathsome misogyny of the music business, on the classical, popular, jazz and experimental scenes, and I thought it might be useful to explore her career in these terms.

Lastly, she was a survivor. She defied the traditional image of the drug addict. Unlike her lovers Jim Morrison, Brian Jones of The Rolling Stones, or Jimi Hendrix; unlike Edie Sedgwick, Tim(s) Hardin and Buckley, or Sid Vicious and the others, she remained alive and dependent until the age of 49, when she died . . . but not of heroin.

I am sorry that Philippe Garrel, Alain Delon and Lou Reed declined to participate, especially as they had the opportunity here to present their sides of the story. The Päffgens of Cologne, too, have sent me and the film director Susanna Ofteringer on a futile trawl through the telephone directory – what on earth can this clan still have to hide after all this time?

I have attempted to chronicle a life that linked Fellini with Warhol, Edie with Jean Seberg, Jackson Browne with Sid Vicious, Ernest Hemingway with Allen Ginsberg, Coco Chanel with Betsey Johnson – without falling into the trap of identifying Nico solely through her name-dropping. As my terribly, terribly close, personal friend Iggy Pop said to me only the other day, 'Nico would go crazy, man.'

Acknowledgements

I am indebted to the following individuals (in alphabetical order, as Nico would have liked it) who gave up their time to respond to my bureaucratic enquiries:

Tina Aumont, Richard Avedon, David Bailey, Binky Baker, Ari Boulogne, Peter Brown, Jackson Browne, Victor Brox, John Cale, Ornette Coleman, Edith & Paul Cottrell, Dino De Laurentiis, Brian Eno, Federico Fellini, Eileen Ford, Antoine Giacomoni, Richard Harrison, Martin Hennin, Philip Jones, Fred Langanberg, Gerard Malanga, Carlos de Maldonado-Bostock, Lilou Marquand, Anne- Sophie Monet, Sterling Morrison, Paul Morrissey, Geoff Muir, Rudolf Päffgen, Nico Papatakis, John Peel, Iggy Pop, Jacques Poitrenaud, Anne-Marie Quazza, Steven Severin, Jack Simmons, Siouxsie Sioux, Aaron Sixx, Pauledith Soubrier, Barry Tyler, Lutz Ulbrich, Vali, Viva, Alan Wise, Helma Wolff, Ulrich Wolff, Zouzou.

I hope the others will not mind if I pay special thanks to Nico's closest relatives, (Tante) Helma Wolff and Nico's son Ari. They will read things in this book which will surprise them, but I hope it will not hurt them.

I am grateful to the following institutions for making their collections and archives available, and also for their advice and hospitality:

Staatsbibliothek, Berlin; the Arts Division of the New York Public Library; the library of *Rolling Stone* magazine, New York; Landes-bildstelle, Berlin; the Polish Institute Library, London; the Andy Warhol Foundation for the Visual Arts, New York; the Library of the London College of Fashion; la Bibliotheque de la Cinématheque, Paris; Kommunikations-wissenschaft Bibliothek, Freie Universitat, Berlin; Adenhauer Archiv, Cologne; the Archive of the US Army, Berlin; the Actors Studio, New York.

In this regard I am especially obliged to Beth Cohen, librarian of *Rolling Stone* magazine, who saved me three days of dull work and who greeted me with, 'Hey, Richard, wanna hear my Nico impression? "Are there any Jewwwwwwwwwws in the audience?" ' Also, I wish to thank Mr Vincent Fremont of the Andy Warhol Foundation for the Visual Arts, who did not blanch at my use of his photocopier. In addition, I am mightily grateful to Natalie Croquet of the magazine *Marie-Claire* in France, who benignly explained to me the historical intricacies of the *haute-couture* seasons over an agreeable lunch, and I'm only sorry that I forgot almost everything she told me.

The careful translations of substantial documents and interviews were made by Natascha Scharmberg (German) and Ben Goold (French). I am especially indebted to Natascha Scharmberg, who bore the brunt of this delicate work in the spirit of *könnten Sie das bitte wiederholen?* Without her patience and cropped hair, the biography would not have been possible. Wherever feasible, the interviewees spoke in English, even in America.

Above all, I wish to record my personal debt to Jenni Bird for the unstinting support she has given me in trying times.

I salute my IBM-compatible friend, who pressed the right keys after I'd pressed the wrong one, Alan Campbell. Thank you Fiona McTernan and Bill Smith for letting me practise on you, Maria Thomas (Scorpio) for her clear thinking, Martin Lovelock for his equipment, and Louise Rennison for the world's worst Nico impression. Finally, I wish to thank Sally Holloway of Virgin Publishing for her wise reactions from one so young, my agent James Hale for his prompt reaction to my vegetarianism (just like Nico, 'except in France'), Lindsey Hucknall for the heavenly interludes, and Andrew Kay for his devilish proposition.

(For acknowledgements of permission to quote copyright material, please refer to the sources listed on pp. 323–8.)

1 1938–1945

All look and likeness caught from earth
All accident of kin and birth
Had pass'd away. There was no trace
Of aught on that illumined face,
Uprais'd beneath the rifted stone
But of one spirit all her own; –
She, she herself, and only she,
Shone through her body visibly.
     (SAMUEL TAYLOR COLERIDGE, 1805)

NICO WAS A BORN LIAR. She lied as a child; it was called story-telling. She lied in her teens; it was condoned with a smile and called romanticising. From the age of 24 to the day of her death she lied her head off and her friends excused this little eccentricity. Only Nico gave her lies their true name: 'I lie to deceive,' she confessed at the end of her life. It was common for her famous friends to lie about their birthdays, their money, their liaisons and vices; as one of them said, 'People like us are in the eye of the press, and it's fun to play games with them.' But for Nico lying was not a question of fun and games. She never dared reveal to anyone how completely she needed to deceive the world. Lying protected her from her own crushing sense of remorse. At the heart of the matter, Nico lied to shield her mad mother and her wild son. She believed she had made one insane, the other untamed. She lied to them and she lied about them because 'I didn't want them to be lost in the land, like me'.

Prompted by the needs of the publicity machine, Nico – The Covergirl Queen, Nico – Mr Warhol's silent Superstar, Nico – Miss Pop 1966, Nico – The Dietrich of the velvet underground, Nico – The Moon Goddess, Nico – The Garbo of Punk, Nico – The Last Bohemian, Nico – As Miserable as Ever, Nico the born liar constructed for herself a generous supply of parallel histories, peopled with phantom families. She mapped them mentally in the form of her favourite gothic image, the palace. Her many memories, true or false and assorted according to taste, were linked together as the corridors and wings of a capricious castle, just like the one Fellini filmed her in for *La Dolce Vita*. Nico rambled around her snaking corridors of memory from one story to another, always invoking fresh panoramas whenever the press called round, because 'they take down everything I say – silly, isn't it?' Before she died Nico decided to devise an autobiography, 'One that is half true and half not true, a mixture that cannot be untangled.' The title was already chosen: '*Moving Target* – because my life follows me around'. When she failed to find someone to write it for her (Nico was inordinately lazy), she left a thin bundle of notes to her son. They were less than half true.

Reporters of the world's press were left to untangle the facts of her life when she died at the height of a scorching Spanish summer in 1988. They found that she was born in Budapest, 1944. Or Berlin, 1943; Cologne, 1942; Poland, 1938. Her parents were Russian; or half Russian and half Turkish; a quarter Russian and Polish and German and Turkish; or, ingeniously, 'Russians who happened to be passing through Germany'. The obituaries carried these details with a discernible degree of nervousness. *The Times* of London qualified its story with 'apparently' and 'probably'. The *Independent* chose 'variously reported' and 'possibly – but maybe not'. The *New York Times* avoided even the hint of a date. *Libération* in Paris printed them properly but fell face down at the hurdle of description: 'Nico – blonde femme fatale-elite groupie-turned-hippie priestess.' The obituarists of the world gave Nico a send-off she might have died for anyway, 'half true and half not true'.

Close friends who had glimpsed her singular passport might have concluded that Nico spread all this camouflage merely to hide her Nazi origins. 'Possibly – but maybe not', she was born in an occupied land during the chaos of World War II, 'apparently' and 'probably' a victim of tyranny long before she struggled out of her Polish–Russian mother's war-torn womb. In fact this fabrication hid much more. She was born before the war. Her parents were German. She was illegitimate. That is why she lied to her child when he asked about his grandfather. 'He was Turkish. He belonged to the Sufi religion. His father was a Whirling Dervish. Your grandfather was murdered by the Nazis in Belsen for helping the Jews.' She longed to protect her boy from the knowledge that he was an illegitimate son of an illegitimate mother. Why she invented a Turkish father was never made clear, but a clue can be gleaned from a claim she once made: 'I do not wish to have any familiarity with the German people. I do not identify with them in any way, except their endurance . . . Turks are the new Jews of Germany.' She often repeated the myth of her father's death in the concentration camp of Belsen. It inspired a German journalist to ask if the family was Jewish: 'No, but I identify myself with the Jewish people. There must have been a Jewish branch of the family. And the first human beings were Jewish, weren't they?'

One of her enemies from the Sixties observed: 'She hardly ever spoke. And when she did she lied. And you felt she was the only one in the room who didn't know she was lying.' But Nico knew it, and she knew they knew it, too. Her purpose was this: she knew the truth, while they could only guess it. They would never work their way down the corridors of her palace, and never, not in a thousand years, would they find their way through the litter of facts and lies and half-finished thoughts to her truth. She thought that as long as people knew she lied, she would never be called on to uncover the crimes she had committed against her family, because whatever Nico said, nobody would believe. Even her name was false – even its gender, a patronym. Nico as Nico the Moon Goddess had no family name and thus no family. She would have been a free spirit if it wasn't for one little thing: 'We should not need passports. They are stupid. They are the opposite of a *memento mori*. Who cares where anyone was born?'

TO PUT IT CRUDELY, Nico's fame rested on her face, her songs, her lovers, and her drugs. She was the alpine-fresh covergirl of the Fifties who pigged on amphetamines to lose weight; the 'Swedish princess' who smoked joints of cannabis on the film set of *La Dolce Vita*; the 'most beautiful woman in the world' who dined on magic mushrooms on the island of Ibiza; the Andy Warhol Superstar who took acid to 'find her head' (and then lose it); the blood-sister of The Doors' Jim Morrison who chewed peyote buttons in his company to conjure bewitching visions in the desert; the composer who smoked heroin 'because I have too many thoughts'; the raddled junkie who smuggled her needles through every customs post in Europe; and finally the Moon Goddess of methadone. 'Everyone goes on about the drugs, especially the heroin,' observed one of her musicians from the final years of her life, 'but I remember her more as a terrible drinker. Beer and white wine, especially beer. Pints of it, bottles of it. That's when she'd start beating people up. You hear the fans go on about the "Moon Goddess" stuff, but they should have seen her backstage hassling for money! She was a real boozer, was Nico.'

Nico claimed that beer was in her blood. She once told a startled fan that 'I like to drink beer. As long as it does not remind me of my birth.' As usual on these occasions, she declined to say more, apart from a routine 'Ho, ho, ho, ho, ho' which was her vague, Valkyrie response to any kind of prying question. But the remark was almost true. There was one beer she would not touch, however parched. Kölsch she detested, for it was brewed in Cologne where she was born. The sight of a certain Kölsch brew gave her special grief. She could not bear to see a beer glass stamped with the label 'Päffgen', a famous brand from a family brewery in Cologne's Friensenstrasse, the Öbergärige Hausbrauerei Päffgen. Nico's real name was Christa Päffgen. The family brewery was forever linked in her mind to the father who deserted her. She tartly dismissed Kölsch beer as 'eau de Cologne', and for many years she could not even bring herself to say the word 'Päffgen'. When journalists quizzed her on her 'real' name, it was not vanity that denied them an answer. Päffgen was her family name, but she never saw a family to go with it.

There were twenty Päffgens in the telephone directory of Cologne the year Christa was born. Of these twenty several were aunts and uncles, a network of relatives comprising the formidable clan of this enshrined and complex Catholic family in this enshrined Catholic city. The surname Päffgen is itself derived from *pfaffe*, 'cleric' or 'parson'. One young cousin she failed to meet until late in life became the distinguished modernist painter C. O. Paeffgen; another was an architect. But she was not considered a Päffgen, not by the clan, and strictly speaking they were correct, for she was not born in wedlock. She never even knew her father. He was the black sheep of the Päffgens, a very tall and handsome black sheep called Wilhelm (after the Kaiser) who voyaged as a student to distant lands on ventures of a soul-searching nature; he followed the bourgeois German traditions of the *Wanderjahr*, the year of wandering. He gave Christa her dramatic modelling height of six feet (1.80 m), her wide grey eyes, her masculine, chiselled chin and neckline. 'He gave me my tallness and an overactive mind,' she believed, 'though he gave me nothing else but poverty.'

She wrote in her autobiographical notes that her father was an opium addict: 'I was conceived an opium addict, nobody would believe me.' On another page she added that he was a converted Sufi who lived in India, Tibet and Arabia; Mahatma Gandhi was a good friend. She resolved at one point to trace her father's tracks to the

Garden of Eternal Spring, the Kashmiri city of Srinagar, but decided in the end that his journey had been sufficient for the two of them. Nico alleged the strangest things about this father whom she never knew. The notion of Gandhi entertaining his good friend the opium-glazed German is merely batty, but to have him a mystic, navel-searching Muslim in the hub of Nazi Germany is inspired, and to make his father a Whirling Dervish is simply fabulous. Nico wandered along her corridors of memory inch by inch. She started perhaps with a book her father may have owned on the mystical aspects of Islam. From there he became an authority on Sufism. A few steps further and he was a converted Sufi. By the end of her corridor he was a full-blooded Turk, a Muslim mystic. She only had to turn the corner to find her castle crowded with Islamic ancestors, whirling away around her head in praise of Allah.

It would have been a terrible shame to spoil her story with fact, even the simple one that Turkey's ruler had abolished Sufism in 1925 on the grounds that its navel-searching rituals were too corny for a country struggling to be as modern as, well, Germany. But Nico could then in turn relish an image of her Turkish father as a heretic, dutiful to his outlawed, underground faith. In fact, he was a dreamer who became a soldier. He had met a tiny woman in her mid-twenties (he was younger than she) and they 'fell in a deep love', as Nico would have it. He was rich and she was poor; he was Catholic and she was Protestant; he had a future and she had none. According to the family lore of Nico's mother, they got married in Cologne in the New Year of 1938 and they promptly conceived a child. The Päffgen family was shocked beyond belief. They badgered the father to annul the marriage before the child was born so that neither the mother nor the child could lay claim to the Päffgens' lush inheritance, because his wife 'was only in it for the money'. He was to enlist as a soldier into the Wehrmacht in anticipation of Germany's conquest of Europe. He did what he was told, and Nico was born a bastard.

She gave the world her first full-throated wail in a Cologne hospital on 16 October 1938, the daughter of Wilhelm and Margarete (Grete) Päffgen. Grete was still a Päffgen by law; the Nazi government had by then forbidden people to change their married names so that Jews couldn't hide behind Gentile titles. Grete was 28 years old, not the youngest of mothers in those days but one of the most attractive. Incurably modish, she would dye her auburn hair blonde and wear it with the fashionable up-sweep of the times, a look later known as a 'Betty Grable'. The trademarks of her family

were the distinctive, sky-high cheekbones from which hung bal-
looned orbs of fine flesh; the family called them 'apple-cheeks',
though Nico said they must have meant cooking apples. Grete had
those cheekbones, a clear and regular bone structure, full lips which
she often painted within the line to lighten their impact, and a gentle
expression to her eyes, her 'soft regard'. She gave all these to Christa,
but luckily for Nico's career did not pass on her height. She was
only five feet three inches (1.60 m), though her husband was a good
foot taller. Their physical combination provided their daughter with
everything she required to become a peerless fashion model. It was
what they didn't give her that fuelled the looming tragedy.

Three weeks out of maternity hospital, the baby was christened
a Catholic, 'to feign family honour,' Nico claimed. She was baptised
Christa, 'daughter of Christ' – rather apt for someone with a
devotional, Mary-like mother and a shadowy, Joseph-like father.
The name also has a more chilling ring to it. Christa was christened
on the eve of Kristallnacht, the night when the shop windows of
Jews were smashed, leaving the high streets of Germany glittering in
the dawn light with countless shards of splintered glass. When Nico
once called herself 'a nice little Nazi baby' she acknowledged that
she had been born into a Nazi paradise. It was a splendid year to
be born in Germany if you weren't Jewish or Turkish or anything
that contravened the Law for the Protection of German Blood and
German Honour. Employment was high. Money had true value.
Good food was back on the tables. Law-abiding citizens (and there
were many laws to abide by then) enjoyed holiday trips courtesy of
the Strength Through Joy leisure service. In the eyes of Grete,
Germany was the success story of the world. In half a dozen years
the National Socialist government had turned the country round
from despair to triumph (and it took the next half-dozen to turn it
back again). The economic havoc at the start of the Thirties was
replaced by fertility and grandeur, and for the next three years Grete's
Germany would rule Europe entirely, a mighty Reich to equal
America and Russia, stretching from the English Channel to the
Baltic, from Norway to North Africa. How lucky is Christa, thought
Grete, to be born in this golden age. She did not know that Christa
was born too late to savour those rewards and too early to avoid
the consequences. The childhood of her daughter would be spent
sheltering from the consummate revenge of Europe, America and
Russia.

1938, however, was a great year for mothers. Grete had given birth in a boom time, for Germany had then greeted one and a half million 'nice little Nazi babies'. Nazis were fervently keen on family life, though the term 'family' was officially reserved for parents with four or more children. Adolf Hitler, the Reich's great Führer, had decreed that his mother's birthday, 19 August, should be a special day in honour of childbirth. Fertile wives were awarded the Honour Cross of the German Mother – bronze for more than four offspring, silver for more than six, gold for more than eight. As Grete Päffgen had been divorced, she was a non-starter. Unlike most of the other 20,000 maternity cases in Cologne that year she could not say 'I have donated a child to the Führer', for the Führer frowned on 'fallen women'. The Päffgens had been obliged to return the thousand marks the state offered newlyweds for their first child, and Frau Päffgen survived on alimony. Even that was reduced when her estranged husband joined the Wehrmacht. According to Nico's notes, she spent eighteen months in a Catholic orphanage, 'the holy sisters being very authoritarian', though there is no record of her stay. Grete and Christa endured lodgings; Nico was to spend her entire life in other people's rooms.

Grete's meagre allowance ended in early 1942, shortly after a parcel arrived from Paris containing a packet of dried dates and a fancy pair of underpants. There followed a letter from High Command informing Frau Päffgen that her husband had been 'killed in action' (Nico once recalled a letter – this or another – referring to 'death by natural causes'). In fact Päffgen had been killed by his commanding officer. He was caught in an ambush and shot by a French sniper. The bullet entered his temple and lodged in his brain. He did not die; he could have been saved by brain surgery and convalescence, but the Germans had no wish then to encumber their Fatherland with the mentally disabled. The rules were clear and the officer in charge acted accordingly, shooting Päffgen dead. It was strictly true, therefore, for Nico to say that her father was killed by the Nazis. That he himself was a Nazi in the first place might have seemed to her a trivial elaboration.

An autobiographical note of Nico contends that her mother and her father would have remarried once the war was over. She added a telling phrase: 'They were very much in love. It was a father and daughter relationship between them because of the difference in their sizes.' Nico was to search all her life for a phantom family; it is not mere affectation that made her call both Jim Morrison and Bob Dylan 'my brothers'. However, the next three years would furnish

Christa a brief encounter with the blessings that family ties often bring. As the drip, drip of alimony disappeared and the British bombs began to dent Cologne, Grete sought solace from her own family, settled around distant Berlin. The 32-year-old mother and her three-year-old toddler took the train east to short-lived bliss. Their carriage was packed with soldiers on their way to launch Operation Barbarossa, the Reich's doomed conquest of Russia. Two years on, mother and daughter would see these soldiers limping demoralised back to Berlin in advance of the communist victors.

The bliss they sought lay beyond Berlin, southeast of the country's capital on the road to Poland. In a little town lived Grete's mother and father, and in making this journey to her roots, Grete was undertaking something that her daughter could never copy. Before she was a Päffgen, Grete was a Schulz. Hers was a large and supportive family; as well as caring parents, she had four brothers and three sisters. The four sisters and four brothers of the Schulz family were raised in Bromberg, a German city long absent from maps. When Grete was born there in 1910, Bromberg was a busy market town on the River Vistula, at the point where the river runs north to face the Baltic Sea. It is now a Polish town called Bydgoszsz, but in the early years of the century it was populated with Germans and was part of West Prussia. After World War I and German defeat the land was handed over to the renewed country of Poland. The Schulzes, along with the other Germans, were invited to 'go back where they came from'. They did, and went west towards Berlin. The Nazis took their revenge on Bydgoszsz twenty years later when the invading troops burned down its synagogues and executed 50,000 townsfolk at random.

Schulz lore says that the family can be traced back to the *Szlachta*, the Polish nobility. Grete's father recounted that his grandfather earned a living in the 1820s as a dancing master, when he taught aristocratic young ladies. A noble family named Pawlowski sent their daughter to Meister Schulz for lessons. Teacher and pupil fell in love. When they married she was sharply disinherited by her titled father. She was Catholic, and if Herr Meister Schulz was ever Protestant, he converted. It is said that they lived a creditable hard-working life.

When the magic of rail touched Bromberg, the town looked westward to industrial Germany while the United Church of Prussia turned it into a centre for an evangelical mission to the east. Most Germans, including the next generation of Schulzes, found the Lord and reaped the economic benefits that the Protestant church could empower – anyone who has lived in Belfast would understand a place like Bromberg. The patronage ceased once the family moved west after World War I, but Protestants they remained. Grete was born one and remained one.

Her downfall, according to the family, came when she was courted by a Päffgen. The Päffgens of Cologne were Catholic and rich, while the Schulzes were Protestant and poor. The Päffgens knew that Grete was 'not one of them'. She was a leech, a heathen leech craving to drain the family blood – that is how the Schulzes viewed the haughty Päffgens' view of them. Grete was disinherited as bluntly as her great-grandmother had been. The Schulzes were destined never to transcend the greed of the rich. No wonder Christa was brought up to believe in fate.

In the grand Schulz family of eight children, mother Grete came third. Her best friend was Number Five, the girl Helma, who was four years younger. It was to the adult Helma that she first turned when evacuating Cologne, for Helma was also married with a young child and without a husband – like millions of wives in the war who had lost their partners. Frau Helma Wolff was then 28. She displayed all of the beautiful balanced features of the Schulzes, though she was more consistently chic than her elder sister. Helma was obliged to bring up her son Ulrich (Ulli) in a Berlin apartment she described as 'one-and-a-half-rooms'. Each weekday morning she would leave her one-and-a-half-rooms in the central area of Schöneberg and travel to her job as a secretary at a military station. She'd found a first-rate kindergarten for Ulli ('nice little Nazi babies' had excellent state provision), but her routine was obliterated by the sudden arrival of Grete at the doorstep, suitcases blocking one side and Christa, in her tiny pushchair, the other. Ulli was merely six months older than his cousin, so they took over the half-room together. The mothers coped by sharing the remainder: 'not exactly *Lebensraum*,' Helma joked. They had at least a form of shelter from the ever-growing pestilence of the war, but it was not the solution that Grete dreamt. The sisters' father and mother wrote to suggest an immediate move to their placid, rural home. A few weeks later, Christa and her mother took the steam train through the heathland southeast of Berlin. They got as far as the little town of Lübbenau when Grete's father, no less, stopped the train to let them out. He was the town's signalman.

When the baby Christa had grown up into the goddess Nico, the born liar began to pluck details from the Schulz family saga and present them to the press as her own. She told the *Los Angeles*

Times that her true name was Pavlovsky. The Russian spelling was adopted to give her Slavic roots a credible appearance; she had said elsewhere that she owned a German passport but could always change it for a Russian one. The *Guardian* reported that her Polish family 'changed their name from Pavlovsky to avoid Nazi persecution'. Some of her melodies, she once told an American fanzine, were like the tunes her grandfather played when he taught dances to young ladies 'before they danced their way to the ghetto'. A remarkable comment followed: 'Why shouldn't I have my own name and then my family name? You know, I come from a city with two names.' The interviewer asked her to elaborate. She would not, of course ('Ho, ho, ho, ho, ho'). Such dualities – Bromberg and Bydgoszsz, Päffgen and Pawlowski/Pavlovsky, Christa and Nico (one German name and one foreign) – served to promote the convenient enigmas she needed, at first to control the images that she reflected back into the world, and then to conceal from herself a disquieting thread of personal revelations. Nico would dwell on Poland, not Germany. She would talk about an apocryphal father rather than her living mother.

'I LOVE NATURE. I like forests and hills and deserts and bomb sites. Cities look best when they are wrecked,' Nico told a journalist in 1978. What a miserable cow she must be, he added, deaf to the vein of serrated irony that often spiked her remarks ('They think if I'm German I have no sense of humour'). The hills and deserts would invade her life in years to come. From the window of the rumbling train to Lübbenau three-year-old Christa could see forests, nothing but forests, flat vistas of unrelieved woodland: birch, fir, pine.

As the train followed the River Spree southeast, Grete felt the weight of war loosen its hold. War came to the city, not the country, she told Christa. A hundred kilometres down the track from Berlin, the train stopped in front of the signalbox marked 'Lbn'. Out of the shed leapt Christa's grandfather, resplendent in the pompous paramilitary outfit of the Reichsbahn state railway. He guided them to his company house across the tracks, where they would live until the war's end.

Herr Albert Schulz was an important man in Lübbenau. Although there were two signalboxes in charge of crossings that sliced through the town's arterial roads, one at either end of the nineteenth-century station, his southern box housed the levers of a pivotal junction. One line led trains from Berlin to Görlitz and Poland, the other to Dresden and Czechoslovakia. He had directed trains full of troops and guns when the Reich invaded Prague. He switched the tracks when Germany entered Poland. He glanced at goods wagons as they lumbered, stuffed with Jews, through to Silesia. Herr Schulz checked the tail lamps of trains as they passed, not their cargo. Work was governed by a printed schedule and increasingly improvised orders, by the book and the clock and the telephone. He was conscientious, his job secure.

No. 4 Güterbanhofstrasse (Freight Station Street) is a comfortable two-storey house of red brick built by the railway company next to the freight yard. 'It was an enormous house, four storeys at least, with a huge courtyard,' Nico recalled. 'Well it wasn't, but then when you're a little child most houses impose themselves,' said her cousin Ulrich, now a distinguished architect. 'I will tell you exactly. There were four rooms, plus the utilities, a large courtyard and a fine garden for the kids to play. In addition there wasn't much traffic and there was the excitement of the trains,' explained Christa's Aunt Helma. Christa was indeed excited by the trains and remained so; whenever the adult Nico saw one she would exclaim to her manager, who tried hard to look interested for the hundredth time of hearing, 'Oh, look! A train! It reminds me of my childhood, you know.'

Christa found brighter entertainment at the other side of the house, a place a thousand times more thrilling than the trains – the graveyard. The land behind the house was linked to a pair of churches that clung together for company. The Catholic church of Saint Mary the Virgin was a 1920s creamstone structure with an onion-shaped dome. It sheltered a red-brick Evangelical chapel. Jesus as an infant hung over the Catholic portal, Jesus as a grown-up over the Protestant. Christ, man and boy, ministered to his secluded cemetery where the bereaved of Lübbenau groomed their family plots behind tall, spiked railings of blackened iron. The names of the buried were carved in gold on tombstones of shining black marble. The hollowed, exotic titles – Togeretz, Poppscholz, Belaschk, Filko – testified to Lübbenau's legacy as a haven for those who escaped the nationalist upheavals of lands to the east. Broken statues of melancholy angels were draped in tendrils of viridian ivy. Dazzling clusters of cut flowers graced pea-green metal urns on the eight raised tombs of the Claudius family. Trees and bushes camouflaged the graveyard's symmetry and offered shaded recess to blackbirds, and little girls. Christa played day after day in a gothic paradise.

'She spent so much time in there, sometimes just wandering

around,' Ulrich remembered. 'I can't think what she found to do. I think she enjoyed its quietness. On the other side of the house was all this machinery and movement, but here it was natural and for children it held a certain mystery.' The mystery was deepened by the rare sight of a funeral. It might be presumed that a town in such a war as that of 1939–45 would entertain young Christa with many diverting rites of death, but the cemetery, no doubt to her frustration, was not equipped for mass burial.

At first there were four living at No. 4 Güterbanhofstrasse: Christa, Grete, and Grete's parents. Then, as Berlin life turned sour and Allied bombs unnerved the capital, Helma and Ulli joined them. The two sisters spent their weekdays at work. Helma continued at the military station and travelled over for restful weekends with her son; Grete found employment at a nearby factory that built flying boats – it was by then mandatory for women to aid the war effort. Their children were nursed by the grandparents. Albert and Bertha Schulz – the consanguinity of their names was never mentioned, apparently – had been benign parents to eight children, a couple whose marriage might have served as a model to others, said Helma, pointedly. Nico, however, remembered the occasional shouting match during which she and Ulli would escape to the calm of the garden shed. Bertha Schulz kept an orderly home and strode across the railway track to feed her working husband meals that were 'hot when I left'. To Christa she looked like a grandma out of Central Casting, a pepperpot matriarch, her durably dark hair scraped back in a bun, solid and squat, a dumpling.

Her husband was known to the children as Opi, the German nickname for congenial grandparents. Within sight of retirement, he remained lithe and active (he died aged 93, still in Lübbenau), and his constant pugilistic expression was the effect of the classic northern features of his face – close-set eyes and a thin mouth – which veiled his open, cheerful character. Above all he was a brilliant storyteller. He fired the imaginations of Christa and Ulli with tales of all kinds: traditional fairy stories, adventure yarns, romances filled with kings and castles and alien creatures, travellers' tales of astonishing landscapes, German myths like the Nibelung, and improvised inventions. The children even forgave him his insistence that they work in the fields each harvest time, picking ripe berries they were not allowed to eat.

'He was wonderful, the most entertaining part of our day was listening to him,' Ulrich recollected. 'You must bear in mind that there were few books around then, no children's comics, no magazines for us, a boring radio service, and, of course, no television. The cinema was very popular but not in Lübbenau – we had to wait until we were back in Berlin. So our Opi was a fantastic source of entertainment to set our imaginations racing.' When Nico wrote lyrics of dungeons, falconers, hunters, gladiators, bandits and the Nibelungen Land, her mainspring was less the current of the times than her childhood Opi.

By her fifth birthday, on 16 October 1943, Christa had become an Aryan's dream, balloon-cheeked and blonde like a picture-book cherub – a wilful, stubborn, avaricious, powerful, pig-headed cherub, according to the family. Apart from the gravedigger's daughter, Ulli was her only regular friend. Just as Christa was a perfect Nazi girl, he was the perfect blond-haired boy. Apart from his pygmy eyes and jug ears, Ulrich was distinguished by his devoted attempts to wear his whippersnapper version of a Hitler Youth outfit inside and out, night and day. Deep down, though, he was a softie, and Christa exploited his polite and calm demeanour to the hilt of his 'Hitler Youth' dagger. He recalls that 'When we played she was funny, foolish and silly. She liked to be entertained. Opi used to put a basin on my hair to cut it. This would amuse her no end. I would have my hair cut to amuse her. She was a very giggly girl, but not in a relaxed way. In fact, she was totally dogmatic. She wanted to control things. She imposed herself in a powerful manner. Nothing else mattered until she had her own way entirely. We would play with toys or cards – we learnt a lot of card games – and she would become engrossed in winning. She developed techniques to control situations.' Christa would drive the neighbourhood to distraction with one routine. Whenever she wanted something, she would wail.

Fifty years on Aunt Helma could still hear in her head Christa's singsong bray: 'Tan-te Hel-ma! Tan-te Hel-ma!' It was a very loud and slow siren. 'I would go to her,' recalled Helma, 'and I would go very quickly because this sound drove me mad and it drove the neighbours mad, too. I'd say "What do you want? Say what you want," and Ulli would be asking her as well. But she'd carry on with this whine until everybody put down what they were doing so that she was the centre of attention.' The cause of the braying was often trivial – another biscuit, a ball – but this speciality of hers taught her how quickly she could command attention. Later in life critics would label her singing 'Wailing, like a banshee'. She would reply, 'Well, that's OK. I am a banshee.'

Christa and Ulrich fooled around and fought. Being wilful, she usually won. When the mothers arrived from war work at the weekends, the Schulzes would report on who did what to whom. Grete defended Christa and attacked Ulli whatever the circumstances. 'She was deeply idolised by her mother,' Ulrich observed, 'and I always felt for that reason she was the "preferred" one in disputes.' It infuriated Helma to see her son regularly blamed for Christa's mischief. Eventually she took him back to the one-and-a-half-rooms in Berlin; they would rather chance the Allied bombs. 'My father wrote one day,' Helma recounted. 'He said, "We can see the sky burning over Berlin. You cannot leave your child there. Come back." The air attacks grew stronger. One night I had to run through an inferno of flames with my son in my arms. The strength of the flames lifted us up in the air. I had the sensation we were already burning. I saw my sister Dora waving to us on the other side of the street. She guided us to safety, otherwise we would have been killed. Later my workplace was destroyed. We returned to Lübbenau.'

They were not the only Berliners there. Each weekend Lübbenau was invaded by workers on Strength Through Joy excursions. The marsh at the other end of town was known as the Spreewald, and its river-fed meadowland attracted metropolitans in need of fresh air and plain sailing. The British might liken it to the Norfolk Broads, Americans to a tranquillised bayou. The Schulzes, the Päffgens and the Wolffs enjoyed these doorstep treats and hired one of the traditional, emaciated skiffs to skim around the chain of lakes. Lübbenau seemed at peace. To the townsfolk, war was something they saw in the night sky when the searchlights and enemy blasts flared over distant Berlin, something that trundled through the station to remote regions. A travel guide of the period noted that the people of the Spreewald were 'honest peasants' who 'held fast to simple certainties in a land where sky and water meet by nature's sandbanks'. The honest peasants had not considered invasion by anyone other than tourists, nor the consequences of living on adverse terrain in such a time. They were soon to learn that hell could flow down the River Spree.

NICO REMEMBERED LITTLE about the heaven of Lübbenau but a lot about its hell. 'What frightens me the most? To be in hell. I'm very superstitious. I really do believe in heaven and hell,' she told the German journal *Twen* in 1969. *Twen* was a monthly magazine devoted to readers in their twenties, and possibly because she was required to respond in German, Nico gave less cloudy answers than she might to English or American writers. Even so, there was a catch. 'Yes, I remember the war years very well. But that was not me, that was another girl. I seem to myself to be a criminal who spends her entire life with faked documents. I can't identify myself with the past. Life consists of experiences which one accepts or refuses; you are formed by the things you accept. My memory consists of shreds and short flashes, never the whole picture.'

She had clear memories (she said this many times, too, to friends) of trains taking Jews to Auschwitz. 'Our neighbours waited by the railway fences to give them food and water, but the guards whipped them away from our reach. I remember how many hungry people I saw when the trains came to a halt. Freight trains and barbed wire windows . . . I was sighing to my cousin Ulli that I refused to wash with soap made from human bones; the material for clothing had been made from human hair, lampshades from human tattooed skin.' She wrote in her notes of dead bodies lining the pavements of Lübbenau and Berlin: 'It had to be this way . . . One did not analyse the questions and answers.' Not when you were six, certainly.

Whether or not the skin lampshade and the bone-marrow soap were clichés of propaganda that she adopted in later years, there was enough in Lübbenau to disturb the young Christa and the mature Nico. Ulrich took another view. 'I can understand it when she said that she remembered only certain moments. After all, that is how most adults recall their childhood. But what she remembered is strange. I have no memories like that. I imagine that she linked together two things from the end of the war, when she was six. Firstly, prisoners on trains, military prisoners. Secondly, the chaos when we fled from Lübbenau. There were a lot of Russians, there was stress and discomfort. I think she rationalised or dramatised certain associations from these moments. Why she did so is another matter.'

Those moments began in the autumn of 1944 when Christa and Ulli started school at the age of six. Their photographs were taken alongside their mothers in the Schulzes' backyard, clasping the traditional paper-wrapped bunches of flowers to present to their teacher. In return they were taught everything their million and a half contemporaries were learning throughout the Reich – the basics of language and arithmetic, to love their mothers and honour the Fatherland, to hate the evil Russians, and not to worry about the war because their Führer had a secret weapon. The only secret weapon they saw, however, was a cupboard full of canes that one of their teachers, the stern Herr Jönte, kept in his classroom ('We were all afraid of him,' confided Ulrich). They were not told that the Soviet army had pushed the Germans back into Poland, though they had begun to see in the streets the unsupervised soldiers and refugees drifting towards Berlin. Nor were they told at Christmas that the Allies had gained Belgium and France, though they learnt that communists ate children for breakfast (but not to worry; they would never get into Germany thanks to the Führer's secret weapon). By March the Russians were close to Lübbenau.

The Führer did not, of course, have a secret weapon; the children saw merely the crippled remnants of Nazi pride, the Ninth Army and the Fourth Panzer Division, taking defensive positions in the town and around the Spreewald. They could hear monstrous explosions of tank fire and the demolition of the autobahn south of Lübbenau, carried out by the German army on Hitler's command. Because of the marshes and the springtime river, the Spreewald was the last area in the east to hold out. On 16 April 1945 General Zhukov had already started the final offensive on Berlin. He was staggered to learn that his colleagues were still facing difficulties in a rural backwater. 'We are in Berlin. Where are you?' joked an officer in a note. On 23 April, Lübbenau surrendered to soldiers of two Soviet army divisions, the First Ukrainian and the First White Russian. Seven days later the Führer swallowed cyanide as the Russians beat down the doors of Berlin. He was reported to have written 'The Germans do not deserve me. Let them rot.' How ironic that Nico would often say the same.

Of all of their enemies, Germans feared Russians the most – hardly surprising, in view of Operation Barbarossa. The communists had come for their revenge. Townsfolk were warned by retreating soldiers that their watches and rings would be ripped from their hands, their houses denuded and their larders stripped bare. The enemy had set up 'trophy brigades' to collect anything of use to Mother Russia. As a final warning, they were told: this scum will rape their way through the town. They will see a woman and shout, 'Frau, komm'. That was their catchphrase, the people were warned.

'My grandfather saved our town. He could speak Russian, of course, and he told the general to leave us alone. I remember the soldiers. They were old Mongolian peasants.' That is how Nico put it. The Slavs of the Ukraine and Belorussia (White Russia) lived as near to England as to Mongolia. These Central Europeans spoke a similar language to each other that used loanwords from Polish, a neighbour to them both, and that was how Albert Schulz was able to make friends with the communists and why Colonel Myzkov and his batman Vanya were billeted at No. 4 Güterbanhofstrasse. Helma remembers the time best. 'We had to accommodate the officer in our house. Vanya slept in a nearby barn for some reason. Grete and I already had the best room and our father was clever in the way he gave it to the colonel, because his real concern was to get us out of the house and away from the Russians each evening so that there was less chance of us being raped. We would slip away each night and stay with friends. He once said to some soldiers, "If you touch my girls I will make trouble for you", and he could, because he had an officer in his home.'

Helma continued, 'One night an extraordinary event happened to Christa. The two children slept together in one of the upstairs rooms. Suddenly Christa screamed, "Vanya's coming through the window! Vanya's coming through the window!" She believed that she could see him hanging from the window, trying to force it open to get into the room. He couldn't do it; the window was locked. She saw his dark face shrouded in a white sheet, like a ghost. The problem was, she was shouting for her mother. The children did not know that we deserted them each night. My father did his best to comfort her, but she was disconsolate. I really don't know to this day whether she saw Vanya in the window or in a dream.' Nico told a friend that two ancient Mongolians stayed at the house. 'They would watch me pissing at the toilet. They liked to watch me,' she said.

Unlike so many others in that pitiful time, Christa's Opi was never short of work; the Russians needed the railway just as much as the Nazis. On 7 May 1945, when the Reich ceased to exist and the communists formally liberated Berlin and eastern Germany, troops were ordered to dismantle the healthy rails they found in the western half of the capital and haul them eastwards to towns like Lübbenau that needed to repair their tracks. General Zhukov had already calculated how Berlin would be carved up between the Allies and took advantage of his army's sole presence to asset-strip the land he couldn't keep. Thanks to this, Lübbenau was better served than Berlin, as Herr Schulz insisted to his daughters, both mothers, both out of work, both eager to make a new start for themselves and their children. But the women could see little future in this defeated, tiny town held under communist control. They needed Berlin.

As the days crept by and the capital became caught in a bizarre tussle between the four Allies, their father could see no way of sending Grete and Helma on safely. Thousands of refugees were wandering around, trigger-happy Allies were hunting down Nazis, and the few unbarred routes were forlorn lanes where looting and gang rape were common. One day Herr Schulz learned that rolling stock in a goods siding was required in Berlin. He told his daughters that their chance had come. They must climb onto the roof of a wagon and grip tight for the 70-mile trip. Laden with anxiety they did so. They waited a dismal hour without moving; there was no locomotive to lead the train. It arrived four days later. They clambered back up and clung to the roof of the juddering wagon. Five hours on they trudged along the muddy earth of Aldershof just short of Berlin; despite their terrible journey, they had not escaped the Russian zone.

Nico would often tell the tale of little Christa and the wagon-roof ride to Berlin. It was one of the few stories she never embellished – the locomotive, the wagon, the juddering journey, the five-hour drive, the muddy goods yard were described just as they had been. There would hardly be a dry eye in the room when Nico told her simple story. The only problem with the adventure was that it happened to Ulrich, not to her: the Wolffs took the train, the Päffgens stayed behind. Three months on, when the road routes were more settled and passage easier, Grete and Christa joined a lorry bound for Berlin. Though the journey was physically easier, it was by now illegal to travel without permits and passports. Grete and Christa were no longer residents of Cologne, but communists living in the Soviet zone. In order to meet up with Helma and Ulrich, they would have to act illegally and cross borders, not as citizens but as refugees.

CHRISTA WAS BORN in a country that was heaven for her but hell for Jews. By the time she was old enough to distinguish between the two, she only knew hell: 'I cannot be surprised by hell, which I do believe in. I have seen hell, I have smelt hell, which was in Berlin when the bombs destroyed it. Hell is like a city destroyed, and it is beautiful to see.' Christa would spend her next ten years in hell, beautiful hell.

2 1946–1955

To tempt the dangerous deep, too venturous youth,
Why does thy breast with fondest wishes glow?
No tender parent there thy cares shall sooth,
No much-lov'd Friend shall share thy every woe.
Why does thy mind with hopes delusive burn?
Vain are thy Schemes by heated Fancy plann'd:
Thy promised joy thou'lt see to Sorrow turn
Exil'd from Bliss, and from thy native land.
(SAMUEL TAYLOR COLERIDGE, 1786)

'MY FAVOURITE GERMAN WORD is *Schwarzmarkt*,' Nico told a writer. 'When I was a little girl I thought it was a place in Berlin, a building like the Opera House. My mother bought everything at the *Schwarzmarkt*, but I was annoyed that she'd never take me there. Now I understand. *Der Schwarzmarkt*. It is longer in English, and it doesn't rhyme – it is the Black Market.'

There were few buildings of any kind standing in the Berlin of 1945, let alone a black market. What Christa encountered was best described by William Shirer for the *New York Herald Tribune* that summer: 'This is more like the face of the moon than any city I have ever imagined . . . The spacious avenues, once the pride of the city – the Friedrichstrasse and the Leipzigstrasse, the Kurfürstendamm and the Unter den Linden – were so covered with debris that bulldozers had to be set to work to clear a passage even for tanks and armoured vehicles. And everywhere came the smell of decaying flesh to remind the living that thousands of bodies still remained beneath the funeral pyres of rubble.' Eyewitness Wolfgang Leonhard added: 'The city was like a picture of Hell; flaking ruins and starving people shambling about in tattered clothing – all of them looking terribly tired, hungry, tense and demoralised.'

Nico called the city 'a desert of bricks' and remembered as a six-year-old, turning seven, 'seeing dead bodies lying in the rubble as I walked through a wilderness at the end of the street where we lived. That is the image that still comes in my dreams. It is something that I use in my lyrics, that hides behind my lyrics like scenery.'

19

Nico

Many of her songs are set in shorn landscapes, at frontiers and crossings, opaque and frosted:

> Friar hermit stumbles over
> The cloudy borderline;
> Frozen warnings close to mine,
> Close to the frozen borderline.
> *(Frozen Warnings, 1969)*

Since August 1945 Berlin had sprouted four borderlines – American, British, French, Soviet – dividing up little more than 25 million cubic metres of rubble. Its remaining citizens saw their omnipotent Führer replaced by four military dictatorships whose soldiers could not and would not discriminate between Germans and Nazis. The zones were drawn to give each army command of equal resources and population. The Russians governed 40 per cent of the geographic mass, east and north, but they already owned the surrounding country. The city stood like an atoll in a Soviet sea. From the time that Christa moved there until the year of her death, the Cold War was quartered in Berlin. The city, no longer the capital of the Grossdeutsche Reich, endured countless stupidities as capitalism and communism clashed across its streets. 'It really is a foolish city, like Manchester or Minneapolis,' Nico complained. 'I can't think why they bothered. The Americans put a lot of money into the western half and turned it into a big shop window full of fur coats and sports cars. The East said "We don't waste money and everyone has a job". It is a pity they rebuilt Berlin. They should have left it empty. It would make a marvellous museum now. The National Museum of Destruction. That would be fun, wouldn't it?'

WHEN THE PÄFFGENS ARRIVED in Berlin, the city lay in a civilian chaos that allowed them, illegal though they were, to pass unhindered through the sentried barriers of the four zones. They joined teeming crowds of refugees in search of shelter. Many fugitives had innocently assumed that the city's buried residents would bequeath countless empty bedrooms for the use of the living. But scores of houses were now piles of loose bricks, and the military had commandeered the hotels. Half of Berlin had been killed off by the war. Most of the two million left were female: a typical street scene comprised grandmothers, mothers, sisters and their children – multiples of Grete and Christa, Helma and Ulrich; men were foreign, wore helmets, drove jeeps. A report noted that the war in Germany had enlarged the number of 'surplus women' fourfold ('surplus' is a neat Nazi word, though an American wrote it). 'All their women, all our soldiers. We'd better build an orphanage first,' a Russian general wisecracked. In the ravaged streets of Berlin, it was not his men alone who drawled, '*Frau, komm*'.

Helma's one-and-a-half-rooms in Schöneberg had survived. There was a bonus, too. Schöneberg was governed by the Americans, who ran the ritziest black market in town. The 'Amis' traded corned beef and fruit juice, coffee and candy bars. Nico recalled nothing of this, save for one detail: 'I think the first English word I learned was "Hershey". Later I went to New York and I was shocked to see so many Hershey Bars in rows, like they were nothing.' The soldiers sold by the back door and they sold high – a packet of twenty cigarettes could cost 135 Reichmarks, the full monthly wage of a manual worker – and their huckster style did nothing to soften the stern impression they'd set. Berliners called them 'Russkies in pressed pants'; rapes were reported. Despite their posters proclaiming 'We are conquerors but not oppressors', the soldiers believed they were there to penalise the Germans, not to rehabilitate them. It took two years to transform a negative strategy of 'non-fraternisation' into the more positive frame of 're-education'. Christa would experience the full force of this change, for hitherto she had spent but two terms in a backwater Nazi classroom. Now her schooling was consigned to Uncle Sam.

Uncle Sam hedged. Incriminated Nazi teachers had been removed from their positions. They were supposed to be replaced by those who had not been model members of the National Socialist Teachers' League. The Americans set up a unit charged with the dual task of weeding out the best Nazis, as well as the worst Nazi schoolbooks, and replacing them with a 'democratic alternative', though nobody was sure what that meant in a society where 80 per cent of the entire teaching profession had belonged to the NSTL and the pre-Nazi books were as lumpenly nationalist as the ones the Americans were now dumping for fuel. One English teacher remembers a conversation with a visiting consultant who considered that 'the dreadful thing about the Germans was that they'd all had Grimm's fairy tales, which were so cruel, and they ought to have nice things like Winnie the Pooh'. One American professor suggested they should scrap the German system and replicate their own in order to 'transform German thinking'. Professor Hocking of Harvard thought the opposite, because 'German education standards had been perhaps superior to any other in the world'. The debate did not help to open schools. The army was exasperated with children of Christa's age creating trouble for them in the ruined streets when they could be creating trouble in classrooms.

The first primary schools were opened on 1 October 1945, unheated and staffed by unblemished old Nazis, no doubt reading, to the delight of their audiences, the grimmest of Grimm's fairy tales. Christa was offered a place in a Wilmersdorf–Schöneberg school, to be taken up once she had a permanent address. Grimm or no Grimm, she was not delighted by the prospect.

Although lodgings were dreadfully scarce, Grete had found a room in Schöneberg, along Nürnbergerstrasse, not far from the Kaiser Wilhelm Memorial Church, whose war-bombed tower is now a much-snapped tourist sight. It was the southern end of this street that Nico deemed a 'wilderness . . . that hides behind my lyrics like scenery'. Nico described the dwelling in her notes. She recalled that the room was one in an apartment where couples and individuals led lives that were 'shy, or I should say, discreet'. She and her mother had to use the toilet on the floor below, and rain leaked into the room. 'Ever since I was born I hated getting wet, perhaps because the wetness gave me a bad chest – a weak chest and the power to overcome this weakness by wanting to be a big singer.' That sentence, incidentally, is the only hint by her on record that she contemplated a singing career before she reached her mid-twenties (but then she wrote it when she was 47). The ambitions of this seven-year-old were fixed on a dry chest, a warm bed, and nothing remotely academic. Her mother ushered Christa into the state primary school nearby in Regensburgerstrasse, then began to look for work.

Grete was obliged to register with the American military command and complete a document, known as a *Fragebogen*, which contained 133 questions. On the basis of her answers she would be placed in one of five categories. Class Five guaranteed exoneration, Class One execution ('or South America', Berliners quipped). By the time she undertook this 'de-Nazification' test, the Americans had acquired access to the National Socialist file; scrutiny of Berliners' answers was tightened in response to a spate of false claims nicknamed *Persilscheine* because the Germans had 'washed themselves whiter than white'. Grete was classed Four, which limited her to manual labour, a penalty for her 'fellow travelling' war work. She'd won a respectable status, however, and she gained her full due in ration cards. It was hard for her to find work, but easier to make it. Grete had nursed ambitions to run her own clothes-making business, having sewn clothes for Christa and others in the family, which had earned her little money but much respect. She decided to practise from her room as a seamstress. Her running costs were surprisingly low thanks to the limited logic of a British air-force supervisor. He had read of the 'surplus women' of Berlin and concluded that they might be best occupied in dressmaking. Aid programmes had begun and through one he raised a monthly order for 40,000 packets of machine needles, 30,000 sewing and darning needles, 150,000 gross of safety pins, and cotton thread without limit. Once she'd found a sewing machine on the black market Frau Päffgen was in business.

At first she sewed at home for a couturier. Assiduous and nimble, her work was so well regarded that neighbours enquired if she would take on direct commissions. No, she thought, the cost of cloth was not yet in her reach. But the more she did, the more she was trusted, the more she earned and the more creative became the commissions. Word soon spread that she sewed for Frau Eberhard, the wife of the classy songwriter who had composed '*Aufwiedersehen*' ('Until the Next Time'). Grete could afford on occasion to fill the room with flowers and treat her daughter; Christa was the kind of child who enjoyed a lot of treats – chocolate, of course, but also opera. The opera house was then controlled by the Soviets, who made certain that the tickets were sold dirt cheap to induce poor families like the Päffgens to visit a cultural shrine to communist goodwill. 'My musical upbringing was solely opera. The Berlin Opera House [the State Opera] on Unter den Linden was our weekly refuge from our room in Schöneberg, which after a while turned out to be a room in a concentration camp,' Nico wrote in her autobiographical notes. Christa didn't play with dolls or pets (she never kept a pet), but killed time with clothes. Her mother was gaining confidence in designing her own variants of fashionable wear, and Christa would watch her experiment in front of a large mirror with swathes of cloth. The child then stuck the hats on her own head, draped the adult skirts and suits around her cygnet frame, and checked the effect in the mirror. It is said that outdoors she would kick her way through the rubble and act the tomboy; inside she played the *soignée* princess.

The tomboy and the princess played alone. 'There were children around, doing the same as her,' Aunt Helma recollected, 'but I don't think she ever made friends as easily as Ulrich, yet, of course she always wanted to be the centre of attention, whoever was there. She was devoted to her mother. It was a very strong bond, but I do once recall her telling me that she wished I was her mother. I don't know what brought that on. It may have something to do with the fact that my sister and I were very different mothers to our children. I think my sister was rather cloying. I also remember that Christa liked to fantasise a lot. She would tell all kinds of stories about herself that were cute but ridiculous. I would say, "Oh, stop telling stories", while I think my sister encouraged her, or maybe she took no notice.'

It could not have been easy for Grete to live and work in one room and take notice of her demanding daughter, toiling for long hours by the light of a fifteen-watt bulb as she did, nourished by thin monotonous rations – little more than a thousand calories a day – kindled lukewarm over a small kerosene stove. But Grete was resilient and ambitious. She lived among resourceful folk who were working for better days ahead, and there was more than the black market to help her along. Few apartments survived those postwar days without 'Kleiner Gustav', a brilliant illicit gadget that made the electricity meter run backwards; the more power you used, the less you paid. Silk was stripped from old parachutes, leather from helmet straps. It irked the military controllers to be confronted with the unceasing invention and independence of the people they had conquered ('but not oppressed'). A German historian slapped a label on the creative boom he saw around him: the Golden Hunger Years. He pointed to the new genre of movies called Trümmefilm (Rubble films) that told social–realist tales of postwar life. They replaced the celluloid dreams of the Nazi bourgeoisie, but an alternative to Rubble films existed in the popular form of comedies such as *Tell the Truth!* (*Sag die Warheit!*), about a young man who says exactly what comes into his head. Nico half-remembered her mother taking her to see this film, starring the matinée idol (and hero of *Metropolis*) Gustav Fröhlich, one of her favourite German actors: 'It was this one, or another – well, I like the title,' she wryly admitted.

The Golden Hunger historian singled out literary groups of radical writers who worked to 'shrivel up the slave language of the Reich'. He even included postwar cabaret – there was an excellent club opposite the Päffgens in Nürnbergerstrasse – where songs and jokes satirised the half-tones and subtleties of survival in the face of defeat. The Golden Hunger Years grew more golden as the Western allies constructed a new currency to rival the Russians' Reichmarks; it was launched with a gift to each adult, Grete included, of 40

Deutschmarks. Hunger enveloped these years when the communists counterstruck by banning traffic and power into the Western sectors. Thus began the Berlin Blockade, imposed in the summer of 1948 and sustained through the bitter winter that followed for ten harrowing months. Christa enjoyed her tenth birthday in a gloomy room brightened by birthday candles.

'You think I can remember something like that? I was just three when it happened,' Nico told a Dutch journalist, though in truth she'd reached double figures. She remembered being underweight and eternally hungry – it was from this time that she learned from her mother how to cook simple dishes, a skill she would later refine when she played a *Hausfrau* to impress the undernourished rock stars of her phantom family. She certainly remembered that her mother was forced to work late in the night when the electricity in the sector was limited to four hours out of the 24. The outdoor radio she dimly recalled; it was a station named RIAS, a prosaic acronym still in use – Radio in the American Sector. Neighbours would group nightly at street corners to hear, out of hung loudspeakers, the Americans' propaganda music and news programmes. She even recollected the constant growl of planes entering and leaving the Tempelhof airfield nearby. This is not surprising; the Western allies' sensational answer to the Soviet blockade was known as the Berlin Airlift. At its peak, in April 1949, a million tons of food and goods were delivered, including Grete's cotton; at one point craft were landing every 22 seconds. Berlin kids did not play with toy cars but with planes. Late in life Nico could still fashion a lurching model plane out of old newspaper, 'though no one ever asks me'.

When pressed, Nico told a bizarre memory of the Airlift. One morning she picked out of the gutter a rubber balloon. It said something about 'Schmoo'. A card attached to its mouthpiece told the finder to take it to a certain office where she would receive a special prize. Christa foresaw a glittering future; no more heatless, lightless rooms, no more tepid food, no more school. She waltzed with her mother to the office and displayed her Schmoo balloon. The Americans there congratulated her on her find and handed over the glamorous gift. She took home a tub of lard.

NICO, 'MR WARHOL'S SILENT SUPERSTAR', scorned looking back to her childhood because it reminded her she was no longer a child. Yet whenever she touted for sympathy, out would come one-eyed stories of the rubble or the tub of lard. Her friends in Manhattan – uptown or downtown – didn't quite follow her drift, and not only because she never told a story neat ('Ho, ho, ho, ho, ho'). Surely, they mumbled behind her back, she was talking about Berlin not Beirut, Western society not the Third World? Berlin, an imperial city, snug in American hands; surely it was not the hell on earth she had portrayed? 'Nico should have been in Vietnam, then we would have made more sense of her,' declared Viva. A fellow Superstar and an astute companion to Nico in the Sixties, Viva reflected Nico's character and concluded: 'She was in need of heavy therapy, that girl. She thought she was the Queen of Sheba. Nico was a spicy combination of insecurity and arrogance. The truth was she was an emotional cripple. When she told me these little stories about the war, I realised how badly it had screwed her up. We would have recognised the condition today as post-traumatic stress disorder. Vietnam veterans overcame it by long bouts of emotional counselling. But, of course, who would have recognised that in Nico, when she never got her story straight?'

It is a perceptive notion. Post-traumatic stress disorder is a form of anxiety that displays itself after a distressing event. The disorder might be brought on by the horrors encountered in wars or earthquakes or fires. Its central symptoms are flashbacks, a sense of personal isolation, morbidity, lethargy, remoteness, estrangement, unpredictable behaviour. All very Nico. One medical definition of the disorder states that 'prolonged physical deprivation (such as that experienced in a concentration camp) may scar people psychologically for life'. Nico told friends and journalists of crystallised incidents: an opium-induced conception, an orphanage, Jews in rail wagons, the guards whipping them out of reach of the food and drink she held, her father murdered in Belsen, the soap of human bones, a lampshade of tattooed skin, the rumble of bombs, the Russian soldier who tried to climb into her room in the night, the Mongolian couple who liked to watch her piss, the refugee journey, bodies in the Berlin rubble, rain through the ceiling, and the endless hours in glacial lodgings 'which turned out to be a room in a concentration camp'.

But a rented room in a Berlin block is not exactly the same as a concentration camp. Not flowers, nor chocolates, nor even a tub of lard, were handed to the victims of Belsen. While opera for some is nothing less than 'prolonged physical deprivation', Christa was unlikely to be 'scarred for life' even by Herbert von Karajan. Yet she was scarred for sure. She hid the hurtful truths inside fantasies. Some of her memories dealt with fact, some perceptions. Some probable, some not. Yet they were all the same to her in the end; she observed the fact and the fiction out of harm's reach, detached. As she confessed to the German journal *Twen* in 1969, 'That was not me, that was another girl . . . My memory consists of shreds and short flashes, never the whole picture.' She later added: 'I always picture Christa alone, but then I never see the whole picture.' When she disclosed the whole scene, she filled in the gaps with fantasy. Nico and Christa, the two of them, carried the symptoms of the stress disorder – flashbacks, a sense of personal isolation, morbidity, and the rest. The cause, however, was less the stress of battle than the strain of loneliness. In order to turn her insularity to account, she tried to transpose the despair of Christa's isolation into the triumph of Nico's independence. That's what Viva saw when she stood face to face with the Queen of Sheba's 'spicy combination of insecurity and arrogance'.

For the last eight years of her life Nico had a manager, an Englishman, a Jew, whose role was one-third bank teller, one-third combatant, one-third therapist. Alan Wise considered that Nico dropped these war-worn shards of memory into conversations to grab both attention and sympathy. 'It was her way of saying sorry. Or to explain her behaviour. By doing it she would remind you that she'd lived in terrible times, struggled with horrible experiences. She may have punched you in the face, but she tried to make you feel remorse for it. Sometimes you saw it was a trick, but not everyone did. And you have to remember that all the stories had the same validity to her. She could no longer discriminate between what actually happened and what she feared had happened. I soon understood that she could not distinguish between what lay in front of her eyes and what lay behind them.' Christa passed through a difficult childhood, but Nico gave her an unbearable one. 'I had a terrible time. I was a miserable girl,' she told a journalist. Christa encountered episodes of sheer pleasure, but Nico allowed her none. She never reminisced so eagerly about Omi, the big house, card games, the Spreewald, her cool cemetery, opera, chocolate, the Schmoo balloon, dressing up, her mother and her cousin and her aunts.

It is difficult to follow the threads out of which Nico wove her stories. Each strand of reality is tangled in a skein of fantasy, and she could never spin the very same tale twice. Her friends might notice a slip of detail or a change of name, in the manner of many people saddled with flawed memories, but on occasion she would transport entire events through time and tell the listener about something trivial that had happened a week before as though it had taken place in Schöneberg, as though she was talking about that unconnected little girl called Christa. Her associates have each remarked on her singular sense of time, both exquisite and deranged, but nobody has accused her of backwardness. 'She was an intelligent woman with a childlike mind,' affirmed her Warhol confidant Paul Morrissey, 'and I'm careful to say childlike, not childish.' There is a common view of those who knew her well: she was somehow rooted to that time in ruined Berlin and she acted the ten-year-old even when she was 40. 'The past, the present and the future become not relevant when they go into a big melting pot,' she said of her dreams. 'They all begin in Berlin, wherever I am . . . A wilderness of bricks.' Nico never revealed how old she looked in that envisioned wilderness of bricks.

CHRISTA WAS ALMOST ELEVEN when the wilderness of bricks along her street vanished forever. First of all they were numbered, each one. Their cankered plaster was chipped away and the land beneath them rolled smooth. Berlin's bricks were cemented and rendered into homes, sweatshops and stores, 'full of fur coats and sports cars'. The city's swift recovery began on 12 May 1949, the day the Russians lifted their blockade. The American sector's commander wrote that 'Berlin was now a symbol of liberty; its inhabitants had earned the right to freedom; they had atoned for their failure to repudiate Hitler'. Exactly as Nico had said, the United States poured money into their part of town and pushed their coats and cars against the noses of the communists. They labelled Berlin 'The Shop Window of the West'. Those parts of Germany occupied by the British, French and Americans were drawn together on 1 September as a Federal Republic. Berliners were dismayed that the chosen capital was not their city but a boring little town called Bonn.

The republic assigned Berlin a 'special status'. This sidestepped many issues and irritated its citizens. They were offered, for instance, a separate 'Berlin' passport in contrast to the West German style. Nico carried a Berlin passport all her life; she rather liked it because it was 'not really German'. The atoll in a Soviet sea remained one, though risingly rich. The 'wilderness' at the south end of Nürnbergerstrasse was transformed within a year into a modern shopping street. It remained a wilderness to Nico.

Christa supposed she had entered another wilderness in October 1949, when she reached the age of eleven. Berlin was not a 'symbol of liberty' to her, for she was now obliged to enter a new school, a secondary Volksschule. 'I went without pleasure. In these schools one is only suppressed. It is a cruel education method; one is graded. You are not allowed to be truly different there, but some children are unusual. I was a very sad child – now I'm happier – but they thought I was impenitent.' Nico summarised it this way for *Twen*. She showed off in class but had nothing to say. Christa bragged, lied, and invented stories to draw attention to herself, but nobody was impressed. She romanticised, impenitently. Her grades were low, her reports poor; she was moody, withdrawn and wilful, and would not concentrate on her lessons. Helma believed she was simply bone idle.

It was not as though she was still stuck in a sad little room with her mother. They had found a smarter two-roomed apartment near the elementary school at No. 5 Regensburgerstrasse, on the corner with Ansbacherstrasse, a dignified six-storey block that had survived the war and was now cut up into twelve flats. The area was slick and thriving. But Christa felt utter solitude. She often said later she felt as though she were looking down at the earth through a microscope, as though much of human living was minute and negligible and worthy only of observation from a towering distance. 'I often feel I share very little in common with other people. I was alone for a lot of my youth, in a kind of wilderness, and that feeling has developed with me all these years,' Nico later reflected.

The young Christa was not short of ambition, however. She knew she was very pretty (and very tall and rather awkward) – everyone agreed, however begrudgingly – and Christa knew there was only one thing that very pretty girls become. A ballerina, that would be just the job for her, she thought. To be a dancer was then the most extraordinary, rarefied career a girl like Christa could follow – a perfectly romantic gesture in her drive to be the unparalleled centre of attention. It combined the physical and the aesthetic; the stardust world of ballet transgressed the limits of common life. She pestered her mother. Her mother resisted, but not for long.

Grete, now nearing 40, was not above flamboyance. Her room would always be full of flowers and fruit whenever she earned extra cash. Cakes and sweets were acquired with little regard for lean days ahead. 'She didn't save,' observed Helma, 'she would fritter her money away on little things. Her daughter learnt from her example;

she thought that was what you do.' Above all, Grete indulged in the gramophone records of her favourite singer, Zarah Leander. 'She would listen to her and cry, cry, cry. She'd cry buckets. She couldn't stop. It melted her heart to hear Zarah Leander,' said Helma.

Leander was a sweetheart of the Nazis. She sang glutinous ballads, some skilful and haunting, about rainy days and splintered love – 'The Wind Has Whispered Me A Song', 'You Should Not Send Me Roses Anymore', 'Fettered Hands', 'Deepest Longing'. Leander starred on screen in clotted melodramas filmed in Berlin's Babelsberg Studios at the personal request of the Reich's Propaganda Minister, Goebbels. There was a slight irony about her sovereign position as the great German diva. She was Swedish. The same age as Grete, she was tall with naturally red hair and an exceptionally handsome face. 'She had a "cow face" as we call it, beautifully calm, large Swedish eyes like Garbo or Ingrid Bergman. However you shot the face, it was always good looking,' said the film director Detlef Sierck (who was better known to Hollywood as Douglas Sirk). Goebbels promoted her to pre-eminence when his attempts to bribe Marlene Dietrich back into Nazi Germany failed. He would be traumatised today to learn that Zarah Leander, who died in 1981, has become a camp gay icon of the Fatherland. When Grete played her records and wept, Christa listened to a remarkable, exotic singing voice. Zarah Leander sang very, very low with a velvet timbre and a restrained vibrato. When Nico started to sing fifteen years later, she simply reached back to her Berlin days and evoked the voice of her mother's favourite singer, the one who made her cry, cry, cry.

Christa planned to be a prima ballerina, not a coryphée, not a ballerina. When she reached the age of twelve, her mother took her to the very peak of the profession, at least in Berlin, for an opinion. Tatjana Gsovsky had been prima ballerina at the Berlin State Opera during the Nazi period, when she danced to the jackboot beat of the young Herbert von Karajan. Being White Russian by birth, she had assumed that the Soviet soldiers knocking on her door in 1945 had come to gun her down. Not so: they saluted her as an artistic treasure. Luckily for Gsovsky, Russian commanders had demanded to see a vibrant cultural life in the conquered city; the theatres were mandated to open as swiftly as possible. Like the signalman of Lübbenau, the prima ballerina of Berlin was valued by Nazis and communists alike. She retired from the stage but retained her supremacy as the Opera's ballet mistress, until the West–East divide placed the State Opera in the East and her private school in the West. The popular magazine

Für Sie ('For You') devoted its front page in March 1946 to a portrait of Tatjana Gsovsky embracing one of her students on the stage of the State Opera; she looked like a raddled bear, wrapped in a monstrous furry coat, crushing a fleshy mound of tulle, teeth, and panstick.

This was the woman who inspected Christa. She stared at the gangly, puppyfat thing not far off puberty. 'Well . . .' she grunted, 'your daughter can never become the prima ballerina she dreams to become. She is too old, for a start. She should have begun her work at the age of five. She won't do.' Christa did not believe it and begged for ballet lessons to prove Madam wrong. Grete saved up for the expensive weekly course. Christa found it tough going but persisted, until lamed by indolence. She grew bored with the disciplined routine, the five positions, the crushingly dull exercises at the barre, and the staggering lack of glamour. She complained that this was no route to the top. One day her mother could bear it no longer and returned to Madam Gsovsky: 'Does it make sense for Christa to continue if she only wants to be a star?' No, of course not: the ballet mistress was bitterly clear. Christa's lessons were cancelled.

To pad out time between her detested school and the nebulous stardom she craved, Christa skulked among the cinema queues and the magazine racks. At the conclusion of the war Goebbels had shut down every place of entertainment, but he dared not touch the cinemas. The Russians promptly reopened everything he'd closed, but the cinemas remained the favoured centres of leisure. Christa preferred the most gushing romantic slop she could find. 'It used to make me laugh,' she claimed, a mite defensively.

Otherwise she scoured magazines for fashion and make-up tips, and she was not short of reading matter. 'Surplus women' were a prime target of the newly licensed publishing houses. There was *Constanze* from Hamburg; *Heute* (Today) from Munich; *Lilith* from Berlin; *Caprice, Chic, Quick, She, You, For You, Monika* ('for the Catholic mother & daughter'), *Bunte, Eve At Home*, and *Needle, Thread & Thimble – A Woman's Gift*. Among the hand-drawn adverts for Tosca cold cream and Chip perfume ('brings the air of Paris to loving couples'), the articles projected a surprisingly serious tone in their coverage of women's issues. It was not difficult for Christa to find features such as 'Bad Habits Spoil Your Face', a doggedly thorough treatise on each trivial aspect of the comely, feminine figure ('Our body is a motor!'), but there were others on social issues. *Constanze* printed a series on drug addiction entitled 'It's Easy to Get Drugs':

> Today it is not so easy to smoke cocaine, heroin or marijuana, because the German and foreign police are working together to put an end to the smuggling. But the black market does not depend on smuggling. Chemists help put drugs into the hands of addicts. Morphine, for example. The health department gives an official total of 40,000 addicts. But we know more.

Christa could have read articles about 'Women who Live as Men' ('Just once I slipped into the uniform of a hotel page. It was as though the jacket was made for me'), another on the horrors of a catwalk career. Her future was mapped out in these pages. Everywhere Christa looked she saw the elegant face of Germany's premier film star, a tall, sultry blonde named Hildegard Knef. In her late twenties, Knef not only endorsed the postwar wonders of Luxor soap or Bellinda nylons, but was prominent in news photographs, pawing at young celebrities of the day such as Jean-Pierre Aumont ('Monsieur Dreamboat'). She appeared in *Bunte* or *Sie* every week. Knef was an industry, a postwar industry (she made her screen debut in 1946) representing all that was fresh and bright in federal Germany. Nico hated her. She once struck out at a man who said she sang like Hildegard Knef, though it was an excusable comparison. In America, Paul Morrissey considered Knef's success in combining an acting and singing career as a good model for Nico. She swiftly dismissed the notion, revealing that 'My mother never liked her.'

Nico denied that she took any German role models. Aunt Helma believed that whatever influences she found at this time were more likely to be foreign – Marilyn Monroe or Gina Lollobrigida, for example, or the Belgian-born actress Audrey Hepburn – for the publicity machine that reinvents the lives of cinema stars filled the news pages of German magazines with the kind of cosmetic tosh Christa enjoyed, half true and half not true.

WHEN SHE WAS THIRTEEN Christa was raped. A black American army sergeant stood in the doorway of a dark and quiet street one evening. He called to Christa, talked to her, then attempted to touch and kiss her. When she resisted the soldier pushed her down, tore her clothes and raped her. He did not say '*Komm, frau*', but it came to the same thing. Christa dragged herself back home to an empty room, to wait for her mother who was being entertained elsewhere. Violated and scarred, but not impregnated, Christa's nightmare did not end there. Grete reported the rape to the authorities. The sergeant was charged and court-martialled. Christa was obliged to attend and give testimony. It transpired that the sergeant had raped other girls, who also confronted him in the courtroom. He was hanged.

That is how Nico told the story to her friends; it seems she mentioned it whenever she was accused of racism. On occasion Nico made a disparaging point that 'Negroes are not like us'. Her bigotry was drawn from a terrible moment in her childhood, she revealed, and if you knew what had happened, she said, you would excuse me. Nico may well have told the traumatic story exactly as it occurred, but there is nothing now to back it up, simply no information at all. The United States Army archives hold no record of this case. The Military Staff Judge Advocate's office knows nothing of it. Berlin's daily newspapers did not report it, though by 1952 such a case would have been newsworthy. The papers frequently carried items such as the following story from April 1953:

PLEAS FOR CLEMENCY
FOR A NEGRO SOLDIER
Numerous Germans have sent pleas for clemency to the American military court in Würzburg in support of the negro soldier Edwards who is sentenced to death. Edwards strangled a 24-year-old German woman, after she had made contemptuous remarks about the colour of his skin.

Frau Helma Wolff and her son Ulrich were recently startled to hear of Christa's rape, of which they had known nothing. Her manager, Alan Wise, remembered Nico recounting it because of a small detail: she called the soldier an officer, yet her description of the stripes on his sleeve clearly demoted him to a sergeant's rank. 'If the story's true, it would explain a lot of things,' reasoned Viva. 'If it's not true, it would explain another lot of things.'

The rape story bears an unnerving resemblance to another of Christa's nightmare tales. A foreign soldier, a doorway or a window frame, a prone girl, night time, mother elsewhere – the elements are similar to the story of Vanya, the 'Mongolian' intruder. Nevertheless, it is disconcerting to be told such a disquieting story of rape and disbelieve it. As Helma said when faced with a similar enigma,

'I really don't know to this day whether she saw Vanya in the window or in her dreams.'

THE AMERICANS RAN A SURVEY of 250 Schöneberg schoolgirls in 1946. They sought to grade their career aspirations. In decreasing order of desire, their ambitions were to become: salesgirls, dressmakers, clerks, teachers, hairdressers. When the survey was repeated five years later, little had changed save that hairdressing was now more popular than teaching. Christa, on the other hand, had chosen rather differently. She wished to be discovered. At what she did not care so long as it made her the centre of attention; it would be the task of the discoverer to work out her talent, but she would work fearlessly doing what people who wished to be discovered had to do. She would mooch around the fashionable streets, the smartest cafés and the poshest stores. Christa was nearly fourteen, an age when she could leave school for ever and ever and embark on her fabulous career of being discovered.

Grete was not impressed by her daughter's plans. She gave Christa two options: she could continue at school and consider a distant goal of college, or she could go to work as a salesgirl, dressmaker, clerk, and so on, just like the others. But Christa could never do things just like the others. In the summer of 1952 Christa finished her desultory education and began her chosen career of lounging around the home. 'OK, something has to happen now,' argued Grete. 'You have to help me and earn some money for the two of us to survive.' There was a nervous pause. 'I have a job lined up. It's ideal. You will like it. You will be a shop assistant.'

When Grete talked to Christa she used a babyish diminutive. She talked to her as though she was still weaning. *Töchterchen*, she cooed, 'little-tiny-daughterkins'. It would embarrass Aunt Helma to hear their foetal conversations. Christa would respond with 'mummy', 'mummykins', *Mütterlein*, *Mütterchen*. '*Töchterchen*, you must help me and be a shop assistant,' soothed Grete. 'But mummykins, I'm too clumsy. I'm all thumbs. I can't serve customers.' Grete was firm. 'You'll have to try. I've got you an apprenticeship in a clothes store.' Grete clearly had connections, because jobs were scarce in a city of high unemployment. An apprenticeship scheme was common; it involved the drawing-up of a contract between the boss and the parents. Thus, at 9 a.m. one Monday morning in 1952, Christa began her first and last shop-floor job.

Her task was terribly simple. It concerned the ceiling-high rows of shelves neatly piled with large cardboard boxes containing a certain size of vest or corset. A senior shop assistant would ask Christa to climb a ladder, bring down a box, wait, and put it back. Christa got as far as ascending the ladder. She grabbed a box. She held it for a moment, let it twist and slip through her fingers and crash to the floor. She watched the staff turn round and gape at the scattered heap of vests. Then she grabbed a second box, and the same thing happened. Then a third, to ram the point home. The manager was brought in to view the mess. 'I can't do this job. My hands are too clumsy. I'm not a shop assistant, I made that clear to mummy. You'll have to fetch her to see what a mess I've made. My mummy can stand on her head and beg if she wants, but I'm not cut out to be a shop assistant.' Grete came and talked quickly to the boss. Christa's contract was 'terminated by mutual consent'. The other assistants were left to tidy up her damage. She had spent less than one hour out of her entire life in retail. Yet she told a member of The Velvet Underground group that her film career began when she was discovered by the Italian director Federico Fellini, working at a checkout in a supermarket. 'I could have done well in a shop,' she lied.

From then on she had her way. Her mother could not, in any case, find her *Töchterchen* another apprenticeship. Christa was alone and at liberty to tread her daily career path, the one that led out of the apartment block, up Ansbacherstrasse to the main road and round a corner to the biggest department store in Europe. Formally called the Kaufhaus des Westens, the store was known to all as the KaDeWe (Kar-day-vay). New Yorkers might compare it to Bergdorf Goodman, Londoners to Harrods. Christa perched daily by its doors, waiting to be discovered. She would certainly be noticed. Having shed her gosling character, she was arrestingly tall and athletic in her looks (though she avoided sports – too German); a girl–boy. She would often try to look like the gamine Audrey Hepburn out of *Roman Holiday*. Her neck was long 'like a vase', setting off a sensational, symmetrical face that harmonised the ancestral features, in particular the bee-stung lips and the ultrahigh cheekbones. Shoppers and staff could not avoid a glance at this androgyne layabout. Christa had innocently assumed that fashion designers and photographers used the KaDeWe like a corner shop. She had not yet understood about seasons, the patterned, annual rituals by which the high-flown fashion trade garners its wealth. So she slouched around pointlessly, waiting to be discovered. But one day it worked.

The king, and queen, of German fashion was Oestergaard. Like Hartnell in Britain or Halston in the States, he designed exclusive dresses and outfits in the elevated tradition of *grande couture*. It is a cruel and simplistic notion of foreigners that Germany is a land without fashion: 'What does he design – uniforms?' a fashion writer asked of Heinz Oestergaard. Unfortunately for his international reputation, he did; industrial giants such as Beyer and Hoechst were among his customers. However, on the fashion floor of the KaDeWe he ran a salon. There, beautiful young women were engaged as models with the misogynist name of mannequins, or dummies ('Walk, dear. Turn, dear'). They displayed the latest, brilliant Oestergaard gowns to snortily rich customers, the wives of Beyer and Hoechst. It was not a pleasure but an honour to work for Oestergaard, the mannequins were calmly reminded, and only the ambitious amongst them survived their daily ordeal. His agents were eagle-eyed for new talent; one spotted Christa on his way to plot the KaDeWe autumn show of 1953. He returned to the entrance with Oestergaard's chief assistant. The two fashion scouts cruised round Christa while she feigned not to notice. They approached her; thus at the age of fifteen she stopped posing in shop doorways and started posing for Oestergaard. Discovered. Discovered! Having proved her mother wrong, she could even support her out of a decent wage. Her faith in chance had paid its dues, though she never called it chance; her mother had taught her to call it fate. It was her fate to be discovered. Discovered! ('Ho, ho, ho, ho, ho.')

Nico remembered these days: when they weren't in view, contriving to make the clothes look more comfortable than they were, Christa and the other mannequins were hidden behind a screen sweatily swopping outfits, painting on fresh make-up, pinning hats, combing wigs, untangling the finery scattered around the floor, and trying to find out what came next in the task to meet the whims of wealthy women. Christa was determined to be a professional: 'It was like an alternative school. I understood why everything had to be just as it was, which I never understood at school. I could see the effect of a walk, a turn, a position. And I was the centre of attention.' She never took the job seriously, but she took herself seriously and that was enough to keep her in work. 'The money I earned then', she claimed in 1985, 'was enough to keep my mother in comfort without her having to work, but she could not think what to do instead, so she carried on with her sewing.'

Christa's mind dwelt for the first time on her mother's loneliness and the family name she carried that had no family to carry along with it. One day she took the express train from Berlin to Cologne. Her mother had remembered an old address there, and the sixteen-year-old Christa knocked on the front door of the smart house. According to Christa, she told the woman who answered, 'My name is Christa Päffgen. I believe my father was your brother.' Christa reported to her mother that the woman replied, 'I'll tell you who you are. You are a bastard,' and slammed the door. The bastard caught the next train back to Berlin, in tears, comprehending for the first time her complete solitariness.

'WHEN I WAS YOUNG in Berlin I was not interested in many boys. Well, I was interested, but nothing more. I was shy. I have always been shy, this has been my difficulty. Some people think I am distant, while I think I am shy. When I became a model I met handsome boys, really the most handsome boys you could meet. They were homosexual. The most beautiful boys were interested in the most beautiful boys – I can understand that. I wanted to be a boy myself. I mean, why should I want to be a woman? I liked my homosexual friends the best.' Christa's closest friend was a gorgeous young photographer named Herbert Tobias, then twenty years old. She wanted to be him and he wanted to be her.

Tobias – always Tobias, surname only – made his money in the small but busy fashion market of federal Germany, supplying studio portraits of the latest local fashions to newspapers and magazines. He used mannequins like Christa and turned them into covergirls – models who worked for the camera rather than the catwalk. He was valued for his camp, ornate, romantic style of a high, professional order. One of his earliest portraits of Christa was taken at the end of a trade show for jewellers. She had been voted best mannequin at a parade to show off new items, and as a reward, the traders let her keep the rings she had displayed. Tobias photographed her bejewelled hands. He also gave Christa her first full-colour portrait in the magazine *Bunte* of January 1955, when Christa was sixteen. It was accompanied by a coy text:

A summer night party: tired of dancing, the young woman sits down between the coloured Chinese lamps in the summer house. Is it the photographer she's waiting for? In any case, it is Tobias from Berlin – making the most of an opportunity to fill our magazine with the latest advance in colour photography.

They also shot, in monochrome, clothes and jewellery for *Bunte* and *Constanze*, though there are few printed credits to either of their names. The freelance fees Christa earned from these sessions would be spent on evenings of gentle hedonism, dining out with him, sometimes dragging *mütterlein* along, or drinking in the more sedate of Berlin's gay bars. He was her 'Bad Samaritan', she claimed, though in time she would meet Samaritans who were really bad. Above all else, through Tobias Christa was introduced to three great turning points of her life: Paris, Ibiza and Nico.

3 1956–1959

To Imagination

So hopeless is the world without,
The world within I doubly prize;
Thy world where guile and hate and doubt
And cold suspicion never rise;
Where thou and I and Liberty
Have undisputed sovreignty.

What matters it that all around
Danger, and guilt, and darkness lie,
If but within our bosom's bound
We hold a bright, untroubled sky,
Warm with ten thousand mingled rays
Of suns that know no winter days?

(EMILY BRONTË, 1844)

'I WAS SIXTEEN when I met Ernest Hemingway in Paris. Maybe I was seventeen. I was staying on the Left Bank in a little hotel in Place de la Contrescarpe and he was staying next door. I was sitting in a bar and he made an excuse to talk to me. My French was very simple, and so was my English. But he was a big man and he hypnotised me. He said he was writing a book and he would put me in it, a pretty young girl sitting at a bar. I don't know which book this is. Do you know it? I am probably in many books like this, scattered about in the bookshops, and I will never know. (Do you know in a record store I found my records under "V", for Velvet Underground, not "N"? Lou Reed wasn't under "V". It is better to be under "N" because there are not so many "N" people. So, even when I have my name on something, I still can't find it.)

'Ernest Hemingway invited me to a party near the rue Bonaparte. I did not understand a thing at this party. There was all these people like Jean-Paul Sartre and Jean Genet. But Hemingway was very kind to me and I think he wanted to make love to me, but he was more like my father. He was old with a beard; he was like a bear. He tried to feel me. He said I was a princess, but he said Princess Nico sounded as if I was Swedish. I think that is why I said I was Swedish to many people. I am supposed to be Swedish in *La Dolce Vita*, did you notice?

'He said that if I was Swedish, then I should be a blonde, instead of my dark hair. I was mistaken often for Audrey Hepburn then. You know, he was blond, but a blond from old age, not a blond from the hairdresser. He had just won the Nobel Prize and I thought that if a winner of the Nobel Prize told you to do something about your hair, there is something to consider. I could be a Nobel blonde. I did this eventually. It was not so easy then as it became, to keep your hair blonde. But it was good for me to do it. Don't they say "blondes have more fun"? Well, I don't agree. It is more correct to say "blondes have more money".'

Her friends recognised this story as 'typical' Nico. Bits of it may be true, they agreed; certain facts fit, though to admit this only devalues Nico's sense of romance. Hemingway was awarded the Nobel literature prize in 1954, he stayed in Paris during the autumn of 1956 though he lodged at the Ritz on the Right Bank, and it's true that the grizzled veteran, nearing 60, still fancied teenagers, but he was there with his wife. As for Christa, she had certainly left Berlin for Paris at the age of seventeen. The precocious Tobias had arranged with a scout from *Elle* magazine for Christa to work on regular assignments with a leading Paris fashion photographer, Willy Maywald, who just happened to be German. 'I have to ask my mummy,' she told *Elle* in Berlin. Mummy said no. 'I think her mother was afraid to be alone,' suggested Aunt Helma. 'They had been together all these years, so terribly close, and Grete had no one else. She had been with the occasional boyfriend, and maybe she was a little bit flamboyant or "loose-living", as we would say in those days, though I don't want to give the wrong impression. Perhaps we would say she was *modern*, she had a *modern* outlook on life. I think Christa took this up from her mother. My sister was not unsociable, but still she could be rather lonely.

'Well, there was a lot of pressure for Christa to take this opportunity,' continued Helma. 'I mean you can imagine what a thing it was, to be so young and offered this work with the top fashion designers in the world and the top photographers and the top magazines. Paris was the centre of the fashion world; you could not go higher. Imagine what she would earn! Imagine the fame! Finally her mother agreed. I remember Christa flew from Berlin, and they were both crying buckets at the airport, crying buckets. In a way, neither of them got over this detachment. While Christa was in Paris, her mother started to suffer from the separation. It almost broke her heart. I believe it was this time that my sister started to have her mental problems, or at least the seeds were planted. But Christa would not have seen that, or even understood it.'

Elle magazine arranged for Christa to stay at her 'little hotel in the Place de la Contrescarpe' in the Latin Quarter and it seems it was there, for a brief moment, that the big bear of writing hypnotised her ('Oh, she was full of these crazy stories,' said a friend, 'and the names changed every day'). Before he shot himself in 1961, Ernest Hemingway worked on three books. There are bars on every page in every one, and plenty of girls in those bars, all young and pretty and drinking like fish. But the book he wrote in 1957 is a memoir of Paris in the Twenties. It is called *A Moveable Feast* and, had she read it, it could have stood as a model for Nico's own memoirs, *Moving Target*. It opens in 1921:

> Then there was the bad weather. It would come in one day when the fall was over. We would have to shut the windows in the night against the rain and the cold wind would strip the leaves from the trees in the Place Contrescarpe . . .
>
> A girl came in the café and sat by herself at a table near the window. She was very pretty with a face fresh as a newly minted coin if they minted coins in smooth flesh with rain-freshened skin and her hair was black as a crow's wing and cut sharply and diagonally across her cheek.
>
> I looked at her and she disturbed me and made me very excited. I wished I could put her in a story, or anywhere, but she had placed herself so she could watch the street and the entry and I knew she was waiting for someone. So I went on writing.

'LOOK. SHE NEVER READ A BOOK, dear boy, she never read a thing. I don't think she *could* read, really. She was virtually illiterate. She hadn't an idea in her head. She could hardly even speak; just a sentence here, a sentence there, in broken French, broken English, broken German, broken everything. She made a lot of gorilla noises. "Ho, ho, ho, ho, ho" – that was her reply to whatever anybody said. "Ho, ho, ho, ho, ho." It covered everything up, you see, her ignorance, her lack of savoir-faire, her uncertainties, her fears. She was a lovely, lovely, lovely girl. A wonderful face, sensational and regular in her features, and a hefty body. She was fabulous, beautiful, a magnificent child. We had such a delightful time, walking around Paris, running through the streets, "Ho, ho, ho, ho, ho," along the Seine, the quays, in the cafés. She was always joking about little things. She had the mentality of an eleven-year-old. There will never be another Nico, never, never.'

It is unlikely that there could ever be another Carlos de Maldo-nado- Bostock, either. He is now a rather famous figure around the Place des Vosges, the cloistered square near the Bastille where film stars like to live. He patrols his huge hound round the narrow streets of the Marais, a modern Hemingway in his stalking outfit topped with a feathered hunting hat which changes daily. He still retreats into the countryside to shoot game: the Bostock circus family, from which he is descended on his mother's side, virtually invented the lion-taming act. Maldonado's distinguished Spanish name and heritage masks his thoroughbred English education ('I went to a rather decent public school, dear boy'), though he argues with the dog in rasping Spanish. Maldonado-Bostock calls himself a 'dilapi-dated toad' but when the teenage Christa met him he must have been around 30 years old, seductive, dashing and devil-may-care.

'When I first met her she was eighteen or so, or seventeen, no more. I was a photographer. She was all alone, sitting at the brasserie in front of the Café de Flore at St Germain des Prés. She sat at one table, I was at another. It was summertime, and she wanted to know me, simple as that. And we spoke and we spoke and we spoke, yet she had nothing to say. Everything was a kind of abstraction. "Ho, ho, ho, ho, ho." And she couldn't care less. She liked the atmosphere of emptiness of nothingness, even then – I don't think anything ever really changed in her attitude from a young age to an old age. She was disaffected with humanity; but she had an air of loneliness and this disturbed her a great deal, I believe, and that's why she sought out friends. We were friends, which is what she wanted most, not lovers. She had romances, crushes on men, crushes on women. But not lovers, never. Nobody could love her. She was unfuckable.'

Placing Hemingway back on the fiction shelf for a moment, Maldonado-Bostock was the first of a chain of men Nico met in this way, by the rule of chance that she had learned to call *fate*: 'I met so many wonderful people in Paris over the years. They were all beautiful and exciting, but the ones I met first of all seemed to be the most exciting. It is a shame I cannot remember them,' she sighed in 1985. 'I met my second father in Paris, too. Later he became like a father to my child, but first he was like a father to me. He was my photographer and my father – what would Freud have said of that? Ho, ho, ho . . .' Her father–photographer was known to the fashion trade as Maywald. His christian name was Wilhelm, like Nico's first father. Prestigious, accomplished, senior, Wilhelm Maywald, then 50 years old, had worked in Paris since the early Thirties supplying photographs of the latest *haute couture* fashion collections for magazines such as *Elle* and *Stern*. Some of his classic shots can be bought today in postcard shops, including the famous *Grès* of 1954 where a demure woman is otherwise naked in a vertically slit toga. His loyalty to Paris caused him grave discomfort during the Nazi Occupation, as he was patently homosexual – he lived for a long time with his boyfriend Bobby and his sister Helene. Maywald was interned in camps until he sought refuge in Switzerland. Returning in 1947 he was swiftly employed as the photographer of Christian Dior, and his pictures of Dior's sensational success, the New Look, were used by the press world-wide.

Maywald wrote about his encounters with Nico in an autobiography published in German just after his death in 1985: 'I was retouching photographs on a summer afternoon at my big working desk, and the door to my garden was open as always. A sound in the room made me look up. In front of me stood a most beautiful girl with bright eyes. She was tall and well-proportioned, and her hair was cut short. She gave me a shy glance and introduced herself to me . . . I had just had the assignment to shoot some ready-made clothes at the Côte d'Azur. And because Nico was exactly the right look for that I hired her at once.

'As always, Helene, Bobby and Ursula accompanied us. We took pictures in a lot of small villages in Provence. While I was still selecting the shots we had taken the day before, and preparing for the next day, the others had already gone out for fun. Ursula had been invited on an English yacht, and Nico had fallen in love with an American cover-boy. She had met him just then in La Jungle, a nightclub in Cannes. We all met up there later that evening and we danced and amused ourselves. But Nico's love adventure did not work out the way she wanted it, and I had to run out after her on to the beach to stop her from running into the sea to drown her grief. It was all tears and dramas. And when we came back to the hotel late at night, Helene was screaming down the steps at me, "You really should take better care of the child, because you are responsible!" There is a saying, which came to my mind right then, "It is easier to look after a sack of fleas than young girls." '

Christa was fortunate to find a benign German father in Paris, though she claimed it was fate rather than fortune that brought this particular sack of fleas to his home. Maywald became her 'Good Samaritan'. Tobias, her 'Bad Samaritan', had craved to chaperone her from Berlin to Paris, but he was forbidden by the police from entering the city he adored. The problem was that what he adored were its pissoirs. On his last visit he had been caught by the cops in a *vespasienne* urinal, touting for rough trade. Tobias was a foreigner, a German pederast fouling gay Paris; he was smartly deported and barred from ever returning. This hurt him greatly, for he had fallen helplessly in love with a handsome young man, a divine figure he had seen on the city's Left Bank but never managed to meet. Back in Berlin, the exiled and terminally romantic Tobias decided to invent his own version of the man, and love that instead.

One day he said to Christa, 'You cannot carry on calling yourself Christa Päffgen. Even Christa is wrong. It's not international. Krista is better, but it doesn't suit your character. You are pure, androgyne. Models have one name, just like photographers and designers have one name. I am Tobias. I have a name for you, and you must use it from now on. It will be good for business, at any rate.' Christa asked him where he got the name from, whatever it was. 'I will only tell you because you are my sister,' Tobias replied. 'The most wonderful man I have ever seen lives in Paris. I am in love with him. He is fabulous. I have seen him at the Café de Flore and in the club La Rose Rouge. He is a friend of the writer Jean Genet, and I discovered not only that he owns La Rose Rouge, but I also found out his name. It turns out he's not French at all – he looks dark – he's Greek but he was born in Ethiopia. His name is Nico Papatakis.'

From that day, in the Berlin of 1956, Christa was Nico, taking the name of a man loved by another man. Tobias had created a substitute Nico, as untouchable to him as the real thing, but available to his bidding. Christa was freed into fantasy. She was no longer a bastard Päffgen, no more a dim schoolgirl, and her penniless past was erased in a single stroke. As Nico, she could be anything – rich beyond wealth, Swedish or Slav, male or female, an Audrey Hepburn clone or an ageless enigma. She recognised even then that Nico as a name was a brilliant, indefinite, ambiguous choice. In most countries Nico is incontestably male. It is taken from the Greek, a diminutive invariably adopted from Saint Nicholas. As the patron saint of

Russia, children and pawnbrokers, he is the ideal patronymic for Miss Nico Pavlovsky. As the patron saint of Greece, he fits Nico Papatakis to perfection. Yet in other countries Nico is considered a short form of something such as Nicola, the female form of Nicholas. 'Is it male? Are you sure? I never thought about it. Nico, male? I just thought it was foreign,' admitted one of her British fans. As for the real Nico, it was not his full name anyway. Though he was properly Nikos, he was recognised by everyone as plain old 'Papatakis'. She would not meet Papatakis for another three years, when they would eventually be known, like a circus act, as The Two Nicos.

When she presented herself to Maywald she had already named herself Nico: 'She gave me a shy glance and introduced herself to me. She said her name was Nico. The photographer Tobias from Berlin had sent her.' Nico herself offered the press and her relatives four different accounts of why she was distinguished by this solitary word:

(i) She was living on the island of Ibiza with a photographer whose best friend Nico had disappeared after a fight. The photographer started calling her Nico and she quite liked it so it stuck.

(ii) Her full name was Nico Pavlovsky, but nobody can spell Pavlovsky.

(iii) Nico is an anagram of Icon, and Salvador Dali gave her the name because of this.

(iv) She worked for the fashion designer Coco Chanel, who was a lesbian. Chanel, who already had a curious nickname in Coco, gave her models the names of boys, and proposed this nickname for Nico after an affair with her.

Astonishingly, Nico confided the Chanel story to Aunt Helma. It is an intriguing Nico paradox that she chose to remove the gay slant of one story and replace it with a lesbian angle to another. Typical, too, of Nico to drag Dali and Chanel into her life – Dali changed her name and Hemingway changed her hair. Throughout her life Nico ornamented her stories with the names of celebrities, however implausible the connection ('They take down everything I say – silly isn't it?').

The first account is the true one, of course, Nicofied into something more exotic and ambiguous. 'She played this sort of game all the time,' Carlos de Maldonado-Bostock observed. 'She was exotic because she didn't say anything and she had nothing to say anyway. When she did respond, she "Ho, ho, ho'd" her way out of a corner, and it was neat and ambiguous, because people believed she meant something by it, or perhaps they *wanted* to believe she meant something by it. She was a beautiful little girl surrounded by sophistication, and her reaction was as sophisticated and mysterious as a little girl could manage – "Ho, ho, ho." She was impressed, but she had her own careful way of reacting to things and she was never sure herself if she cared or didn't care.'

Nico started to tell admirers she was called Prince Mouchkine: 'I gave the impression of being a boy, with my short hair and low voice. In those days I had a weakness for gay men and wanted to be one myself, so I told everyone that I was . . . Nico was a man and Mouchkine was a boy.' Her friends agree that she flirted with men and women in equal measure. 'But you have to understand this,' stressed Carlos de Maldonado-Bostock, 'she hated men and she hated women and she wanted men and she wanted women, but she didn't want any of them in the end, not as lovers, she wanted friends. Nico was lonely so she took friendship very easily and so she was open to exploitation. This beautiful girl, she was full of romance, you have to keep reminding yourself of that, she was *elsewhere*.' He concluded that 'there was nothing sexual about Nico. She was asexual. She was neither female nor male. She was uncontaminated. We used to joke about it, I'd say, "It's such a shame you haven't got a little penis." She played the game in society, she had to, but she wasn't passionate with anyone. She was very uncomfortable with people she thought were on the make. She was always frightened that they were about to say any second, "Open your legs". She detested those people. She didn't want anyone to touch her cunt.'

Nico played with her gender to protect her sex, not to explore it. It is often assumed that women like Nico, who seek out the company of gay men, do so because gays are not, in the end, a threat. But she was lured by the look of bodies that controlled their own seductive image. Nico desired Tobias and the others because, simply, they were 'beautiful', and seduction is a matter of foreplay, not congress. She did not associate with them as a *latent* homosexual herself; she would never entertain such a position because she was open about her desires, however vaguely she presented them. Neither did she judge herself bisexual, because she thought that everyone's sexuality was 'open, not split'.

She empathised with gay men because she considered they shared her distaste for the constrained conventions of bourgeois life. They acted outside the unliberating moral code. When she hated men, she hated the men *inside*, the unamusing men; she hated unimaginative women in the same way: 'Women in general like to have security, financial and moral support without moving a finger . . . Women are poison.' Tobias – her brother, like Andy Warhol or Jim Morrison was her brother – was a true bohemian in her eyes, because he confronted the dominant moral code even in his biology. He was seditious in mind and body. She thought the same about Allen Ginsberg too. They were 'queer', and as far as society was concerned, so was she.

This does not explain her insatiable desire to seduce, nor the constant contradiction of desiring and detesting that would allow her to hold opposite opinions next to one another. She used her beauty as a honey trap to capture friends, but when she found that friends could rarely be found this way, she turned frustrated to the most physical reactions she could muster from her lexicon of romantic gestures learned from films ('It was all tears and dramas'). Her seduction, the lure of her image, was the game she played; the goal was not sex, but respect. These games, and their recurring dramatic ends, recall her pastimes with Ulrich in Lübbenau: 'She imposed herself in a powerful manner. Nothing else mattered until she had her own way entirely. We would play with toys . . . and she would be engrossed in winning.' She won the right to be *elsewhere*.

NICO CONFESSED that she was often intimidated by the Paris of the Fifties, especially the air of condescension she found there: 'I could not admit that I was out of my depth, but anyway I found a way to overcome my shortcomings. You might think it was easy, because the men in any case did not assume you had intelligence. But that was a trap, or do I mean a convention? I didn't want anyone to assume I was a stupid girl, because I don't believe I was. I was uneducated because of the restraining system of the school. I found instead an underground way to learn. You can study most from other people not when they are formal, but when they are relaxed.'

In other words, the 'little girl' learnt nothing from classrooms, but everything from nightclubs.

Maywald made sure she worked all day and played all night, 'because modelling relies on the same energy as a dancer and you cannot let your body soften,' as Nico put it. 'I could say that I reserved all my energy in Berlin for Paris. I was never so lazy in Paris because Willy Maywald was strict and he counselled me. But when you are eighteen in Paris, you do not want to be lazy, in case you miss something. I tried to miss nothing, but I understood nothing as well.' This became her Paris *cri de coeur*: 'I did not understand . . . I was intimidated . . . I pretended . . .' She used it whenever she was asked to conjure up the Paris of the Fifties: 'I worked and I had fun and the rest was not important, or at least I don't remember. I was too shy, and I did not understand very much because of the language.' She said she felt she was 'the centre of attention in a city that was already the centre of attention'.

Being in a job where she was the unceasing centre of attention helped to get Nico out of bed of a morning, but it was even easier when she moved into Maywald's apartment ('*Raus!* Nico, *raus!*' he would command). At first he chaperoned her to evening restaurants or they ate communally at the home of friends. He showed her what to eat and how to eat it: 'It is never easy to eat when you are a model. You are hungry but you are frightened you will lose your figure. For a time I took some pills that suppressed the appetite, but they were not correct for the complexion. In the end I didn't care and I ate more because I was large anyway and that was a part of my character. I avoided to slim with a diet, so I would eat normally or eat nothing. But when I ate, I ate like a sparrow – a big, German sparrow. Sometimes I felt this was the hardest part of my work, either to eat, or not to eat. Is there any other job like that? I'm sure there isn't. Oh, aside from dancers – they are neurotic, too.'

Maywald was meticulous in his tutoring of Nico over food and drink, because he knew that in France food and drink meant company, socialising, fellowship; Nico needed friends above everything. He made sure she appeared cordial but never *arriviste*. His *milieu* was stuffily debonair, rarely bohemian, but Nico accepted whatever came her way and did not object to the bourgeois ambience – not while she was in training. She was dazzled. But once she had stopped being Audrey Hepburn and developed, with Maywald's help, her 'Hemingway' blonde look, with the long, eyebrow-level bangs to hide her ample forehead, she out-dazzled the lot of them. Nico resolved that all heads should turn her way, men and women, bourgeois and bohemian: 'You could say I looked the same from 1957 for ten years, until I changed the colour of my hair for Jim Morrison. Maybe my hair grew a little longer or shorter depending on the cut, otherwise I never bothered to make a change. Whether it was quite the fashion I didn't care, because I had found my fashion. It gave me a security.'

Secure, she could start to seduce. It was commonly said of Nico that she knew how to turn every head in the room, though she denied it: 'I was tall, I was blonde, and I was dignified. Nothing more is needed to make an effect. It is short people who need technique. Andy Warhol had technique, I had none.' She admitted in 1985 that she desired to seduce all the beautiful people she met, and in so doing seduced everyone, because she wanted 'beautiful friends (rather more than beautiful sex)'. In the restaurants and bars of Paris, with Maywald at her side and surrounded by *le beau monde*, the goddess-in-training honed her primitive technique of seduction: she looked fascinating, said nothing, and if cornered went 'Ho, ho, ho, ho, ho . . .' It worked.

'I MODELLED FOR COCO CHANEL, and she corrupted me. That is why they say I went with women.' Nico was lying. She never worked for Chanel. She worked with the models who worked for Chanel. Madame Chanel was 73 when Nico started modelling in Paris, and at the time she liked to use a mixture of mannequins and princesses, the latter because 'they're bored. Their mothers and grandmothers had a different occupation: love.' In any case, Nico would not have taken kindly to the sort of snotty advice Chanel offered her staff in the form of savoury aphorisms:

> The greatest flattery that one person can offer another is carnal pleasure, and only carnal pleasure, because reason has no share in it and there can be no question of merit, and because it is addressed not to the character of the person but to the person himself.

Madame Chanel hired German models for a short time in the early Sixties, when Nico was far too established as a covergirl. Chanel was obsessed with kinetic grace, which Nico tended to neglect: 'I like those tall patrician German girls because they walk well naturally. First they thrust their thighs forward, like animals; the calves and the feet follow. The French and the English girls do the opposite: they put their feet out first, and that's ungraceful.' The nearest Nico came to Coco Chanel's corrupting grasp was when she joined the matron's modelling team round the back of the Chanel establishment on rue Cambon in the afternoons after work, in what they called the *cabine*. 'We were like a gang, we young girls,' observed Anne-Marie Quazza, a distinguished Chanel model of that time and now a businesswoman and mother. 'Nico would call round, say hello to us girls – "What are you doing tonight? Where shall we go?" '

They would go as a team to chic nightspots like the Epi-Club, which was the place to be seen then, on Boulevard Montparnasse; the songwriter Serge Gainsbourg was starting up there, while the philosopher Derrida was a regular. It was run by the Castel couple and it was attached to a grocery, an *épicerie*, hence its name; the Castels later opened Le Castel which became a favourite haunt of Nico's in the Sixties. 'There was also Régine's, the old one on Rue du Four,' recalled Anne-Marie Quazza. 'The Chanel models were regarded as something rather special, because we were not all conventional mannequins. We were not a *cabine des mannequins*, but we went around in a group just the same. You can imagine what it was like for this gang of girls to enter the club and sit at a table. I think we must have been very intimidating! But the table would soon be surrounded and the other tables emptied. Nico would join us on these outings, and we liked her very much. She would laugh a lot, very bright in manner.' The Swedish model Anne-Sophie Monet added, 'She was not at all sombre, you know, but I must say she was a bit strange. She carried around with her a book by the philosopher Nietzsche. I never saw her actually read it.'

In Paris, Nico was a covergirl, a print model, but not a mannequin. She worked solely with photographers, in their studios and on location, displaying the latest fashions for the magazines, either exclusive *grande couture* or *prêt à porter* for the department stores. Out of season she would advertise beauty soap or scent (not eau de cologne, if she could help it). One of the first Paris studies of her is the most sensational, and advertises nothing. It was taken by Jeanloup Sieff in 1957, who was hardly older than the models who posed for him. She sits on a stool in a dressing room, naked and fleshy, looking as though she has just wiped away her make-up, or her tears. She is coiled round, curling her neck to catch the camera. Nico looks like a gazelle.

'Nico was considered a healthy, country girl,' commented Anne-Marie Quazza. 'It was her big, red apple-cheeks and large-boned body that gave her this image, and she had by then ash-blonde hair. Nico would laugh a lot, which emphasised this impression. If I remember rightly she was not promoted as a girl from Germany but

Switzerland or Sweden. There were two German models around us in Paris then in this position, Nico and Anka, but they were not considered Germans. I don't know if this was something any more to do with the war, because I imagine that should really have been left behind by this time.' Coco Chanel had outlived the attacks on her Nazi collaborations. She lay low after the war and only in 1954 felt able to open up her salon again to challenge the supremacy of Willy Maywald's employer Dior; she never thought that men were the best designers of women's clothes.

Anne-Marie Quazza continued: 'Nico looked powerful in print. She was *volonté*, strong-willed in her appearance. She conveyed a real personality in her pictures. In fact, I would say this is a difference between the late Fifties and today, the expression of the model as a personality. In those days you would open your magazine and recognise certain models by their individuality. Monica Chevalier, Marie-Hélène Arnaud, Nicole de la Margé, Suzy Parker and Ivy Nicholson from America, Sandra Peterson, Danielle Loder whose father was a British film star – I forget everyone now, but they had a particular personality that they disclosed in the photograph. I think that later on, in the Sixties, models were used more to represent the reader, and now a certain anonymity has crept in. There are exceptions in the first division, of course, and in my time there weren't so many models around, anyway. The equivalent of Nico today, at least as a print model, is someone like Claudia Schiffer, another German.'

By the age of nineteen, Nico was earning an exceptional amount of cash. She obtained work from a pioneering model agency in Paris run from a skimpy office near the Trocadero by the astute Dorian Leigh, a sister of Suzy Parker's. 'Nico would earn between 80 to 250 francs an hour, or between 500 to 800 francs if she was booked for the day,' Anne-Marie Quazza calculated, 'and I remember only too well that it was *Elle* and *Vogue* that paid less than the others, because they considered themselves more famous! At the end of each month she would have earned at least 10,000 francs net [at least £80,000 net a year at 1992 values]. She didn't save it – when you are that age, who saves? You just *live*!'

Nico *lived* her nights best of all when she escaped the teasy-weasy world of Willy Maywald and joined her model friends in the underground *caves* of St Germain, her Nietzsche by her side: 'Everywhere good was in a cellar, beneath the streets, and it was like a speed drug to be there. It was the true idea of the bohemian.' She was a little late to be a true bohemian, for they had died out in France a century earlier – brazen young artists who detested conventions, wore unkempt clothes and, worst of all, kept *irregular* hours. *They* were Nico's true *bohémiens*, the 'gypsies of society' who affected to come from nowhere, and nowhere was their destination. It is ironic that one of Nico's favourite operas was *La Bohème*, Puccini's sanitised tale of romantic, bohemian love set in a chocolate-box Paris (she redeemed herself with a true touch of class when she added, 'but my favoured composer is Donizetti'). Down in the *caves*, the bohemians Nico joined were beatniks, as bohemian as she could find in the post-war world.

She sat on wonky stools in the cellar bars amongst the real rebels, the phony rebels, the disaffected and the disinclined. They were gathered together to maintain the image of the wartime Resistance, inspired by its underground intimacy and its mission of benevolent subversion. The press called them 'beatniks' in derision, after the Russian *sputnik*, with a hint of communist deference. For the first time, however, Nico felt there was some kind of intellectual vocabulary that addressed her estrangement from society: 'It took me a long time to understand anything, because it was a foreign language inside a foreign language, but I knew I was not alone in my thinking.' It was here she met the man who invented Dada, Tristan Tzara, then in his sixties – a kind of dadaist Hemingway who coloured her head rather than her hair (she said he taught her to play with words).

She hated the dank, hazy atmosphere – she didn't smoke in those days – but enjoyed the disorder, and the arguments: 'I understood something of politics, which was discussed with intelligence. It was the time of the imperialist war in Algeria, and my secret support was with the Arabs against the French Army, but I could not say this to my society friends, who were often the opposite, but I could say it in these clubs. I always dislike the invader and, of course, I am part Arab because of my father.' She liked the way politics merged with style in the simple black clothes ('Like Arabs – isn't black the perfect colour? For everything?'). Above all, she was curious about the music.

Nico said she learned to love modern jazz at the Hôtel Louisiane, where she heard 'Dizzy Gillespie, Bud Powell, and others I forget. I did not understand the language until later, when I met a professor of jazz who taught me everything. But it was a wild music, against all the conventions that I knew then. So it was a music I could admire but never play. And it was a man's music, anyway.' She learnt instead, she said, to play the cannabis pipe at the Hôtel Louisiane. As she didn't smoke, she disdained a cigarette mixture of marijuana and nicotine, 'though I smoked a hash pipe like a child smokes a first cigarette – coughing and coughing until I was dark red. Then I laughed too much, and I do not like to be vulnerable in this way.' As it made her tired the morning after, she decided to smoke cannabis, if at all, only on Saturday nights.

In the dank cellars she listened to 'what do you call them? *Chansons*? But all kinds of songs are *chansons*. They were like protest songs, but they didn't *protest*, they *reflected*, which was an inspiration to me. I think they were *ballads*, actually.' At the height of this form in the Fifties, Jacques Brel, Boris Vian, Joseph Kosma and Georges Brassens composed brilliant, radical *chansons* that have yet to be equalled for their deft poetry and illuminating thoughts. Nico adored the simplicity of the performance – often just a singer, a stool, a guitar: 'That's all I did when I started by myself,' though, idle as ever, she needed someone else to handle the guitar. Nico came on to the scene at the end of it all, along with the tourists, when her favourite singer Juliette Greco had already progressed from the cellars of Le Tabou and La Rose Rouge to the large concert stage of the Olympia. 'Brigitte Bardot had been discovered in one of these places, and so now all the girls hanged around waiting to be Brigitte Bardot,' Nico smirked, forgetting how the Audrey Hepburn of Ansbacherstrasse had started out. At its best the bohemian scene of St Germain had furnished a rebellious intellect like Nico's with a satisfactory approach to life and death ('there is next to nothing'). At its worst, it offered up to a scornful press and then to a sneering Hollywood the sullen figure of the black-clad, blank-faced, bongo-thumping beatnik.

Back in the studio, Nico the beatnik-in-training could tolerate the peculiar world of modelling because 'I was an alien . . . I did not take it seriously. I could laugh . . . because I was playing the part of Nico.' She arrived on time (or thereabouts), she was compliant, and she ho-ho-ho'ed her way through the session. 'She was professional and very friendly, and yet . . . a little unusual. She made up stories like a child will, saying she'd just seen a celebrity in the street when you knew it was quite impossible. But we didn't mind; we accepted that as her character,' observed Mme Quazza. The best of the print model's work, she added, lay outside the studio. Assignments to the cities and shores of unfamiliar countries were a perk of the covergirl's job, and Nico travelled more than most: Switzerland, Austria for a backdrop of snow; Italy, Spain, the Canaries, for the bright sun: 'I can't remember anymore where I went. Everywhere looked like a magazine. I became blasé. Anyway, I was working. But I can never forget my favourite place to go: Ibiza . . . I think I would like to die there.'

TOBIAS, HER 'BAD SAMARITAN', took Nico to Ibiza for work; she knew nothing of this mountainous island off the Mediterranean coast of Spain. He had worked there on some photo shoots for magazines and booked Nico for the rest of them – it was their chance to be together now that Paris was denied him. She fell in love with the isolated island and was enticed by the cheap houses available for rent there; the climate was steady, the landscape unspoilt, and the sun furnished extremes of effulgent light and deep shadow. Better still, it was an 'after hours' kind of place. It kept faith with its time-worn reputation as a haven for hedonists and pirates. A small colony of bohemian artists settled there, 'about 50 foreign artists, mainly Americans,' recalled Victor Brox, one of their number. 'There were writers like Joseph Heller who wrote *Catch-22*, poets, jazz musicians, but mainly painters – Bob Thompson, Frank and Jean Schwarky . . . They were there for the light and the idyllic ambience. The very few tourists we saw were mainly Germans, for some reason.' Spain was still a fascist state run by Franco's police ('Germans feel at home in Spain. They can wear their jackboots to the beach'). A German paper, *Der Kurier*, printed an effusive feature on Ibiza in 1953:

> Between these ancient walls, which have seen the centuries pass by, the people can live cheaper than anywhere else in the world from local fish and vegetables, bread and goats' milk. Germans can take lodgings here at less cost than any other resort in Europe.
>
> You whitewash houses and gates twice a year, spring and autumn, and you gather together at the quay in the morning light when the steamers from Valencia call with goods, just as the Phoenicians and Carthaginians sent their ships to the sun-kissed islands to trade for the gold juice of the olive. Here is happiness.

The sun-kissed, olive-drenched conclusion of the report revealed how perfectly the island suited someone as languid as Nico: 'You do not ask questions on Ibiza. You do not count the hours, nor worry about their passing.' The trouble was, that's how she acted everywhere.

'One day we heard this story from the locals,' said Brox, 'that the most beautiful girl in the world was coming to live in Ibiza, but a lot of restrictions had been placed on her by the Guardia Civil. Namely – she must remain completely covered at all times in public view, she must leave the house as little as possible in the daytime, she must adopt no provocative attitude whatsoever, and she must keep herself entirely to herself ['You do not ask questions on Ibiza']. We were told she was extremely beautiful but unusual and fragile in her personality. It was decided amongst us bohemians that we would only think *very good vibrations* about her – that's the sort of thing that went on in those days.' The beatniks of Ibiza could see her walking through Ibiza town dressed completely in black: a black scarf around her head, black sunglasses, black gloves, and a long black robe down to her feet. She was swathed from public view like a docile Muslim. 'It was stunning to see,' reflected Brox, 'extraordinary, quite extraordinary.' Most extraordinary of all was Nico's acceptance of these sinister restrictions. Nico could explain these things away by saying she was playing Nico. Nevertheless, she knew she never looked better than when she wore black.

Once in Ibiza, Nico decided that her mother should come too, for a holiday. She paid for the journey, met her tearfully at Barcelona and brought her to the island on the ferryboat. They arrived at the port of Ibiza, for the main town in the south and the entire island take the same name. Nico found a little house to rent at 500 pesetas a month in the crammed and noisy walled town district of sa Penya, but her mother hated it and Nico found her a separate house a mile down the port in calmer Figueretas. Paying for two houses, her ready money soon went: 'We had two months of glory until I ran out of money and I had to borrow some for the ship and train to Paris.'

Ibiza became Nico's port in a storm for the rest of her life, and, once Nico had leased a house a year later, her mother's too (though her mother's storm in a port). The attraction was not merely the warmth, the idle pace and the reassuring sense of timelessness. Nico was increasingly attracted to the island by the drugs and the studs she could ferret out after dark, once the black shroud lifted up and she could make friends in the bars. On one side of the town there were the Beats, thinking very good vibrations about her, and on the other side the loaded playboys on breaks from mainland Spain, of whose luxury assets Nico's mother thought very good vibrations indeed.

It was in Ibiza, on routine rests from Paris, that the Nico of nineteen and twenty and twenty-one years slowly dug under the bohemian skin. Every generation has its renegades, and every generation reclaims them. The appropriation moves ever faster and each sign of defiance is absorbed and enfeebled with practised speed. When Christa was a child the Germans sired *navajos* and the French *zazous* to rebel against the Nazis. The defiant kids were rounded up, spurned with derision and hanged. It took all of five years for the tourist coaches of San Francisco, Manhattan and Paris to stop by the clubs and bars sheltering the Beat Generation of the Fifties. The hippies of the mid-Sixties were ridiculed for all of a year before kaftans and granny glasses were sold in suburban markets. Seventies Punk was a consumer trade within six months. The ravers of 1988, who danced in Ibiza while Nico died, were already consumed. Back in the Fifties, at the age of nineteen, however, Nico decided she would rather like to live the aesthetic life of the dissident bohemian: she wanted to believe in 'nothing at all' because 'everything is stupid' and 'everything we do is harmful'. She wanted to be 'aimless'. She agreed that the beatnik artists were 'making something from them-selves', they were 'searching', and that was the only way to live in a society based on 'exploitation . . . and narrow-mindedness'. But the giggling covergirl, ho-ho-ho-ing her way through photo sessions and dinner parties, was covertly drawn to the prime meaning of Beat – beaten up, world weary. Jack Kerouac wrote in 1955: 'Here we are dealing with the pit and prune juice of poor, beat life itself and the pathos of people in the Godawful streets.'

Ibiza was not a pit-and-prune-juice kind of town. Its beatniks had little time for the overly glum line that Nico trailed; they were having good fun in the sun. The artists had rather fine drugs to help them in their demanding task of thinking very good vibrations. As the saying goes, they 'wrote in their smoke'; marijuana and cannabis resin were as much a part of their diet as wine. Most supplies were ferried in from North Africa, Morocco especially: 'It was so easy to find cannabis, like picking it out of the garden,' Nico told a Dutch journalist who was unsure how literal she was being. 'It is foolish to have it illegal. Nothing should be illegal anyway, but once coffee was illegal and now it is a business. One day we will buy cannabis in the grocer shop just like coffee – freeze-dried in big jars. No, it would be better sold in a delicatessen. You could sample it first like goat's cheese.' Her beatnik friends could not pick hard drugs out of the garden, but with the right amount of fake discretion they could buy them in the backs of bars.

Nico cruised between the two social sides of town, both groups linked by their devotion to marijuana; the rich young playboys liked to smoke with their heavy drinking ('Everybody drank Cuba Libre those days, because Battista was still ruling Cuba'). In the privacy of their boats – motor crafts and yachts moored in the port – the parties to which Nico would be invited were fuelled by soft drugs. Nico claimed to recall one young man who shared with her one or two joints of marijuana. His name was Juan Carlos, she said, Juan Carlos de Borbón y Borbón. He is now King Juan Carlos of Spain. 'It is not the only royal personage I have met. And he is not the only one to have taken drugs. There is Princess Margaret of England, for example, and the Monaco people are all junkies. But I think it must be better to be a prince than a king. He must be very boring now. He was a puppet of the fascists for many years, and I think people like him went to Ibiza to escape from this boring condition. Soon after I met him he married a princess from Greece. I could have gone to the wedding, but I had to have my baby instead. They could have timed it better.'

Her mother was already planning a marriage for Nico. In the harbour of Ibiza she had spotted the perfect husband. Ostentation was his by-word, and Grete considered him the most debonair ladies' man of a port stuffed with playboys; clearly, ostentatiously, he was the most affluent among them. Nico was advised that 'he had royal blood in his veins . . . [he] was the black sheep of the family and liked to walk barefoot.' But he was known around town for another reason. 'Oh, him! He was the town playboy. He was a prat. He was always drunk. It was all show, and he appealed to susceptible girls. I thought she'd have had more sense,' laughed one of the island's residents. She didn't. She got to know him, all too quickly. Nico was eager to stay on his yacht that he told her was 'standing in the harbour'. This was literally true: it was an old boat cemented to the side of the Club Nautico, and its engine had been removed. 'We got drunk a lot and nothing happened,' she confided.

Now Grete was putting pressure on her nineteen-year-old daughter to marry. She may have been embarrassed that she was relying entirely on her daughter's earnings, or perhaps she saw no other way to restrain Nico's childish romanticising, or maybe she wanted to curb her extraordinary career. But it does seem odd timing to attempt this at the start of Nico's career in one of the highest-paid professions a woman could find. As Helma said, Grete never paid much attention to money. The pressure she placed on her daughter rose, rather, from her own unfathomable loneliness.

Nico decided that her mother should now live permanently in Ibiza instead of Berlin, and be as near to heaven as earth allowed. 'Our entire household in Berlin my mother sold for 1,000 Deutschmarks,' wrote Nico. She sold everything, including her clothes-making equipment. Her sister Helma, however, saw that Ibiza was no heaven for Grete: 'She went to Ibiza and she had nothing to do any more; she had given up her profession and she was not yet even 50 years old. The house in Ibiza, which was hired on a lease, was furnished to my sister's choice. The furniture came from Valencia. There was also a beautiful chimney breast, I remember. But there was no one to meet. Nico thought it would all be wonderful, but she hadn't thought out the practical problems, and in order to have the money for the house, Nico had to work in Paris and Rome and so on. She was not there with her mother very often. I think my sister made friends with a German schoolteacher on the island, a woman, but I don't think their friendship lasted. There were no men. Not one. My sister became ill, ill in the head. I don't think Nico understood this tragedy. It got worse and worse, and my sister was forced to face it alone.'

'ANDY WARHOL TOLD ME that you do not need to know many people in a place to know the others worth knowing. This works as long as the people you know in the first place are the right ones,' Nico declared. Those she met in Paris were certainly right for Nico – that is, they were famous. She had already built her phantom family: Maywald was her phantom father, Maldonado-Bostock her phantom lover, Tobias her phantom brother, and the mannequins her phantom sisters. Paris was her phantom Berlin, Ibiza her playground Lübbenau. Now she needed friends, not family; she needed famous friends. Nico never sought out famous people for reasons of snobbery; it was their glamour that attracted her. All her life she remained the teenage girl in the back row of the cinema, ogling at the breathtaking demigods on the screen. Now she saw them in real life, on the social round, in clubs and bars and dinner parties. Pride of the pack were the Marquands.

The Marquands were the French Fondas. Christian Marquand was a lusty leading man of Spanish–Arab descent, a handsome actor in French and Hollywood films who began his career in Jean Cocteau's *Beauty and the Beast* straight after the war. Nico first saw him on screen opposite Brigitte Bardot in Roger Vadim's film *And God Created Woman*. His brother Serge was also a renowned actor. There was Nadine, the film director, married to film star Jean-Louis Trintignant; and Tina, Christian's wife, was the Hollywood-born daughter of the glamorous Maria Montez and Jean-Pierre Aumont, the 'Monsieur Dreamboat' of the German magazines the teenage Christa had devoured. A dinner at the Marquands' could make Nico drool; it comprised a double feature of movie gossip.

The Marquands were the 'not many people' who led her to 'the others worth knowing'. Through them she met two stars who helped her into films. First was the elegant actor Maurice Ronet, who had just finished shooting *Carve Her Name with Pride* in England. He led Nico into an adventure that ended with the birth of her child. Second, she met the stunning Sylvano Mangano, who was not only known as a film actress – most famous today for her role as the boy's mother in *Death in Venice* – but also as the wife of Dino De Laurentiis, the international producer. Nico was invited to stay at their apartment in Rome, an offer which led eccentrically to her film debut.

Nico told the press three different stories, at least three, of how she got a part in *La Dolce Vita*. She could have told as many versions as she liked; both Dino De Laurentiis and Federico Fellini said, 'I really don't remember how it happened.' She already stayed in Rome twice a year. The couturiers of Rome were trying terribly hard to oust Paris as the centre of the trade, and they used top models like Nico to help them:

> The Italian fashion industry has gone ahead by leaps and bounds. Couturiers as well as manufacturers are studying the colours, designs, and textures of cottons and fine woollens, as well as the traditional silks and coloured furs ... the problem is the lack of organisation. It would be nice to say that Rome is a city that mixes business with pleasure. Unfortunately, it mixes pleasure with more pleasure, which is bad for business.

The London *Times* of April 1958 made its report in the year the press began to give generous space to the Italian fashion collections. Half the buyers in Rome were German, and Nico displayed the latest designs for the magazine-reading *fraus* of Hamburg, Munich and Berlin, much to her distaste. But Rome washed the bad taste away. Rome became her phantom Paris: 'Italian boys are so beautiful. You sit at a café and watch the street on Via Veneto and it is like an assembly line of gods. Anyway, you have to sit and watch because the service is terrible.' A few Italians were beginning to agree with the carping foreigners, Nico and the *Times*. They observed that the rich of Rome were living a sweet and empty life, *la dolce vita*, and the poor were paying for it. The economy was in a state of continual crisis, and the air of decadence was choking social development. While Nico tried her first snort of enervating cocaine in the back of a Rome bar, the film director Federico Fellini was planning a film to reflect the hollowness of *la dolce vita*. But he was still looking for a title.

NICO THOUGHT that everything in Rome was blessedly chaotic, and none more so than her part in the making of *La Dolce Vita*, the notorious film that launched her out of modelling and into the real, fake world of stardom. The longest version of the three stories she told about it incorporated the more retarded features of the other two: 'I was staying in Rome with Sylvano Mangano, who was a friend, at her home with her husband and their children (who are now themselves producers). It was in the summer of 1958, after the spring fashion season. Sylvano had a lot of advice to give me, because she had been a model and changed her profession [not quite, but she was Miss Rome 1946]. She liked gambling, and she introduced me to roulette, to which I could have been addicted; ever since, I have loved to gamble. One day at the apartment there was this big row, two men shouting at each other, it was very noisy and I heard something smash. I went down and saw Mr De Laurentiis trying to stop Fellini from leaving. It is amusing to watch Italians arguing. They are like wrestlers who have been separated. They flick their arms around a lot, but there is just air in front of them. It is invisible wrestling. But here was a film producer and a film director making invisible wrestling. Fellini saw me. He was not so old then, about 40 years old I guess [he was 38], and he is a charming man. Mr De Laurentiis was much older [he was also 38]. I think Fellini saw me and was interested in me. But he was in a bad temper and he stormed away.

'I discovered afterwards that Mr De Laurentiis had given Fellini a lot of money to make a new film [$100,000 pre-production costs] and he did not like the ideas. Of course, the film was *La Dolce Vita*. He wanted an American star in it and Fellini wanted Marcello Mastroianni. I think De Laurentiis wanted James Dean [no, dead; it was Paul Newman]. But Fellini wanted Sylvano to star in the film also; so he owed this money to her husband, and it was this typical crazy film business shit. Mr De Laurentiis insisted that the script would not work, and in the end, you know, he was right because Fellini had to change a lot of things, and make improvisations, and it was a v-e-r-y long film. In the end they had a film that was ten hours long [this is apparently correct]. Andy Warhol would have put it on two screens and cut the time in half, but the Italians are not so *experimental*. So they made edits and they wear out their scissors. It is still three hours, which is a long time for Italians to sit down in a cinema. I think this is really why the Pope tried to ban it.

'The next summer I was staying there once more and I met some friends at the cafés of the Via Vittorio Veneto who said they were working on this film, and it was crazy because Fellini did not know how things would go and nobody understood the story. He also wanted to do an orgy scene, but nobody knew how to do an orgy. Well, I thought, I can help them, though I have never been in an orgy, of course. So they took me to Cinecittà which is the big studio Mussolini had built to make bad films. I was with my friends and there were some props on a table. I picked up a candlestick with a false light on it, and I was just holding it up. No, it was a candelabra. And Fellini saw me and ran over to me and said, "I have dreamt of you. I recognise your face. You will look wonderful with candlelight. You must be a star in *La Dolce Vita*." I must have entered his dreams when he saw me at the house. He introduced me to Marcello Mastroianni, who was very attractive for his age [he was 35]. "What is your name?" he asked. "Nico." "Nico is perfect. If I say the name before you appear, then the audience will think a man is coming. Then they will see you, and it will be a sensation!" And that is exactly what happens in the film.

'What I found so funny was that the first scene with Mastroianni was to be at a café on the Via Veneto. You know, then it was very chic to be on the Via Veneto. All the tables had umbrellas for the sun, and it was a very animated atmosphere. Everyone tried to look beautiful and . . . well, they were Italians and so they tried very hard, except that Italians are like little midgets. I am always afraid to step on one. So, I thought we were filming the scene on the Via Veneto.

But – it was amazing – they had built a fake Via Veneto in the studio. I had left a real Via Veneto to travel to the same thing, but more flat. This is why I think this kind of film-making is so stupid.'

It has to be made clear, for those who never knew Nico to be such a raconteur, that it took three conversations with a writer for her to say this much about *La Dolce Vita*. The pauses, of which there were hundreds, have been edited (in the Italian fashion). Fellini, back in 1959, played on this trait of Nico's. She was worried, she told him, about acting. He had asked her to play Nico, a model. He believed that she would be playing herself. She believed she was already playing a role; Nico the model was the role she already played. She did not know how to play this role twice, 'one on top of the other'. Fellini's first advice to 'act naturally' was the worst he could have given this twenty-year-old woman with 'the mentality of an eleven-year-old'.

In order to help her, Fellini asked her to do something quite contrary to her nature. That way, he estimated, she would have to play the role. He asked her to talk, to be garrulous, to talk and talk all the way through the scenes. The only time she could shut up was when Mastroianni was talking to her. She could say anything she wanted, in any language, because they could always dub something else on afterwards – a typically Italian notion, and the bane of many filmgoers. Nico practised talking. She invented her own languages, and gabbled away in gobbledygook. Mastroianni enjoyed this. It became a feature of their improvised dialogues:

Marcello: What language are you speaking now?
Nico: Eskimo. Ho, ho, ho, ho, ho, ho, ho . . .

Nico's appearance in the film is so essential it is little wonder that Fellini pounced on her. *La Dolce Vita* follows the dissolute and rambling exploits of a bored journalist, Marcello, and his snooping photographer called Paparazzo (it is a sign of this film's eminence that he lent his name to the prying photographers of the sensationalist press, the *paparazzi*). They drift through nine meandering sections, each exposing the tension and malaise that lies at the heart of *la dolce vita*; how ironic that the film is now exalted as a symbol of an entire era. In its first half, Marcello's actions fluctuate between two women: his old lover Maddalena, and a sensational sex goddess who visits Rome. This role is played by an ex-Miss Sweden, Anita Ekberg, blonde, voluptuous. The film is in black and white, and she is silver. The older Maddalena is played by Anouk Aimée, dark, hermetic.

The rest of the film searches for this visual, dynamic balance. Nico's ash-blonde hair and sparkling presence restore a certain harmony. They made her Swedish, like Ekberg. Her entrance, as Mastroianni predicted, is 'sensational' (it is Scene 75, for anyone counting). He walks through the raucous throng of the café society on the Via Veneto, and spots Nico, off screen:

Marcello: Nico!
[Nico enters camera right, her back to the camera, a mass of vivid blonde hair. She turns, full face]
Marcello: Nico! How are you?
Nico: Marcello! I'm going to Bassano, to my fiancé's castle.
Marcello: Why not take me along? Paparazzo wants to photograph you for a fashion magazine.
Nico: I finished modelling a year ago. Enough's enough.

They find a car, driven by the Old Duchess with her dachshund, and go to the castle. Nico, in a feat of virtuoso dramaturgy, manages to talk all the way through the scene. At the castle, called Bassano di Sutri, there is a party. It is held in honour of Nico and her fiancé, a prince:

Maddalena: There's Giulio and Nico, his Swedish lover. She'll be a princess.
[Nico laughs and bites the thumb of her fiancé]

Later, Nico takes the armoured visor of a knight and flounces around with it on her head.

'That's how I remember her from the Sixties. Coy, but a bit cheeky. She was just like you see her in *La Dolce Vita*. She certainly didn't need to act in that film!' claimed the photographer David Bailey.

'When I knew her she was just like you see her in *La Dolce Vita*. You know that scene where she's giggling a lot in a castle? She puts a metal visor on her head and horses around. That's how she could be, like a child, playing, sweet and real fun,' recalled the composer Jackson Browne.

'I remember that scene in *La Dolce Vita* where she bites the thumb of the guy. That's what she was like,' said the composer John Cale, more darkly.

They may have remembered her face, but nobody could remember the name she was given in the credits. It was Nico Otzak, and nobody knows why.

During the filming Nico met Anouk Aimée, who played Maddalena. She said the film star told her, 'It's funny, you have the name Nico. My husband was called Nico. We're divorced now. He was Greek, and he used to run a nightclub in Paris.'

Nico didn't dare breathe a word.

HER LINE 'I finished modelling a year ago. Enough's enough' came from the heart. Nico had been a covergirl for four years, a model for six, and enough was enough. She was almost 21, absolutely aimless but totally ambitious. Filming was not the fun she thought it to be; there was too much hanging around, and the technicians seemed to be more the centre of attention than she was – 'crazy!' But there must be more to life than posing, she thought; there must be something creative she could do. She pondered on the options while she meandered around the spiffy social scene of Rome for a couple of weeks after filming. Nico started to see how drugs, drink and mischief fitted neatly together when she was bored, but most of all she got a taste for gambling.

She loved the card games, and roulette. 'When you gamble in games, you either believe that everything depends on chance or on fate. I was born a Libra in the middle of the month, so I am very fatalistic. I love to gamble, at least, when I can afford to lose. But I like playing these games, and I like better to win them.' It was in Rome, Nico recalled, that she first came to understand the importance of astrology. 'It is not a matter of rational thought, but you can explain it that way, this is what I learned. Look at the sea. The tides are controlled by the moon. We cannot control the sea, but the moon can. It is the same with our lives. The planets and the stars determine them, from the moment we are brought into the world. It is the same with women's problems [menstruation]. They are moving like the sea.'

The stars might have been handling her life, but not her diary. She suddenly remembered she had been booked to make another film, a real proper organised one. Nico sailed out on the ferry to join the film crew on the magnificent Italian island of Ischia. The work had been arranged for her through her friend Maurice Ronet, the suave screen actor (and later the director of an odd cult film called *Bartleby*). The film was in French and called *Plein Soleil*. At various times in its celebrated life it would be known throughout America and England as *Purple Noon, Blazing Sun* or *Lust for Evil*, depending on the coarseness of its distributor. Its subject was deceit and duplicity. An elegant version of a Patricia Highsmith novel, this *film noir* thriller was to be shot on a yacht, a kind of setting which was the speciality of its director, René Clément. He'd just won a foreign film Oscar for *Forbidden Games*, his portrait of two children (very like Christa and Ulrich) who spent their days crafting a cemetery for dead animals. He detested studios and delighted in the technical problems posed by small and awkward spaces.

Clément was meticulous, obsessive for details. He had no time for idlers. He certainly had no time for Nico. She arrived to find that her role had been handed over to a regular French actress, Marie Laforêt. Nico was doubly shocked: she had wasted her chance, and she discovered for the first time that her part was the lead female role (though it was very much a 'man's film'). It hurt her even more when the film played to good houses and triumphant reviews. The principal actor came over and lent her his shoulder to cry on. He offered to take her away for a few days, somewhere interesting, as consolation. The amorous young lead was Alain Delon. Nico was in seventh heaven when she met him; he was the prettiest man she had ever seen. She knew, she said, that fate had drawn them together. Her mother had goaded her to get a husband, and here was the very man.

'We went away for a short time and fell in love,' remembered Nico, though it's doubtful that Delon remembered any such thing. His regular lover then was another German, the spellbinding actress Romy Schneider, who also appeared in the film – a woman whose sad life would in many ways match Nico's. The 23-year-old Romeo had once been a parachutist with the French marines, and there was an astonishing contrast between his butch physique, his rugged bearing, his compact frame, his elegant demeanour, and his cute face. Delon was the French James Dean, and Nico met him at the glittering start of his astounding career. He remains to this day an iconic film star, adored and hated and followed remorselessly by gossip writers. Even when Nico first knew him, Delon was demonically ambitious. Within five years he was to set up his own production company, through which he would aggressively dispose of his pretty-boy image and turn tough-guy, an impression he would revel in, on and off screen. Nico called him 'the most dangerous man I ever met'. Delon bragged of his associations with the underworld, and this fascinated her even more. 'He was like a gypsy,' she claimed, 'with strong eyes and dark hair, and I wanted him for myself. I had never felt so possessive before. It was a very emotional feeling whenever I saw him. My hand shook, like my mother's hand shook when she was ill, I could not control it.'

Away from the film set of *Plein Soleil*, Nico claimed that he took her around the island for a few days of 'falling in love'. After a mere few days of 'falling in love' they went to their separate work – Delon to Rome and Visconti, Nico to Paris and Maywald. A friend who knew them both said that 'it would have been better for both their lives if they had both drowned then and there in Ischia – anything to stop them meeting again and doing what they did.'

4 1960–1964

How Clear She Shines!

And this shall be my dream to-night –
I'll think the heaven of glorious spheres
Is rolling on its course of light
In endless bliss through endless years;

I'll think there's not one world above,
Far as these straining eyes can see,
Where wisdom ever laughed at Love,
Or Virtue crouched to Infamy;

Where, writhing 'neath the strokes of Fate,
The mangled wretch was forced to smile;
To match his patience 'gainst her hate,
His heart rebellious all the while;

Where Pleasure still will lead to wrong,
And helpless reason warn in vain;
And truth is weak and treachery strong;
And Joy the surest path to Pain.

(EMILY BRONTË, 1843)

'I WAS 21 WHEN I MET William Burroughs in Paris. I was staying at a little hotel in Place de la Contrescarpe and he was staying next door. I was sitting in a bar and he made an excuse to talk to me. He said he was writing a book, and he would put me in it, a pretty young girl sitting in a bar. I don't know which book this is. Do you know it?' Nico's musicians stared earnestly at the floor. One of them finally piped up: 'But, Nico, didn't you tell us the same story about Ernest Hemingway last week?' 'Oh, yes, he was there too.'

Nico invented tales of chance encounters ('It was a question of fate, not of chance. Roulette is a game of chance, but I think life is a matter of fate'). Nobody could fathom out why; she could have told far more remarkable stories of chance that were actually true. Yet she felt obliged to tell lies if the truth threw light on her family, either her physical or her phantom family. That's why she never told anyone the remarkable story of the day she met the real Nico. The real Nico, however, had less to hide: 'It was 1960. I was living at the time in New York, though I also had an apartment in Paris. And I knew a girl of Chinese origin called China Machado – she was a fashion editor of *Harper's Bazaar*. And we decided that summer to come to Paris for a break, though work was never far away. She arranged a photo shoot for Dick Avedon in Paris, in part to take advantage of the visit. Well, China invited me for dinner, which they held in the studio during the photo *séance*. We were sat around this big table – Avedon, Machado, the models, me – and all of a sudden China called to me, "Nico!" At that moment the girl next to me at the table turned and stared at me. "Nico?" I said yes. "You live in Paris?" Yes. "Did you have a night club?" I did. She replied, "My name's Nico too, because of you." From that moment we were never separated. For two years we chose to live together, Nico and Nico. Until that business with Delon.'

Nico Papatakis was then 42, an alluringly handsome man whom Nico would have wished to seduce, however weak her opening line. His mother was Ethiopian, his father Greek, and he had been born in Addis Ababa. Young and active in Paris after the war, he opened a nightclub on the Left Bank, La Rose Rouge, the Red Rose. Together with the Tabou, it was a centre for the 'new generation', eager for chic bohemian entertainment in dank cellars. Papatakis catered to the social world of the rebellious intellectuals – the bohemians that became the beatniks – and as ever when intellectuals turn rebellious, their world was composed of drink, drugs, sex and song. He supplied the drink and the song. After the philosopher Jean-Paul Sartre had paid a visit to hear the singer Juliette Greco, the press labelled the whole scene 'existentialist', though Sartre replied that 'it was as existentialist as a toilet'.

When Papatakis married the film star Anouk Aimée in 1951, their best man was Jean Genet. They did not know that their best man was soon to be sanctified, though not by any church. He became known as Saint Genet within the year, thanks to Sartre's book of that title, in which he sketched the history of how Genet the unrepentant thief and homosexual prostitute became an eminent writer who 'put good into hell and evil into heaven'. Papatakis was a close friend of Genet's – so close that he produced his notorious film *Un Chant d'amour* ('Love Song'), a metaphoric, silent, black and white study of homosexual love in prison. The film was banned in France and elsewhere for more than twenty years. Papatakis today is a respected director of seven cult films whose subjects relate unceasingly to those of Genet. His first film as director, *Les Abysses* (1963), was drawn from Genet's play *The Maids*, and was in turn outlawed following near-riots at its presentation at the 1963 Cannes Festival. His latest, *Les Équilibristes* ('The Tightrope Walkers') (1991), is based on the true story of a Genet lover who died from a fall. It contains a character called Christa Päffgen.

'We lived together, Nico and Nico,' Papatakis recalled. 'Whenever anybody called out "Nico!" we'd both look round. It was strange, certainly, but rather beautiful to have this little game between us.' Papatakis was one of the original jet set who flew over the Atlantic on the latest aeroplanes in a devoted mission to merge business and pleasure, Europe and America, eternally. He invited Nico to join him, swinging between the continents. Through links like those of *Harper's Bazaar*, she obtained enough covergirl work in New York to pay her own way over and *live*. Their relationship was 'playful and innocent with bouts of rage', according to their friends, 'more brother and sister than husband and wife; they were more like siblings than lovers'. Papatakis was twenty years older (Maywald had been older by thirty years). He replied that, 'Nico had a wonderful spontaneity. She could be naïve about things. She was really very shy but, at the same time, she could be too confident. This was a result of her introversion; yet she was facing the public eye all the time – she was contradictory.

'She took me to Ibiza the next summer [1961] to meet her mother, and it was apparent from this where the source of some of her problems was. Her mother was nervous and agitated about things that we would take for granted. She thought the neighbours were plotting something against her, that they were being evil to her behind her back. The thing is that Nico was very attached to her mother. She would take care of her, support her like a mother, though she did not identify the problem. This protective aspect of Nico was something that was very strong, very strong and important to understand in her life.'

Papatakis accepted the strangeness of Nico because he was overwhelmed by her astonishing physical beauty: 'Nico's looks were sensational. She was never what you would call a classic beauty, but entirely unique. Peculiar. I couldn't get over how the structure of her face, rhythmically speaking, was so exceptional, and then these huge bones . . . But she couldn't rely on this look for her life. I saw that there would have to be a change in her career. Models soon come to an end. It starts in their early twenties, and I wanted Nico to prepare for this. This wasn't easy because she never even took her modelling seriously, though she was professional. She was ambitious. She wanted to be an *artist* . . . it's not surprising because there were artists all around her throughout her life . . . somehow an *artist*.

'I had spent a lot of time listening to singers, and talking to them, because of *La Rose Rouge*. There wasn't only Greco in those days, I heard and dealt with so many. I got to the point where I could recognise by their speech if someone could sing. I had recognised talent and supported certain artists, and by the time I met Nico I could recognise a singing voice in a speaking voice. Nico had this deep tone. In New York once (I would say 1961), I asked her, "Do you sing? You could do." She hadn't thought about it. So I took her to a voice teacher there in New York. I can't remember who it was now, just a singing teacher. She went there and also to acting school – the one run by Lee Strasberg, the Actors Studio.'

Papatakis was right to look ahead. Already, Nico was taking on modelling work that flung her too far in all directions. She posed in the latest Madeleine de la Rausch creations for *Harper's Bazaar* on one assignment, only to be followed by a cheap advertisement for cold cream. It's patently clear how her name came to be put forward for that particular job:

> NEOCOL really does rejuvenate the neck and obliterates all imperfections. I guarantee optimum effectiveness from the full treatment of Neocol.
>
> Yours sincerely, *Jeanne Piaubert*.
>
> Try it at home – Neocol.

One edition of *Elle* features Anne-Marie Quazza on the cover in the newest Chanel jacket of red and gold wool, while inside a straw-blonde Nico stands superciliously in a salmon-checked housecoat, gripping the latest in Electrolux dishwaters: 'Everything clean . . . The washing-up of five people clean in six minutes!' Carlos de Maldonado-Bostock surveyed the ad: 'Christ, she looks bored to tears already. How old is she in this photo? 21, 22, 23? She looks ghastly, like a *hausfrau*, like her dreadful mother. Thank God nobody sees this stuff of hers today.' Anne-Sophie Monet, the Swedish model, stressed that Nico was 'a good model, very professional, though it was obvious by this time that she didn't take it at all seriously. I think she just wanted to earn the money and do something else, though what I don't know. I think she took a lot of jobs on, whatever was on offer – she was always in work. She earned an awful lot of money.'

Nico and Papatakis, with Carlos and Anne-Sophie (who married each other), soared through the seasons on transatlantic flights. At the time Papatakis was working with the director John Cassavetes on his first film. Cassavetes, whose parents were Greek, had put aside some of the money he earned as TV's *Johnny Staccato*, the cool dude private-eye of a popular series who solved crimes and blew jazz in bohemian bars, and with these savings made *Shadows*, a provocative portrait of racism, which Papatakis co-produced. Meanwhile Nico signed up with the world's most famous model agency, Eileen Ford's in New York.

According to Nico, Eileen Ford took her to Ford's own doctor, who regularly gave Nico strong amphetamine pills to lose weight. (Amphetamines were not yet illegal.) This, said Nico, is the moment from which her future drug dependencies derived. At least, that was Nico's claim. Eileen Ford, still the president of Ford Models Incorporated, has no recollection of any Nico. Anne-Marie Quazza, on the other hand, certainly worked for Eileen Ford during 1962. 'She was like a mother to us. There was such a few of us and we were like her babies. She arranged your work and where you stayed and your leisure, she made your *visage*, she made you work and she knew you. Eileen Ford would take you out in the evening and chaperone you, and you quite needed this – we little foreigners in this strange, big city! Ms Ford really made you work, too. The first day I arrived, messy and tired, "jet-lagged" we'd say now, she made me do a photo *séance* with Irving Penn. It must have been the worst session I ever did in my life! But I have to say that I can't recall Nico amongst the group, and Eileen would certainly remember somebody like Nico. Maybe Nico worked for another agency – I think there was one called Plaza Five, but it did not have the *cachet* of Eileen Ford.'

Nico wrote that 'at this point in my life nothing was too much work for me, aimlessly running around Manhattan Island. I guess the "speed" (or diet pills) . . . kind of gave me more energy.' She lived for a time in the West Village and often saw the poet Allen Ginsberg in the street; they developed a 'nice noddy acquaintance', she wrote, in a nodding acquaintance with the term.

Aside from her singing and acting lessons, she learned to drive. The notion of Nico driving a car remained a long-standing joke amongst her many musicians, but their chortling derision was of the 'woman driver' variety. She would merely flash her American licence at them and ask to see theirs. Once she could legally drive she bought a red Ferrari sports car, a model appropriately named Berlinetta. 'She didn't keep it very long. She had a fling with some man who stole it off her and disappeared,' Aunt Helma grumbled. 'She just didn't know how to deal with all the money she had, no idea at all. She enjoyed giving parties, she invited the whole world to them. She loved bathing in money.'

Carlos de Maldonado-Bostock remembers the time like this: 'Everything was rather jolly. I had a place in New York on East 48th Street, and every night it was packed with friends. So far as I know there was no drug scene there; we knew how to have a good time anyway. We'd go to a club called the L'Interdit next to the Gotham Hotel. We'd go in there and steal Ferraris, pranks like that. We had no money at all, we were poor as church mice, but we still had a fine time. We used to travel around . . . but, it's funny, you know, I just can't recall where the money came from.'

Anne-Sophie stressed that 'Nico always had money and was always buying things for everyone. Meals, drinks, little gifts. Whenever she came to see me she would come with flowers. I think some people took advantage of her generosity. It was certain that she wanted to make friends. The generosity was genuine, but also she wanted to promote her friendship. I know there is talk of lesbianism. Yes, she did, she did like lots of girls. She adored them, but I don't think it was much more than a desire to be friends with them. I think the storytelling was part of this. She made up stories, always inventing things, making them up on the spot. She did it to have something to say, to keep you interested.'

'I had an affair with Jeanne Moreau,' Nico alleged to her manager. She later added that 'Jeanne Moreau was working on a film then with François Truffaut about a love triangle [*Jules et Jim*, 1961]. I wonder if you can tell from the picture that she is happy from the love of a woman, not the men you are meant to believe in?' In the esteemed *Jules et Jim* Moreau is both ingenuous and knowingly seductive. She was ten years older than Nico then, and certainly more slender. 'She was not a typical woman, at least,' hinted Nico. 'She is beautiful and shadowy. She commands your attention with a look, which is how strong people should be.' Nico was once asked who her favourite film actress was. 'Bette Davis,' she replied, 'or her sister – what is her name?' 'Her screen sister was Joan Crawford.' 'No, you mean Jeanne Moreau.'

'Nico had these romances with women, and I remember her telling me about Moreau,' Carlos de Maldonado-Bostock reflected. 'She had this notion that it was chic to be a lesbian. It was like the idea of her reading Nietzsche; she probably carried the book around because it was a fashion. The same with her dress – she didn't care what she looked like outside of the studio. That was a fashion, too, the fashion of bohemianism. It's a kind of put-on rebellion, and she picked it up from other people. She was beautiful anyway, she could get away with it, she could wear anything and look sensational. But she didn't care. Bohemians fight society, but she wasn't fighting society so much as fighting herself. She was a nihilist. She wasn't a nihilist from reading Nietzsche either, she just liked that atmosphere of emptiness, of nothing. It was already there in her life, you see, she didn't need to intellectualise it. Other people probably did that for her, you know, gave her the trappings that made it seem more put-on than it was. They were probably the same people that took advantage of her, used her money, I wouldn't be surprised. What the hell did she do with her money?'

THERE WERE MANY TIMES when Nico called herself a nihilist: 'I'm a nihilist so I like destruction, I have to admit, but there should be a reason for someone to destroy themselves.' Elsewhere, 'As far as religion is concerned, luckily from early childhood, nihilism seemed to be the most suitable ever since I started to think.' The Nietzsche book the covergirl carried around was *Beyond Good and Evil*, or rather *Jenseits von Gut und Böse*, for she owned the original German version – in doing so, Nico was being more rational than pretentious. Though her friends understandably assumed she never read the thing, her outlook on life was guided by the tract, as far as she understood it. 'His style is old-fashioned, like he had just copied out the Bible.' This was truer than she knew, for Friedrich Nietzsche's previous book had been *Thus Spake Zarathustra*, which he composed in the style of the scriptures. He warned in his *Beyond Good and Evil* of 1886 that people would fight against the meaningless of life they had observed now that 'God is dead'. They would supplant the absolute they lacked with a new one, nationalism; the nation would invest their life with new purpose.

To come to this conclusion Nietzsche examined the origins of morality, and did so by tracing the etymology of the words *good* and *evil*. He believed in two kinds of morality – crudely, the privileged morality of the Masters, and the corrupt one of the Slaves. It was the Slave morality that defined codes of Mastery as degenerate. Pride was considered by them sinful and was replaced by humility. Liberty they squashed into obedience. When Nico read this sort of thing, she felt vindicated. The moral code of Mastery was more like hers – nobody ever accused Nico of humility or obedience. Pride and autonomy were her hobbies. Here, too, was a foundation for her contempt for nationalism. In being a nihilist, Nico thought, she stood against the repellent, hypocritical fervour for oppression and genocide that marked a nationalism she had not only glimpsed, but lived through.

She fought on two fronts when she touted her Nietzsche round the chic cellar clubs of the Left Bank. First of all here was this *Mädchen*, this Aryan German girl, clutching the work of one of Hitler's favourite philosophers. All she lacked was a swastika armband and a riding crop. It wasn't only her looks, either. She liked to provoke a reaction in conversation by pretending to adore fascism, though always in a tone she considered ironic. One of her associates was the film actress Zouzou, someone who seemed to prefigure Nico in her career moves – from model to actress to singer – and her affairs. In 1961 Zouzou starred in Bernard Blier's first film, *Hitler, connais pas* [Hitler, I don't know him]. Nico would taunt Zouzou, 'I knew Hitler, and he was OK.' Her close friends never thought her a Nazi, but she easily courted pretension and derision. Her cardboard companion Nietzsche had been an influence on Sartre and the existentialists, but only an influence, not the source. As the years went by Nico would quote more decisively from her version of Nietzsche, landing herself in all manner of trouble. The pickets in Denmark were not the only ones who would call her a fascist cow.

Secondly, she was a covergirl. Later she was a covergirl who got into movies. Later still, a covergirl who turned to singing. Finally, a beauty who became a junkie. At thirteen, the age of her apparent rape, she was a girl; at 21 she was a covergirl; at 26 she was 'new girl Nico'; at 35, a 'girl singer'; even at the age of 44 a reviewer called her 'good old girl Nico'. When she wasn't a girl, she was a girlfriend. A boy reading Nietzsche is a sign of advancement, but a covergirl reading Nietzsche is considered to be merely posturing. Her contradictions and her constant inventions stemmed in part from the simple fight she undertook in order to transcend the stifling environment placed around her by those she trusted and loved ('Not lovers. Never. Nobody could love her. She was unfuckable').

NICO TOOK NIETZSCHE jet-setting with her. America, she was told in Ibiza (by Americans), was the home of Beat. Encouraged to read *On the Road*, the bible for beatniks written in diesel oil by Jack Kerouac, she got halfway through the book before deciding 'it had too many words'. Instead of reading it, she declared, she would live it, on the road. First, however – like a true beatnik – she had her career to think about. There was her course of singing lessons, la-la-la-ing up and down the scales, and then her acting. She paid her fee and turned up each week at the Actors Studio, and, as she remembered it, her timing was perfect, for the Studio was then not full of the egocentric nonentities generally found in these places; instead, 'Marilyn Monroe was in my class. It was very exciting.' No one can deny Monroe was there, as the Studio did not keep registers then. It is quite possible that in late 1961 Marilyn Monroe and Nico (alternatively, Norma Jean Baker and Christa Päffgen) sat in the same room to watch Lee Strasberg push around a bunch of recruits. Marilyn Monroe had certainly made use of Strasberg, and did drop in to the occasional session even at this point late in her life. She venerated Strasberg, as did Nico.

A Polish Jew, Lee Strasberg grew up in New York's Lower East Side and trained as an actor in the socialist theatre companies of the Thirties. His many admirers assert that as 'the artistic heir to the great Russian actor and director Constantin Stanislavsky, Strasberg taught generations of the world's finest actors and actresses, including John Garfield, Marlon Brando, Geraldine Page, Paul Newman, Eva Marie Saint, Marilyn Monroe, Jane Fonda, Steve McQueen, James Dean, Dustin Hoffman, Anne Bancroft, Al Pacino, Dennis Hopper, and countless others.' His technique was known as the Method – his detractors said because he was 'a quack who turned actors into meths drinkers'. Although Nico was a 'countless other', she was proud to say that 'I was a student of Lee Strasberg' (however, those who attended were not considered students but *members* of the Studio). 'At the Actors Studio I learned how to be myself,' she said, which is some claim. It is hard to think what on earth Lee Strasberg could have taught her.

There are three stories concerning Nico and the Actors Studio. She said herself that in November 1961 she was working with

Strasberg's son John on the play *Hello, Out There* by William Saroyan, sometimes at 'the small apartment on 78th Street and Park Avenue, an old townhouse, while Lily Moor, a friend and model, went to Lapland for the winter [!], subletting her place to me', and sometimes 'at the Central Park West residence of Johnny's parents'. It would have been fascinating to hear Nico tackle Saroyan's all-American speeches, though one of Marilyn Monroe's husbands, the playwright Arthur Miller, did think of Saroyan as 'an unattachable man with a great appetite for friendship and loneliness and no idea of the value of a dollar', which makes him sound like a candidate for Nico's twin brother.

Secondly, Nico told a garbled story that, for some murky reason to do with immigration, she was advised not to tell 'the people of New York' of her true origins, and so she was suddenly an Albanian. Nico worried, though, about her clear German accent, and she hoped that the sessions with Strasberg would help her lose her 'immigration sound'. Strasberg dismissed this notion, as it would have been 'absurd to lose [her] European quality'. She concluded that she would remain a foreigner rather than an immigrant: 'one should really be Jewish in order to be an authentic immigrant'. She related this thought to Elia Kazan, the Greek-born film director of *On the Waterfront*, who was then working on the film *America, America*, about immigrants. Kazan taught sometimes at the Actors Studio, though not in the early Sixties. Nico met him anyway, maybe first through Papatakis, and she claimed he told her: ' "Whatever you do, do it in your own time. Don't do it in anyone else's." I have taken him at his word ever since.'

Lastly, Nico once told the story against herself. When she spoke English her vowels sounded elongated, stretched like her bones; the tones she made would later become a standing joke with the Andy Warhol team. At the Actors Studio Lee Strasberg devised a breathing exercise where he asked an actor to sing 'Happy Birthday' with the syllables dilated but the melody retained. He sang, 'Haaa-peee.' Strasberg shouted, 'No, longer.' The actor sang, 'Haaaaaa-peeeeee.' 'No, longer.' He sang, 'Haaaaaaaaaa-peeeeeeeeee.' 'No! Longer!' 'Haaaaaaaaaaaa-.' Strasberg turned to Nico: 'Now you try it.'

'HAAAAAAAAAAAAAAAAAAAAAAAAAAAAAAAAAAAAAAAAA AAAAA . . .'

'No! Shorter! Shorter!'

One night in November 1961, while she was learning the all-American lines from *Hello, Out There*, she phoned a man who she read had just settled in to the Saint Regis Hotel and said 'hello out there' to him. He invited her over. She had not seen Alain Delon for two years, but her hand shook. He was still the prettiest man she'd ever seen, and still 'the most dangerous'. They swept up and down Manhattan in her sports car and 'got stopped by the cops three times for speeding' (she didn't specify if her kind of speeding was a matter for the traffic police or the drugs squad). Nico was obsessed with Delon, and he allowed her obsession. She slept with Delon at the hotel and they conceived their son. Delon refuses to be drawn on the subject, but it is not likely that he was a complicit donor. There was a convention for orgasm in those days – the man withdrew just before climax. Contraceptive sheaths were a 'macho' tease, the pill had barely conceived itself, and the other unwieldy gadgets had yet to be invented. Both Delon and Nico were Catholics of a kind and did the natural things that Catholics are taught to do, but they 'fucked and fucked it up', as a friend observed. Others felt that Delon took advantage of 'a girl who was willing to go the whole way', or that Nico took advantage of his desires. But the whole affair was over by the morning, Delon thought.

'I was just leaving for Paris,' recalled Maldonado-Bostock, 'when Nico came round, very happy and excited: "I've just slept with Alain Delon!" It was like Snow White had met her prince. She was obsessed with this ghastly man for some reason.' Four months later in Paris, Nico turned up at the Chanel *cabine* during the spring shows of 1962. 'I remember her turning up one day, all brown,' declared Anne-Marie Quazza (Nico had been on assignment in the Bahamas). 'She said to us, "I am the most happy girl in the world. I have found the most beautiful boy in the world. I wanted a baby and now I am going to have one by him!" We all looked at her. "Who is he?" "Alain Delon!" You can imagine the silence. "But, Nico, he's not your boyfriend." "Oh, no, no," she replied. "Nico, you're crazy!" "But I didn't want anything from him. I didn't ask for it. I just want now a baby of my own." It was like a fairy tale to her.'

She wrote to her mother, to tell her the wonderful news. Grete was mortified. She saw her own past sweep back before her. Christa was born a bastard, and the bastard was breeding another bastard. She wanted Christa to marry, not to spawn. As her sister kept saying, 'It was like a Greek tragedy'; fate had infected the family line. Grete told her daughter she must have an abortion, now, immediately, before it was too late to stop the catastrophe. Christa was adamant.

Nico

She would do what her mother had first demanded. She would marry, she would marry the father; things had just happened the other way round, that was all. Mother and daughter were both lost in a world where the man is free to escape the responsibilities of genesis, and the woman obliged to compensate.

Nico Papatakis was still Nico's partner, but he learned of the pregnancy after all the others. 'I was in Paris at the time, dealing with Cassavetes' film, *Shadows*. If I remember correctly, Nico was in Paris but she telephoned me. She was very strange, it was obviously a hard thing for her to admit. She said, "I'm pregnant and the father is Delon." OK, I said, if you love the man and you want to keep the child, it's up to you. "I want to keep the baby," she answered. I said, are you sure? "Yes, yes." Why? "Because I want to take the baby to Alain Delon and show him and marry him." I was surprised. I said, OK, but we'll separate. We had to separate because of what she had said, which was dangerous. Then I warned her, I really warned her, "This man has had many affairs, and he couldn't care less. Please don't try any blackmail on Delon. Don't blackmail him." The whole thing to her was not like something in reality, but like something in a film.'

FILMS WERE ON HER MIND. *La Dolce Vita* had won the Palme d'Or at the 1960 Cannes Festival, though the announcement was drowned out by enraged boos from Christian zealots. The movie, much to Nico's delight, was branded 'a nihilist parade of depraved and idle scum who have nothing to offer society except a filthy smell'. But everyone remembered her face; she was promptly studied for other productions. Fellini told her that he would dearly love to use her again, but, frankly, she was too lazy for the discipline of filming. However, she was considered for the *femme fatale* lead of another seminal film of the Sixties, *Last Year at Marienbad* ('L'année dernière à Marienbad'). It would have been an excellent choice for Nico, considering its subject – the enigma of memory – and its setting, a palace of endless corridors with a casino attached. While the young Delphine Seyrig was cast for this role, Nico was contracted for something a touch more terrestrial. She would take the lead in a major film with a built-in multilingual title, *Strip-Tease*.

The director flew with the contract to the Bahamas, where Nico was doing a photo shoot for *Harper's Bazaar*. Jacques Poitrenaud was 40 years old and a 'real trooper'. He was one of many directors, Papatakis included, who hung on the coat tails of the French 'New

Wave' film resurgence at the start of the Sixties to get their own projects realised; never had the French production scene been so busy as it was now in 1962. Poitrenaud must have been startled to find his leading lady pregnant. The baby was due in August, the film not much later. Nico would be fine for work by November, she promised, and she would have a perfect babysitter on hand – her mother.

The Swedish Anne-Sophie and Carlos accompanied the pregnant Nico to Ibiza. Anne-Sophie recalled that 'We spent the months of June and July there. Nico had leased a house for her mother, it was up a hill just outside of the town of Ibiza. It was frightening to see her mother, because she was so obviously ill. She was developing Parkinson's Disease but there was also something mentally wrong. To put it simply, she was paranoid – everyone was against her, trying to poison her. There was a kind of reversal in the relationship between the two of them; the mother had become the child of the daughter.' Carlos de Maldonado-Bostock added, 'This little house was sort of sub-bourgeois; it gave me the creeps. There was this incredible woman, the mother, who was like a *Frau*, and Nico the nice little *Gretchen*-girl. But they were physically the opposite – the mother was tiny and Nico tall – and then mentally the mother relied entirely on Nico, because she was absolutely lonely otherwise. I thought she was abominable. Maybe I'm being hard, but that's how it appeared.'

Anne-Sophie assumed that the mother would remain in Ibiza, but Grete refused to stay. She wanted to be with Nico at the birth; she insisted that though she might be ill, at least she was experienced. 'Nico wanted the baby in Paris, she wanted her baby to be French, so we had to return with the mother,' Anne-Sophie recollected. 'You cannot imagine how difficult this became. For a start, Nico was not allowed to fly with the pregnancy, so we had to do the trip to Paris by boat and train. We spent a night in Barcelona – Nico, her mother and me. The mother started to howl. She became hysterical, thinking that strangers were after her, frightening hallucinations. Nico asked me to take her mother on to the beach at Barcelonetta – I think she thought that would calm her down. We sat there for two hours or more, and she was unpredictable the entire time. Then we had the train journey, and this was nerve-racking, because the mother would react in an unstable way that drew attention and could not be controlled. In Paris I had a small apartment on the rue Jacob, and I gave that up so that Nico and her mother could stay together for the birth.'

Nico entered the clinic at Neuilly-sur-Seine, a smart suburb west
of Paris, on 9 August 1962. Nico Papatakis took her to the clinic.
'He had nowhere to stay around there,' remarked Carlos, 'so I
phoned my friend Jeannique who gave him a bed. Then there was
the delay. On the night it happened, the 11th, we were all at Regine's,
the old one, not that frightful new place. Papatakis was with us. He
was in a terrible state, waiting for a phone call from the clinic,
waiting for news. I have to tell you that Papatakis was well known
for his temper – he's a strong man, you know. I remember once there
was a Brazilian painter called Mandela (he's dead now) and
Papatakis defended him in an attack by three Algerians . . . Anyway,
there was a phone call from the clinic. I've never heard anyone so
violent on a phone! He was insulting everyone down the line. It
transpired that the surgeon had decided to do a caesarian operation
to cut the baby out of Nico. Papatakis was beside himself with fury.
He defended her for a natural birth. I tend to agree with him. He
slammed the phone down and flew out of Regine's to the hospital.'

Papatakis added: 'I was angry with this arrogance of the surgeon.
These kind of men always want to open people up! He had no right
to assume this with Nico, who was in no condition to argue. So, I
arrived and so did the baby. As I was around at the time I could
follow one of the formalities and 'declare' the baby at the town hall,
which is the French custom. Unfortunately, I believe the family is
supposed to do this, and Nico was not familiar with this, nor was
she in a position to deal with paperwork.' The baby was a son,
named Christian Aaron. They wrote down the mother's supposed
family name, Päffgen.

Three things came from this: a signature, a scar, and the name
of her son. The only piece of paper connected with the birth was a
witnessing document signed by Nico Papatakis. Why him? Was it
because he was really the father? One of Nico's friends expressed a
view that was rumoured at the time: 'She was living with Papatakis
at the period of the conception. Delon denies responsibility. Nico
had a crush on Delon. She invented a lot of things. The boy has a
darkish complexion.' The evidence is against this, however. Firstly,
the boy grew up to look like Delon; it is one of the first things you
notice about him. Secondly, Papatakis did not take responsibility for
the child, he only witnessed the birth, whereas Delon's mother later
accepted liability. Thirdly, there is the testimony of Maldonado-
Bostock: 'Papatakis was a decent chap. He had integrity in the
matter. I think he only wanted to see that Nico was treated right.

He had lived with her for two years, and he was kind to her in all that time. I think they had a romantic liaison with very little physical intimacy. He was simply being honourable, unlike Delon.'

Then there is the scar. Later in life, Nico often mentioned a body scar inflicted in a fight. Sometimes she said she got it from John Cale, sometimes Iggy Pop, or the rapist, or a black lesbian in a bar. She never mentioned its source, the caesarian operation. Aside from Papatakis's indignation regarding natural birth, it must have crossed his mind that Nico was a model whose body had to be perfect. Even worse, she was just about to make a film where she was contracted to appear naked.

Finally, the baby's name, Christian Aaron. C for Christa and A for Alain (Alain Delon has sired at least two other children, Anthony and Anouchka), of course. He is known today to all as Ari, the diminutive of Aaron. Ari believes that Aaron came from the Paul Newman character in *Exodus* a film about Israel, and his mother simply liked the name. However, his full title partners a Christian name with a Jewish one, which is a very Nico thing to choose. Above all, Aaron means 'little lion', and Ari was born under the sign of Leo, the lion.

Nico left the clinic and stayed with her mother at a fine studio in the Marais that Papatakis had leased for her. She did not know the law regarding citizenship. She assumed that Ari was now French. 'She did not consider the need to put anything on paper,' commented Madame Pauledith Soubrier, the half-sister of Alain Delon. 'She was German and she wanted a French son. It was not possible under law because there was no father, nothing registered in the name of a father, nor of anyone French. As a German citizen she should properly have gone to the German Consulate in Paris, her equivalent to our town hall, for the purpose of registering Ari. So he was not German, he was not French, he was not anything. When he came to the age of majority, which is fourteen in France, he was stateless. It was a total absurdity, and it was her naïvety that caused it. But then, that was how she lived. She wasn't a German citizen herself, she was from some small planet somewhere, the poor girl.'

Within six weeks of the birth, Nico decided it would be rather nice to take her baby to Ibiza (it was also a useful ruse to get her mother back home out of harm's way). Nico rented a suite for herself in a new block of flats by the harbour. Decked in black once again to satisfy the Guardia Civil, Nico would carry little Ari out of her apartment to her mother's house up the hill every time he became a handful. Curtains drawn and quiet, Nico could then relax alone and learn the lines of her *Strip-Tease* script. To help her learn she had bought the latest thing, a tape recorder, a monster of a machine that weighed a ton. She soon discovered, however, that she could put it to better use. On numerous evenings from the suite above hers she could hear sessions of modern, improvised jazz played on a mixture of instruments. She taped them, just for the sake of it. On occasional days in the mild autumn heat she would hear from above the mellow tones of a flugelhorn playing impromptu rhapsodies ('it was a trumpet practising'), and she would tape that, too.

One morning the sound from above was not a flugelhorn but a football, a kick and shout and a plop as it dropped on to her balcony. Minutes later she answered a tentative knock on her door. She opened it to the handsome young Victor Brox, a jazz and blues musician from Manchester, England. It was his football, his flugel-horn and his jazz group that Nico had caught. She invited him in and she stunned him by promptly playing a tape of the group. 'We bohemians on the island had been told to leave her alone,' he recalled, 'and we did, so I was as nervous as a little kid – "Please can we have our ball back?" She was simply breathtaking to look at (black clothes and long blonde hair), but she was very shy. She'd been curious about the free music group I ran and she wanted to know everything about jazz and blues, absolutely everything. She started to come upstairs and I'd talk her through the history of the forms, the styles, the key musicians, the singers like Bessie Smith – just everything I could tell her and play her. She just sat there and listened intently, though I had no way of knowing how much she took in. Then she came over to the improvisation sessions. There was a rule for entry – you had to bring an instrument. Nico brought her tape recorder.' They soon had an affair together, lasting a few weeks, while *Mütterlein* minded the baby.

Victor Brox remains today, in his fifties, untouched by all things illegal but otherwise a true bohemian, sleeping no more than five hours a night, trekking around Europe or California with a tattered flugelhorn case, hitching rides to get to the next gig before his devout audience leaves. But when Nico met him in 1962 he was in the bohemian vanguard exploring 'free-form' jazz in parallel with Ornette Coleman, and, like so many other jazz musicians, was waiting on Ibiza for the arrival of the black composer Charlie Mingus, who had written in his autobiography at that time that he was fed up with New York and was rather tempted to leave it for somewhere bohemian like Ibiza. He never showed up. Nico, conversely, was on hand and all ears and began on that timeless island to understand that music was a language that can be composed in advance or in real-time, and that the composition that lies at the heart of music is the starting point, simply the starting point, of a performance. She later said that 'it was a professor of jazz . . . who introduced me to music'. Clearly her singing teacher in New York had introduced her to something else. Nico never forgot the kindness of Victor Brox, her 'professor of jazz', though she never saw this particular lover again for over twenty years. 'One day around 1985,' laughed Brox, 'I got a phone call completely out of the blue. It simply went: "Victor? It's Nico. Do you have any smack?"'

NICO NOW HAD three mouths to feed – Ari's, her mother's, and her own. She could not play jazz and jazzmen all season long; she left her mother on Ibiza and flew with the baby back to Paris for her work on the film *Strip-Tease*, where she called herself for tax purposes 'Krista Nico'. When she arrived there Maywald had arranged a surprise. He put Nico and Ari in the studio and shot a colour portrait for *Elle*. It came out as the cover of the Christmas edition, 1962. Nico and Ari, Madonna and child. The film, on the other hand, was a little less than holy:

EN PLEIN CINEMA

In the Madison Club off the Champs Elysées, Jacques Poitrenaud (director of *Les Ports Claquent, Les Parisiennes*) is working for Lambor films on *Strip-Tease*. I talk to him during a break for cable-laying. Nearby, the stars Krista Nico and Dany Saval are eating a piece of cheese.

What lies under this blatant title, *Strip-Tease*? 'A sentimental comedy. My film tells the story of a young foreign ballet dancer who is bored in a small company. This girl likes the vocation, but she aspires to greater heights. One day she meets by chance Dany Saval, a stripper who likes her work and makes a good living. The girl is lured into this world. My film starts from the moment the girl prepares to take off her clothes. It reveals her isolation, the rejection of her friends, and all she encounters, including a handsome young playboy who likes her character but not her profession. She reviews her life and gives one final performance, flinging away everything, including her jewels.

'It is a film with two main themes: the solitude of a beautiful girl, one who is vulnerable and foreign, but also the life of Paris between midnight and morning, the life of those that fritter their existence away.'

The 8 December issue of *La Cinématographie Française* echoed other papers in their strenuous efforts to turn something softly pornographic into something deeply profound. This would have pleased Krista Nico no end, for otherwise it is odd to think that she never mentioned this film to anyone, even though it is the only mainstream movie she ever made, and indeed one in which she starred. Miss Krista Nico, like *La Dolce Vita*'s Nico Otzak, never made an appearance again, at least not under these names. When *Ciné Monde* obligingly asked Nico what her most difficult moment was, she thought long and hard before her answer:

It was the sequence where I am completely naked. They did it as I preferred. They cleared the set.

I then drank several glasses of port. And they played a haunting tune to carry me through the ordeal.

As for the rest, a woman always finds out how to keep on top of the situation.

Filming must have been purgatory for Nico, but hell for the director. Nico could not have enjoyed the ironies of the script, nor the demand to learn screeds of dialogue. At least she could get away with a foreign accent. But she couldn't get away with the cheesy clothes and the gruesome wig she was given. In any case the corny double bluff, of the serious artist who takes up stripping for the sensation of adventure and fulfilment, would not have convinced her artistic friends, not even Ernest Hemingway. In atonement, the Nietzsche-carrying covergirl could count the money at the end of the job; she needed every franc to feed three mouths. Once she had the cheque in her hand, she forgot the film entirely, which was just as well in view of its press. When *Strip-Tease* was released in May 1963, the reviews traded her accent for her body:

One should certainly raise objections to the foreign accent of the principal actress, Miss Krista Nico. Her diction is dreadfully laboured, the accent a touch crude. But, nevertheless, there is the compensation of Miss Krista Nico's glamorous physique, not only the beauty of her big eyes, but also the sculptural allure of her body.

Only a bombastic paper like *Le Figaro* could complain about crude accents in a sex film. The movie's finest review came from the Catholic watchdog journal, *Fiches du Cinéma*:

Type: Psychological drama.

Moral valuation: In spite of some comical capers and its description of the dangers that face a young girl eager for the limelight, we are obliged to proscribe this film as too many of the scenes and images are not acceptable from our point of view.

Commentary: The road to hell is paved with good intentions. We thought our interest would be held by this – alas! – banal story of a young girl who strays into the arms of dubious types. But, frankly, it's nothing more than a pretext to present a spectacle that does not respect human dignity. This is why we reject this film finally as empty and degrading.

Strip-Tease (starring Krista Nico) opened in Paris the same month as Visconti's *The Leopard* (starring Alain Delon), Fellini's *8¹/₂* (starring Marcello Mastroianni), and *Whatever Happened to Baby Jane* (starring Bette Davis). In three years' time Nico would do more than outstrip them all.

BUT FIRST SHE HAD a baby to bring up. Nico and a recruited wet nurse nurtured Ari the best they could. Willy Maywald, her *mécène*, her patron, her phantom father, did what he could to help. He delivered an open invitation to Nico and her baby to his busy apartment for company. It was not the first time he had seen women bearing the consequences of men's venality: 'Models usually lead a life rather different from the kind you might imagine. Not all of them have rich men to lay a fortune at their feet. On the contrary, I hardly know a model who was not misused by men. I can still see these creepy fellows, waiting like pimps in front of my studio to take the money off the girls that they got from me.

'One night, in the kitchen of the model Catherine Harley, the girls were preparing some dinner. It was incredibly hot. The girls wore only bras and slips, over which they had tied aprons, and without the time to take off their false eyelashes they stirred big pots with wooden spoons. A record player – the old, mono sort, a Dansette – was playing loud pop music. Kiki, a small model who always posed for me in baby-doll dresses, was racing around from one room to the next in absurdly high heels, followed by a lot of small yapping dogs. Meanwhile the boyfriends of the models were waiting for the food, impatient with knives and forks in their hands, sitting at a huge table. In an adjoining room, my sister Helene was sitting next to the bed of Nico and her baby. She said to Nico again and again, "Now finally you have to inform the father. I will dictate the letter to you . . ." '

Delon did nothing. He could not imagine why he should: Delon did not consider himself responsible. Throughout Nico's remaining life – 25 years – he vacillated from a Gallic shrug of the shoulders (as though it was, you know, 'one of those things') through to outright denial. He told his mother, she claimed, 'that Bosch is responsible; she's the guilty one'. After the French daily *Libération* printed Nico's obituary, in which Ari's paternity was cited, Delon's lawyers forced a denial to be published.

ARI PAS DELON
Ari: Alain Delon, father of Anthony Delon, denies *in the most categorical manner* (as he always does) the information of the 23rd July in our paper concerning Ari, 25, son of the chanteuse Nico.

Nico was devastated that Delon had taken no interest. In the meantime he married a young 'actress' called Nathalie, 'and it ended in a murder four years after,' snapped Nico. She tried to make contact with him time and time again, but she was rebuffed by the loyal friends of Delon who defended the ambitious star. She was mindful, too, of Papatakis's apprehension that the baby was a form of blackmail, and when she thought of that, she feared for her life. Delon, she declared, was a devil with the face of an angel.

'Children never grow up as you'd expect,' Alain Delon's mother told a German journalist in 1984. 'I think my son is as evil as I am good . . . All of the people, important or unimportant to him, who come close to my son get damaged . . . When he does something stupid then everyone has to pay for it. Once I was called to school. All the boys were fighting, except for Alain. The director told me that everyone was fighting for or against my son. Wherever he is concerned, you start as a winner and end up a loser. He is charismatic, a born seducer. You can only capitulate. There is no middle ground. For a woman it is worse; for a woman with a very strong character, it is terrible for the both of them. And nothing is clear with him, nothing.' Nico had met her match.

Willy Maywald decided that if he could not get Delon, he would get Delon's mother – someone who would understand the distress of another mother, who would acknowledge her grandson, and force her son to accept his responsibility as a father. Maywald was surprised to learn that Delon's mother still worked for a living, at a little souvenir shop in the staid southern suburb of Bourg-la-Reine, near the Château de Sceaux. Madame Edith Delon, Ari's Mama Edith, was no longer a Delon but a Boulogne. She told the German journalist that 'Before I had my son Alain, I lived with his father for four years. His father died in my arms.' She had remarried and started another family, one which included Delon's half-sister, Pauledith Boulogne, whose singular name was derived from her parents, both of them, combined. Pauledith (now married and known as Madame Soubrier) is now more commonly known to the family as Didi, Ari's Aunt Didi – Mama Edith was Ari's second mother and Aunt Didi his third. The confusing complications of these changing names (Soubrier–Boulogne, Boulogne–Delon, Wolff–Schulz, Schulz–Päffgen) occur whenever writers write of women, who are born with the name of their fathers and marry into the name of their husbands, and never seem to have a name to call their own – except, of course, for Nico.

Mama Edith accepted Ari as her grandchild. She would do, she said, whatever she could to help, but her son would be furious once she got involved – 'I am his guilty conscience.' Nico, in any case, pointed out that her own mother would take care of the baby while she was working, though she forgot to mention that her mother lived on a remote Mediterranean island. The Delon link secured, Nico left with Ari for Ibiza. She was pleased that she built for her security two kinds of family. There was her phantom family of men – Maywald, her phantom father, Papatakis, her phantom husband, Maldonado-Bostock, her phantom lover, Tobias, her phantom brother. Then there was her real family of women – Grete, Tante Helma, Mama Edith, Didi, and finally her baby son, the 'little lion'. She thought she had forged an excellent foundation on which to build up her life as a working mother and a spare-time bohemian. She failed to see that by consigning her little lion to Ibiza, she had put him in a cage.

For a full year and more Nico worked entirely as a model in Europe and America and took what came her way, earning money to pay for the three mouths, though Nico saw it as two mouths and one head: her mother had started to see a specialist and the help she needed could be found only on one of the island's private clinics, for which Nico was supposed to pay. Sometimes she forgot the young mouth and the ageing head, and her mother would wait, empty-handed, until the next arbitrary visit from her aberrant daughter. When Nico arrived, she would watch her mother shaking with Parkinson's disease and sense a sickening smell of putrefied shit. Grete had been leaving Ari for hours on end without observation or attention. Once, on the island, Nico was walking in the street with her mother when Grete had some kind of fit. She asked a passer-by for assistance to get her mother to the clinic. The man turned out to be D. G. Päffgen, from Cologne, a distant and now uneasy relation.

After this incident Nico could no longer bear to go back to Ibiza: 'It broke my heart to see my mother in pain. I could not bear to see it.' She knew perfectly well that her mother was no mother to her child, but she was obliged to work and impelled under cover of fatalism to disregard the consequences of her absence. When a doctor left a message through Maywald in January 1964 that her mother needed to go into hospital for a period of treatment, Nico despaired. Maywald reminded her that the Boulognes were disposed to help. He phoned; they agreed to assist Nico in bringing Ari up in Paris. Nico promptly flew to London for an assignment and left them with the problem. 'I was given the task of going to Ibiza to collect Ari from the grandmother,' recalled Pauledith – Aunt Didi. 'I arrived and I was shocked. The boy was kept in a room, quite dark, and he was afraid, crouching like an animal. That's what I remember most, that he was more like a little frightened animal than an eighteen-month child. Nico's mother would not let him go. She wouldn't give me his entry papers, so I couldn't take him. I had eventually to fly back to Paris empty-handed. My mother decided she must go there and take charge. I have to add that this was not easy for us, because we had to pay for our own travel. Nico never paid a penny.'

Edith Boulogne got hold of Nico in London by phone and made her send a copy of her papers with Ari's name on them: 'With these papers I went to the French Consul in Ibiza to explain what I was doing. Then I saw the doctor, to get a note that the grandmother was not a fit guardian, as she was in hospital with Parkinson's disease. I got another letter to enter France with Ari. What I did was kidnapping, lawful kidnapping! We kept Ari at Bourg-la-Reine. My grandchild was so wonderful. Suddenly Nico turned up and asked to 'borrow' Ari so she could take him to London. Well, she was the mother. They flew to London. But three days later Nico phoned me, 'Please come and take Ari back.' Now I had to go to London to collect him. She never asked me if I had enough money for these journeys. I went to London, stayed a couple of days and brought him back to Paris – for the last time, I hoped. But there's never a last time where Nico's concerned.'

NICO PROMOTED CLOTHES, kitchens, soap, scent, dishwashers, make-up, beds, face cream, gramophone records and washing-up powder ('Oxydol! The best yet!!'), in France, the USA, Canada, Italy, Germany, Belgium and Spain. She was bored stiff, on her last legs, desperate for something new. She thought she'd soured her film career with *Plein Soleil* and *Strip-Tease*; nobody asked her to act, and no one but her singing teacher had heard her sing. Just as she had ten years before, Nico decided that it was time again to be discovered. In May 1964, springtime in Paris, by the chance she called fate, she met a dishy new singer who heard her singing one of his songs. He told her to shut up; not because she was bad, but because he didn't like women singing his songs. That distinction was significant. In trying to stop her singing, he provoked her into a fresh career. It was not quite the same as discovery, but for Nico, 25 years old, it was a kick and a start.

Robert Zimmerman was a middle-class Jewish boy from the American Midwest who changed not only his name but also his accent (to a yee-har Oklahoma twang) for the sake of his folk-song profession. In that way, Bob Dylan was as much a persona as the Swedish model Nico. When she met him he was 23, two years younger than her. His second LP had been released; it was a sensation, and not only in Nico's view. He had started out as an imitator of folk and blues in a manner typical of teenage American bohemianism until, in 1960, he discovered the music of Woody Guthrie. The veteran Guthrie, composer of 'Bound for Glory', was a brilliant creator of sharp-edged 'protest' songs. Dylan donned his mantle so successfully that he rose to a consummate position as a singer–songwriter who has yet, in the view of his many devotees, to be equalled. Nico didn't understand a word of his music. '*Twing, twang, twing, twang, baybee*: that's how it went.'

Dylan had played in London to promote his LP, and had received more acclaim than anyone had then expected. He was a new icon, as Nico would have known before she met him. Dylan had decided to move on to Paris for a few days, not to play but to meet Hugues Aufray, who translated his songs into French. In this way he came by chance to Nico. They met in the street, introduced by their mutual friend. Bob Dylan said he remembered her from *La Dolce Vita*, and feigned interest enough to get swiftly invited to her studio apartment. They stayed there for an evening and a week: 'He was so charming. I had not quite met someone like him – assertive and delightful, and young. He did not treat me very seriously, but at least he was interested in my story, which he found to be a sad one, especially about my baby. As I was from Berlin, he asked me if I knew the playwright Brecht. I told him that Brecht had run a theatre in Berlin, but we were forbidden to go there because it was in the Soviet sector. He said, "You see? That would never happen in America. At least we are free to see things." I said, "But it's the Americans who are stopping us walking through." For a man who was preaching about politics he did not know his history too well. Anyway, what about William Burroughs? Wasn't his book banned in his own country? I could buy it in Berlin.

'So, then we went together to Greece for a short time, a little place near Athens, and he wrote me a song about me and my little baby. I was the first to sing it in public [not true, Judy Collins was]. But he didn't like it when I tried to sing along with him. I thought he was being chauvinistic and a little annoyed that I could sing properly – at least in tune – so he made me more determined to sing to other people.' The song is titled 'I'll Keep It with Mine', and its opening verse runs:

> You will search, babe,
> At any cost,
> But how long, babe,
> Can you search for what's not lost?
> Ev'rybody will help you
> Some people are very kind
> But if I can save you any time,
> Come on, give it to me,
> I'll keep it with mine.

Nico kept him with her for those short weeks in France and Greece, but while Bob Dylan went back to fame and fortune, she went back to clothes and kitchens, scent and soap (to which she added cognac when she made a series of corny TV ads for Spanish television). She had mentioned to Dylan that she'd like to sing in public, and he suggested she try one of the clubs in New York, like The Blue Angel, where *chanteuses* could get work. When modelling jobs next took her over to Manhattan in the autumn of 1964, she happened to meet a man who knew a fixer who knew a booker for The Blue Angel looking for a singer to play a few nights. The place had been named after the Thirties film starring Marlene Dietrich as a sadistic cabaret singer, and Nico took this as a timely omen. The club was a chic uptown venue where folkies like the Clancy Brothers and Tommy Makem went to 'sell out' to richer patrons; Nico got her appointment there as 'That Girl from *La Dolce Vita*!' (they were probably hoping patrons would think of Anita Ekberg). Backed by a piano, bass and drums trio, she sang standards acquired from her singing lessons and the history lessons of 'Professor' Brox. Her favourite solo was 'My Funny Valentine' by Rodgers and Hart. 'I first heard this song played by the jazz man Chet Baker. He played his trumpet and then he sang it. I thought this was very clever, like a beautiful magical trick. Do you know that Chet Baker introduced me to heroin?' The writer asked her if she had shared a needle with him. 'No, no. I mean I first saw heroin. He first showed it to me. I was about 24 or so, in New York when I first started to sing – he was around. Of course, everyone thinks I started when I was a baby. They know nothing. Chet Baker was so handsome, such a beauty, but he was in love with drugs too much to be in love with me.'

She couldn't bear The Blue Angel, she claimed. It was more *Strip-Tease* than *Dolce Vita*. 'The men were horrible. They were drunks, blind drunks. They would offer me drinks and shout dirty things at me and try to maul me. It was degrading, this behaviour. They would not have done this to Marlene Dietrich, so I would not stand for it. I answered them back, or I declined to continue. So, it didn't last.' It was more correct to say that she didn't last. Nico would turn up late, forget lines of songs, and grumble about the audience (she thought in all innocence that they had come to hear her). The consolations were tiny but memorable: 'One man talked to me who knew Garbo, who lived then in New York in seclusion; I don't blame her – anyway, everyone lives in seclusion in New York. He said I was like her. I was flattered to know that I shared her character and her appearance. When she died I think something entered me, something from Garbo. Isn't that romantic?'

'She came back to Paris to do some modelling work and to see Ari,' recalled Pauledith Soubrier. 'She was a ridiculous mother, really. Quite unprepared to deal with it. When she arrived she said she had brought him a present. Can you imagine what she brought her tiny child? A Camembert cheese.'

5 January–June, 1965

The fields from Islington to Marybone,
To Primrose Hill and Saint Johns Wood:
Were builded over with pillars of gold,
And there Jerusalems pillars stood.

Her Little-ones ran on the fields
The Lamb of God among them seen
And fair Jerusalem his Bride:
Among the little meadows green.

Pancrass & Kentish-town repose
Among her golden pillars high:
Among her golden arches which
Shine upon the starry sky.

The Jews-harp-house and the Green Man;
The Ponds where Boys to bathe delight:
The fields of Cows by Willans farm:
Shine in Jerusalems pleasant sight.

(from 'To the Jews',
WILLIAM BLAKE, 1815)

'I KNEW THERE WAS SOMETHING WRONG the moment I saw the table. She had laid it out very nicely for tea, but there was an extra pot. A pot of rum. Strange, seeing it there in the daytime. Then once more, at breakfast, a pot of rum.' It was Aunt Helma who noticed the rum when she visited her lonely sister in 1965, and Grete who drank it. Nico had neglected her mother, who remained captive in Ibiza; a recent pang of guilt had driven Nico to post 200 American dollars to her aunt in Berlin. 'Take a holiday from your work and visit my mummy. You will enjoy the break,' she urged. Helma was not fooled. She knew that Grete was desperately lonely, and had sensed her isolation from her nervous and melancholy letters, but it was only when she arrived on the Spanish island that she realised Grete was more than isolated, she was sick. 'At breakfast her hand shook. She tried to hide it from me. At first I thought it was another sign that she had become an alcoholic. But eventually I guessed it was Parkinson's disease. I had last seen her in Berlin six years ago. The difference was terrifying. She lay in bed a lot. I did all the shopping for her, and she told me the Spanish names for eggs and bread to help me. But she didn't come out. I did the shopping and the cooking. She had nothing to do. There was no sewing machine, even. Nothing. Nowhere to go. I can't even say she lived in a paradise, because the time I went the weather was a terrible mixture of rain and storms. I had to wait ten days in Barcelona for a ship to ferry me over to the island. She was a prisoner there, drunk and in need of a doctor. But she couldn't afford a doctor any more. Nico had not sent her the money.'

Nico had no money, not to spare, not at 26 and a timeworn mannequin. By that age models generally go to grass and their agents discharge them with firm advice: buy up boutiques, breed horses, but, above all, marry into money. Models a decade older than Nico became ennobled by wedlock as Lady Astor or Baroness von Thyssen or Princess George Galitzine. Those who were to follow her retired into the arms of rich managers and rock stars. Nico, with her young son, was trapped between them. In any case she had little desire to serve time in conventional submission; marriage, she now decided, was merely one career move among many. She would find something else. She would be discovered, again. It had worked at the doors of the KaDeWe; she simply needed to find the new doors, the new KaDeWe, the equal of Berlin. Everyone said that the 'happening' place was now London. 'They've seen *La Dolce Vita* and they want to live it. London's a kind of Rome without car horns,' Maywald had told her. Her agency had an office there, she still looked good enough for work, and London ran a booming fashion industry. She went. Sadly, she had selected the wrong city.

Nico's problem was not only her age, it was her style. London's fashion queen was Mary Quant, the miniskirt pioneer, and she did not think much of mannequins like Nico. She said, 'I want model girls who look like real people, to wear my clothes which are for real people. I want girls who exaggerate the realness of themselves, not their haughty unrealness, like the couture models do.' Nico never looked like a 'real' person; 'haughty' and 'unreal' would haunt her to the grave. Her glamour was distinct from that of Jean Shrimpton, the gamine model who defined the new London look. Shrimpton was promoted by the star photographer of the time, David Bailey, who claimed that 'Jean wasn't the stiff, dummy kind of posed shop-window mannequin. She was somebody you felt you could have touched, almost.' Nico was not the type to be touched, not even almost. Her immediate problem was recognised by the agent Cherry Marshall:

> By 1965 skirts had crept up four inches above the knee . . . I regarded the trend with some horror; seeing my elegant five feet eight models transformed into gargantuan spiders . . . Who would have known that under cover of calf-length skirts were hidden thin, stick-like legs boasting a nice turn to the ankle but with boney knees and shapeless thighs? The younger models revelled in them, but models over twenty-five and five foot eight had a rough time.

Nico was 26 and five foot eleven. To make matters worse, she had tried to give up amphetamine and her weight increased. 'Everyone took speed – diet pills – then, when it was legal. I hardly knew anybody who didn't. That's why we could work so much!' admitted David Bailey. He noticed her weight problem immediately: 'It never occurred to me to ask Nico how old she was. She looked young enough. But she was fat – well, plumper than the others, I mean. Weight was obviously a problem for her. It wasn't under control. To be a model in that period you had to be seriously skinny. She had the right haircut, I remember, like a long helmet, the kind that Shrimpton pioneered. She was a bit of a hustler, but that was OK. You felt she was trying to prolong her career. I did some shots of her for *Vogue*, but I don't think they were used. She wasn't very commercial; she was unusual, stunning but unusual.'

Nico appeared in mediocre adverts for the upmarket magazines such as *Town* and the spanking new additions to the newspaper culture, colour supplements. She spent a cold March day, for instance, in Trafalgar Square, working on an American campaign for London Fog raincoats (Andy Warhol spotted the advert and pasted a copy into his scrapbook). Looking down forlornly at the ground, all long hair and lips, she avoids the eyes of the young, modish man, careworn and melancholy, stood aslant at her side. The advert's copy plays on their autumnal demeanour while cramming in as many touristic references to London as the page allows:

> Are there London Fogs in London? Don't ask Scotland Yard. Just look around you. You don't have to be Sherlock Holmes

to spot a London Fog, even in a London Fog. Drape a raincoat à la Mod. Go to Soho. Pick your way through Piccadilly. Take time out in Trafalgar Square. No matter where, there'll always be a London Fog standing up to the elements like a Coldstream Guard. Are there London Fogs in London? Are there tempests in a teapot? London Fog.

This was a text of the times. Short sentences. Telling you what to do. Dictatorial. The advert for her last-ever London assignment ran a text that Nico took to be ominous:

Life today is bolder. Better off. More fun. Things are changing. Everywhere. And today more and more people are enjoying extra smoking pleasure with Grandee cigars.

'It was true, there was a change, and I wanted to change too. But I thought I should leave it to fate to decide. I will not contradict my fate – that is what I thought. It is wrong to push ambition into one thing all your life, isn't it? There was a lot to choose in London, and it was a good place where not to choose. Everything was open, and the one thing I wanted was not to close anything to my future. When I hear a door close behind me, it makes me cry. It is like walking in a palace, like the castle in *La Dolce Vita*. You walk around the corridors and the doors behind you close, and you can only walk ahead but you know that one day you may return to that door in a different way and now it is closed to you, and you have reached the end of something that had been in your life. It is necessary to avoid that, and so I always look ahead and let chance lead me around to escape from nostalgia, which stops artists from advancing.' Nico said this in 1985 to a writer who then pressed her to say more about London. 'Oh, it rained the whole time and there were lots of parties.'

ESPRESSO BARS, motor scooters by Lambretta and Vespa, boys in snappy suits and sunglasses, pizza parlours, casinos: London was indeed turning Roman, as Maywald had claimed. Aspirant London had turned Italian (London, they were reminded, was a Roman name) in reaction to the rock'n'roll American-ness of greasy bikers, Wimpy bars and The Flintstones. Nico enjoyed any kind of cultural discord. She especially remembered reading about the Mods fighting the Rockers on the promenades of atrophied seaside towns ('It's funny to see people fighting for nothing at all, like football fans. I prefer it to people fighting for something, like Nazis'). She also favoured the crumbling quality of London's landscape, caked in soot, 'like Berlin could have looked if they'd left it alone'. Later, once London was cleaned up, she would say the same about Manchester.

The editor of the American journal *Encounter* had written in 1964 that London was 'the only European metropolis that has managed to maintain a combination of greenness and greyness, vitality and yet a certain gentleness. Paris hasn't got it. Rome is oppressive. Berlin is a special case. All the others are just villages.' Foreigners noted too that London was overrun with young people: 'It is as though the entire youth of Britain has come to live in its capital. Any full-blooded American will understand what happened to our old ally. Yes, once the war was over it was time to make babies. Now London, like New York and Los Angeles, is full to the brim with baby-boomers (over one million more than the last generation) of which The Beatles are only four,' observed the *Encounter* editor, wrongly, as The Beatles were born during wartime.

He was one of several who wrote of London as 'an old town full of young people' and Berlin as 'a young town full of old people'. The rise of 'Swinging London' was analysed and debated long before that catchphrase was coined by an American journalist for *Time* magazine in April 1966. Nico, the eternal jet-setter, considered it some kind of chance event: a bunch of influential people grew bored with City X and moved over to City L. This shift of attention could not be explained except by caprice, she thought, a basic human need for change and novelty. Though 'it was cheaper to live in London than Paris', she was puzzled as to why this should be: 'I find that when you have a certain amount of money, you do not need any more because everything becomes free. In London you did not seem to need anything at all. But that was a matter of psychology, not economics.' She conceded, however, to the following political argument she said she had picked up second-hand at a dinner party and rather liked: her cohort blamed America's foreign policy for fuelling inflation and the Tories for saddling the new Labour government of Harold Wilson with their own financial snarl. 'I believe in conspiracies and the vileness of governments, especially those who control other countries,' she said pointedly. 'Well, it is not unusual to blame the foreigner.'

The national deficit, of no benefit to the native, made Britain a cheap place for foreigners to produce work, especially the cultural industries that could exploit the country's veteran studio skills. Nico found the myriad social explanations more confusing, because she said she lacked an understanding of 'class' and 'classlessness'. It was simpler for Nico to believe that young adults enjoyed high employment, and earned wages to spend on dissolute weekends and the trappings of courtship. The retail trade rejuvenated itself to meet their novel needs. Tiny clothes shops became 'boutiques', hairdressers were elevated into stylists housed at earth-toned, spotlit 'salons', and John Stephens turned a back alley into the trading splendour of Carnaby Street ('It was shit. I liked Biba the best').

Nico said that she noticed two types of people in London, 'those who spent their money in the week and those who spent their money at weekends. I was told at parties that this man was Lord So-and-So and this man came from the East End but they were both good fun and they had the same money, but one of them (the East-Ender) would only spend it at weekends. I was told that their background was not a problem any more, but I was always told their background anyway, and I was always told it was not a problem. It seemed to me that everyone was fixed [obsessed] with backgrounds. Of course, I came from a poor background but they never thought to ask me because I was not English.

'They assumed what I was. I realised [then] that I could say I was anything in London. I could be a princess because I had the bearing of a princess. It didn't matter what I was to them as long as they accepted my appearance. Of course, I wanted more, because this was superficial. It was like the rules were no longer there, and I thought that was good for them but bad for me ... Do you know what I thought? It was [as though] the young, rich people were running out of money and were looking for something to do. And they took poor people to act as models for them. I mean it! To test the way ahead. They bought shops and did what tradesmen did, but they turned these jobs into something more debonair. I felt sad for David Bailey because they would say he was successful despite his education. They kept saying it behind his back, and how it wasn't a problem. Well, I was successful too, despite my education, but when I said this they thought I was making a joke.'

Nico's Lord So-and-So was Lord Snowdon, the Queen's brother-in-law and a photographer by trade. He joined an assortment of trend-setters constantly celebrated by their dear, dear friends in the magazines of *Town*, *Queen*, and *Private Eye*. The satirist Jonathan Miller wrote that 'there is now a curious cultural community, breathlessly *à la Mod*, where Lord Snowdon and the other desperadoes of grainy blow-ups and bled-off layout jostle with commercial art-school Mersey stars, window dressers and Carnaby Street pant-peddlers. Style is the thing here – Taste '64 – a cool line and the witty insolence of youth. Tradition has little bearing on any of these individual talents and age can go stuff itself.' Nico often felt she was the oldest thing at the party.

'IT WAS VERY SIMPLE, like in a factory. A lot of parties, a lot of talking, a lot of looking, a lot of flirting, a lot of drinking, a lot of drugs – that's how it went,' Nico summarised. First she had to live somewhere. As usual she loitered a few days in a hotel, the Grosvenor at Victoria railway station (a little grander than Güterbanhoffstrasse, Lübbenau); then she moved a few streets away into a Belgravia apartment rented by a model friend. She needed money for clothes, taxis and her slender share of the rent; everything else she picked up at parties, including deluded escorts to settle the subsequent bills at stylish restaurants. Her fashion contacts dragged her round the trendy places: neighbouring Chelsea (then quite cheap), Mayfair, The Ad Lib and Annabelle's clubs, The Marquee where rhythm and blues bands played, the Chelsea Potter pub on cultish King's Road, and Esmerelda's Barn, a club owned by those modish East End crooks, the Kray brothers. But she was indifferent to the places. It was who she met, not what she met, that she valued; thoughts of Ari and Grete gnawed into her hedonist desires, and she hunted around for her new benefactors, sources of wealth, the new Oestergaard, the new Tobias, who would help to soften her guilt. When she first came across The Beatles, she decided that Paul McCartney would be the one of which her mother would approve, 'but his timing was always wrong,' she grumbled, referring rather to her timing and his girlfriends.

In order to catch the benefactors she dressed impeccably in the fashion trends of the time. Her hair was shoulder length and arrestingly ash blonde, and she ensured her clothes remained as chic and *à la mode* as heaven and Mary Quant allowed. The style of the moment took the label 'Modernist', a term commonly reduced to 'Mod' – Modernists wore Modernist clothes. Mods wore a dramatic mix of Italian fashion merged with British art design. The clothes were geometrised and given acid tones. Boys donned smart suits and subtle face make-up; girls wore short, knitted dresses and prints with op-art or paisley designs, their face cosmetics very pale to emphasise the thickly toned eyes, the lids of which were weighted with one or two sets of false lashes. The golden rule was 'Skin bad, make-up good'. One boy told *The Sunday Times*, 'I don't want to be like my father. I want to be smart.' Nico loved the look. She felt in accord with any style that crossed simple elegance with innovation, though she adopted Modernism in a rather *haute couture* way.

'She was the epitome of Cool,' an observer of the Chelsea scene testified, 'standing in the corner in the half-light but the centre of attention. She was tall, and that helped, and she had these brilliant, powerful eyes that gazed steadily through the haze of cigarette smoke. She was slightly come-hither, you just knew she meant business, but she was so beautiful – very noble – that you couldn't resist staring back.' David Bailey remembered that she was fun to be with, charming and demure, chuckling, generous: 'She really was just like you see her in *La Dolce Vita*. She certainly didn't need to act in that film!' Friends asked her why she had made no more screen appearances since Fellini (Nico told them nothing of *Strip-Tease*). She couldn't really answer. She recalled that Papatakis, who was, after all, a film producer and director, told her she was '*un peu aberrant, comme* Monroe' for the discipline of filming (by implication, she supposed, he suggested it would destroy her, '*comme* Monroe'). She believed that her career may have been blocked by the Delon affair, which had been a juicy item of gossip behind her back, and she considered her own insularity to be a severe problem: 'I am too shy to act. I cannot pretend to be somebody else because I am already somebody else.' She feared that her private life was in danger of destroying her public future. It was a mistake that Garbo and Dietrich never made. From now on, she resolved, they would be her phantom managers.

Yet, if she wanted to cultivate a screen career, she had picked the right place. Ever since the James Bond films trained the attention of the international cinema trade on to the production parks circling London, Hollywood emigrés and European modernists patronised these relatively cheap and efficient studios. So, at one party Nico met the French actress Catherine Deneuve (who was later to marry David Bailey), four years younger but far less naive – Deneuve was then filming in South Kensington for Roman Polanski's chilling *Repulsion*. At another, Nico encountered the Italian director Antonioni who was preparing to work on *Blow-Up*, a seminal film about Swinging London. She told a friend that around this time she had a one-night fling with the French filmmaker François Truffaut who was directing his version of an English science-fiction story, *Fahrenheit 451*.

It seems odd that Nico never found an opportunity to act in these European films while in London. She had the contacts – though no agent – and she cultivated encounters, if her Truffaut story is true. Perhaps she was known less as the stunning Swedish model of *La Dolce Vita* and more as the troublesome, one-time cohort of Alain Delon who, that very year, was taking a rough tumble in Hollywood. The London-made films of these Europeans, or of the American exiles Stanley Kubrick (working on *2001*) and Joseph Losey, or the British directors John Schlesinger, Lindsay Anderson and Jack Clayton all include a part that Nico might have played, had she got up in time, on the right day, and learned the right lines. None of her friends can explain this flaw in her life. They said she combined, at one and the same time, moods of profound desire in a perversely disinterested manner, compelling ambition with a bashful tone, world-weary reflections with a delinquent heart, all in a muddy mixture of strength and self-doubt, discernment and delusion. They couldn't make head or tail of it, and that was why (they considered) she never got the breaks she was due: 'It was the fear of dealing with another Monroe,' said one director. 'She was the first girl I met that put me off with her charm. She scared me.' There is a scientific definition of 'aberrant': an apparent displacement of a star.

One night in early March 1965, Nico met The Rolling Stones. All five members of the foremost beat group – the term 'rock group' had not yet been invented – Mick, Keith, Brian, Bill and Charlie, had assembled for a record company party to celebrate a successful tour of Australia and the release of their second LP, the one with the famous Mod cover by David Bailey. It was a further step in the astonishing two-year rise of the London band and epitomised their entire career, for The Stones' life consisted entirely of making tours and making records (and, in Brian Jones's case, making babies). Nico made sure that first of all she met their manager. She had been told he was looking for 'girls to turn into stars'. Having hitherto encountered the old-style executives of the music business, the dull suited backroom shysters, she was startled to meet Andrew Loog Oldham.

For a start he was four years younger than her. Ginger-haired Oldham was an audacious young Mod who wore his sunglasses indoors, make-up on his face, a silver identity bracelet on his wrist, and his smug assurance on his sleeve. His name was one of the few unaffected things about him: an illegitimate child, he had been given the surnames of both parents, the Loog from his Dutch–American father who was killed in the war flying over Germany. Oldham had succeeded in placing The Rolling Stones on a publicity par with The Beatles (their manager was his former boss); *Vogue* termed him 'a young tycoon', but he was happier at promotion than budgets. His youth and ostentation did not sit pretty with the jobsworth producers of municipal venues and variety bills; to avoid a culture clash he promptly teamed up with a show-business veteran named Eric Easton who managed a fixed-grinned ham guitarist called Bert Weedon and the hefty honky-tonk pianist Mrs Mills.

While Eric Easton sold The Stones to the trade, Oldham sold them to the world. Without the band's knowledge, for instance, he had written sleeve notes for the second LP that generated brilliantly bad publicity and raised angry questions in the House of Lords:

> Cast deep in your pocket for loot to buy this disc of groovies and fancy words. If you don't have bread, see that blind man, knock him on the head, steal his wallet and lo, you have the loot. If you put in the boot, good, another one sold.

Oldham remorselessly fed the press with brash claims and insolent slogans such as 'Would you let your daughter marry a Rolling Stone?' For the benefit of enduring media coverage he had raised The Stones as satanic rivals to the sanitary Beatles – seditious, sexy Southerners defying lovely, clean lads from Liverpool. Behind the scenes, however, he'd made a polite anti-clash deal with The Beatles management to assist the record release schedules of both groups. 'He was good at cultivating the bad moments,' Mick Jagger recalled. 'Actually we got on OK with The Beatles. It was all a publicity game.' Oldham could never be accused of running a tactful strategy: 'Pop music is sex and you have to hit them in the face with it.'

Nico told Andrew Loog Oldham about her modelling, *La Dolce Vita* and her friendship with Bob Dylan. He was immediately intrigued. He had been trying for some time to launch the supreme female singer. One year before, in February 1964, he had surprised The Stones by detaining them in their regular Denmark Street studio to record the backing for an eighteen-year-old black vocalist, Cleo Sylvester. They were abashed to remember her from a year earlier as a girlfriend of Jagger's who had failed an audition as their backing singer. Now, with their help, she recorded 'To Know Him Is To Love Him', a song from 1958 originally produced by Oldham's American hero, the fanatical Phil Spector. Too little happened to the

1964 version, though Oldham was brave to try – it would have been a remarkable and pioneering action to project a young black singer into the racist British music scene (the exception that proved the rule was Little Millie's novelty song 'My Boy Lollipop' in April 1964). But this lack of success never prevented Oldham posing as the Spector of Denmark Street.

It was said of him that he had little idea what a producer did, but 'Andrew used to think anything was possible if you put enough echo on it.' Down in the studio his grasp of the precise technical jargon was limited: 'That's D for Divine, that's *very* wankable indeed.' He pushed out tacky instrumental singles played by a bunch of studio sight-readers dignified with the name The Andrew Oldham Orchestra. He had hunted for young women who could sing in a gutsy manner embodied by shameless imitations of black soul. He searched, too, for singers who could copy soul's suaver neighbour, the distilled satin mezzo-soprano of Dionne Warwick; her American chart successes, composed by Burt Bacharach and Hal David, would soon be covered across the ocean in crude fashion by two white imitators, Dusty Springfield (real name Mary O'Brien) and Cilla Black (really Priscilla White, a deeply ironic reversal of name). Oldham was too late to muscle in; he failed to find his starlets in time. To indulge his fixation he booked Phil Spector's own female singers, The Ronettes, as the support act for The Stones' first headlining tour of Britain. But then he observed a trend that shook him dramatically into reverse.

It started with The Singing Nun. Pallid, acoustic, and righteous, The Singing Nun's LP was the best-selling record in the USA for no less than ten weeks at the start of 1964. Then there was Joan Baez – pallid, acoustic and righteous. Peter, Paul and Mary, the very same. Folk and folk–gospel trends had cut into the Top 100 charts. This signified to analysts the possibility of a market niche that was the polar opposite to black soul. Indeed, it flowered at the very time that Motown emerged as a commercial force. Key elements were first assembled from acoustic folk – a thin and reedy voice, reflective lyrics. At the broadest level it brought back to the music trade the insipid and vulnerable timbre of the white adolescent voice.

Pop–folk evolved into a revival of cool bohemianism. As it bloomed it grew variegated, remaining white and scrawny in all its varieties. In the folk–rock vocabulary of the music press, male singers were labelled 'troubadours', females 'chanteuses', and their songs 'ballads' in a crude attempt to validate the style with a white

European literary heritage. In its most refined phase, their songs and their singing were blanched and lean, self-absorbed and engrained with questions and ironies. The ballads served as anthems for the introspective, uncertain daughters and sons of war-hardened parents, eventually giving long careers to Joni Mitchell and Leonard Cohen. In its early and least refined phase it offered up Sandie Shaw, Twinkle and Andrew Loog Oldham's most triumphant discovery, a seventeen-year-old convent schoolgirl called Marianne Faithfull. He had met her at a party. 'How did he know you had a voice?' quizzed *Vogue*. 'He didn't. I haven't.'

Here was another party, one year on, and another fab girl, thought Oldham. He was looking at Nico and weighing up the options. She was no svelte schoolgirl, but she talked first-hand of Fellini and Dylan and was game to get on in the world. There was another factor in Oldham's professional dealings with women. He was not only supplying singers for his business, he was equipping his group with girlfriends. At the party where Oldham first met Marianne Faithfull, Mick Jagger had contrived to pour champagne down her dress in a terribly subtle attempt to attract her attention. Now, Oldham noticed that Brian Jones was staring ardently at Nico; the come-hither look was crossing both ways. He acted accordingly. 'Let's meet up again and talk careers,' he offered. 'How about tomorrow?' asked Nico, rather too eagerly. 'We're starting a tour. Come and catch us somewhere. We can talk after the show.' That is how Nico described the conversation.

The show she caught was in Paris, on 17 April 1965. Willy Maywald had found her a small assignment in the city and she was able to visit her son Ari. She was astounded to learn that her actress colleague Zouzou had spent some time with Brian Jones; at least she was then in a position to take Nico past the Olympia's security staff into the backstage rooms. Her visit is recorded in a book with an unfortunate title, *The True Adventures of The Rolling Stones* by Stanley Booth:

> Brian was with a French model named Zouzou. After one of the shows, a girl came backstage. She said in a German-sounding North Italian accent that her name was Anita. She was a model and had acted in Italian films. A few years before, when she was seventeen, she had gone to the United States and had lived in a house in Greenwich Village where the poets Frank O'Hara and Allen Ginsberg also lived; at the time, she

had been scared to death. Now she was no longer seventeen, no longer scared to death. Brian knew nothing about her and had no thought that he would die loving her.

He would not die loving her and her name was not Anita. The on-and-off period of three months that Nico spent with Jones is firmly documented. There are various memoirs and biographies, not one of which correctly identifies her. Like the *True Adventures*, they confuse Nico with a later lover of Brian Jones's. Anita Pallenberg was a nineteen-year-old model, strikingly attractive with long blonde hair. She looked a little like Nico and was, for Jones, a probable replacement. To those men of the press and the aides of the group who later wrote their memoirs, one 'German chick' was the same as the next.

Anita Pallenberg said that she first met Jones after a concert in Munich on 14 September 1965. Bill Wyman confirms this in his deadly precise and date-riddled autobiography. The photographer in May, therefore, who saw Jones and Pallenberg enter a Los Angeles hotel room to resurface a full two days later on an acid binge, saw Nico. It was a typical moment in their affair, too, if Nico is to be believed. 'It was fascinating and frightening. Jim [Morrison] had the best sex I ever had inside me. But Brian gave the best sex, when he could. He took too many drugs. He was like my little brother, and I had to stop him sometimes from destroying everything, including himself. At least that was one thing I could do that Anita Pallenberg couldn't.'

Brian Jones was 22 and the prettiest in the band. 'As a guitarist he was good looking,' a *Melody Maker* writer dryly noted. He petulantly competed for public attention with the group's singer, Mick Jagger. His light hair was grown long and shaggy in a pudding-basin cut that became a trademark he used to gain the attention afforded Jagger's thick, sexy lips. In the early days he was the group's businessman and hustler; they were once called 'Brian Jones & Mick Jagger & The Rollin' Stones'. But he was also the proverbial rich kid turned rebel. An affluent childhood in Cheltenham and a public school education had evidently prepared him for an adult life of indulgence and excess. During his affairs of late adolescence he'd fathered four boys with different women. Two of the boys were both called Julian, after his jazz hero Julian 'Cannonball' Adderley. The group's tour photographer, Al Aronowitz, wrote of him:

Brian was always a dandy. In the end he was like a princeling who had run out of toys to play with. Once he kept a box-score of his women and it added up to sixty-four in one month, a pace which doesn't allow for the luxury of a one-night stand.

Kathy Etchingham, one of his more durable friends, recalled that 'sometimes there would be two or three chicks because Brian often liked more than one at a time. One time I went over there after he called and he was in bed with two chicks. He just threw their clothes on the bed and said to them, "Do you mind leaving?" '

Jones was very keen on drugs, although they invariably caused him physical problems because he was asthmatic and required regular medical attention. The poet Brion Gysin wrote that 'Brian was the kind of man who would take anything you gave him. Offer him a handful of pills, uppers and downers, acid, whatever, and he'd just swallow them all.' The press accounts of Brian Jones parade a man so utterly cracked that it beggars belief that 64 women, let alone Nico, a month would wish to spend a split-second in his company. 'It's really very simple,' claimed Nico. 'He was sexy. He seduced girls. He was charming, until he locked the door.' Nico said on another occasion that she preferred The Rolling Stones to The Beatles (whom she had met at parties) because the latter were 'show business' and The Stones 'were living on nerves and more my idea of rebels. You know that Mick's girlfriend Marianne Faithfull came from a convent [school]? I came from a convent, too, a convent style. I wanted to be in the centre and at the edge, do you follow? The Beatles could give me a n-i-c-e time, but I wanted then a b-a-d time. I was foolish in that way.'

Jones was a sadist who could turn submissive. Nico never admitted a tendency to masochism, though she preferred anal sex to straight ('She didn't want anyone to touch her cunt'); she said she liked it 'the Turkish way – my father was Turkish'. Nico gave five examples of her encounters with Jones, and in each case her account is the memoir of a submissive. On one occasion he had taken some amphetamine pills which rendered him nervous and impotent. He wanted sex with her but couldn't manage an erection. He slapped her around and punched her in the face, leaving a bruise. Another time, while tripping, he attempted to stick a brooch pin through her vaginal lips, cutting her. She also said that he placed a loaded gun into her vagina as a dildo. She talked of his love of ceremonial candles, their golden flames, the dripping of hot wax on to his nipples, and the pouring of the stinging wax on to her vaginal hair, which Nico had to cut off with scissors once the wax had cooled and congealed. Jones also used candles as dildos, she said. On the occasion of the Los Angeles hotel sighting by a photographer, they had both taken LSD, the drug that induces adventurous hallucinations and mood shifts – the 'good trip' or the 'bad trip', depending on results. Jones tied Nico down for anal intercourse, which he conducted without a lubricant. She bled profusely, inducing a bad trip, but she dared call for medical help from the hotel only once she was finally alone and had 'come down'.

These were the stories Nico told twenty years on. Zouzou, however, contends that Nico intimidated Brian Jones. 'He was scared of her, sure he was, and he was frightened of our confrontations with her. We would be at parties and if Nico came into the room Brian would say, "Oh no, you'd better disappear for a bit." She was a big, threatening woman.' Indeed, Anita Pallenberg took the dominant role in her affair with Brian Jones. Their friend Ronny Money observed that 'at that particular time he was out for as many kicks as he could get. Anita was great. She excited Brian – whatever young guys only read about he was getting on a plate. She was into the bisexual number and arranged scenes.' Two years after his encounter with Nico, when Anita Pallenberg had finally abandoned him for Keith Richards, Jones was put on trial for drugs possession; the judge ordered him to visit a psychiatrist in order that the court might enjoy a report on his mental health. It was noted with some irony that the expert he saw, a Dr Neustatter, had a German name. The psychiatrist wrote:

Mr Jones' sexual problems are closely interrelated to his difficulties of aggression ... He is still very involved with Oedipal fixations. He is very confused about the maternal and paternal role in these. Part of his confusion would seem to be the very strong resentment he experiences toward his dominant and controlling mother, who rejected him and blatantly favoured his sister.

Nico had thought of him as 'my little brother', which was none too bright a thought under the circumstances. It might have been fun to overhear Brian Jones and Nico discussing their mothers.

*

Nico

'SHE WAS A PRISONER THERE, sick and in need of a doctor. But she couldn't afford a doctor any more. Nico had not sent her the money.' Aunt Helma went back to Berlin from her 'holiday' in Ibiza. She could hardly believe the state of her sister, whose body was shuffling into paralysis. The insidious progress of Parkinson's disease – the impulsive trembling of limbs and the shaking of the head, the growing stiffness – could have been controlled by drugs, had Grete received steady medical advice and the resources to cover its cost. The money she needed for drugs was being spent on drugs by her daughter. But Nico was buying LSD, not Levodopa; she was paying to enhance her sense of 'inner truth', not to ease her mother's miserable life. Aunt Helma wondered if Nico knew or understood the severity of the situation. Her mother had no health insurance, and Nico was defaulting on payments on the villa's lease. Helma tried to get in touch with Nico. It was logical for her to assume she was living in America, the last country from which Nico had contacted her. That's where she wrote. But logic rarely held sway over Nico's endeavours.

WHEN NICO SAID she was drawn to Brian Jones because he was 'sexy', she was telling half a truth. There was also her anxious attraction to business. Jones was her adjunct to the open-all-hours door of his manager, the man who had said 'Let's meet up again and talk careers.' In fairness to Grete's daughter it could be said she saw Oldham as the show and Jones as the audition. She needed a new career and here, according to *Vogue*, was a 'young tycoon' who wished to discuss it. She knew, too, that he was not in such a great hurry as was she. Nico endured the sadistic whims of Jones to establish her presence near Oldham. She had also craved for their relationship to be one of a genuine correspondence. Nico tried to discuss poetry with Jones, and then music, but 'he was really too stoned to talk about anything, and often so was I'. She considered him 'too lazy [!] to be a genuine artist, but he was gifted and could have made some original music. I kept saying that, but he called me a *nag*.'

It annoyed her to have her public and private life fused together in this crude fashion – her phantom managers, Garbo and Dietrich, would never have allowed it. She knew, though, that Jones had little more to offer her, for he had been quoted in the rock press then as saying: 'I haven't tied myself down with a girl yet [an unfortunate turn of phrase]. After all, how many girls could I find who would make me tea, cook me meals, tidy my house and talk intelligently to me while I sit and watch with my feet up?'

The talk with Oldham, however, would soon take place, in exotic circumstances, and a bargain would be struck. Before that, however, Nico was to meet up in Paris with a man who would give her so much more. Maywald, in his memoir, put it succinctly: 'She had the gift of ferreting out interesting people. One evening (1965) we were together in the nightclub Castel when she made herself known to a group of Americans. One of them was the young American artist Andy Warhol. A short time later she went back with them to America, learned singing, and became one of the stars of The Velvet Underground.' If only it had been so simple.

Andy Warhol was 36, a decade on from Nico and not as 'young' as Maywald assumed; Warhol was ageless, just as Nico was ageless. It wrangled him no end that he was known as a weird pop-art personality and not a serious artist. When Ileana Sonnabend first risked a show of his electric-chair paintings at her gallery in Paris in 1964 he was thrilled for two reasons: it was his European debut, and it would confer kudos and validation on his work. But everyone knew Sonnabend had been married to his agent, Leo Castelli; her selection was not considered to be entirely impartial. Now, a year on she was showing his new work, the flower paintings of poppies, and the show was a comparative success. The flower image hinted at everything from drugs to death; it suited a city just reconciled to Impressionism after a major show; it appeared uncannily modish at the dawning of 'flower power'. Sonnabend had paid the cost of four return flights from New York. Warhol brought his new 'girlfriend', and Sonnabend didn't mind paying the extra, Warhol recognised, 'because she knew that an artist would get more attention – especially in Paris – with a beautiful girl on his arm'.

The quintet of Americans Nico encountered in the Castel comprised a stick-insect, silver-haired Warhol, his stick-insect, silver-haired 'queen' Edie Sedgwick, and their respective escorts, Warhol's assistant Gerard Malanga ('He looked good, like Elvis Presley, but not so fat – well, I don't know, though. Ho, ho, ho . . .'), Edie's friend and organiser Chuck Wein ('I can't remember anything about him at all. Can anyone?'), and the man who gave Nico the excuse to walk over to their table, her regular, friendly American in Paris, called Denis Deegan. Nico made herself known to the others in the usual way, name-dropping and adding The Rolling Stones to her list of intimidating celebrities. 'Edie was too occupied with her lipstick to listen, but Gerard told me about the studio where they worked in New York. It was called the Factory. He said I would be welcome to visit when I was next in New York, but Edie interrupted with some stupid comment about my hair colour. Andy was interested that I had been in films and would be working with The Rolling Stones.' Of course he would. When Warhol wrote in his chattering memoirs of the Castel he described it exactly like Nico would have done: 'They'd just finished filming *What's New Pussycat* at Castel's and it seemed like the whole place was popping with stars like Terence Stamp, Ursula Andress, Peter Sellers, Woody Allen, Romy Schneider . . .'

Naturally, it all depended on what Nico meant by 'working' with The Rolling Stones. Unless she had thoughts of making tea and tidying house for Brian Jones, she was clearly pursuing delusions about a conversation she had not yet had with their manager. But, once again, her instincts were proved right. Andrew Loog Oldham gave her a chance to sing 'with' The Stones. He made the offer, according to Nico, in the Los Angeles hotel where the band was staying for a few days in May to record the next single '(I Can't Get No) Satisfaction'.

One afternoon, so Nico said, Oldham drew her aside. She claimed that he took her to a secluded toilet nearby where they each snorted a line of his high-grade speed. 'It's time to do a deal,' she recalled him saying. 'I'm going to start up a Rolling Stones record company. They'll be the producers and so will I, and we'll be able to give the breaks to people we love, like you, Nico. Once we've got the business sorted out with the legal people there'll be a contract for you. I'm thinking three singles for a start. We commence releasing midsummer, so think of a summer-style single. All you have to do is sign and sing. OK?' Oldham had forgotten that Nico had been signing business deals for a decade. She was no novice and agreed to think it over, she remembered telling him, once she had sight of a contract. Deep down she was gratified. 'I thought, every cut of Brian is worth it. Then I thought, I'm standing in a toilet with this man!'

But Oldham had not told her the whole story (if Nico's account was indeed her whole story). At the raddled old age of twenty, he was on the verge of retirement as manager of the Stones. By 1965 the group was such big business he had to admit in private that he could not fully cope with the demands. His acumen lay in image-building. The Stones had little image left to build, and as the practical matters of finance grew ever greater, Oldham found solace in drugs.

He finally recognised the group's disquiet about the calibre of his work with Eric Easton. In the States he had met up with Allen Klein, an accountant whose crass and caustic manner was a winning approach in the bookkeeping profession. It was agreed between them that Klein would take over as executive manager (a new Easton) while Oldham would nominally retain his position and set up his own business, to be called Immediate Records. They chose to keep the entire matter under wraps until August, when The Stones' contract with Decca came up for renewal. However, Oldham could not quite keep quiet, and the *New Musical Express* gossip column for 28 May included a cryptic note: 'Andrew Oldham hopeful of recording Nancy Sinatra in Hollywood.' History would judge Klein's involvement in a phrase cattishly known to the trade as 'a De-Klein'.

Nico flew back to London. She immediately went party-hopping and was surprised to find Gerard Malanga there with their mutual friend Denis Deegan (they had been scouting around town to find a gallery for a Warhol show). It was then that Malanga gave Nico the phone number of Warhol's Factory, to use 'the next time I was in Manhattan'. But Nico put it to one side. She had one thing only on her mind: she must find a song for her debut single. She considered the best choice to be Bob Dylan's ballad that he wrote with her in mind, 'I'll Keep It with Mine'. His songs already helped to propel careers: 'Blowin' in the Wind' had boosted Peter, Paul and Mary, while 'It Ain't Me Babe' was such a big hit for The Turtles that it was given a respray as 'I've Got You Babe' to launch Sonny and Cher. If only Dylan would let her sing it. Once more she was in luck. Dylan was lounging around London. He'd just completed a sensationally successful tour of Britain, the one captured in candid detail by D. A. Pennebaker in a film documentary called *Don't Look Back*. Nico had missed the final concert at the Royal Albert Hall but found him, inevitably, at a party. 'He tooked terrible. Bob was completely drugged up and moody and arrogant as ever. I had not seen him so thin and white, like a matchstick.

'He was asking me all the time about The Stones and their clothes. What do they wear now? What shirts? What boots? He was wearing a leather jacket, but not a biker jacket, with a blue tab collar shirt. It was so ordinary. He looked like a handyman and he wanted to be a Rolling Stone. It was funny because there were these boys trying to look like him! He wanted too much to be in the fashion, but it took him a long time to get comfortable with the changes. He was always paranoid about these things, and about the people around him, when there was a photographer there – "would it be bad to be in this photograph?" When he first saw *Don't Look Back* he was shocked. It wasn't his behaviour that gave him the shock, it was how he looked, his image to the world, captured for ever on this film, a matchstick in a leather jacket. He wanted to be Brian [Jones] or Jim [Morrison], not a folk singer, and that's why he wanted to ban the film at first. It's strange because he had his own look, when he stopped trying to be somebody else – the Dylan hair, you know? All artists go through this passage. They make themselves beautiful a little bit at a time. Sometimes they force themselves and lose respect – look at Lou Reed. It's not a vanity always; it's done for the sake of the followers, to be a hero, a perfect idol.'

Nico told Bob Dylan about the record deal. 'He was not very flattering to me. He didn't like women singing. Joan Baez had followed him on this tour, you know, but he wouldn't let her sing. He was jealous because she was more famous in America. She had more success with singles than him.' Nico reminded him of 'her' song, and she remembered him saying, 'Well, I'm going down the coast for a break. I'll be back in a week or so to record some stuff with some British guys. Why don't we try it out then?' She would regret her nod of consent, and not only because 'down the coast' meant the coast of Europe. Dylan, his *Playboy* bunny girlfriend and his portly manager Albert Grossman allowed a mixture of Portuguese food, drink and drugs to take their toll. Joan Baez recalled, 'Everybody said "I'm tired of being in England, let's go someplace where there's a good restaurant." I mean, you live with Albert Grossman, you're gonna eat. Everybody took off and came back sick. And I don't know whether Bobby had tonsillitis, syphilis, or just a stomach-ache or what.' He spent three days in a London hospital.

Once discharged, the last thing on Dylan's mind was working with Nico. But she hung on tenaciously, and he was eventually lured into a London studio to follow up a private session he'd undertaken. He had wanted to grasp the mechanism of moving from acoustic to electric and from solo to group. He'd tried it in secret with an English rhythm and blues band, and it had fallen apart. Now, in this rambling session, they picked up the pieces as best they could. Nico hung around for hours and hours: 'I sat around with the girlfriends. Did you know, girls were called "chicks"? We were like the chickens [hens] waiting for our rooster. I felt too old for this. No, not too old but too experienced. But that is how we were then. We waited for the men. I don't like waiting for men. I like people to wait for me – that makes it more equal.' By the end of the day Dylan was drunk, yet he vamped at the piano so Nico could sing 'I'll Keep It with Mine' – one rehearsal, one take. The recording was turned into an acetate demonstration disc (a 'demo'). It was not bad, not good, but rushed. Before Nico even got a chance to check it, Dylan told her, 'This is going to be my next single. Whaddya think?' He launched into a song at the piano. Nico replied tartly that it was not as good as 'her' song. He had played her 'Like a Rolling Stone'.

6 July–December, 1965

She walks upon our meadows green:
The Lamb of God walks by her side:
And every English child is seen,
Children of Jesus and his Bride,

Forgiving trespasses and sins
Lest Babylon with cruel Og,
With Moral & Self-righteous Law
Should Crucify in Satans Synagogue!

What are those golden Builders doing
Near mournful ever-weeping Paddington
Standing above that mighty Ruin
Where Satan the first victory won.

Where Albion slept beneath the Fatal tree
And the Druids golden Knife,
Rioted in human gore,
In Offerings of Human Life.

> (from 'To the Jews',
> WILLIAM BLAKE, 1815)

S IX MONTHS ON from her decision to be discovered again, Nico had been wonderfully discovered, by the man who managed The Rolling Stones. She would shortly sign a record deal; a prestigious song of Bob Dylan's would be released. Nico would soon be a very famous singer, as famous as . . . she knew there was no *chanteuse* to *be* as famous as. There was Joan Baez, 'who looked like a horse', and Marianne Faithfull, 'who looked like somebody's girlfriend'. There was Mary out of Peter, Paul and Mary, 'but I noticed her name came last'. Nico could think of just two divas she could emulate in her ambition to be supreme, 'and they had the same name'. She was thinking of Marlene and Marilyn, Dietrich and Monroe.

'Somebody said something amusing about Beethoven,' Nico reflected in 1986. 'They said he was a great composer because he had a great manager. You see, we never think of great artists having managers. Who was Michelangelo's manager? Do you know? But nowadays, whenever I meet a musician, I meet his manager, too. I realised that it was necessary for me to have a manager, just like Michelangelo – or at least Bob Dylan.' So Dylan's manager would do, she decided. Albert Grossman was known as the Floating Buddha on account of his huge girth. He was a 40-year-old businessman famed for the protection he afforded his performers and notorious for the hard time he gave anyone who stepped in his way; his style is amply evident in *Don't Look Back* when he howls a hotel manager out of the room. As well as the iconic Dylan, he managed the most popular folk group of the time – Peter, Paul and Mary. Nico had a drink with Grossman and mentioned the impending record deal. Would he be interested in managing her, she wondered? 'Sure,' he replied. 'I've already been thinking about it, since Bob talked about you. Sure, I'd be interested . . . in the States. That's where I work. I'm looking for a girl singer right now – in America.' Nico giggled. She'd left the States to make her name in London, and now she had the chance of a deal with the most powerful manager around, but back in the States. She said she'd be in touch, and promised to send him a copy of her debut single. The first step was the record, something tangible to sell him.

Grossman was not the only manager looking for a female singer. One executive had told him, 'If you can find a girl who looks like Marilyn Monroe and sings like Mary Travers, you will conquer the world.' Grossman already had Travers; she was Peter and Paul's Mary, long-haired, blonde and wanly beautiful. He fathomed the reason behind his friend's advice. It was this: bands were the next big thing, they were the new hard edge, tribal, electric; bands were like gangs, bands were boystown (and the girls could loyally dote on Brian or Mick, George or Paul). In contrast, the soft edge must be feminine, cool, passive, self-absorbed, inscrutable, acoustic. These were how the options were shaping up in 1965. The music business was not clairvoyant, however. It could not have predicted powerful mavericks like the black virtuoso Jimi Hendrix or the white blues of Janis Joplin. But it might have considered more carefully the imminent drift to androgyny. Nevertheless, Bob Dylan had already made his choice. Grossman placed a group behind him, The Hawks, which eventually crowned its career with the ultimate group name, The Band. Now Grossman needed The Girl.

Nico was not a girl as boys' girls go. She felt deep confusion and discontent for the assumptions being made about her. She was not a girl, a chick, a bird, or a doll. Nico was a woman of 26 with her mother and her child to support. As Paul Morrissey had explained, 'She was an intelligent woman with a childlike mind, and I'm careful to say childlike, not childish.' Yet she was in need of work and induced by that pressure to invent a girl singer called Nico for a fat man aged 40 and a thin one aged 20. 'I was acting a role that I had to do. It was like being back with Strasberg. It was fun, really. But it was not acting a role on a stage or on a record. I was acting for contracts. I was making an audition each time I met Andrew, or Brian or Bobby. I was too shy to be me, and it's easier to play someone else, isn't it? It's like when I was a child, being nice to Americans to get some chocolate. But it's OK, because you become a success and you can live your real life out of sight. That's what Garbo did, and Dietrich. That's what I could do.' She never got that far.

THAT SUMMER OF 1965, London was drowned in dirty rain. In the wettest summer for years, not even a London Fog coat on a Coldstream Guard could cope with the elements: 'The city was like Venice in winter, and I wanted to be in Ibiza. But I had to make my "summer" record in the rain.' Andrew Loog Oldham had formed Immediate Records with Tony Calder, the producer of Marianne Faithfull's successes. They offered Nico a standard contract. Oldham told her that the label would be distributed by a major, Philips, and specialise in new talent singing their own material or covers of American hits. In Nico's case, he added, she had no material of her own and so they were searching for an American song. She played him the Dylan demo. 'It's a great song,' he reacted, 'but it's too downbeat for a debut. It'll make a good follow-up.' Nico learned to her dismay that her contract precluded her say in matters such as this. Brian Jones told her not to worry as Oldham was experienced and knew the trade 'inside-out' ('I wondered which trade he meant. The drugs trade, I think'). Jones promised to help her, coach her in whatever song was chosen, and furthermore play guitar in the recording session.

Oldham went as close to Dylan as he could get. He chose an A-side song by another Grossman act, the young Canadian composer Gordon Lightfoot. In those days he was a rather glamorous figure whose songs were covered by Elvis Presley, Dylan, Barbra Streisand and Johnny Cash. Once he'd been outed as 'Canada's Mister Folk of 1966', however, his prestige sank. Nico was indifferent to the song, a sentiment in keeping with its title. 'I'm Not Sayin' (as it is spelt on the label) is a typical Lightfoot number, influenced by Dylan in its extended lines and clever twists of thought:

> I'm not sayin' I'll be sorry,
> For the things that I might say that make you cry,
> I can't say I'll always do all the things you want me to,
> I'm not sayin' I'll be true – but I'll try.

The recording took place one day in the Soho recording studio down Denmark Street (at five pounds an hour). Oldham produced. He sought a lively, pop sound and hired David Whittaker's string orchestra to fill the texture, with a glockenspiel adding a cutesy, tinkling countermelody. Jones strummed his guitar upfront, accompanied by a drum kit that together effected a wretched pattern all too reminiscent of 'The Swinging Busker'. Nico was encouraged to sound like Marianne Faithfull, which she resented – 'You have to remember I was the oldest person there and they wanted me to sound like a little virgin.'

It is surprising to hear this record today and instantly recognise Nico's strong voice. Her trademark contralto tone is there from the start; Lightfoot's song was finally transposed down to B flat major to give Nico deep notes to sing, notes that lie below the conventional range of 'girls' voices' and belong in the shadowlands of Zarah Leander and Dietrich. For the only time in her vocal career, a Marianne Faithfull bleat can be detected, an embarrassingly thin and nervy attempt at vibrato that Nico darkened the next time she worked in a studio. The *New Musical Express* chirpily reviewed the single:

> Folksy and commercial, with a bounding, driving beat – that's
> *I'm Not Sayin'* written by Gordon Lightfoot who has pre-
> viously composed songs for Peter, Paul & Mary. It highlights
> the most attractive voice of girl singer Nico. Flip side is more
> of a protest song, titled *The Last Mile*.

Over the years this record has become a cult collectors' item on the strength of the 'protest song', written by Jimmy Page for Nico's session. Andrew Oldham had jotted down some lyrics of his own that Page shaped over a matter of minutes into a passable song:

Rivers were made for flowing
So why not let them flow?
People were made for showing
So why not let them show?
Show a little laughter, show a little smile,
'Cause we've started on the last mile.

Children's minds are crippled,
Black is what they see,
Man's mind is murdered,
So why not let him see?
Show a little laughter, show a little smile
'Cause we've started on the last mile.

This truly terrible farrago is little more than a paraphrase of the goofy speech Oldham delivered in New York City's Times Square to announce Klein's takeover: 'The sound, face and mind of today is more relative to the hope of tomorrow and the reality of destruction than the blind who cannot see their children for fear and division.' (Perhaps the blind divided from their children were the ones who had their heads kicked in at Oldham's bidding on the sleeve of The Stones' album five months earlier.) No wonder Nico resented playing the girl for such irredeemably dim boys.

It was not the song alone that caused the cult attention this record now commands. More magical is the combination of Nico with a guitar duet backing by Brian Jones and Jimmy Page. Page was then a jobbing, 21-year-old session guitarist who was recruited into Immediate as Oldham's house producer. He had played on all manner of singles in the pop charts, including those of The Stones, but most remarkably on The Who's 'My Generation' and 'It's Not Unusual' by Tom Jones. Few guessed then that the delicate, asthmatic session man would grow into a seminal figure of rock music, the creator of the group Led Zeppelin and a shamanist hero. Collectors hear the growl of The Great Beast behind 'The Last Mile'. They know that Jones and Page pursued the occult, and they suspect Nico, too, of rambling down the dark side of black magic, as far as 'the last mile'. But then this is the sort of thing record collectors tend to think.

Nico did once ask a writer, 'Do you know Brian was a witch? We were interested in these things and he was very deep about it. Mick knew and was his enemy. It was dangerous sometimes.' She said on another occasion that Jones was keen on the occult but 'he was like a little boy with a magic set. It was really an excuse for him to be nasty and sexy. He read books by an old English man who was the devil. I told Brian that I knew the devil and the devil was German!' The old English devil was Aleister Crowley (1875–1947), who named himself The Great Beast. Jimmy Page later bought his house and gathered memorabilia of the master. Three men have separately testified to Jones' fixation: the poet Brion Gysin, the film director and occultist Kenneth Anger, and the late blues historian Alexis Korner, though Korner cautiously added, 'He was more interested in the paraphernalia than the philosophy.' As for Nico, here is another half-truth compounded by mistaken identity. Anita Pallenberg has made little secret of her authority in the magical arts. When she was arrested for murder in Salem, Massachusetts, in 1979, she was also investigated for witchcraft (Salem has that kind of reputation). It seems that, even for record collectors, one 'German chick' is the same as another.

Nico was lured to witchcraft like she was to *The Anarchist Cook Book* and the *Kama Sutra*. They were slightly subversive, disobedient alternatives to dominant culture. She was part of the generation which sought alternatives in everything. Many of Nico's associates shared a distaste for the constraints of conventional materialism. One or two might have been placated by discreet adjustments to the drugs laws or the minor concessions of liberal government. Others were made of sterner stuff. Nico later summed up their options to a rock journalist: 'There were two ways to go. You could walk outside on to the street, or more inside to your mind.' (She was thinking once again in terms of her *Dolce Vita* palace.) Those who walked outside into the stale air sought change through communal action, civil rights and agitation. The others explored an inward path to self-enlightenment, a blasting away of the grime of orthodoxy, or 'mind blowing' as they would then say. Nico believed she had seen the effect of mass change and feared it: 'That's what the Nazis did. That's what happened to Germany.' She chose to stay indoors, seeking the 'inner truth', just as she imagined her father had. Not the soldier father – the Sufi father.

The search for alternatives often starts with opposites. Through the early Sixties, as the Christian churches pulled themselves apart between the cloistered traditions of privilege and the populist endeavours of the 'swinging vicar', the studies of pagan religions and the occult published trebled in number. A certain sect of Baptists launched a ludicrous campaign ('Is the devil up your high street?') that gave good publicity to those they attacked. The popular Sunday newspapers ran regular stories of housewife witches and seedy suburban covens. It was not hard to get engrossed, and like many bored boys of his generation, Brian Jones was fascinated. He read what he could find and learnt to love the occult's deviant spirit. Nico, of course, relished intimacy with options that were hidden or forbidden, and she was intrigued by the inverse uses of Christian symbols. There was a visceral thrill to be had from touching on taboos; in such matters Jones and Nico were of like mind and easily led. But, as usual, Nico was too lazy to go very far.

She had told the German magazine *Twen*, 'I am very superstitious. I really do believe in heaven and hell.' It was the spaces she referred to, not their owners God and Satan. At the same time she had said, 'I am a pagan. But I am religious, too. I guess religion also exists in a pagan, like pagan exists in religion, because it was there first.' She declined to amplify. Pagan means everything and nothing in this way, which makes it a perfect Nico word. She literally used it in that moment to signify 'pre-Christian', though she normally used it as a substitute for 'atheist' to convey 'non-Christian', in order to hint that she was drawn to religion but did not pursue it. Like Brian Jones she was 'more interested in the paraphernalia than the philosophy'; little Christa hung around the cemetery, not around the church. As far as 'The Last Mile' goes, it is foolish to burden it with powers beyond its seven-inch merit.

On 1 August 1965, Immediate was launched with a painstakingly dull press conference at which The Rolling Stones' management shake-up was implied in as anodyne manner as possible. Nico sat starkly at the centre of the top table, the only woman amongst a mixture of swinging and stuffy businessmen: Oldham, his partner Tony Calder, and the old-school-tie company manager of Philips. Alongside a photograph of this odd crew, the *New Musical Express* of Friday 13 August faithfully reproduced, as it always did, Oldham's press release:

> Three singles make up the inaugural release of Andrew Oldham's own label, Immediate Records, next Friday (20th). They include one produced by himself, 'I'm Not Sayin' ' by new girl singer Nico; an American hit 'Hang On Sloopy' by The McCoys, and a disc by the new British group the Fifth Avenue called 'The Bells of Rhymney'.

That Friday evening Nico did something prestigious that provided her with more free lunches than anything else she ever did in England. She appeared on *Ready, Steady, Go!* This trend-setting television programme was particularly renowned in America where nobody had seen it. Crammed into a London studio full of scaffolding, it showcased pop stars performing live in front of a fab crowd of groovy guys and gals, as they would have said in those days. The show led off with its racy slogan 'The weekend starts here!' and tethered the songs together with habitually fluffed links from a young lady known as the Queen of the Mods, whose microphone often worked. Nico promoted her A-side, appearing in the show with Sonny and Cher, The Animals, The Walker Brothers, and, following in the rear with that month's enormously popular novelty record, Jonathan King singing 'Everyone's Gone to the Moon'. Soon after, the tape of the programme was wiped clean, no doubt with good reason.

A fortnight later *Melody Maker* ran a gossip item in its Raver column: 'Nico says her next single will be a previously unrecorded Bob Dylan song.' She had obviously told a writer about the demo of 'I'll Keep It with Mine'. The follow-up was not released, however. Nico never made another recording for Immediate, and her contract remained unfulfilled. She complained that Oldham had not done his work properly, failing to find a chart placing for the single and running poor distribution. Here is the first sighting of a typical Nico trait; she would blame the manager for structural problems beyond his direct control. If the distribution was poor, he had made it poor; if she was not taken seriously by promoters, it was because he was letting her down. The manager represented to her the entire system, and she personalised her grievances. In Oldham's case, this was naive. He had landed an immediate success with 'Hang On Sloopy'. It hit the number one sales spot for six successive weeks; the market had resolved that this was where the money was to be made, thus all of Immediate's business resources followed. In truth, Nico had done tolerably well out of Oldham. He had built an adequate campaign, put her on TV for a pre-release boost, got her photograph in the music papers and her name in the gossip columns. Nico would not be placated. 'He was an idiot,' she grumbled, twenty years on.

Nico found comfort from the words of an ageing record company man she met at a party and whose name she could not later recall. He said to her, 'Singles are history. Each year people buy less and less. And girl singers only account for 20 per cent of the sales. You're on a hiding to nothing. There is a future – a future for groups and a future in albums. And I'll tell you what – a girl leading a group, that would be a winner!'

'TIME ISN'T IMPORTANT because it's the same thing all over the world. It can be ten o'clock in London or ten o'clock in Budapest. So I can't remember time very well. But I do remember places. It's very easy to remember them. The taxi in New York is yellow. In London it is black. In Berlin there is the U-Bahn. In Paris it is the Metro. In Ibiza there are boats. That is how I know where I am. And the sun.' It's odd that Nico never mentioned language; by now this recalcitrant Volksschule pupil knew four – English, French, German, Italian – and enough Spanish to buy bread and marijuana. She had not learned them but had 'picked them up', though she did not protest when admirers assumed she had endured an expensive education in private schools around Europe. 'I have received a good education in more than one country,' she admitted with the strictest candour. In the second half of 1965 Nico exercised her languages by skipping from country to country in search of . . . work, certainly, as Maywald had small assignments for her, and the assignments were not coming in so readily. Yet she was not only in search of work, but also her son, who still lived with the Boulognes in Paris. She longed to see him right then, it's conjectured, because she had just undergone an abortion in London, having discovered she was pregnant by Brian Jones (there is only Nico's vague word on this; she would have been ashamed to mention such a thing, especially after her row with her mother over Ari). At some point she took the three-year-old Ari for a short break to Berlin.

Her cousin Ulrich was now a tenderfoot architect, married and stable and not at all a member of Nico's bohemian netherworld. He remembers taking a meal in a Berlin restaurant with his family, Nico and Ari. He had to stomach more than the food: 'It was completely embarrassing the way she ignored her son. I mean that he would be roaming around other diners, pulling plates and cutlery off tables, playing with other people's food, making a noise and a mess. She carried on talking as though she had nothing to do with it, as though someone else was the boy's mother. She had no desire to dispense discipline, not of any kind, however sensible. He was completely free to do what he wanted, but he had no social character because of this. Yet, if he hurt himself or sought attention from her, she would comfort him generously. She acted both thoughtlessly and thoughtfully. It was extraordinary to treat a child in this way.'

Aunt Helma must have reminded Nico then how sick her mother had become, as Nico did visit Ibiza once more. It is easy to imagine her reacting to Grete and Ari in the same way, offering little more than a suntanned shoulder to cry on. She knew deep down that her mother could not survive in this manner, because she would talk in half-tones at stoned moments of her sad, sick mother to her American friends, though in half-tones only and nothing more. But she could not cope with the enormity of it, not when she met it face to face, and she lacked the money to indemnify herself against its hurt. At this time, alone with cheap magazines in harbour bars, the contrast in her life appeared most acute. She read in their pages about her 'friends' The Rolling Stones, Bob Dylan, Alain Delon and Andy Warhol. She saw photos of herself adding glamour to low-grade goods. She had access to fame but it was the men who had access to the money. And none more so, the magazines seemed to say, than the silver-haired stick-insect in Manhattan. Surely this time, she thought, she could keep the business side and the private side uncoupled from each other. After all, this Warhol was no dreamboat.

By early November Nico had flown to New York, where she found The Rolling Stones, Bob Dylan (who had just married in secret the *Playboy* bunny Sara Lowndes) and his manager Al Grossman. There was a little modelling work to be had, including a trip upstate to have her hair plaited and tugged by deer in the snow to advertise 'Bernhard Altmann's cable stitches of baby-sized braids on rich-as-whipped-cream cashmere'. Back in Manhattan, Brian Jones took Nico to Warhol's factory, which, she was disappointed to discover, was nothing more than the fourth floor of a warehouse on East 47th Street. It was covered in silver foil ('Silver makes everything disappear', Warhol noted) and was full of trendy people doing lots of things or nothing at all. Nico greeted Warhol and Malanga with a copy of her Immediate record. This was a wise move, for that disc proved to be her audition for The Velvet Underground and her ticket to fame as Andy Warhol's new Superstar and the tag Miss Pop 1966.

Nico was immediately given a screen test. This was not exactly an exalted moment in her career. Everyone, including Bob Dylan, took this test ('an entrance examination') when they first visited the Factory. They sat on a chair in a well-lit corner of the warehouse while Gerard Malanga pointed a camera at them for all of three minutes. Nico's test was evidently a success, for a few days later

Nico was placed in a real Warhol film, a two-reeler titled *The Closet*, in which she lives in a cupboard with gay boy Randy Borscheidt for 70 minutes of non-adventure. The connotation is gay; 'coming out of the closet' defines a public admission of homosexuality, though this was lost on Nico. It was the first of six Warhol films she was to make, any one of the others more memorable than her debut.

Beneath the silver-foiled ducts and clouds of dope, she met the Factory gang: Billy Name who covered the Factory in foil, a beatnik called Ondine who described himself as a 'running, standing, jumping drug addict', the porky Brigid Berlin whose father ran the Hearst Corporation, and scores of others, of whom the most glamorous was the wafer-thin model Edie Sedgwick, whom Nico would soon replace as First Lady of the Factory. Above all of these, the most *useful* employee she met was a young man, yet another young man, who fell in love with her. The suave, acid-tongued Paul Morrissey had started to direct the films Warhol was supposed to direct. He also managed Warhol's business affairs, and continued to do so for nine years. Gerard Malanga called Morrissey 'a cross between a New England whaling captain and Bob Dylan'; the gang around Warhol were nervous of this sharp-witted spark plug, as much as he was intolerant of their drug habits and artistic pretentions. His irrepressible, Irish whimsy was a characteristic that Nico much enjoyed in their perennial, platonic (unrequited) relationship. He is, after all, the man who summed up Andy Warhol's career as 'a window dresser who moved into painting when he was told his stuff looked like modern art'.

Paul Morrissey's story of Nico the Superstar starts in the once-upon-a-time manner of Opi Schulz: 'We have to go back a little, before Nico set foot in the Factory; I mean no later than the start of November. Andy had begun getting a fixed income from the Leo Castelli Gallery. But he wasn't doing any art. He withdrew from the art world for a number of years to put his price up and make the earlier stuff more collectable. He got a thousand dollars a week. And he didn't want to pay any taxes, so he decided to spend the leftover to make little films; an hour's worth of developed 16 mm black and white film cost $200. Well, for $200 we weren't exactly going to compete with Hollywood. But this guy, Jonas Mekas, used to rent an off-Broadway theatre on a Monday night when it wasn't showing plays, and called it the Cinematheque. Now, Andy was always looking for ways to keep his name in the papers, and it turned out that the film critic of the *New York Times* reviewed this stuff at the Cinematheque, so we'd put something on there and it'd get Andy's name in the *Times*. These films were truly experimental, no one in their right mind thought there'd be an audience. When Andy started, the camera didn't move, not at all. Then I said, "Andy, let's try moving the camera," and Andy'd say, "Gee, um, I don't know." He was terribly indefinite about everything. I really became his manager in the sense that I did all the talking; I also had to suggest what to do. Andy would get up in the morning and say, "What do I do today?" and you had to tell him what to do. I'd say, "Let's make a picture," and he'd say, "Great, what shall we do it about?" and I'd say an idea, or he'd have something in mind he'd heard from somewhere else . . . not exactly Hollywood.

'We started to move the camera and shoot two reels – we did one reel and then, "Oh, well, let's do another, maybe it'll be better." So, I'd project a reel for 30 minutes and there was no cut in it so it just went on and on, the camera maybe zoomed in and out a couple of times, but it was pretty boring. One day I got fed up with this and put the other reel on at the same time on the other projector to see if there was anything of interest in either, and putting them together made them better. I told Andy, he said, "Oh, gee, um, OK," and so we started showing films at the Cinematheque two reels at a time. That's how the multi-projection thing started up that we used in The Velvet Underground shows and got us all that *avant-garde* reputation.'

Morrissey and Warhol were always on the lookout for ways to bring new money into the Factory and get 'employment for our employees'. Anything would do, they said, simply anything. Nevertheless, they were amazed when an old theatre producer called Michael Myerberg phoned with a plan to have Warhol host a discotheque he was building: 'For some godforsaken reason he wanted to open up a discotheque in an aircraft hangar in the district of Queens, where nobody in the world went. There weren't many discotheques in New York and they were all small like Arthur's, Ondine's, The Scene – that was some rich kid renting a basement with a dance floor the size of a toilet seat. We went to Myerberg's office above the famous Sardi's restaurant, and he said to Andy, "You go to discotheques and you've got that girl Edie Sedgwick and you both have your names in the papers all the time going to clubs. I'd like to hire you to come to this discotheque every night." Andy was always interested in people offering him money, but the problem was here that nobody would believe Andy was really going to Queens every night!

'This guy was trying to accommodate us and he suggests, "I'll call it Andy Warhol's Discotheque. Or you can think up a name." We were sitting there a bit startled by now, but Andy said, "Er . . . er . . . The Up. Andy Warhol's Up." Of course, this guy had no idea that Andy was being a little naughty: "That sounds fine to me," he replied. We said we'd think about the deal. Outside, I said to Andy that we could go to his stupid discotheque and he could pay us, but it didn't make sense unless we had some financial stake. In those days discotheques had records *and* live bands. I told Andy we'll find a rock and roll band and then we'd have a reason for going there because it was our group and Andy would be like Brian Epstein. He said, "Ooh, that's great." And I told him not to worry about the art part because Cocteau once managed a prize fighter. So suddenly Andy was sold on this idea of managing a group, and it just came from me trying to accommodate this guy Myerberg.'

Morrissey phoned Myerberg that Andy would do the deal if he'd promote their band for the opening. Myerberg said, 'Fine. What's the name of the band?' Morrissey gulped. He had no band. He garbled, said he'd let him know. He sat around the Factory for a week, head in hands, trying to sort it out: 'It turned out that the Factory kids didn't like to go and hear bands,' complained Morrissey. 'They'd only go if it was an *event* like The Rolling Stones.' Gerard Malanga had a friend, Barbara Rubin, who knew a young singer called Lou Reed. She asked Gerard to film a new group that Lou had joined that was booked for a three-day residency in a West Village venue called the Café Bizarre – 'Or was it the Café Wha? They were next to each other. These cafés were leftovers from the Fifties beatnik thing; they had folk singers and poets and all that crap for the tourists, and they were controlled by Italian interests – the West Village is very mafia.' Malanga borrowed Warhol's Bolex camera and asked Morrissey to help him work the light meter and load the camera. That was how Morrissey got to see The Velvet Underground, who had taken their name from a cheap sex paperback.

Morrissey thought they were fascinating: 'John Cale had a wonderful appearance and he played an electric viola, which was a real novelty; but best of all was Maureen Tucker, the drummer. You couldn't take your eyes off her because you couldn't work out if she was a boy or a girl. Nobody had ever had a girl drummer before.

She made no movement, she was so sedate. But you had to have three things to run a group: a guitar, an amplifier and a manager. Well, they didn't even have the amplifiers. Maureen was only brought along because her brother had one to lend. I asked them, "How would you like Andy Warhol to be your manager? We are looking for a band, we can guarantee employment, we can open you in a big discotheque with lots of publicity, we'll sign a contract with you and find you a record deal." If things hadn't worked out the way they had, there wouldn't have been a group a week later. That's the power of coincidence. I brought Andy along the next night. He said, "Ooh, yeah, great. I love that word 'Underground' in their name." But he always said yes. He just wanted something to happen.'

Nico made her Factory entrance that very week. Morrissey recalled the occasion: 'Andy said "Oh, hi!" but he would say hello to a wall. He'd met her in Paris but he could never remember these things. He always covered himself with a grin and a "Hi!" ' Nico gave them a copy of 'I'm Not Sayin' ' which they promptly played and 'sort of liked'. Morrissey immediately saw a solution to a problem he had with The Velvet Underground: 'Andy, the problem is these people have no singer. There's a guy who sings but he's got no personality and nobody pays the slightest attention to him. They need someone with a bit of charisma.' The singer with 'no personality' was Lou Reed, and the solution was 'the most beautiful girl in the world', standing right there in the Factory. They took Nico that night to see the band. Afterwards Morrissey broached the deal. He offered some money that the band could live on and cover their rent, and some equipment. 'But,' he added uneasily, 'you'll need to sign a management contract and you need a singer . . . and, er, we know this singer and, er, what if she sang with your group?' They listened to Nico's record. Morrissey watched their reaction: 'Right away that sour little Lou Reed bristled. He was hostile to Nico from the start. I told them I thought that Nico could be part of The Velvet Underground and just fit in there under that name.' Lou Reed replied, 'Let's keep Nico separate in this. The Velvet Underground – and Nico.' Even in the name alone, second billing. 'That's because I was the girl,' Nico grinned.

'Now, you have to remember,' reminded Morrissey, 'that we'd gotten hold of this group only because of Myerberg's discotheque deal. But he kept stalling, the date kept getting postponed. Finally, we got a date in April 1966. The Velvets were going to open the place on the Friday. On the Monday before, I phoned Myerberg but he said, "There's been a change of plan. I can't use your group. We're gonna open with The Young Rascals." The Rascals were a group of New York Italians managed by the kind of people who run West Village cafés. I shouldn't really have been surprised. However, there I was, sitting in this room with a band who think they start work on Friday in a big club. But, coincidentally, that very same day . . .'

That very same day Nico announced to a journalist that her public life was flourishing wonderfully, and her private life was – 'it was flourishing also, but no less than before'. At the age of 27, she was the centre of attention wherever she went, and everyone thought, 'she was between twenty and ageless . . . with the mind of a child and the looks of an archangel'. Nico confessed in 1985 that she was a child who played a woman, and her life went best 'when I met a boy who played a man. Ho, ho, ho . . .' The boy was Warhol. After four months in his presence, she decided that he was more of a dreamboat than she had presumed. It was not that he was handsome, but that he was 'brotherly'. Nico said in 1986 that the two of them were like 'Hänsel and Gretel . . . though I think he wanted to be Gretel'. It is an unhappy consequence of these games that Nico had to be reminded how Hänsel and Gretel were doomed – no, *fated* – to meet their wicked witch: 'Oh yes, we met the wicked witch. Her name was Valerie.'

7 January–June, 1966

Time, Real and Imaginary

On the wide level of a mountain's head,
(I knew not where, but 'twas some faery place)
Their pinions, ostrich-like, for sails out-spread,
Two lovely children run an endless race,
A sister and a brother!
This far outstripp'd the other;
Yet ever runs she with reverted face,
And looks and listens for the boy behind:
For he, alas! is blind!
O'er rough and smooth with even step he passed,
And knows not whether he be first or last.

(SAMUEL TAYLOR COLERIDGE, 1828)

ON AN UNKNOWN DAY of an unmarked month in the Sixties, days and months and seasons floated off into the ineffable cosmos, leaving a blissful stretch of indissoluble space. There, unfettered by time, golden children of the universe inhaled giant spliffs, decoded the *Kama Sutra* to the incantations of concept albums, studied with microscopic care The Fabulous Furry Freak Brothers and stared expressively into an empty space through which they distinctly saw space gypsies, hobgoblins and certain kinds of God. 'I can't remember a single date. I don't think anybody can,' complained Nico. Her film star friend Tina Aumont tried valiantly to recall a visit she made with Nico to the hippie paradise of Italy's Positano: 'It was in the Seventies, 1978? No, it was when I did Fellini's *Casanova*. When was that? 1971? 1968? Well, it was sometime then, between 1968 and 1978.' They were not alone in their amnesia. The photographer David Bailey begged, 'Please don't ask me to remember dates, or even years. In the Sixties I don't think we even knew what year we were in when we were in it, let alone after. It all sort of merged together rather nicely.'

Now that time is back with us, it is a challenge to top and tail the Sixties. The author Robert Hewison contends that they started in 1963 and faded away in 1975; this makes stylistic sense. His adversary, the conservative Christopher Booker, binds 1956 to 1966 as one long exuberant dream followed by the nightmare that commenced in 1966 and gave way to the grim reality of 1969; but then he would, for he framed his theory back in 1970. In whatever way the morphology is fixed, 1966 and 1967 stand out as sensational years. Nico thought they were spectacular, a view not shared by her mother and her son: 'I have always been in the wrong place at the wrong time. But when I was with Andy Warhol, I seemed to have got it right,' she claimed. She certainly received unparalleled attention, which is how she liked it, whether the place and the time were right or wrong.

The right place was Manhattan, but she had not yet found the right place within Manhattan to live. At first she stayed at the Chelsea Hotel, 222 West 23rd Street. Nico would return to this wonderfully impossible warren time and time again, often forgetting she still owed rent from the last visit (it is believed that she owes rent still). The Chelsea was ages old, converted into a long-stay hotel from its origin as a cooperative apartment block by the Bard family, who still run it; Stanley Bard and his father must have argued bills with almost every artist and bohemian in need of New York shelter: Dylan Thomas, Brendan Behan, Edith Piaf, Arthur Miller, Katherine Dunham, William Burroughs, Jackson Pollock, Virgil Thomson, Allen Ginsberg; and then the rock stars, including Janis Joplin, of whose stay there Leonard Cohen wrote a famous song. Within a year of her debut visit, Nico, too, would sing a Lou Reed song about the druggy scenes of its contemporary crop of Warholites – Bridget Berlin, Ingrid Superstar, Mary Woronov, Susan Bottomly (who called herself International Velvet):

> Dear Ingrid's found her lick
> She's turned another trick
> Her treats and times revolve
> She's got problems to be solved
>
> Poor Mary, she's uptight
> She can't turn out her light
> She rolled Susan in a ball
> And now she can't see her at all
> Here they come now

See them run now
Here they come now
Chelsea Girls

Nico was not a Chelsea Girl for long; she found that she could not face a winter with the hotel's historic heating system. She soon joined a modelling colleague in a West Village apartment and took control of the place in her customary regal manner. From there she would strut down to the Factory ('It was more of a sashay, kind of like a feline goosestep,' noted Warhol). Her walk from the Factory lift into the fourth-floor studio was never less than an Entrance, as though she was parading a Chanel gown, even if she had on her regular pants suit ('very mod and spiffy in white wool pants, double-breasted blazers, beige cashmere turtlenecks, and those pilgrim-looking shoes with the big buckles on them', Warhol wrote, with his queeny eye for fashion detail). Although the Factory was stuffed with folk in love with themselves, she would still turn their heads. Paul Morrissey told Warhol that she was 'the most beautiful creature that ever lived'.

There was also her distinctive voice, and her accent. Americans adore classic foreign dialects and will shamelessly bribe owners to make aural idiots of themselves for home amusement, as many Europeans can testify. In Warhol's book *Popism*, there is an anonymous quote about Nico's voice that has since been used in countless articles and commentaries: 'An IBM computer with a Garbo accent.' The phrase is attributed to Warhol, which is wrong. It is assumed that it refers to her singing voice, which is very wrong (he writes of her singing voice later). It is considered precise rather than facetious, which is very wrong indeed. It is actually a Nicoism, half true and half not. Her voice was deep, like Garbo's voice and Dietrich's voice and millions of women's voices in Germany and Scandinavia and other regions around the world, for a low voice is not a racial trait. But she had a little trick she had evolved to ensure people paid full attention and did not interrupt. It was a refinement of the Lübbenau Whine, her childish siren that boomed through Güterbanhofstrasse, 'Tan-te Hel-ma! Tan-te Hel-ma!' She would simply dilate her sentences to immeasurable length. Firstly she prolonged the vowels, secondly she added incongruous pauses, thirdly her meaning would be as vague as her vocabulary allowed – at best oracular, at worst deranged.

There are four attempts to capture Nico's voice in Warhol's

Popism book: 'No, it's not truuuuue'; 'I want to sound like Bawwwhhhb Deee-lahhn'; 'We should siiiiit here on the flooorrrrr and waaaaiiiiit with the candles burrrrrning and praaaay'; 'I only like the fooood that flooooats in the wiiine'. The last phrase is perfect, enigmatic Nico. To her, it is a simple and obvious thing to say; she means she likes to suck on the slices of fruit that float in a jar of sangria. She is thinking of sangria, oranges and jars, and speaks of it. You might not be thinking of sangria, oranges and jars – they might be the last things on your mind; that is your misfortune. John Cale of The Velvet Underground said, 'It was unnerving. She had this weird timing. You'd ask her an innocent question, maybe "How ya doin'?" and she'd look inscrutable for ages. Once you'd given up waiting for an answer, you know, like ten minutes later, she'd suddenly say, "Oh fine." And it was up to you to remember what was fine. Everyone had this problem with her. She kept control of the situation this way. It always worked to her advantage.'

A typical Nico conversation was captured by her final manager, Alan Wise:

Alan: Are you saying that Jim Morrison was *like* Jesus Christ, or that he *was* Jesus Christ?

Nico: I'd like a new car.

Alan: Oh. What kind of car would you like?

Nico: About 2,000 years old.

Alan: The car?!

Nico: No, Jesus Christ.

Folded into these surreal phrases was Nico's sense of wit. Warhol noticed it immediately and loved her for the icy rejoinders she threw. He assumed they shared a vein of humour, rooted in middle Europe, for Andy Warhol was really Andrew Warhola, born of Czech parents in the industrial town of Pittsburgh. They shared much more than humour; Warhol's father died when Warhol was thirteen and he still looked after his mother, Julia, for whom he had bought a Manhattan apartment. 'Andy and Nico liked each other's company,' said John Cale. 'There was something complicit in the way they both handled Lou Reed, for instance. Lou was straight-up Jewish New York (his name is Louis Firbank), while Nico and Andy were kind of European (like me – I am Welsh). Lou was very full of himself and faggy in those days. We called him Lulu, I was Black Jack, Nico was Nico. He wanted to be queen bitch and spit out the sharpest rebukes of anyone around. Lou always ran with the pack and the Factory was full of queens to run with. But Lou was dazzled by Andy and Nico. He was completely spooked by Andy because he could not believe that someone could have so much goodwill, and yet be mischievous in the same transvestite way that Lou was, all that bubbling, gay humour. It was fun for the rest of us to watch all of the shenanigans going on, with René Ricard and those spiteful games you just had to laugh at because they were so outrageous. But Lou tried to compete. Unfortunately for him, Nico could do it better.

'Nico and Andy had a slightly different approach, but they caught Lou out time and again. Andy was never less than considerate to us. Lou couldn't fully understand this, he couldn't grasp this amity that Andy had. Even worse, Lou would say something bitchy, but Andy would say something even bitchier, and – nicer. This would irritate Lou. Nico had the same effect. She would say things so he couldn't answer back. You see, Lou and Nico had some kind of affair, both consummated and constipated. At that time he wrote these psychological love songs for her like "I'll Be Your Mirror" and "Femme Fatale". When it fell apart, we really learnt how Nico could be the mistress of the destructive one-liner. I remember one morning we had gathered at the Factory for a rehearsal. Nico came in late, as usual. Lou said "Hello" to her in a rather cold way, but just "Hello" or something. She simply stood there. You could see she was waiting to reply, in her own time. Ages later, out of the blue, came her first words: "I cannot make love to Jews any more." What a good start to the day that was!'

SUPERSTAR WAS A TITLE, like Lady, or Countess, or Queen, and it was given to the faithful courtiers and the glamorous women – rarely men – who escorted Andy Warhol to parties and gallery openings. It was also withdrawn when the time came for the reigning Superstar to be dumped. Warhol was discarding one of those when Nico first entered his Factory. Edie Sedgwick was the stick-insect escort Nico had met in Paris, the one she found to be 'too preoccupied with her lipstick to pay any attention'. Like all of the past and future Superstars save Nico, Sedgwick was the child of an ostentatiously rich family. From her New England home where spoilt folk had gushing names like Saucie and Fuzzy, the 22-year-old Edith Minturn Sedgwick moved to uptown Manhattan from where she was driven about in a lavish Mercedes limousine to parties and more parties and ever more parties. Miss Sedgwick was known to all as Edie, just as Miss Päffgen was known as Nico. She was a perfect Mod, androgyne, doe-eyed, amphetamine-skinny, and caked in make-up ('Skin bad, make-up good'). Warhol remarked: 'I could see that she had more problems than anybody I'd ever met.' Edie was, therefore, his perfect Superstar.

The Superstar burned out slowly. Up to the end of 1965 Edie had been Andy's good little rich girl. She had starred in Warhol's films (*Vinyl, Poor Little Rich Girl, Kitchen, Bitch* and ten more); she had cropped her hair and dyed it silver to match his wig; she had reclined with him in her Mercedes and been driven to numberless receptions; she had paid entire meal bills; she had worn her leopard-skin furs and pouted brilliantly for the paparazzi; she had made every kind of momentously petty sacrifice a Superstar had to make. But she also took all the drugs they offered her ('I think drugs are like strawberries,' she said), began to run out of family money, and – the most dangerous sign of all – started asking about her 'career'. Edie was no longer a glittering ornament, but was becoming dissident; the poor little rich girl was turning into a largely poor and knowing woman.

Bob Dylan had lately been dating Edie and seduced her with ideas of stardom. He was giving her ideas way above her station, as far as Warhol was concerned; he suspected, too, that Dylan had introduced her to heroin. As Paul Morrissey remembers, 'Dylan was calling up Edie and meeting her at a discotheque called Arthur's all the time, and Edie was seen going around with Dylan, which annoyed Andy. She was still the Edie we all knew – a lively, funny and cute girl – but she now had people saying she could be a big star and that this Andy Warhol guy was wasting her talent. Once, I had dinner with Edie and Andy in The Ginger Man, and I'll always remember her saying, "A wonderful thing has happened to me. I'm going to be managed by Albert Grossman. And Bobby says I'm going to star in a film with him. But Mr Grossman says – you know those movies I made with you? Don't ever show them. I never signed a release, and I think they'd be bad for my career." The only reason people were so interested in getting a piece of her was because these films of Andy had made her famous in the first place! It was shocking to see she could be taken in.'

There was no Dylan film to be made. The Factory crew had speculated that it was merely Dylan's device to keep Edie available for his own nefarious use, but they were not then aware of her story's uncanny affinity to the one Nico was shortly to tell them. Neither did Edie know that Dylan had just married the *Playboy* bunny; she never expected to join a queue for anything, let alone love. Behind her back, the crew were sniggering that Edie was 'a stupid cunt'.

She had known her starry days were ending once she had met Ingrid Von Scheflin. Von Scheflin was Factory-christened as Ingrid Superstar because she looked like 'an ugly Edie'. They cropped her hair like Warhol's wig and trowelled on the make-up to make the corrupt resemblance painfully acute. It surely burdened the both of them to be treated in this malign manner, though neither was a threat to the other. Nico pitied them both: 'Edie was the opposite to me in many ways. She had never known anything but richness, can you imagine? I think she made a fool of herself to impress these men. She should have had more dignity. She moved around too much. But she was sweet, like a little boy, a lovely boy who played with the make-up for the first time. Ingrid was fine and sad. She was abused and she did not understand it, though she guessed it. Edie has a ghost, a melancholy ghost. I know this to be true.'

Warhol thought that changing from Edie to Nico was like switching from silver to crimson. 'Nico and Edie were so different, there was no good reason to compare them really,' *Popism* claimed. 'Nico was a new type of female Superstar. Baby Jane [Holzer] and Edie were both outgoing, American, social, bright, excited, chatty – whereas Nico was weird and untalkative. You'd ask her something and she'd maybe answer you five minutes later. When people described her they used words like *memento mori* and *macabre*. She wasn't the type to get up on a table and dance, the way Edie or Jane might; in fact, she'd rather hide under the table than dance on top of it. She was mysterious and European, a real Moon Goddess type.'

Nico was a goddess and Edie was a nuisance. Sedgwick was put out to the upstate pastureland of Woodstock where Dylan and Grossman had their home and their wives. Retired at 22, Edie would return now and again to the Factory, wearing long sleeves to hide the needle scars of her heroin addiction. She wore them long right through to her final overdose and funeral at the age of 28. Nico was horrified to see her descent. 'Andy didn't like Bobby Dylan because he had stolen a painting and Edie from him. But I couldn't at first associate Edie and Bob and her heroin problem, not like Andy could. Some things you are born to, and Edie was born to die from her pleasures. She would have to die from drugs whoever gave them to her. Anyway, drugs are the surface of something deeper. When we say drugs, we are talking about something else. They are the symptom.' Nico pronounced it 'Symp. Tom', and gave a little giggle.

When she was asked to amplify her opinion, she said, 'You either live outside or inside, and some drugs help you to live inside. Edie Sedgwick wanted to live inside because there was nothing outside for her to see anymore. But she was a husk. She died because there was nothing inside, either. Brian Jones died because there was too much inside. They died the same age, you know.'

When Warhol chucked Edie he lost his sugar-daughter (the limousine lined up ready, bills settled, glamour pictures guaranteed). But he had replaced someone who tried to look like him with someone who behaved like him. Instead of a twin, he now had a sister: 'two nuns, not on the run', quipped Viva. Catholic herself, Viva saw the Factory as a sort of Vatican. They were two European Catholics from poor homes who succeeded in society by saying nothing and staying cool. Ultra Violet (who hid her real name of Isabelle Collin-Dufresne) was a subsequent Superstar who noted in diary form that 'I am fascinated by Nico. I see her as Andy incarnated into a singer. She is as lifeless as he, although I once saw her shedding slow tears while singing at the Dom . . . When she and Andy first meet, neither knows what to say. They just stand there and feel each other's vibes. A conversation between them goes like this:

    Nico: Hi, Andy.
    Andy: Oh, hi.

(Silence. After a while . . .)

    Nico: Andy.
    Andy: Hmmm.
    Nico: I . . .

(Silence)

    Andy: What?
    Nico: I . . . thought . . .

(Silence)

    Andy: What?
    Nico: . . . thought you . . .
    Andy: What were you saying, Nico?
    Nico: Nothing.'

NICO REALISED HER IDENTITY through men. Many women of her age recognised that marriage conferred the status they sought in life.

Through it they bore a new identity, graphic and fixed, rendered by the family name of the man they married. Nico, who rated singularity above submission, gained her status by other means. She tried to resolve her evident crisis of authenticity, and did so in a time before the thoughts of feminism sponsored other options. Firstly, she adopted a male forename, and then she embraced the style she had most admired in straight society – that of the quiescent, mannerly gay men who survived most eligibly in orthodox society through their public silence and their cryptic private lives. Andy Warhol was her model, a virtual mute who stood his still ground surrounded by screaming queens ('I prefer to remain a mystery,' he said). 'I didn't really know anybody in America except Andy. I just stood close to him. Whatever he did, I followed him. I was in love with him for a time, I guess, though we never broke our friendship,' she told *Twen* in 1969.

'Andy likes other people to become Andy for him. He doesn't want to be always in charge of everything. He would rather be me or someone else sometimes. Like the radio interview when I couldn't show up, he went on and took my part – said the things I would say. It's part of pop art, I guess, that everybody can impersonate somebody else, that you don't always have to be you to be you. If tomorrow I find somebody else who is pretty much like me and I put her here to sing, she can be Nico while I go to do something else.' She said all of this in March 1967 for a curious magazine called *In New York – Guide to the Swinging Side of Single New York* (it was later used to form the liner notes of her first solo LP). The writer concluded that, 'She is beautiful. And in a world where so much can easily be possessed on a whim or for a promise, she is unpossessable.' Except, it seemed, by Andy Warhol. Gerard Malanga, however, added that, 'Although Andy and Nico were a very good match, Nico was independent in a way that Edie wasn't. Nico was never really needing anything of Andy, and Andy wanted women to need things from him, so he could deny them.'

Nico's revealing comment, 'You don't always have to be you to be you', is the kind of aphorism that might be found in the sayings of Warhol, though his books, like *Popism* written with Pat Hackett, were often written 'with' or 'by' another author who wrote down the sort of thing Warhol would say, rather than the things he really said. When Nico proposed an autobiography titled *Moving Target* that would be 'half true and half not true', her friends assumed that she was weakly aping Warhol yet again, and none too wisely. There is enough evidence, however, to show that Nico could coin a barbed maxim or a cute axiom before she had even met him. Warholisms and Nicoisms were morally next of kin; in her phantom family, he was her shrinking-violet sibling who died of boredom just before she did ('I will have Andy to gossip with in the grave'). As Paul Morrissey said, they were a brother and sister – one who died rich and the other poor, 'and both unhappily'.

Yet from the New Year of 1966 until Warhol's near death in the summer of 1968, Nico would live 'the happiest days of my life – ho, ho, ho . . .' She would spend them drifting between lovers, drugs, films and music, and she would learn to compose fine songs and play them. The luxury of drifting she encountered for the next two years was something sustained by Warhol's friendship, Nico believed. She would thank Warhol above all, because 'he never stood in the way when I opened doors. He watched me do it in the same way that I watched myself. We were both voyeuristic. Nobody understood that about our affinity.'

IN JANUARY 1966, The Velvet Underground – 'and Nico' – were ready to play. They had signed a management contract with the Warvel Corporation. The War(hol) Vel(vet) directors were Warhol and Morrissey, who racked up 25 per cent of the Velvets' earnings and 25 per cent of Nico's earnings from the work the Corporation got them. Paul Morrissey already earned 25 per cent of Warhol's earnings, 'which made it a bit complicated, because I got something stupid like 15.625 per cent of Nico and Andy got 9.375 per cent – well, we never made a buck so it doesn't really matter in the end!' The financial stake was large enough to warrant a few try-outs before their debut, then still imminent, at Myerberg's discotheque out in Queens. They started with a film made by a boggle-eyed crew for the WNET cable station. They had come to make a short feature on Warhol which he subverted into a filmed rehearsal of the group at the Factory. He taped an introduction for the film crew in which he gauchely chattered for the considerable length of thirty seconds:

> We've sponsored a new band that's called The Velvet Underground, and – erm – and we're trying to – erm – and since I don't really believe in painting any more, I thought it'd be a nice way of combining – erm – and we have this chance to combine music and art and – er – er – films all together and

– and – we're sort of working on that and the whole thing's being auditioned tomorrow at 9 o'clock and if it works out it might be very glamorous.

The Velvets were not auditioning nor had they the slightest wish to be merely 'very glamorous'. They were alarmed to see the Factory people chipping in very glamorously, especially Gerard Malanga who had thoughtfully brought along his whip to perform what he termed his Whip Dance. They didn't really care about Paul Morrissey playing with his projectors, because he was projecting something obscure and out of focus on to the wall behind them. But it all seemed to be a bit of a circus. 'That is what Paul would have called our Selling Point, I think,' commented Nico. She was none too happy with the chaos either, because it detracted from the matter she considered to be the most vital on earth to resolve – how many songs she got to sing, and what she did when she wasn't singing. 'Lou said, "Nico, you can always knit." I said he could go to hell. He looked around and said, "Well where do you think we are now?"'

On 9 January the group, with Nico and absolutely everybody else, gave an unorthodox public rehearsal at the New York Society for Clinical Psychiatry's annual dinner at the dapper Delmonico Hotel. Warhol had been asked to give a lecture, and instead he proposed a 'performance'. There are some photographs of the occasion showing Edie dancing the watusi next to a notably rigid Nico. Ultra Violet was there, too, and described the event as 'Andy and the Underground giving shock treatment to the 175 well-dressed shrinks and their perfumed, carefully coiffed wives'. The clinical psychiatrists must have seen several past and future patients posing on the stage, not only Lou Reed but also Edie, a resident of many asylums. They would never get to summon Nico, though. 'I would rather take drugs than be in a nuthouse,' she declared.

'What am I supposed to be doing in The Velvet Underground? What's my role? When am I going to get paid?' This was not Nico complaining, but Edie. The Cinematheque had organised an Edie Retrospective for February 1966 – all of her Warhol films, plus the debut of her latest. Because of the Edie–Dylan debacle, the whole project was replaced with a try-out for The Velvet Underground spectacle, twice nightly for a week. Warhol showed only the new film, *Lupe*, where Edie played the Mexican diva Lupe Velez. In its final scene she was made to retch over a toilet bowl, which was Warhol's way of saying 'Adiós Edie'.

Succeeding the toilet bowl came The Velvet Underground – and Nico. She was given two songs to sing and a tambourine to rattle behind Lou Reed ('We couldn't have chosen a worse instrument to give to Nico. Her sense of rhythm was – unique,' said Cale). The whole evening was not quite called *Andy Warhol's Up*. There was an appropriate amendment:

ANDY WARHOL, UP-TIGHT
presents live
THE VELVET UNDERGROUND
EDIE SEDGWICK
GERARD MALANGA
DONALD LYONS
BARBARA RUBIN
BOB NEUWIRTH
PAUL MORRISSEY
NICO
DANIEL WILLIAMS
BILLY LINICH

Next to the newspaper advert with this roll-call of Factory regulars sits a photograph. It shows Warhol with the Velvets – and Edie. 'My name was somewhere near the bottom, I remember, and I cried,' noted Nico. 'Andy told me not to care, it was only a rehearsal. Edie tried to sing along, but she couldn't do it. We never saw her on stage again. It was Edie's farewell and my premiere at the same time. They played the record of Bob Dylan's song 'I'll Keep It with Mine' because I didn't have enough to sing otherwise. Lou wanted to sing everything. I had to stand there and sing along with it. I had to do this every night for a week. It is the most stupid concert I have ever done.'

Nico advanced to chief roadie when the Factory crew gave concerts at two universities during March, at Rutgers in New Jersey and Ann Arbor in Michigan. The show was no longer Up-Tight but Erupting Plastic Inevitable (they soon decided the title could be immeasurably improved by altering 'Erupting' to 'Exploding', a very Sixties notion of progress). 'I still had my American license and I was the only one who could drive. Edie used to be their chauffeur, or I mean, her chauffeur was their chauffeur. Now I was their chauffeur and chanteuse.'

Warhol gave a dramatic account of Nico's driving in *Popism* ('It was all shit, but he didn't write it anyway,' she said in 1985): 'Nico drove, and that was an experience. I still don't know if she had a license. She'd only been in this country a little while and she'd keep forgetting and drive on the British side of the road ... Nico's driving really was insane when we hit Ann Arbor. She was shooting across sidewalks and over people's lawns ... Ann Arbor went crazy. At last the Velvets were a smash. The strobes were magical, they went perfectly with the chaos music the Velvets played, and that long piece of phosphorescent green Sylvania tape that Gerard was now using for his dance numbers, whipping that around, looked terrific when the strobes flashed on it.' It is typical of the Factory that it could chronicle a concert in terms of its light show.

Then the fateful Monday morning came when Paul Morrissey learned in horror that The Young Rascals had taken the Velvets' place in Queens. 'But coincidentally, that very same day,' he continued, 'I had to go with Andy to a coffee shop so he could have his photograph taken with Allen Ginsberg for some god-forsaken reason or other. I'm sitting there telling Andy we've got a group and no gig, when guy at the next table leans over and says, "You've got a rock and roll band and you need a hall to play in? We've just done a dance recital on 8th Street, it's called The Dom. It's a large hall, has a stage and a bar. If you go over there now you could probably rent it for the weekend." So I went over to Saint Mark's Place where it was – not the chic area it is now – met this guy called Stanley, who was Polish, because the club was a Polish national social club (Dom means home), and rented it.

'On Tuesday I say to Andy "We've got to come up with $2–3,000 for the hall and an advert in *The Village Voice*, and the deadline for the *Voice* is, like, this afternoon." It was a lot of money, way over budget, but he said, "Well, um, if you're sure ..." I mean, he was wonderful that way; he didn't read contracts or anything, he'd just trust you. Frankly, he was very fortunate that things went always so well. So I got over to *The Village Voice* and took a full-page advert, that's the only publicity we had time for, nothing else, just this artless, cheap ad.' A copy survives in Warhol's scrapbook:

DO YOU WANT TO DANCE AND BLOW YOUR MIND
WITH
THE EXPLODING PLASTIC INEVITABLE
live

ANDY WARHOL

THE VELVET UNDERGROUND
and
NICO

Live Music, Dancing, Ultra Sounds, Visions, Lightworks
by Daniel Williams, Color slides by Jackie Cassen,
Discotheque, Refreshments, Ingrid Superstar, Food,
Celebrities and Movies including: Vinyl, Sleep, Eat, Kiss,
Empire, Whips, Faces, Harlot, Hedy, Butch, Banana, Etc,
Etc, Etc,
ALL IN THE SAME PLACE AT THE SAME TIME

Program repeated Saturday April 9th for Teenage, Tot and
Tillie Dropout Dance Marathon Matinee $1.00.

Poor Ingrid Superstar, ranked between the food and the refreshments, though at least she had a place, unlike Edie. The advertisement
succeeded beyond expectation, and 750 came to blow their minds
on the Friday evening (sadly for posterity, no one can recall how the
Teenage, Tot and Tillie matinee went). The form of the evening was
based on the tried and tested structure of the Happening, a performance of simultaneous events pioneered a decade earlier by the
veteran composer John Cage (it embarrassed John Cale that people
confused him with the older composer, whom he respected, 'and I
sometimes got the royalty receipts of J. J. Cale, and I think the
bluesman got mine!'). Cale considered that 'So much of what Andy
did seemed to be a diluted version of the Downtown *avant-garde*
scene. I had previously worked with the composer LaMonte Young
and we were concerned with philosophical attitudes to art. LaMonte
was concerned with durations and longevity, and so we viewed
Andy's dollar bills and Elvises and soup cans with grave suspicion.
LaMonte's work was about long duration, and Andy dealt in
repetition. We got the feeling that strong ideas were being recycled
and thinned out by people like Andy. Yet, he made it popular, and

Ulrich and Christa, aged four, 1942. Ulrich proudly wears his imitation Hitler Youth uniform

Christa and her mother Grete in September 1944, on Christa's first day at school in Lübbenau

Ulrich, Helma, Christa and Bertha in Lübbenau, 1943

Grete in 1941

Helma, Christa's aunt and 'other mother', 1941

Berlin, the south end of Christa's street, 1948
(Landesbildstelle, Berlin)

Christa displays rings at an exhibition at the
KaDeWe, Berlin, 1954 *(Herbert Tobias)*

Christa models for *Bunte* magazine
(*Herbert Tobias*)

Prince Mascalchi (played by Prince
Zadim Wolkonsky) offers his
fiancée Nico (Nico 'Otzak') a pearl
necklace at the Odescalchi Palace at
Bassano di Sutri, in Fellini's *La
Dolce Vita (Kobal Collection)*

Nico advertises the latest
dishwasher in *Elle* magazine, 1961

Nico in the film *Strip-Tease*,
directed by Jacques Poitrenaud and
filmed in December 1962, five
months after the birth of Ari

Nico with Andy Warhol in a
publicity shot for *The Chelsea Girls*
(BFI)

Nico and Andy Warhol as Batman and
Robin for *Esquire* magazine, 1967 *(Globe
Photos, USA)*

Nico and Philippe Garrel in *La
Cicatrice intérieure (BFI)*

Nico in the film *La Cicatrice
intérieure*, directed by Philippe
Garrel, 1971 *(BFI)*

Nico and her son Ari, 1981
(Antoine Giacomoni)

Nico on stage, 1985 *(Paula Cox)*

Nico in a London cemetery, for use on the
cover of the *Drama of Exile* LP, 1979
(Antoine Giacomoni)

the way he formed this multi-media thing around the Velvets is an example of how this copying could work to the good.'

The *New York Times* mentioned the event, on the Women's page. 'The first story about The Velvet Underground was on the Women's page of the *Times* and it was all about Nico,' recalled Paul Morrissey. 'You can imagine how well that went down with Lou Reed. It was really about Nico being the new girl of the year. Then it talked about this extraordinary event that did things that hadn't been used before – strobe lights, films, five Carousel slide projectors – oh, did I tell you about that? That was Andy's one contribution, I must say. He took some coloured gels (green, I think, and red) and took a cutter for making holes in paper – he remembered this from his art-school days! – and he made holes in the gel and put them in frames to sit in the slide projectors. These little things worked wonders because they went over the black and white films we were showing. The colours were just bouncing around the hall, it was so kinetic. You can sort of see how they worked because we put them on the original cover of the Velvet's first LP. Then we used them in *The Chelsea Girls* movie. Nico has these holes on her face.

'The next month we were invited to take the Exploding Plastic Inevitable to the West Coast, to the Whisky a'Go-Go in Los Angeles and the Filmore Auditorium up in San Francisco (the Swillmore Vomitorium, I called it; it was run by that guy Bill Graham, the most goddam awful human being I've ever met; he was crying and begging us to go there, "You must come over, it means so much to me." Awful fool. Once we got there he told Sterling, "I hope you mothers bomb"). Now, San Francisco always reckoned it invented the light show. But what they had was this shed where there was a camera obscura and some oil in a glass bowl. They'd move the oil around and throw the picture up on the wall. It was just this abstract gook floating around, really boring. No strobes, no slides, no lamps, no energy. So we became a real big thing right away, the Velvets became famous within a month, and they never got over that. It happened real quick.

'We got this residency in California because of a guy who came down to the Dom and asked to help out. He said, "I know the rock scene backwards, I've worked for Al Grossman, I'll take the gate and make your receipts, and I can start getting bookings for your band." Well, I hadn't got them any bookings apart from those universities, and there were no proper booking agencies for bands in those days – Grossman was both manager and agent to his people

– so I said OK. He got us this residency at this place The Trip. It seemed to work out fine (the ads read: "Flip Out! Skip Out! Trip Out!"). One night Jim Morrison of The Doors came to see the show; that must have been the first time he saw Nico. But a few days in, the two managers are fighting each other and the place goes bankrupt. Because of the union regulations we have to stay around the entire contracted time in order to get our money. And that's when that shark Bill Graham showed up, a-crying and a-begging.

'You have to remember also that there wasn't this big rock industry structure yet. A good example was accommodation. I went to LA a few days in advance to check dumb things like whether the club had enough sockets to plug the projectors in, and the toughest job I had was finding somewhere for the band to stay. Hotels did not take bands. I put Andy and the "respectable" folk in the Tropicana motel, but they wouldn't take the Velvets or Nico. They said that bands rent houses, and I got put on to this wonderful guy called Jack Simmons. He was James Dean's best friend and now he ran this big place called The Castle. It really is a castle surrounded by a park. Nico got to love the place and later she stayed there for a time with Jim Morrison. So, you see, however straight you tried to run these operations in those days, you still ended up with these crazy, exotic alternatives.

'We got back from the West Coast end of May, and I stupidly went back to Stanley at the Dom and said that I'd like to rent the place again from September. "Guess what," he said, "that guy who worked for you has leased it for a Mr Grossman." They opened it in the fall and they called it The Balloon Farm. So the guy came to see me and said, "Your band isn't working." No, I said through gritted teeth, it doesn't seem to have an agent. "So why don't you work at The Balloon Farm?" The son-of-a-bitch! He'd taken the lease. It was exactly the same thing that we'd set up in those few days back in April, except now they had control. And then eventually they sold the lease for a fortune to this guy who was working for the Columbia coffee company who wanted to promote coffee to teenagers, and they turned the place into a giant crazy coffee-shop-cum-discotheque affair called The Electric Circus, but that's another story . . .'

Nico could not understand any of this. "I always thought that what The Rolling Stones did was very simple. They travel and make concerts and they sit in a studio and make records. They are paid for these and they live their lives from the money. I thought it was chaotic because of disorganisation, not because it needed to be. And then when I had to do it myself I saw again how simple the idea was and how complicated the reality. It was because it was people selling people to other people who came to see them. It was all people, no machines. I saw then why Andy wanted to be a machine. He said he wished he was a machine so that he did not have to make decisions or hurt people [he actually said "I don't want to be hurt"]. I understood that. But I did not understand commotions every day and the little fights, or why we were famous but didn't have work to do. I was glad in the end that I had some independence. I looked for every way to strengthen it. But when you are a woman these people think you are just being difficult, not intelligent.'

'Presence is what she is about, and it is a formidable one. Having her sing to you is not unlike having the Statue of Liberty sing to you; her gestures are frozen, her complexion looks as though someone had sculptured it out of eggshells, and her lighting has all the amber reverence accorded by the Louvre to the Venus de Milo.' This quote is not about Nico but Marlene Dietrich, by Sheridan Morley; but had he seen Nico at the Dom, he would surely have written the same. She knew that on stage she was the centre of attention. It was not exactly difficult. The three men of The Velvet Underground often wore black and stood with their backs to the audience. The lighting was low to allow Warhol's films to register on the back wall. Nico was an inch taller than the gaunt John Cale. As Lou Reed insisted on singing most of the songs, every action Nico made was significant. She wore a pantsuit of white leather, velvet or wool, and she stood centre stage, frozen, her face caught in the beam of a bright spotlight. She didn't move and she didn't smile. 'Paul said I should never smile in photographs or on a stage. He was like my photographer and the concert was a shoot.'

'Off the catwalk I think Nico never wore a dress in her whole life,' observed Paul Morrissey. 'She wore slacks – like Hepburn, Garbo, Dietrich. It was considered a kind of androgynous look, because it was a powerful image on stage, but overall I would say she looked terribly dignified, set against the rest of the group in that white/black way. Everything was geared so that she just had to stand there to command attention. Lou couldn't do that. Nico'd had ten years of practice.' A more direct note on Nico's sexuality was recorded by a subsequent Superstar, Ultra Violet. She went to the Dom and declared in her autobiography that 'Nico has a unisex, atonal voice. She looks like a girl, with long blond hair, a well-designed, pretty mouth, high cheekbones, long lashes, and pale, luminescent make-up. But when she sings, it's hard to be sure of her sex. You're not even sure if she's singing, so little life comes out of her mouth. Still as a statue, she repeats in a low, low register, in a strong German accent, words you cannot comprehend because of the loudness of the band.' A reviewer suggested that 'she hypnotised the audience with her divinely sensual but sexless look'. Another wrote that she looked, and sounded, like a breathtaking alien.

Even the most cynical reviewer would soften before Nico. An exceptionally vituperative and prurient article in the *Boston Globe* began, 'About the best thing I can say of Warhol's Expanding Plastic Inevitable is that it is not expanding, not plastic, and certainly not inevitable ... At its worst, which was most of the time, the three-in-one film spectacle centred on sadism, rather like an inverted Cecil B. DeMille epic impassioned with simple-minded passion instead of piety. I don't think you'd want me to tell you all of its demented details, but here are a few specifics which set the savage tone: a young man was flagellated with chain and whip while strapped to a chair; a female impersonator growled through a song ('I Feel Pretty' changed to 'I Feel Funny') without a note of music in his voice; a wild hood did the Monkey to unheard music; a woman, supine on an operating table, was worked over by two men, one of whom fiddled with a darning needle near her left ear, and one who threatened her right lobe with pliers. All these vignettes were run simultaneously, the images sometimes clear, sometimes enlarged, sometimes shortened. When he ran out of film, finally, Mr Warhol began another sequence. He brought on the dancing girls, I mean boys with long, tangled hair, plus a rock'n'roll combo, and a beautiful blonde singer named Nico dressed in white culottes, belted velvet jacket – a willowy flower in a garden of weeds. Nico displayed a sang-froid manner that would warm a beatnik's heart.' Nico would have been deeply offended by the description 'willowy'.

But this flower among weeds was still stuck at second billing. She sang for three songs then slapped her out-of-time tambourine behind the dry voice of Lou Reed. He was possessive with good reason. The songs were his and he sang them well. Nico wanted so much to sing 'I'm Waiting for the Man', but her later recordings of it simply show that Reed could sing it better. Paul Morrissey and Nico would separately test him time and again about the matter, finding an excuse for her to sing a song or for him to write one with her in mind, but he resisted. John Cale reflected that 'right through the Seventies and Eighties I hoped Lou would write her another song like 'All Tomorrow's Parties', 'Femme Fatale', or 'I'll Be Your Mirror', but he never did. I'd tell him I was working with Nico on her new LP, whichever it was, and he'd just say "Really?", nothing more, not a flicker of interest. He could have written wonderful songs for her. It's a shame, and I regret it very much.' Cale suggested that the 'three psychological love songs' were written while Reed was in awe of Nico, though the group's lead guitarist, Sterling Morrison, cautioned that 'You could say Lou was in love with her, but Lou Reed in love is a kind of abstract concept.' When the relationship turned sour ('I cannot make love to Jews any more') Reed co-wrote three further songs, including 'Chelsea Girls', then nothing more, ever.

'Leaving aside the personalities for a moment, there was a real, practical problem with what to do with Nico in the songs she didn't sing,' Sterling Morrison observed. 'She'd kind of wander on and off like she'd seen singers do in old movies. You know, like there's George Raft sitting at the front table and Marlene Dietrich swans over to get her cigarette lit – that's what Nico thought you did. Andy said, "Let her play a tambourine", and Paul said, "Let Nico sing all the songs." It just couldn't go on like this.' Indeed, there is a review in the smart magazine *Status* of June 1966, in which the writer, once recovered from the 'tackiness' of the Dom, describes a Nico promenade: ' "She'll turn once more to Sunday's clown, And cry behind the door," sings Nico, who then glides effortlessly into the wings, eludes the grasp of an inebriated fan and folds herself gracefully into a protective nest of admirers.'

John Cale described an additional point of tension: 'Nico took an age in the dressing room, if there was a dressing room, and then on stage she had a candle somewhere and we had to wait while she'd light this candle. It was a little ritual – it was for her own good luck or something – and she held up the band, held up the gig. Lou had very little time for women and their accoutrements, and this ritual would really irritate him. The comic thing was that she'd do all this to help her performance, and then she'd start off singing on the wrong beat! Where she started in the song was a real focal point of the night! Lou would hiss across the stage, "We know what *we're* doing, Nico." '

Nico knew what she was doing and didn't like it: 'I wanted to be a singer. I was on a stage with a microphone, and there was a group, but I was like a mannequin. Andy wanted me there for visual reference. I was a model on the stage. I was doing the same thing I had done for ten years and I was sad because it was not a development. I knew my fate was to change my life at this point. This was not a change, it was a nuance [variation]. I told this to Andy and he said that Paul was saying about recording an album of the songs. He said that would be good for me because people would hear me and not see me. I said I hoped that I could sing more songs so they knew I was there.'

In June Paul Morrissey made history in this way: 'We rented a recording studio for two or three nights, and it cost $2,000 or so. Andy paid as usual and I sat there and the Velvets played their songs. Lou didn't want Nico to sing at all. I had to fight with him. I'd say, "But Nico sings that song on stage," and he'd reply "Well, it's my song," like it was his family. He was so petty. Even today he looks unhappy, like a walking disaster. What's wrong with him? He married a man, he married a woman . . . Anyway, Nico sang three songs, that's all. It wasn't enough, but it took an awful lot of arguing to get that far. That album, *Andy Warhol presents The Velvet Underground & Nico*, that album has been in print for 25 years but Andy and I never saw a penny from it. Once we'd made the tapes, we tried to sell them to a company who would manufacture the album and distribute it. Nobody wanted to buy the tape. It was too far out. We were sort of stuck with it for a time. Andy said, "Other people succeed who have no talent. Here we are with you gorgeous people and we can't make it." '

John Cale stressed that the session held few surprises for the Velvets. 'We used to tape our rehearsals, to check. Nico was very vulnerable to this. We'd listen and hear her go off-key or hit the wrong pitch at the start. We would sit there and snigger, "There she goes again!", which might seem a little cruel now. She was deaf in one ear [she had a perforated eardrum]. This made for interesting times. Every now and again she went "weeergh" and lost control of the pitch; she was very sensitive to all this and when I produced her albums later on I would have her sing and the musicians play in separate sessions. But I mention the playbacks we'd do, because people would say we were just improvising and making a noise on stage, but actually what we did was disciplined and intentioned. Basically, Lou would write these poppy little songs and my job was to slow them down, make them "slow'n'sexy". Everything was deeper, too. A song written in E would be played in D. Maureen didn't use cymbals. I had a viola [not the higher violin], and Lou had this big drone guitar we called an "ostrich" guitar. It made an horrendous noise, and that's the sound on "All Tomorrow's Parties", for instance. In addition Lou and Nico both had deep voices. All of this made the record entirely unique.'

'Then this label Verve bought the rights,' said Paul Morrissey. 'Verve was a jazz label, of all things. MGM owned Verve, and MGM was musicals. Nobody did rock and roll much then. There were labels like Capitol who did the English groups over here, but they just wanted pop songs for the radio. The man at Verve was called Tom Wilson. He was a very interesting man; he was terribly tall, he'd been to Harvard I think, and he was a negro. Tom Wilson had a big reputation. He had discovered Simon and Garfunkel for Columbia records, and they were a goldmine for that company. He said, "I think that Nico is great. I'll buy the tape off you," – he gave us probably the cost of it. And he bought the record because of Nico.

'Then Tom said, "Listen. The only thing I don't like about the record is, there's not enough Nico. You've got to get another song from Nico. And there's nothing here we can use on the radio, so why don't we get Nico to sing another song that would be right for radio play?" (They never released an album unless they could release a single at the same time.) Between the time they bought it and the time they released it, it was about a year. It was released in March 1967, and by that time we weren't doing business with the Velvets any more, and Nico had her solo act. So, Lou comes up with this song which is terribly insipid, called "Sunday Morning": "Suuunday Mor-ning, Withooout a war-ning," Yech, it's so dopey.

'It sounded alright for Nico because she brought something weird to everything, "Surn-day Mourning." Tom said OK, and we went into a studio paid for by MGM–Verve. Somehow, at the last minute, Lou didn't let her sing it. He sang it! The little creep. He said, "I wanna sing it 'cause it's gonna be the single." Tom Wilson couldn't deal with Lou, he just took what came. Then later, he got Nico back into the studio and gave her a verse or put her with Lou's voice or something, I can't quite remember. Tom Wilson had to force Nico to take this option, you can imagine. We were always fighting tooth and nail to get poor Nico on. She didn't fight this sort of thing herself, she was very shy and self-effacing. She would make a little remark. Or then she would giggle a lot. She'd giggle like a girl.'

Nico rarely spoke ill of Lou Reed. He had provided her with three of her most famous songs; she sang 'All Tomorrow's Parties' up to her death, often with the right words. 'Lou was very lovable,' she admitted. 'Everybody loved him around the Factory, he was rather cute, you know, and he said funny things. We quarrelled a lot. I cried. But he could be nice to me.' Seven years later Reed composed a distinguished LP titled *Berlin*. Nico believed that some of the songs were written about her life, and that she was the girl called Caroline (the cipher 'C' for Christa). 'No,' declared John Cale, 'that was another girl. Her name was Darryl. A real lost soul who had two children, one who was taken away. A beautiful girl, exquisite features, one who would attract dangerous people.' Its longest song, 'The Kids', is set far too flush against Nico's life for comfort:

> They're taking her children away
> Because they said she was not a good mother
> They're taking her children away
> Because of the things that they heard she had done
> The black Air Force sergeant was not the first one
> And all of the drugs she took, every one, every one.

Perhaps Darryl, if indeed this was Darryl, was the woman Nico needed to be Nico 'while I go out to do something else'. Nico often spoke of 'being separate to' her life: 'I shall call my book *Moving Target*, because my life follows me around'; 'That was not me, that was another girl'; 'I've been disappearing from myself'; 'I am a child who played a woman'. Nico once said that the split appeared most strongly when she heard herself singing 'Femme Fatale' on the playback of the recording session, reinforced soon after when she saw herself in the film *The Chelsea Girls*. It is then, in the summer of 1966, that Nico realised most vividly that she was living two parallel lives; one was superficial, the other she had suspended. She decided then to make amends. She would bring her son back to New York where he was conceived, and she would be responsible for his development. She would earn money as Nico the Superstar and spend it as Christa, the good mother.

8 July–December, 1966

It was a climate where, they say,
The night is more belov'd than day.
But who that beauteous Boy beguil'd,
That beauteous Boy to linger here?
Alone, by night, a little child,
In place so silent and so wild –
Has he no friend, no loving mother near?
(from 'The Wanderings of Cain',
SAMUEL TAYLOR COLERIDGE, 1798)

'A LL OF HER LIFE WAS STRANGE. Even the way she arrived at the house was exceptional. She would just turn up, "Hello", as though you had seen her last one hour before. There was never a warning, an arrangement. She arrived, and after she had exhausted your hospitality, she left.' Madame Pauledith Soubrier was raising Nico's son in Paris. They were preparing to celebrate Ari's fourth birthday when Nico said 'Hello', for the second time in his short life, to take him away. 'She said she had a good place in New York where she was singing. Well, she was his mother, so she had her rights to do this. But she was always in opposition to herself. She didn't want to employ somebody to take care of him there. She was afraid for him if he wasn't with her. But when she had him, she was preoccupied with her work and he was not supervised at all, I believe.'

She took him to America where he instantly became a film star like his father. Ari played the part of Ari, just as Nico played Nico, in *The Chelsea Girls*. One day a 'grotesque, ugly waste of celluloid', the next 'the most famous underground movie ever made' once it grossed half a million dollars at the box office, it was agreed by all to be little less than 'a searing vision of hell', Andy Warhol's sarcastic retort to flower power. It caused as much rancour and ethical fuss as *La Dolce Vita*. Nico compared the two in her own sweet way: 'I cannot say which was the best for me. I cry all the way through *The Chelsea Girls* and I laugh all the way through *La Dolce Vita*. I think that is the only difference.'

Between the summer of 1966 and the spring of 1967, Ari was

photographed as many times as a crown prince. He spent his days playing in the Factory with Warhol's team, and there are many charming images of Ari on Warhol's knee or sitting among the Superstars. His appearance struck an innocent tone in a setting readily deemed decadent and venal. It was suggested that his presence had been exploited to give the Factory a cleaner, cuter look. The *East Village Other* had described Ari's new friends as 'amphetamine monsters sucking desperately at the acrid dregs of their sexuality', though the *New York Herald Tribune* peeked into the studio and found only sober sorts 'innocently tinkering with cameras, answering telephones, looking for lost earrings'. It was true that the police raided the Factory frequently that autumn, once *The Chelsea Girls* had been screened, but the conduct of the little boy with long hair would hardly impress the enforcers of law. Being untutored in social protocol, or Factory feuds, he was free to roam around between the factions and make as much mess as he liked. Ultra Violet recalled that Ari had 'the best time of us all'.

The police may not have seen the film, but they would have read the righteous reviews and the gawping news items that described 'visions of rampant homosexuality, drug addiction, nudity and blasphemy: the horror of our time in miniature'. Not quite so miniature; the film would have taken seven hours to show had Paul Morrissey not split it into two to be screened side by side. It comprised twelve reels, each of 35 minutes' length. The original notion was simple: each reel would record a scene in a room at the Chelsea Hotel: Room 416, *The Trip*; Room 116, *Hanoi Hanna (Queen of China)* and so on. Lou Reed's song 'Chelsea Girls', which also lists the room numbers, was commissioned to accompany the film, though he didn't finish it in time, which annoyed Nico a little as she wanted to sing it on the soundtrack; instead the ballad made its debut on her solo album. The movie's room numbers were dropped when Stanley Bard of the Chelsea filed an injunction. Its unadorned structure was enriched by Morrissey's double screen; Warhol dryly advised that 'if you get bored with one you can always look at the other'.

Nico had mixed feelings about her contribution: 'I am on the screen for an hour, and I prefer one scene to the other. There is a scene where my face is coloured with patterns and it is supposed to be, oh, psychedelic. Isn't it called *The Trip* in the order? It is only psychedelic if you are stoned watching it. Otherwise it is a portrait with colour added. It is beautiful in a certain way, but it is like a silkscreen that Andy has made, except I cannot put it on my wall. It only goes on the walls of cinemas. Andy never made a painting of me, because I could not afford to buy it. He only made them for rich people who would pay him money. But in this way he can make his money from this silkscreen of me he has made on film. And each time he sells the film he makes more money. Well, I would have preferred a painting, because I could always sell it for cash. But I cannot sell the film.' She was paid a fee of $2,000 once *The Chelsea Girls* had made its unexpectedly good gross.

Her two sections framed the remaining ten in the order most commonly presented in the early days. It was perhaps intended that Nico's elegaic beauty contrasted with the camp and bitter tantrums of the remainder. The respected critic Raymond Durgnat, writing in a British magazine, gave the film one of its few intelligent reviews. Warhol kept it in his scrapbook:

> The theme of life-within-image recurs in balancing the opening and closing episodes. The first shows the blonde singer Nico in her kitchen, peering obsessively in a mirror and clipping invisible lengths of hair from her brow, while chatting to a man and a child. The last shows her face (its expression curiously mixing Catherine Deneuve in *Repulsion* with the 'umbrella girl', Eunice Levy in *Herostratus*) bathed in coloured lights and stroboscopes.

At some point in the film's exhibition the order was changed to deliver a raunchier start, for Nico's sections were exceptionally dreamlike. Now it is more likely to be opened by the bad boys. On one screen a young and pretty Eric Emerson trips and strips. On the other, Ondine acts the Pope and condemns a woman to the death of living eternally off-screen. 'Ondine should be Pope and Bob Dylan should be President,' Nico later decided. She enjoyed Ondine, a splendidly outlandish gay actor of her own age, 'the Olivier of the Underground', whose real name of Robert Olivo was queenified in honour of his favourite Audrey Hepburn role (the nightclub Ondine had nothing to do with him). But Nico was troubled by Ondine's violent lapses and misogyny. 'The Factory was at the edge of something. It could be tense. You could be drawn into violence, like Ondine or Gerard were, if you did not keep your dignity.' This would explain why Gerard Malanga himself wrote that 'Nico is the true star because she keeps her distance and is socially professional'.

There were two scenes in *The Chelsea Girls* that disturbed Nico, she said. One was a comedy. The veteran Marie Menken plays Gerard Malanga's mother. She is garishly angry that he has married Hanoi Hanna (Mary Woronov, lounging at the screen's edge). Nico didn't like the way the improvised dialogue turned. 'You love your toys,' hollers Menken at her supposed son. 'I love my child. This is not the way it should be; eat, drink, cigarettes . . . I want you to be great in the world! Never mind all the creature comfort stuff! Every mother says this: that children never come up to their expectations. Oh, my God, that I should have brought you into the world! I should have had an abortion!' It tapped into Nico's guilt about her mother and her son. In public she converted this to a loyal concern for Warhol. 'I think there was something about Andy and his mother at the back in this scene. It is amusing and terrible at the same time. I never understood Andy doing this without a fear.'

The second scene Nico disliked was the one starring Ondine as the Pope of Greenwich Village. Charged up on an injected dose of amphetamine, Pope Ondine berates a young woman who has called into his room for a confessional ('I want to get you into heaven. That's what I'm here for, isn't it? To lead my flock into eternal bliss. Where is heaven?! You work it out, Mary. I'll give you a road map'). In actuality the actress, Rona Page, was not a Factory regular; Ondine had not met her before. During the improvised scene she calls Pope Ondine a phoney and he explodes. He slaps her, thrashes her around, and crafts a stunning scene of such misogynist contempt that it could be defended later only on the grounds that they were 'acting'. They weren't. Nico knew this and felt an acute discomfort. Even more disturbing was Pope Ondine's tirade: 'You're a bore, my dear, a bore! You filthy horror! How dare you! How dare you! You motherfucker. I'm a phoney?! You're a phoney!! You little creep!' Nico never liked that word *phoney*.

In 1979 Nico saw *The Chelsea Girls* for the first time in a decade, and she wept. She did not remember seeing it presented in the way she saw it now. On the left side of the screen she viewed herself in colour, iconic, 'tripping'. On the right side Pope Ondine was projected in a monologue, justifying his attack on the actress:

This may be a historic document. I don't like to hit people. I think it's ugly and boring. But when I see something as stupid as I just saw here, just sitting here and *pretending*, I have to reel out. I have to hit it and put it in its place. And its place is below me. Beneath me. Somewhere where it doesn't want to be a little smarter. God forgive them – Me, I forgive them.

Ondine looks down across the screen to his right. There, in the perception of the audience, sits Nico, 'below him, beneath him'. He is staring at Nico when he speaks of 'something as stupid as I just saw here, just sitting here and *pretending*'. Nico found this unbearable. 'You can never know how your image is used. Andy would say it was chance that decides this, but I believe in fate more than chance.'

Her other scene, *The Kitchen*, portrays Nico in over-exposed close-up, snipping at her blonde hair and making small talk with Eric Emerson and Ari. 'Andy never had a script, you know. There was never a plot. Instead you were in a situation. You would respond in this situation. For my scenes, Paul and Andy could not think of a situation for me. I could not play the Pope or the Virgin Mary. I was already Nico. So for one scene I was nothing but Nico and they put lights on my face. In the other, we were in this white kitchen. I think they wanted somewhere white, isn't that it? A white girl with blonde hair in a white room. Ari was there, and I think they wanted to keep Ari in control, so Eric was there, too. Then Andy said I must do something. But they wanted me in close-up for the whole reel. I could make a meal in the kitchen, but no, this was too busy ["I don't think she could cook food too good, anyway," said Viva]. There were some scissors, and maybe Paul said "Cut your hair". I didn't want to. But it was something I could do that was in shot of the camera. The bastards made me cut my hair.'

In one hand she holds a double-sided mirror with a chrome frame, in the other, silver-coloured scissors. Everything is white and silver and reflective ('Silver makes things disappear,' as Warhol had said). It is a scene of sensual narcissism, to which we are voyeurs. When Nico starts to cry, the tears glide down without apparent reason; the camera films on relentlessly. 'I wanted to stop. In many films of Andy, you will hear someone say they want to stop. Have you noticed? They never do. They never stop. I was tired, and I was thinking of Ari and Eric as his father. At one time I wondered if I could find another father. Maybe I thought of Eric, I don't remember now, anyway.' The credits of the film revealingly list Nico's co-stars in this way:

Blonde in kitchen and in light projections	Nico
Man in kitchen	Eric Emerson
Boy in kitchen	Ari Emerson

Eric Emerson would only have added to her problems, though she was indeed having an affair with him when *The Chelsea Girls* was filmed. A handsome bisexual who claimed he 'took every drug and fucked every hole in the Factory', Emerson caused the *Velvet Underground and Nico* to be withdrawn from sale in 1967; Warhol had included a photograph of Emerson on the back cover. Needing money for drugs, or for his defence on a drugs charge, or for both, he decided that suing MGM for unsolicited use of his image would net him some cash. MGM promptly withdrew the album from the market, to the group's profound dismay, while Warhol airbrushed the photo off the sleeve. A year later, after he had made Factoryite Susan Pile pregnant, Eric Emerson died of a heroin overdose.

Nico joked later that perhaps Ondine would have made a better father. 'Ondine was handsome to look at, you know. He had good features. He could have played my scenes, but I could not be hysterical [histrionic]. The men make all the movements, I think.' It has not escaped the notice of analysts that Edie, Nico and Viva play a special role in Warhol's films. It was most bluntly put by Amy Taubin: 'Women functioned at the Factory not so much as objects of desire, but as models for drag.' On the wall of the Factory hung a silkscreen of the gay icon Marlene Dietrich; Warhol produced film parodies of the stars Jean Harlow, Hedy Lamarr and Lana Turner ('their feminineness is so exaggerated that it becomes a commentary on womanhood rather than the real thing,' the screenplay creator, Ronald Tavel, suggested); and transvestites such as Jackie Curtis, Candy Darling, Holly Woodlawn and Mario Montez, who leads a reel of *The Chelsea Girls*, held an honoured place in Warhol's films. He wished he were a transvestite himself, though their presence was more visible as the women's roles decreased, in particular around 1968 when drag in public life turned less taboo.

The Factory drag queens, and those such as Warhol who craved to be as daring, revered the stars they never met, the perfect faces and bodies they viewed only in the safety of two dimensions on the screens of cinema and television. As men, they emulated the most extreme paradigm of that which they feared most: women. They did this to transcend their awe and envy of the sex that delivered them into the world. Edie and Nico were their mannequins, pacing round the Factory day after day, disclosing to the men the mechanics of being female. Skinny little Edie was the model for the boys and the Amazonian Nico the model for the men. In the public eye they were icons like Garbo – more an image crafted for contemplation than flesh and bone – but on the Factory floor they were little more than kinetic dummies. 'They saw Nico as an icon, but a reserved one, or an ambiguous one,' Paul Morrissey considered. 'She was like Garbo. She had allure, class, dignity. She even answered questions like Garbo, in roundabout and witty ways.' So did Warhol; but then they had the same teacher, in Garbo.

The Chelsea Girls opened at the Cinemathèque on 15 September 1966 – Nico went along but was 'druggy' that night and recalled nothing. So successful was the response that it was taken to a couple of cinemas uptown for a continuous run. The *New York Times* review ('A grotesque menagerie of lost souls whimpering in a psychedelic moonscape. Seldom has life among the wicked been documented so faithfully') guaranteed full houses and horny bar-stool banter. At the time Paul Morrissey was quoted in *Cheetah* magazine, declaring that 'The opening scene of *The Chelsea Girls*, nothing more than Nico combing her hair, will last when all the druggy rhetoric is forgotten.'

Nico's final comment on the film confirmed that her command of English was strong enough to grapple with mixed metaphors: 'Did you notice that it does not have a title of one word? Andy's films had simple titles. They were simple words [*Suicide, Kiss, Eat, Sleep*] and they were elementary subjects. I thought the film would be special because it had a special title. It was more complicated; I don't just mean three words, but the word *Girls* meant the boys as well. And *Chelsea* as though it had something to do with London, you know, Swinging London, which was a thing then. I knew that they were thinking not only of making a film, but selling it, too. It is a complicated film; it is like a labyrinth, like the Chelsea Hotel is. But it is like a complicated photograph of Andy. He is looking at his friends. A voyeur. And it is like an old theatre, you know? A stage with three walls only, and the camera and Andy presented the final wall. And I am the painting on the wall!'

NICO STILL REMEMBERED what a record company man had told her – 'a girl leading a group, that would be a winner!' In any case, it is hard to say if that man was astute or stupid. There was only one

rock group fronted by a woman that had caught the attention
afforded 'winners'. The San Francisco of 1966 nurtured Jefferson
Airplane, a band with two singers, a kind of Lou Reed and Nico
arrangement that worked a little more comfortably. Grace Slick (real
name Wing) was a year younger than Nico and more earth mother
than Moon Goddess. The other women in American music were
black and sang Motown, or were folkies; not exactly 'a girl leading
a group'. 'I never saw this happen until Punk. Isn't it strange that it
takes so long, at least a decade? Do you think Siouxsie and The
Banshees could have existed in the Sixties? I don't think so. Have
you seen them lately? I saw a video and they looked like something
out of California twenty years ago. Well, perhaps better. They have
hair conditioner now,' Nico observed in 1985.

It was patently clear to Nico that The Velvet Underground could
carry on working whether '– and Nico' was attached or not. The
band never had many concerts to play (it was too weird to be popular
and too young to be a cult), and so every date was a major
opportunity for Nico. Yet on stage she had next to nothing to do.
She sang three songs and played the reposeful goddess to Lou Reed's
driven god. She stood stock still and sang or she lingered around
the stage, looking lost. It didn't even help that the public and the
press thought differently and gave Reed second billing while they
flocked around Nico asking the kind of questions that received her
knee-jerk response, 'Ho, ho, ho, ho, ho'. Reed was incensed by the
effortless way in which she pulled rank; he asserted that Nico must
go, go, go, go, go. She had made no contribution to the songwriting,
he noted ('I thought men write songs and women sing them,' she
maintained), and she was a nuisance with her stupid candles, the
silly distractions and her scant control over her little kid. He was
privately rattled, too (Nico had hoped so), that after leaving Eric
Emerson Nico had begun an affair with John Cale. At the same time
Lou Reed was right to question her professional behaviour; she
certainly tended to drag the band into her own problems. Gerard
Malanga recalled The Velvets driving to a concert in Toronto: 'When
we told her that to get into Canada and back she needed her passport,
she wasn't happy because she thought we'd sneak a look at her date
of birth. Nico was very vain about her age; she never let on how
old she was [she had then turned 28]. She deliberately left it behind
and put the whole group's gig in jeopardy because of her vanity. We
had to go off-route to an obscure border point. We had to hide her
in the back of the roadie's van among the speakers and drums and

smuggle her across, both ways.' It may have been the first time Nico had been smuggled across borders illegally, but Christa remembered another time.

If the group could do without her, then Nico could do without the group; she could sing solo, as she did in The Blue Angel days. Her chronically slim underground repertoire comprised seven songs – one each by Bob Dylan, Gordon Lightfoot, Jimmy Page, and four by Lou Reed, plus whatever she could manage to sing of his behind his back. She had not yet taken to heart Warhol's exemplary advice, 'Always leave them wanting less'. The list was enough to make a splendid twenty-minute set ('Thirty with her entrance,' quipped one of her musicians). The trouble was she couldn't play an instrument, not even a tambourine. She recalled that this handicap hadn't stopped her joining 'Professor' Brox's group on Ibiza, and so she decided to renew her acquaintance with the tape recorder. With Lou Reed's backing tape behind her, Nico launched her season of neanderthal Karaoke.

Paul Morrissey continued his narrative of Nico's Factory days in this manner: 'So it's autumn, and she has a little boy, she's living in New York and she has no money. The band's not working, either. So I went back to the Dom in Saint Mark's Place to see this guy Stanley. He was a very nice guy. Now, The Balloon Farm was upstairs by then, but Stanley had a long bar downstairs and a discotheque next to it – two spaces, and they were sort of joined together. He said, "This discotheque's driving me crazy. It's making a lot of money but only negroes are coming to it. I'm a little bit afraid if somebody fights . . . I'd love to get a white discotheque, not so many negroes. I have an idea. That girl Nico – negroes can't stand her. She has no rhythm for a start. I think if Nico sang in my bar it'd drive a lot of whites in and some of the negroes out."

'Well, OK, I looked around but there was nowhere for her to perform. Nowhere to sit. I figured out this weird arrangement. Picture this. There is this long bar with a barman and drinks. At the bottom end of the bar we stuck up this platform affair, like a little stage set at the level of the bar top. That's where she sat. It really did look a bit bizarre. So Nico was going to open just singing her songs. I looked forward to this, because I don't think the Velvets' audience ever really heard Nico above all that noise – they saw Nico alright, she was so dramatic in the middle of the group, but that was about all. So I wondered how we could make her appear equally dramatic in this little space. I said, "Let's get some movies behind her." I couldn't be there every night of her residency, so I got an 8 mm projector and made loops of people falling out of aeroplanes, sky diving. We put up a screen so you would see behind her people continually falling out of the sky.

'Then I got hold of the band – John and Lou and Sterling, the guitarists, they weren't working much – and I told them, "Listen, Nico's got a job. She needs a guitarist. Do you think one of you could do it?" Lou didn't want to do it – of course he didn't. And he didn't want Sterling to do it. And he knew that John was terrified of him, so that was difficult to negotiate. "Oh, Lou, if you don't want me to . . ." It was so stupid. (I think that later in life John rose up.) Lou said, "It's not good for the group's image." I replied, "This is awful. She needs work, she has some songs. Couldn't one of you help her?" Then Lou said, "We'll put it on tape." So they put their guitar accompaniments on to a tape with this big, ugly machine. This poor woman Nico, she had to sit on this platform thing behind the bar, and she'd bend down and have to push these buttons on this huge tape recorder and bend up again, sing her song, and bend down to press the "stop" button before the next song started up. It was so excruciatingly, agonisingly awful. Somehow she did it, as gracefully as she could. After a couple of nights I just couldn't bear any more. I had to find someone to play live. I think Sterling came down and helped for a few weeks.'

Ten years later, in the middle of the Seventies, Nico could only recall the harassment of the Dom customers that confronted her each night: 'I would never sing in a club again, because of the great memories of that. It wasn't very easy with all the drunks that came in and asked me if I wanted a drink while I was singing. Sometimes I had to be very rude. I was singing, you know, and a person would come up to me and say, "Would you like some champagne? Here baby, have a drink!" It was like The Blue Angel, the same thing.'

Ari went to the club each night where a Factory functionary called Susan Pile would practise her French on him (Ari knew some French and English and a little German even then; Warhol recalled him saying odd things like 'I want to throw hot snowballs'). Paul Morrissey had an apartment nearby in the Lower East Side, and he would take Ari there to sleep after the first set. At the club's close, around four in the morning or later, Ari would return to his mother. A friend of Pauledith Soubrier's lived in New York at the time and he went downtown to spy on the scene at the bar. 'He told me that Ari would wander around, picking up the finished dirty glasses and drinking the dregs of alcohol. Of course, this could only end in a disaster, and it did.'

'I HAD SO MANY ENCOUNTERS with Andy. So many, it is hard to remember. I enjoyed everything I did with him. I once went to a store with him and he made me wear a paper sack and he wrote my name on it. He wanted to sell it but nobody would buy. We did stupid things like that, every day something strange. This is a good kind of life, yes, I guess? To do something different and strange every day?'

Abraham & Straus is Brooklyn's answer to the KaDeWe. The store sponsored a promotion for a paper dress 'in whitest white twill of Kaycel R'. You wore it once and threw it away; it was not wise to wear one in the rain. On this occasion there was an additional gimmick. For the $2 you paid per dress, you got a free box of paints. On the November day of this special promotion the store placed silver foil on screens 'in honour of Mr Warhol', so that the display looked something vaguely like the Factory. In front of these, Nico lay down in a white dress, white stockings and white shoes – the dress not quite a 'sack', to be fair – while Andy Warhol and Gerard Malanga stuffed a mountain of paper under her waist. Then they took an unwieldy wooden frame and silk-screened FRAGILE seven times down the dress. Despite her memory it did not spell her name, though FRAGILE comes suitably close, considering. There is a photograph in a French magazine that shows the scene ('Un humor trés *cool* se dégage de ce *happening*' is the caption, *trés* cool). Nico looks like a pregnant woman laid out on an operating table under the voyeuristic scrutiny of Doctor Warhol. At her raised feet stands Ari, staring, mouth open, as though waiting for a baby sister to pop out. Nico looks distinctly uneasy. It is surely the most eccentric photo shoot she ever endured.

Ultra Violet described the scene in her autobiography, adding that Nico sang 'All Tomorrow's Parties' down a microphone which she then passed to a horrified Warhol. Cornered to give a speech, he declared, 'Nico is the first psychedelic singer with The Velvet Underground. They do two hours of songs with only the buzzing of a burglar alarm in between.' Ultra Violet claimed that 'the spectators look baffled . . . Shyly, Andy takes out of the pocket of his leather jacket some larger-than-life stick-on paper bananas and pastes them on Nico's dress. A thin woman calls out, 'I thought he was going to paint something by hand. That's what I came for.' A store

employee takes the mike: 'It's to show you how you can do it
yourself. The dress Mr Warhol has just executed will be donated to
the Brooklyn Museum of Art.' Indeed it was, and there it stays.

Of all the daily things, different and strange, that Nico did for
Warhol, the oddest was a Mod wedding in Detroit on 20 November
1966. The novel ceremony was leerily recorded in the *Detroit News*,
under the following headline:

Not The Wedding
We Had Planned.

Holy matrimony was replaced by unholy pandemonium in
what was billed as a wedding yesterday at the State Fair-
grounds Coliseum.

Wearing a white minigown, eight inches over her knees and
white, thigh-high boots, Randi Rossi, a 19-year-old unem-
ployed go-go dancer, became the bride of clothing salesman,
Gary Norris, 25, amid a melange of simultaneous 'happen-
ings'.

Some 4,500 shaggy-haired wedding guests swarmed the
arena for the pre-nuptial rituals. Electronic devices screamed,
guitars and drums throbbed and a fiddle added to the din as
purple and orange lights splashed dots and squares across the
stage. 'Hey, we're really witnessing something, it's history,
history!' a young girl shouted.

'It's not the kind of wedding we had planned for our
daughter,' Mrs Rossi said, as eerie screeches emitted from the
stage. 'He's old enough to know his own mind,' Mrs Norris
added, while Nico, clad in a lavender pantsuit, cupped the
mike in both hands and began moaning some song.

After giving away the bride, Mr Warhol, the 'father of pop
art', sat serenely upon a box of tomato soup, autographing
cans. A color film of Nico's face flickered on and off the back
curtains as she read a few appropriate, but indistinguishable
sentences from a yellow book.

The *Detroit Free Press* was there too, commenting in an equal tone
of sniggering irony, that 'Warhol's "superstar" Nico sang a bizarre
and totally unintelligible song accompanied by the electronic tones
of The Velvet Underground, a rock'n'roll band. Nico, a tall, lanky
girl with straight blonde hair, began to sing just as the microphones
went haywire. As a result, she sounded like a Bedouin woman singing

a funeral dirge in Arabic while accompanied by an off-key air raid siren.' Nico, always game for exotic status, would have loved to have been considered a Bedouin, especially in a lavender pantsuit.

It was all very well being a Superstar, she thought, but it was like treading water. 'She was very ambitious, but she was also independent and did not want to live in a conventional way. It was always a problem for her to move on to something else,' suggested the ever-observant Aunt Helma. As 1966 came to a close, Nico notched up her year's achievements. She had once again played in a notorious film, she had joined a rock band and made an album that would soon be released, she had her son back in her care, and her image was once more in the arts and society pages of the world's press. But at all times she was a romantic ornament to Andy Warhol; she could easily be discarded, as Edie had been, and lose everything through severance. She decided she must promote her independence as a singer and cultivate new relations beyond the Factory.

The gushingly jolly Christmas issue of *Hullabaloo* pop magazine printed two photos of Nico, dressed in 'super-mod outfits by New York's flipped out Paraphernalia!!' The slobbering copy reveals how swiftly the facts of Nico's life could be transformed by the gullible press: 'Nico was already a famous name in London. Nico appeared numerous times in England's super *Ready, Steady, Go!* TV show, and cut a hit "I'm Not Sayin'"' . . . The jacket is double-breasted with big bold buttons and the pants are neither tapered nor bells, but cut straight to complete this elegant outfit. The blazer is blue with brassy buttons and beautifully tailored to look fab at any time.' After all she had been through to revolutionise her career, Nico ended 1966 as she had ended 1956, modelling clothes. The next year, finally, everything would change for ever.

9 January–June, 1967

I built my soul a lordly pleasure-house,
Wherein at ease for aye to dwell.
I said, 'O Soul, make merry and carouse,
Dear soul, for all is well.'

A huge crag-platform, smooth as burnish'd brass,
I chose. The ranged ramparts bright
From level meadow-bases of deep grass
Suddenly scaled the light.

Thereon I built it firm. Of ledge or shelf
The rock rose clear, or winding stair.
My soul would live alone unto herself
In her high palace there.

And 'while the world runs round and round,' I said,
'Reign thou apart, a quiet king,
Still as, while Saturn whirls, his steadfast shade
Sleeps on his luminous ring.'

To which my soul made answer readily:
'Trust me, in bliss I shall abide
In this great mansion, that is built for me,
So royal-rich and wide.'

(from 'The Palace of Art',
ALFRED TENNYSON, 1836)

I N EARLY 1967 Nico saw her father on TV. The elderly fellow sat, gaunt and still absurdly tall, in a studio he shared with a combative host who asked him saliently about psychedelic drugs. 'I took my first LSD trip over ten years ago. It was amusing.' Nico was gratified that her father could so readily endorse her way of life; indeed, he could even participate and find it as splendid as she. 'Look, that is my father. He still takes drugs.' The others in the room stared at the screen. 'But, Nico, that's the philosopher,

Aldous Huxley.' Her eyes widened. 'What a strange name. Is he Turkish?'

'You read everywhere that Andy Warhol never took drugs. But it wasn't true. He took amphetamine – a type of amphetamine, I forget its name. He took pills. He told me that pills were normal. His mother took pills, the President of the United States took pills, so it was not a problem to take pills. He didn't like anything more mysterious than a pill. This was our biggest difference. I wanted to go inside, you know, inside my body. Brian Jones said it was the world we had not yet discovered, a world inside. America and Russia had a fight to go to outer space, but we wanted to go into inner space; we would not be Astronauts, we would be *Intranauts*. Andy said, "Oh, Nico, there's nothing inside. I wear my soul on my sleeve." Well, anyway, he took a drug so he would go faster and miss what there was inside. Maybe that's why he got so bored.'

Nico had been taking two different psychedelic drugs for a couple of years. Until that time she had known marijuana, amphetamines, a little opium and a little cocaine: drugs for work and recreation. Drugs had been useful then, she considered, to help her body to speed up (work) or her mind to slow down (recreation). Psychedelic drugs, however, those that 'expanded the mind', supplied something deeper. Through them she felt she was able to think. They gave her the confidence that the people around her had too often denied: 'In work you do not have to think. Outside of work my mind goes too fast and I have too many thoughts. When I take drugs I am able to think more clearly. It is a sign I need to know inside that I can think. Otherwise, people would have me believe I am stupid. Nobody believes that a model has a brain, or a singer has a brain, do they? A composer yes, of course, but I was not then a composer.' Even when she composed, no one ever called Nico a composer.

She claimed that she was introduced to the two psychedelic drugs by Brian Jones. Whoever it was, of course, would have to have been a celebrity. One was the natural mushroom, the other the synthetic LSD (lysergic acid, 'so much more convenient'). She took the chemical drug seriously ('just like a German, ho, ho, ho') and endorsed the psychiatrist Dr Timothy Leary in his evangelical campaign to overcome the world's handicaps by promoting psycho-chemical indulgence. The hounded Harvard lecturer was right, she thought, in his desire for a psychedelic utopia, and the police were quite wrong to hassle him. Leary was giving new life to the endeavours of the Beat generation, and it did not surprise her in the least that the veteran

Allen Ginsberg added a supportive voice. She was at one with Andy Warhol and Paul Morrissey, though, when she contrasted Leary's 'noble venture' with the anile dope-fiends who lived and died for their fundamentalist creed, 'If you can see through it, shoot it.'

'Everything is a drug. Coffee is a drug – oh, isn't that a cliché? Music is a drug, words are a drug, Jim [Morrison] said that God is a drug – those are not such a cliché. It is a medicine, something to cure you of disease. Coffee cures you of tiredness . . . what else did I say? Music? Well, music cures you of time. God cures you of death, I suppose.' Nico never admitted that drugs cured her of melancholy, though she once told a reporter that 'They were called mind-blowing, and I like the idea that I can blow away my memory, which is imperfect.' This was the one time she inferred that she would prefer no memory to a perfect one.

In that imperfect memory of Nico's, 1967 seemed to be the least fractured of the years she stored there, unless it was the one she lied about the most. 1967 was a year the Californian hippies had designated the Summer of Love, a summer she spent with Jim Morrison, and, when she wasn't with him, with Brian Jones, and when she wasn't with them, with Andy Warhol making films or with Tom Wilson making records. It was also the year that you were warned to know which side of society you were on – whether you were part of the solution or part of the problem. Nico thought she could just sweep through the middle, like artists so often do.

Now at the age of 28, she was a decade older than the 'golden children of the universe' who left home to Turn On, Tune In, Drop Out. In the middle Fifties she had seen the beatniks of Paris take a stand against the war in Algeria, and now she wondered if the hippies would take a stand against the Vietnam war, or stroll barefoot and self-absorbed into the psychedelic sunset. As she had suggested, 'There were two ways to go. You could walk outside on to the street, or more inside to your mind.' She never thought that opposition could be fortified by marching – marching was for soldiers, 'soldiers singing *Deutschland über alles*' – but she believed that society could not be changed by better drugs alone. 'You must destroy what is wrong, not ignore it,' she stressed to a journalist, though she was never in a fine position to lecture others on selfless behaviour.

'I was not a hippie. It was never true to say that, not to Jim Morrison either, nor to Brian Jones. We were bohemians. Do you understand the difference? Bohemians know they are not hippies, but hippies don't know they are not bohemians. Shall I tell you something about the hippies that I didn't like? Well, they were always selling you something. They would try to sell you dope, or patchouli oil, or themselves, or what they were thinking. It was like a Black Market, it was *der Schwarzmarkt* all over again. Do you know where they lived so much, in Haight-Ashbury inside of San Francisco? That was their ghetto. It was like Kreuzberg [in Berlin]. It was a Purple Market. That is a perfect hippie colour. A Purple Haze Market. What is that in German?'

Having lived in New York for a year, Nico was inoculated against the excesses of hippie fever by a slender dose of sarcasm. New Yorkers chortled at the flower-power naivety of Californians; up-tight resisted laid-back. 'You like "We Shall Overcome", but I prefer "Burn, Baby, Burn",' said the New York Philharmonic's chief conductor to a placid composer. The beatnik culture of the Fifties had evolved in European capitals as well as New York, that most European of American cities. It had already re-emerged fully armed for combat in its new guise as Situationism, which Nico loved, though she loved it like a tourist loves Paris. Sunny California, however, was dismissed as a backwater breeding ground of petit-bourgeois pretension, Disneyland and surfing. In the eyes of New York modernists, Haight-Ashbury hippies were nothing more than corner-shop beatniks. Hippiedom was just a way to make a cool buck out of soul food and finger cymbals. The East Coasters asked: why were the hippies only a big thing in California, Britain and Denmark and little places like that? Because it was fake rustic culture only fit for hicks and slobs.

Nico was not a hippie nor a head nor a heavy nor a funkster nor a flowerchild nor a rad nor a digger nor a beat. She was a boho. She did not truly believe in the hippies' counterculture because, to her mind, all cultures must be undone before something worth naming a utopia could emerge. Nico once said that she could not identify with one of the songs Lou Reed wrote for her. It was 'I'll Be Your Mirror': 'I can't identify with that – to notice only the beautiful and not the ugliness.' That was her problem with hippie-dom, too. She quite liked its drugs, though.

DOWNSTAIRS AT THE DOM, Nico perched once more on the bar top and sang to a guitar while her four-year-old son slurped his way around the room. The guitar might be held by Sterling Morrison, John Cale, or whoever else her manager Paul Morrissey had bribed to sit there and strum. He talked of those days in this way: 'After a time she wasn't drawing the crowds, not the whites, and certainly not the negroes. I met Danny Fields, who was then working for Elektra Records – he was involved with The Doors, who were on that label and coming to play in New York. Danny said, "Why don't you get Tim Buckley? He's got an album out, nobody's buying it. He could be the second act." So, I got him. Young Tim Buckley played his own songs – he had a beautiful, high, Irish voice – and then, out of the kindness of his heart, accompanied Nico. Finally Tim Buckley had to go away West (and then forever because he died of a heroin overdose). Ramblin' Jack Elliot played on a few occasions. Then Danny Fields suggested Tim Hardin who was on the same label as Buckley. Poor old Tim, we called him Tim Heroin. He was another damn junkie.

'There was a boy used to sit every night in front of Nico and Tim Buckley. He was just eighteen. By the end of the second week I spoke to him. He said, "Tim Buckley's my hero. I came over from Orange County [California] when I knew he was here." He said he wrote songs like Buckley and he played the guitar. I asked him if he could play for Nico. He said, "No, I couldn't play in public. I'm too afraid." So I got him to play for me a bit, right there in the bar. His songs sounded great and, better still as far as I was concerned, he Played The Guitar! I told Danny Fields about this boy. He checked him out immediately, bought his publishing for Elektra, about 25 songs. So this boy wonder started to deputise for Tim Buckley, and he did real well. I think we called him Jack Browne then.'

In Warhol's scrapbook there is a cutting from an anonymous paper. At the centre sits a photograph of Nico and her boy wonder, Jackson Browne. They are surrounded by a description of their show at the Dom that is almost ... almost ... almost ... like a poem of the time, rampant with lower-case letters and deeply meaningful pauses, 'by julie':

a walk on St. Mark's Place ... ANDY WARHOL at the Dom ... the underground bar ... Nico's voice and the guitar of Jack Browne ... 'could you stop my mirror store an' not be afraid of what you are? look around; you've got so much more to pay ... you fall in love with you' ...

applause ... sad eyes ... a smile ... movies ... Lou eats an apple ... hershey bar ... sky divers tumble in colour ... Gerard caresses Mary's boot ...

'The Kiss' . . . a comment on heterosexuals . . . pastel colours
swim wet . . . the ceiling plastered with silver . . . silver ball
swimming repetition . . . projected coloured lights . . . a
whirlpool of spots floating the room into circle dimension . . .
where clocks don't exist . . .

. . . Nico sings . . .
'i tell you all these pretty things' . . .
                         one foot pressing his back, making love
to his neck . . . his breathing is deeper . . . deeper . . . deeper
. . . Nico on the screen . . . moods . . . light rays stream across
his face . . . his voice comes through . . .

'the best is yet to come . . . the best is yet to come . . . you've
forgotten how to smile for real . . . the best is yet to come.'

Jackson Browne had been born in Germany exactly ten years later
than Nico. Two Librans. 'We didn't even think about it,' he recalled.
'I was born in Heidelberg after the war because my father had been
in the American army and was later a journalist there. Nico
wouldn't tell us where she came from, anyway. All I knew was, she
was extremely European. She was older than me, but everyone
seemed to be older than me then! I'd travelled cross-country with
some friends and we stayed in the Lower East Side and we were
kind of following my friend Tim Buckley. He had a band, but at
the time he was playing guitar in bars. He was performing alternate
sets with Nico, who was often accompanied by Sterling Morrison
or John Cale. It seemed to be a different guitar up there each time
I went.

'Paul Morrissey hired me to accompany Nico but he specified an
electric guitar, not acoustic, because "we don't want to be seen as
folk music folk". I had to borrow one from a friend in Long Island.
We didn't play every night. They'd put this sign up saying "Andy
Warhol's Mod Dom" (apparently he liked the name Dom because
it was Mod backwards). I went in there one night when we weren't
on and it was a different place entirely, just ordinary people drinking,
old songs on a jukebox. But on Nico's nights it was kind of like a
freak show. The Dom was suddenly a place for the Factory people
and their friends to hang out. There would be a film on the wall of
Lou Reed glowering at the camera and eating a Hershey bar, also a
sky diver falling endlessly down the wall – you couldn't see the edit
on the loop unless you were really quick.

'They originally wanted Nico to sing inside a plexiglass box. She flatly refused; she often grumbled about this novelty stuff they tried to make her do. We would sit up on the bar and play the same set twice nightly. She would do the Lou Reed songs, which sounded so hypnotic the way she sang them, a Tim Hardin song, a Bob Dylan song – all of them unreleased; it was an exceptional repertoire to hear, basically the songs we later recorded on *Chelsea Girl*. They were all simple songs to play, and none of us guitarists saw it as demanding work. Leonard Cohen would sit there in the audience and write. Even at that time he was an exciting figure, a poet who had just had his songs recorded by Judy Collins. You felt that he was probably the most intelligent, literate person in the room, a genuine poet. He'd steal in to watch Nico time after time and he'd talk with her and about her with open admiration. They became friends.

'He wasn't the only one, of course. She was physically like a goddess. Tall, stunning. Yet she had a very childish laugh and she smiled a lot. So there were men sitting there utterly infatuated with her. At the time there were these twenty-foot-high posters of Nico all over Manhattan, I forget quite why. It was impossible to work around the Village and not see these gigantic images of her. She didn't exploit it herself. At the Dom she sat on a straight-backed chair and crossed her long legs. It was like Dietrich (though I'm uncomfortable with that comparison – it's too easy, it's like saying Peter O'Toole and Richard Harris are exactly the same, you know, two blond Irishmen). She did not tout her sexuality. She didn't need to trade on it. She was dignified in her seduction. After all, this is a woman bringing up a kid, you know? Of course, in real life she had her defenses. She could be icy and distant with certain people, but I did notice that she was always friendly with people who supported her, like doormen and the personnel who'd help her get cabs and folk like that, she was very sweet to them and I think they adored Nico in return. I had this gigantic crush on her, too.' He told a journalist at the time, 'Oh, I just can't believe it! A mere teenager in from sunny California for less than a month and I'm sleeping with *the* most beautiful girl in the world!'

He would stay at whatever West Village flat she had most recently taken over, and she would cook him food ('cauliflower cheese') and they would drink wine and watch Ari playing around with things he shouldn't. Jackson Browne found it all 'very gentle, sweet and wholly domestic'. Nico the good mother was mothering more than Ari the barfly alcoholic, though the style came from the proficiency she'd gained in mothering her own mother. Nico's *hausfrau* ways began to impress most of her lovers from this time on, especially the Americans who were used to hot food in cardboard boxes. The liaison with Leonard Cohen, his infatuation otherwise unrequited, was absolutely oral.

Browne played Nico some of his songs, and she took a couple into her repertoire. She was the first to sing 'These Days' and 'The Fairest of the Seasons', which he'd written with Greg Copeland, 'and then there was this strange number I'd done called "Somewhere There's a Feather" and she liked that. She was the first to record my songs, and I played guitar for her album. But then I had to go back to California . . . Well, I'll tell you the truth. One day Nico accused me of making obscene phone calls to her. Somebody was doing this and it unnerved her. It was straight harassment. So she accused me and I was stunned. I said, "How could you think it was me, Nico? Fuck this, I'm going." Morrissey tried to get me to stay, but I quit.'

He wrote a song about Nico as he left. He never gave it to anyone, and she never saw it:

Oh how sadly sound the songs the queen must sing of dying
A prisoner upon her throne of melancholy sighing
If she could see her mirror now
She would be free of those who bow and
Scrape the ground before her feet

Silently she walks among her dying midnight roses
Watches as each moment goes that never really know us
And so it seems she doesn't care
If she has dreams of no one there
Within the shadows of her room

But all my frozen words agree, and say it's time to
Call back all the birds I sent to
Fly behind her castle walls, and I'm
Weary of the nights I've seen
Inside these empty halls.

Wooden lady turn and turn among my weary secrets
And wave within the hours past and other empty pockets
Maybe we've found what we have lost
When we've unwound so many crossed entangling

> Misunderstandings; but
> All my frozen words agree and say it's time to
> Call back all the birds I sent to
> Fly behind her castle walls, and I'm
> Weary of the nights I've seen
> Inside these empty walls.

Nico once said, 'Jackson Browne, John Cale, Bob Dylan, they write beautiful songs. They are not so easy to memorise, though.'

ARI'S SKIN TURNED YELLOW. He had eaten and drunk whatever came his way, Hershey bars, chips, coke, dregs. The four-year-old 'wild child', as Nico proudly called him, had not been dining richly like his French father but rather more like a little girl would have done in ravenous Berlin twenty years before. It is claimed that she would coat Ari's gums with heroin powder to calm him down. Thanks to his junk diet of contaminated food and the uneven nocturnal life, Ari developed an insidious infection. He got jaundice, a severe attack of it inflaming his liver. Nico the good mother knew straight away what to do. While others called for a doctor, she called for a grandmother. Madame Boulogne received a letter in Paris stating baldly that Ari was pitifully ill and Nico needed something done about it. For the third time in three years, and the fourth time for the family, Madame Boulogne paid out of her own pocket for her flight to take Ari away from his mother and nurse him back to reality.

'This will be the last time,' said Monsieur Boulogne. 'If we keep Ari here, we must organise it properly. He has to go to school now, at least.' By September Ari was five and less a wild child than a schoolchild. No more film roles, no more 'amphetamine monsters sucking at the acrid dregs of their sexuality', at least not in suburban Bourg-la-Reine, if memory serves. Although he would see his mother a few times on diminishing visits (once there was a gap of five years when access was denied), he would be nineteen and Nico 43 before they were reconciled again. Ari would soon share the same view of school that his mother had: 'I went without pleasure. In these schools one is only suppressed. It is a cruel education method; one is graded. You are not allowed to be truly different there, but some children are unusual . . .'

Nico's mother would strongly agree about certain children, had she been in a position to. Grete was too ill to notice anything any more. She was only 57 but could no longer speak in complete sentences. She had received none of the promised money from Nico and could not afford the primitive medication offered for Parkinson's disease in those days, nor the hospital fees. Her sister Helma, with her son Ulrich, made the only arrangements they knew to be possible. 'The doctor in Ibiza had written to us. She had no money, nothing at all. It was so hopeless, like a Greek tragedy.' They paid for Grete to return to Berlin and attend a residential hospital there. Ulrich, now a practising architect, met the cost, draining though it was. Everything in the house in Ibiza was sold off, 'dirt cheap, you cannot imagine,' added Helma.

This was how Nico's family spent the Summer of Love.

'NICO GOT A LOT OF PRESS ATTENTION that spring from her Superstar status – the *Chelsea Girls* movie had been screened for six months,' Paul Morrissey recalled, 'so Tom Wilson, the record producer, said, "Let's make an album." We racked up the songs. It was wonderful really – a Dylan song, a Cale song, a Lou Reed song, a Hardin song, a Browne song – a very impressive list that Nico had acquired, and all well rehearsed because of the residency. The recording was very simple. There was Nico and a guitarist, John Cale for one, then Lou Reed, then Jackson Browne. It was just like she sang at the Dom. I think the best songs were those by Jackson Browne; imagine, he was just eighteen, and Cal-i-forn-ian. Tom Wilson added the strings later, in another session. Then he added a flute, for some godforsaken reason.'

The session was remembered by Jackson Browne because of the producer. 'Tom Wilson was a very charming man who didn't seem to take anything seriously. I suppose he was kind of unusual, a black guy producing folk rock, though we never thought about it really. He was a nice guy with a good reputation, I mean he produced Bob Dylan's "Like a Rolling Stone". But he was a staff producer for Columbia Records and I think they would just assign somebody to a project, like in alphabetical order. I suppose Columbia's biggest competition at the time was Tamla Motown, so it figures that way. But Tom Wilson spent his entire time holding forth on the phone; he had a whole social scene going. He would say, "Just go ahead and do it, don't mind me." It was probably the first recording studio I'd been in, but even I knew that the producer should sort of get off the phone now and again.'

John Cale agreed ('He was a nice guy, but he just sat there

Nico

with this phone glued to his ear, calling up girlfriends'), and
when the English singer Kevin Ayers worked with Wilson for
his first album a full year later, his strongest memory was the
producer, who 'sat on the phone and called his girlfriends all day
long'. It wasn't the producer that Nico complained about, but the
flute he added: 'I cried when I heard the album. I cried because of
the flute. I hate it so much! It is a great mistake. The arrangements
in general were not so good. Even so, I could bear the string sound.
But I wish I could take the flute off. There should be a button on
record players, a "No Flute" button. There could be an "Add
drums" button, too, why not? You would think they could do this.
It would be fun to orchestrate some things and to un-orchestrate
some things. Well, I wish I could un-orchestrate *Chelsea Girl*. The
flute, anyway.'

After 25 years in recording studios, Jackson Browne remains
awed by the speed in which *Chelsea Girl* was cut: 'I think I went in
to play my guitar parts on the day before I was leaving for California.
We did those, and more, in a day. If that's any indication, her album
must have been completed within three days (think of the time they
take now!). Lou Reed was also playing that day. Afterwards he took
me for a big Chinese meal and then on to see the Murray the K Show
at RKO. There was Wilson Pickett, The Blues Project, The Who,
Etta King. What a day.'

Nico was confused by the timing of all this. 'When we made
Chelsea Girl, everyone was talking about *The Velvet Underground
and Nico*, because that had come out just then. I had forgotten about
it, of course, because we had made it one year before. I was talking
about *Chelsea Girl* and people would think I was talking about the
film. The record came out another year later [July 1968]. It is funny,
really, because that is how films go usually. You make a film and
when you've forgotten about it, the public sees it for the first time.
But Andy's films were very fast. You made it in one month and then
you were a film star in the next. But the records took forever. I never
understood this timing of things that go to the public. That is why
I was not good for publicity. I forgot what I was there to talk about.'

She was routinely invited to talk to the press about The
Velvet Underground, far more so than Lou Reed. She pretended
that she couldn't understand quite why: 'I am a solo singer who
sings a lot. They are a band without any bookings.' To promote
the album in April 1967, Warhol and Morrissey put the band into
a desperate residency at The Gymnasium, a place on East 71st Street

174

discovered by the son of Stanley at the Dom. The advertisements showed a photograph of Warhol with Nico but without the band. The copy ran:

A NEW HAPPENING DISCOTHEQUE
THE GYMNASIUM

NATIONAL SWINGER'S NITE
with ANDY, NICO, LIVE BAND
and FREAK OUT LIGHTS

making the wildest swing-in
the EAST SIDE'S ever seen.
SUNDAY, APRIL 30, at 6PM.

The Warhol of *Popism* wrote that, 'The Gymnasium was the ultimate Sixties place for me, because, we left it exactly as it was, with the mats, the parallel bars, weights, straps, and barbells. You thought, "Gymnasium, right, wow, fantastic," and when you look again like that at something you've always taken for granted, you see it fresh, and it's a good Pop experience.' Not many of the paying public thought 'right, wow, fantastic', and the quickly flailing residency merely added to the band's lowering spirits. It was not a band for Intranauts, it was more Jack Up than Drop Out, and it took fourteen years before the band (by then disbanded for a decade) was openly approved as a major force in rock music.

Years later Nico told a woman journalist her views on the band: 'Everybody wanted to be the star. Of course, Lou always was. But the newspapers came to me all the time. That's how I got fired – he couldn't take that any more. He fired me and then he fired John Cale. Have you met him? What do you think of him – sarcastic?' The album, before the company withdrew it from sale, reached 171 in the album charts. In those days, to find any kind of position in the printed ratings was a blessing, but the band did not like to learn that there were 170 albums selling more than theirs. Debut LPs by The Doors and the Mothers of Invention from California outpaced the New Yorkers, and by the summer of 1967 everything was eclipsed by the latest release from The Beatles, *Sgt Pepper's Lonely Hearts Club Band*. Dispirited by a lack of work, weak management from WarVel, and personal passions for disarming drugs, the band did not fare well. It survived another four years with occasional substitutes before disintegrating. *The Velvet Underground and Nico*, however, eventually went gold ($1 million of sales) and even higher; it remains to this day in the sales catalogue. The Velvets, to their eternal credit, distributed the band's royalties evenly, including Nico in the share-out – a privilege later passed on to her son. 'I never got a penny in royalties from it,' confided Nico, lying.

'AVOID PERSONS in black or lemon. You will have romantic inclinations, so aim for people in cream. You'll feel like a tiger, but don't forget you're a lion.' This was the impressive advice given to Nico by Madame Svetlana ('Get them while they last! Madame Svetlana Lucky Souvenir Rabbit Fur Collars, $27.50!'). Madame Svetlana wrote each month for a New York magazine that foretold the horoscopes of celebrities. In March 1967, it displayed a photographic collage of that month's selection. Nico was prominent, with her date of birth clear for all to see: 8 August 1942. She was a Leo, Madame Svetlana supposed. She did not know that Nico was more a liar than a Leo. Ari was the real Leo, 11 August. So was Andy Warhol, 6 August. Librans were advised to 'avoid persons in white'. No doubt Nico wore cream all March.

Pasted next to Nico was Peter Sellers (Virgo), Federico Fellini (Capricorn) and the singer of The Doors, Jim Morrison (Sagittarius; 'Many Sagittarians will indulge in a taste for forgery'). Of all the sage projections Madame Svetlana made, placing Jim Morrison and Nico together was the most prescient. The Doors came from Los Angeles and had played in New York just twice, firstly the previous November and then in March. The common view at the Factory was that The Doors were a rather pretentious band which relied entirely on the carnal power of its sensual Greek god, Jim Morrison. The Velvets most feared another Californian band entirely, the one led by Frank Zappa and called the Mothers of Invention. 'Jim was Brian Jones and Mick Jagger put together. But he was really a cobra. Who were the Mothers of Invention? A man in a stupid beard. Anyway, who wants to hear a concert given by some mothers?' declared Nico, forgetting she was a mother.

When the Velvets and Nico had played at The Trip club in Los Angeles a year before, Jim Morrison had been there. Warhol believed that Morrison had then paid close attention to Gerard Malanga, who had performed his Whip Dance in a suit of black leather. Morrison later gained much publicity by wearing such a suit ('Many Sagittarians will indulge in a taste for forgery'). It is often assumed that Morrison and Nico first came together in the summer of 1967, when Danny Fields from the Elektra record company tried to engineer the perfect partnership. Morrison and Nico would be Adam and Eve in the Summer of Love.

They actually met in March, when Morrison would have noticed those 'twenty-foot-high posters of Nico all over Manhattan'. The drummer of The Doors was John Densmore, who remembered the March encounter from a distinctly percussive perspective: 'We were staying at the dumpy Great Northern Hotel on 57th Street. Convenient location, but the place smelled of old people. I was rooming right next to Jim, which turned out to be better than TV. Not that I was the drinking-glass-to-the-wall type, but the racket that was coming from next door one night was hard to miss. Jim brought Nico, the Velvet Underground's famous German vamp, back to his hotel room, and I'd never heard such crashing around. It sounded as if they were beating the shit out of each other. I was worried but never dared to ask what happened. Nico looked okay the next day, so I let it slide.'

When so many people talk of Nico at this time in terms of 'elegance', 'shyness', 'dignity', 'beauty', 'divine sensuality', and even as a 'willowy flower', it is surprising to read of her suddenly as a bruiser, a scrapper, a boxer of ears. It sounds more like little Christa in Lübbenau playing hard to win with her cousin Ulli: 'She imposed herself in a powerful manner. Nothing else mattered until she had her own way entirely.' It is less surprising to learn that when she drank beer she turned violent. Within two hours the Moon Goddess transformed herself into a lager lout ('I like to drink beer. As long as it does not remind me of my birth'). Beer-drinking became a common feature later in her life; indeed, one drunken bout led later to her exile from America, but it took someone as monstrously lush as Morrison to provoke the first recorded instance. He called himself the Lizard King, but he was more of a lounge lizard. John Cale observed that 'Jim Morrison was like a spoilt, clean-scrubbed schoolboy in his first day on drink'.

Nico often talked of him as her 'soul brother': 'I think he was the first man I met who was not afraid of me in some way. We were very similar, like brother and sister. Our spirits are similar. We were the same height and the same age, almost.' In fact he was five years younger; otherwise she was justified in stressing their similarities. James Douglas Morrison was the son of an officer in the United States Navy. While his father fought, the boy was brought up by his mother and grandparents in Clearwater, the Lübbenau of Florida. He later claimed that the soul of a dead Native American entered his body when he was but four years old: 'The first time I discovered death, me and my mother and father and my grandmother and grandfather were driving through the desert at dawn. A truckload of Indians had either hit another car or something – there were Indians scattered all over the highway . . . and I do think, at that moment, the soul or the ghosts of those dead Indians – maybe one or two of them – were just running around, freaking out, and just landed in my soul.' His father apparently countered, 'It was a dream, Jimmy, it didn't really happen, it was a dream.' Morrison's Natives were Nico's Jews. But his background was effortlessly bourgeois and cushioned. A butch hostility to routine marked this sulky young man jaded with the clean comforts of Fifties America; Nico often strove for the life he disowned. While she watched weepy movies he went to film school. While she saw Ginsberg in the street, he read Ginsberg. While she learned Dylan's lyrics, he wrote his own. 'He was well read and he introduced me to William Blake and also the English Romantic poets who came after him. Jim liked Shelley. I preferred Coleridge. In fact, he is my favoured poet of all time. Did you know they were all drug addicts? Coleridge was addicted to opium. It is better to be addicted to opium than to be addicted to money.

'I did not feel that Jim was a Californian [he wasn't]. He lived in Los Angeles, which is a beautiful name – The Angels – and it was really a city for William Blake, not for Hollywood. But Los Angeles was destroyed, like Jerusalem was destroyed in England [in Blake's poem]. Jim could have built it again, if he had not been surrounded by these tacky women.' Jim Morrison had as many women as Brian Jones (it would have been difficult to have had more). His looks were brilliantly bohemian: a sullen mouth that pouted more than smiled, barely containable stubble, a childish button nose, puma eyes, tousled red-brown hair, and a petulant demeanour set in a heavy frame; for both Morrison and Nico, weight gain was a persistent problem. He retained a little baby fat and looked pampered, but he was physically graceful, at least when he was sober. Jack Simmons, the owner of The Castle, claimed that 'Jim Morrison walked like a panther and swam like a dolphin'. Nico never walked, she sashayed; and she never swam, ever.

Danny Fields considered that Morrison 'really was a terror – he was the epitome of the old-fashioned concept of the brat, a big, brilliant, sexy brat'. He must have known, when he put them together that July in Los Angeles, that Morrison and Nico were not Adam and Eve, but two snakes. 'I thought they would make a cute couple,' he coyly explained. 'They were both icy and mysterious and charismatic and poetic and deep and sensitive and wonderful.' Nico had a more direct view. 'Jim Morrison had the best sex I ever had inside me,' she confided to a writer in the Eighties, 'but Brian [Jones] *gave* the best sex, when he could. Jim was more involved in his dreams. He liked to sleep and to find visions, because there were private things he showed me. I think Brian was more of a musician than a composer, and Jim was more of a poet. You could say that Jim took drugs because he wanted visions for his poetry. It is like people in the office who drink coffee to help them work. It is really the same.'

Nico talked of Jim Morrison and Brian Jones in the same breath because she moved from one to the other early that summer. She moved, in fact, from Paul McCartney's house in London, which she'd invaded for several weeks, to The Velvet Underground in Boston with Andy Warhol and then to Brian Jones in San Francisco and Jim Morrison in Los Angeles, all in one grand sweep. 'You could say it was like a fairy tale; Andy would be the good fairy and Jim would play the giant, Brian would be the witch, Paul McCartney would be the frog who turns into a prince, no, it would have to be the other way round. Well, it didn't seem like a fairy tale at the time. It was a lot of hassle. But I learned a lot of things, and I began to compose my own songs.' As Morrison would often say, quoting Blake, 'The road of excess leads to the palace of Wisdom.' He rarely added that it was one of the Proverbs of Hell.

Nico stayed in London once she had finished recording *Chelsea Girl*. She was there to get medical attention for her perforated right eardrum, as she was finding herself becoming progressively deaf on that side. She could have gone to the 1967 Cannes Film Festival with the Warhol crew to attend the screening of *The Chelsea Girls*, especially as Warhol had the airfares covered, though the visit turned into a fiasco when the festival's Director declined to give the film an official place. Nico made a quick trip to Paris to see the convalescent Ari, then found refuge in Paul McCartney's house. It was her second choice. Nico had turned up one day at the grand Regent's Park residence of David Bailey. 'She just turned up on the doorstep with her suitcases. She wanted to move in with me. I got a bit panicky – I was having too good a time to cope with Nico as well. I think I said, "I'm very fond of you, Nico, but not *that* fond." ' He recommended Paul McCartney's place, and Nico was not one to argue with an offer like that, whoever it came from.

In terms of their stunning career, The Beatles were not doing too well in May 1967. They did not seem to have worked for some time; they were The Velvet Underground of England. The group had just released 'Strawberry Fields Forever' and 'Penny Lane' as a double-sided single and for the first time in three years, the record was blocked from a number one position by a crooner called Engelbert Humperdinck. 'Oh, is he German?' enquired Nico. 'No, he's from India and his real name's Arnold,' replied McCartney, accurately. 'Which would you rather be called – Engelbert or Arnold?' Nico studied the options for some time. 'Whichever is shorter,' she decided.

The Beatles were not really idle; they had worked for five months recording *Sgt Pepper's Lonely Hearts Club Band*. 'It was an *interesting* album,' said Nico, who claimed to have heard it at Brian Epstein's private party before its release. 'It is European. It has brass bands and hunting cries and orchestras and things America tries to steal from Europe. Do you know they go fox hunting in New England? I can imagine Edie with her dogs and a little whip. I think she would rather whip herself though. I think she would go hunting foxes in New England and hunting fucks in New York. What do you call that? A pun? Well . . . There is a song I liked on *Sgt Pepper*, called 'A Day in the Life'. It has a beautiful song and then this strange sound like John Cale would make (he told me it was an orchestra, actually) and then this stupid little pop song that spoils everything so far. I told this to Paul, and I made a mistake, because the beautiful song was written by John Lennon and the stupid song was written by Paul. It can be embarrassing when you speak the truth.'

Nico outstayed her welcome by several days, if not weeks. Although McCartney's regular girlfriend, Jane Asher, was away acting in the States, an amorous American photographer called Linda Eastman had just arrived in London. Linda would later suffer the classic indignity of all wives and girlfriends who enter bands and sing or play; even John Cale once told *Rolling Stone* magazine that 'Nico's sudden appearance in [The Velvet Underground] was very funny. It was like the lead singer has a girlfriend, and she wants to sing, so let her.' Luckily for Paul McCartney's patience, Andy Warhol arrived in London, fresh from his frustrating time at Cannes. Warhol knew that the manager of The Beatles, Brian Epstein, liked The Velvets' debut album, and he hoped that Epstein might manage them and organise a European tour. Whether he was interested or not, Epstein died three months later from an overdose of Carbitrol.

Warhol and Morrissey prised Nico away from Paul McCartney's home on the pretext of a Velvet Underground ('and Nico') concert in Boston. They flew together from London, but when they arrived at the Boston Tea Party club, the trio was dismayed to discover that the band had hired a new manager. Moreover, the Velvets would not let Nico on stage ('We'd been playing without her for a few months anyway'). 'Well, I had made my own album which would soon come out, but they hadn't recorded anything without me.' Nico defied the snub by flying west to the sunnier coast and into the jaded arms of Brian Jones.

This was the time you were told by Scott Mackenzie that, 'If you go to San Francisco / be sure to wear some flowers in your hair,' in which song laid a menacing rhyme that ran, 'All across the nation / Such a strange vibration'. Nico went to San Francisco and neglected to wear flowers ('I like flowers. They remind me of graveyards'). She turned south to the town of Monterey, host, on the weekend of 16 June, to the first rock festival with any claim to fame. The eminent bands played without a fee and the money went to charity: the audience of 50,000 sat sedately on plastic seats; nobody died, got raped, beaten up or swindled, apparently. 'Peace and love found a resting place in Monterey that weekend,' claimed the *Berkeley BARB* newspaper, in an unfortunate choice of metaphor. Jim Morrison was not to be seen; he was singing in up-tight New York. At the peace and love festival, Brian Jones was a Master of Ceremonies.

He and Nico were staying with Sheila Oldham, a young mother married to The Stones' old manager, Andrew. Brian Jones had brought along with him a trunk full of clothes. 'It was as though he had bought Biba up and put it in a valise,' said Nico. 'He would try everything on every day. He would annoy me with asking questions whether this hat went with these boots, this scarf matched this waistcoat, every little thing against everything else. I made fun of him but he said I was quite the same and why should a girl spend more time than a man? I said that I spent some time with simple things trying to get them correct, but he spent all his time with everything and in the end it still looked like he had thrown it on. This would provoke him, which I liked to do, frankly. I think he was trying to compensate with his clothes for his bad appearance. His body did not like a lot of drugs, and he had spots. Spots on his face.' Nico thought he was in need of a good mother.

There is a famous film of the weekend, titled *Monterey Pop*. It was directed by D. A. Pennebaker, who had made the Bob Dylan documentary. All of the bands are seen in action – The Mamas and the Papas with the balloon-shaped Mama Cass, Canned Heat, the adolescent Simon and Garfunkel, the token blacks Otis Redding and Hugh Masakela ('too jazzy,' the press said), Jefferson Airplane with the earthy Grace Slick, Big Brother with the even earthier Janis Joplin, the English contingent of The Animals and The Who; and then two extraordinary acts, the flash and superficial Ravi Shankar for youngsters to practise Hindu sex positions with ('I hated all that going on,' he admitted), and the smash of the festival, guitarist Jimi Hendrix, who was introduced on stage by Brian Jones.

It was the first time Nico had seen Hendrix play. They had common friends in The Rolling Stones; Hendrix was working in New York when Keith Richards heard him and arranged a management deal. The 20-year-old moved to London to begin a sensational career. It was there or in New York that he met Nico. They spent a couple of nights together – where and when is no longer known; Hendrix suffocated on his own vomit in 1970. Around this time she began to tell her friends of the black sergeant's rape, but in the same breath she also bragged of her fling with Hendrix. Nobody who knew both stories could come to terms with the implied contradiction. Her attraction to Hendrix was obvious, however. 'He was the most sexual man I ever saw on stage,' she confessed, 'even Mick Jagger said so. It was not all the vulgar things he did with his guitar, though I enjoyed it when he burned his guitar at the festival. It was his presence. He was like a cat. He moved elegantly for a man. He was suave. Did you know he was half Indian? Cherokee. I think these mixtures are very good. I am a mixture, part Turkish, part Russian. We would have made wonderful children together, such a mixture.'

The movie of Monterey also shows the sights beyond the stage, a scene so vivid that the film is now a noted reference encyclopedia for those who hope, each decade, to resurrect hippieness. Frame after frame reflects the unsettling mixture of Edwardian military uniforms and cool Indian cotton – Sgt Pepper's Indian Empire – that Nico always avoided because it looked 'tacky' (a favourite word of Warhol's that she picked up). There is one moment in the film that is too easily missed. Among the flower children and acid freaks walks a stunning couple, arm in arm. The cameraman immediately notices that he has a star in his sights. He zooms in to the stoned face of Brian Jones. In doing so, he clips off the regal figure of Nico. She is on screen for all of two seconds. A couple of seconds more and it would have been her sixth film appearance – had she been telling the story.

10 July–December, 1967

A damsel with a dulcimer
In a vision once I saw:
It was an Abyssinian maid,
And on her dulcimer she played,
Singing of Mount Abora.
Could I revive within me
Her symphony and song,
To such deep delight 'twould win me,
That with music loud and long,
I would build that dome in air,
That sunny dome! those caves of ice!
And all who heard should see them there,
And all should cry, Beware! Beware!

(from 'Kubla Khan',
SAMUEL TAYLOR COLERIDGE, 1798)

ONE STORY ABOUT NICO and Jim Morrison has passed into rock legend: *Jim and Nico are staying at The Castle that summer. They are both naked. They are both stoned on acid and drink and hashish. Jim takes Nico up the tower. Jim jumps on to the parapet and looks down to the deep drop below. Nude, he walks along the thin parapet, risking his life. He shouts to Nico to follow him. She refuses. He begs her. She declines. He commands her. She disobeys. He risks everything. She risks nothing.* That is how the story has been passed down from Doors biography to Doors biography. It came first from the lips of Danny Fields and Jack Simmons, who were on the spot, and today it is a renowned image of rock mythology to set aside Jimi Hendrix igniting his guitar and Jerry Lee Lewis smashing his piano: the he-man, the cave man, the strutting cock, disobeying death.

But nobody bothered to ask Nico for her side of the story: 'Everybody says it is true and they saw this thing we did,' she reflected in 1985, 'but I remember something they never say. That I argued with Jim. He asked if I would walk along the edge. I said to him "Why?" and he couldn't answer. It was not a positive act, and not a destructive act; it didn't change anything. So why should

I do something that is so vain, just to follow him? It was not spiritual or philosophical. It was a drunk man displaying himself. Did they tell you that about the story? I don't think so.'

Danny Fields once told a journalist that 'Jim and Nico got into this fight, with him pulling her hair all over the place – it was just this weird love making, between the two most adorable monsters, each one trying to be more poetic than the other.' Nico stressed, again in 1985, 'I like my relations to be physical and of the psyche. We hit each other because we were drunk and we enjoyed the sensation. We made love in a gentle way, do you know? It was the opposite to Brian Jones. I thought of Jim Morrison as my brother, so we would grow together. We still do, because he is my soul brother. We exchanged blood. I carry his blood inside me. When he died, and I told people that he wasn't dead, this was my meaning. We had spiritual journeys together.' When asked to clarify this, Nico declared, 'We went into the desert and took drugs.'

Nico wanted Jim Morrison to join her brotherhood, and he obliged. They cut their thumbs in the desert with a knife and let their blood mingle. Such a ritual form of devotion appealed to their shared sense of theatre, but Nico wanted even more. She wanted Morrison to share not just her blood but her son. One night she decided that they should be married, to test if he was stringing her along or serious. As the drunken boor in front of her had offered little more than literary discourse and downright lust, she suggested to him that he might like to propose marriage to her. He laughed himself off his chair. She hit him, they fought and when they got tired, they made up. That was the routine nature of their alliance, day after day – affection–argument–rancour–resolution: 'I was in love with him and that is how love goes, isn't it? He was the first man I was in love with, because he was affectionate to my looks and my mind. But we took too much drink and too many drugs to make it, that was our difficulty. Everything was open to us; there were no rules. We had a too big appetite.'

During their time together in California, between the months of July and August 1967, they often drove out of Los Angeles and into the desert. Morrison found the cactus buttons called peyote, which they picked off and ate. 'Peyote was a spiritual drug. We were in the middle of the desert and everything was natural, you know, in the open air, nature all around, not a hotel room or a bar. And the cactus was natural. You did not buy it from somebody on a street corner. We had visions in the desert. It is like William Blake. Jim was like William Blake; he would see visions like Blake did, angels in trees, he would see these, and so would I. And Jim showed me that this is what a poet does. A poet sees visions and records them. He said that there were more poets in the Comanches than there were in bookstores. The Comanches took the cactus, too. We were like the Indians who lived in this way for thousands of years, before the Christians and as long as the Jews.'

Jim Morrison recorded his psycho-chemical visions and dreams. His notes often comprised the raw material for his poems and songs. He considered that this was how the opium-addicted Coleridge worked, a model good enough for him; one Coleridge poem he read to Nico was titled 'Kubla Khan, or a Vision in a Dream'. Nico just once offered an example of the peyote visions she endured with Morrison: 'The light of the dawn was a very deep green and I believed I was upside down and the sky was the desert which had become a garden and then the ocean. I do not swim and I was frightened when it was water and more resolved when it was land. I felt embraced by the sky-garden.' Soon after, she started to write a song lyric, possibly her first, titled 'Lawns of Dawns', which contained lines such as these:

> He blesses you, he blesses me
> The day the night caresses,
> Caresses you, caresses me,
> Can you follow me?
>
> I cannot understand the way I feel
> Until I rest on lawns of dawns –
> Can you follow me?

The cross-eyed, internal rhymes come directly from Jim Morrison, who wrote 'The west is the best' and even other lines less elegant ('Your milk is my wine / your silk is my shine'). He showed her how he worked on his poems, and in doing so offered her a model. She was reluctant to write anything down, however. It was a major step, to talk about words and then to write them (especially in a foreign language, Nico liked to remind her fans). 'Jim gave me permission to be a writer,' Nico claimed. 'He said to me one day, "I give you permission to write your poems and compose your songs!" My soul brother believed I could do it. I had his authority. And why not? His song was the most popular song in America.' At the time, this was strictly true. The Doors' single 'Light My Fire' had been released in early June, and by the end of July it attained the number one position for three weeks. Nico spent her nights in the desert with the nation's number one pop star who told her to write songs and read to her Coleridge, Shelley and Blake. No wonder she stayed faithful to her boozy, conceited soul brother, when he was the first fuckable man to acknowledge her mind as much as her face.

Nico told him that she did not know how to compose. She could not follow the mechanics of writing. He told her to write down her dreams, literally, write down the images she remembered. This would provide her raw material. He admitted to her that he started by imitating other writers, Céline and Blake for instance, but then he realised that they were writing down their dreams, and so it would be more creative for him to do the same. The songs would be her recounting of her visions, and that was enough. But then she asked him where the melodies came from, and he gave the stock answer he had ready whenever the subject was raised: 'The music came first, and then I'd make up some words to hang on the melody, because that was the only way I could remember it, and most of the time I'd end up with just the words and forget the tune.' The music, then, was the melody, and all the rest was *arrangement*. Nico felt that she had finally passed an examination.

Their affair, a torrid mixture of drinks, drugs, fights and poetry readings, lasted little more than a month before this Adam and Eve left the Garden of Eden without any god's bidding and drifted down their separate roads to hell. They were tired of each other, little more than that; they were exhausted by each other's titanic demands. Aside from the authority she had received to compose, and the slanted introduction to English poetry, she kept two prevailing souvenirs of her liaison: his blood in hers, and red hair. 'He had a fetish for red-haired shanties, you know, Irish shanties. I was so much in love with him that I made my hair red after a while. I wanted to please his taste. It was silly, wasn't it? Like a teenager.' She kept her hair tinted a pale red until he died.

NICO HUNG AROUND CALIFORNIA through the summer, living at The Castle in Los Angeles and spending leisure time 'hanging out' in San Francisco, meeting friends of friends. One day she hooked up with Andy Warhol, Paul Morrissey and Ultra Violet, who were promoting the West Coast premiere of *The Chelsea Girls*. The chic bohemian paper of San Francisco was known as the *Berkeley BARB* and it ran a terribly earnest interview with the Factory quartet. Whatever the West Coasters' intention, the whole thing turned into a sniggering debate about drugs and hippies. Morrissey revelled in relentless satire but Nico showed how tanned and West Coast she had become over the summer:

BARB: *Do you think the hippies have presented us with a viable lifestyle?*

Andy: Well, I don't know. I like them, but it's so weird . . .

Paul: I wonder about drugs, whether it's a long term thing or a short term thing. I think if they do find a lot of dangers, like LSD and children being deformed . . .

Andy: But the funny thing about it is, I mean you can never really know. People really lie. I mean, they can lie just about anything.

Nico: We can get better drugs, too, and make fantastic children . . .

Paul: But there's no reaction against it. The reaction against drugs has never begun yet . . . And it's going to come . . .

Andy: But everyone's freaking out. People are up on downs and down on ups.

Ultra: We blow our minds.

Paul: Is heroin much used in San Francisco?

BARB: *It doesn't seem to be.*

Paul: That's funny. You know, a year and a half ago in Los Angeles, I already thought that LSD was going to become a joke – like even to mention LSD a year ago seemed so tacky. And it's just got bigger and bigger, and it's still the going thing. And there're still no references to anything derogatory. I mean, I'm looking for a resurgence of alcoholism.

Andy: Oh, but drinkers are so terrible, you know, they're always fighting.

Nico: Well, they're more destructive towards other people. With the drugs it's more towards yourself.

Andy: But I don't see why the love people are against amphetamines and things like that.

Paul: . . . On LSD they're so silly and slap happy, like a prize-fighter who's spent a lifetime in the ring and comes out of his career with a broken nose and a stupid way of talking ... I think heroin's much better.

Andy: Oh, but heroin is really awful.

Paul: No, I think I'm really for heroin, because it doesn't affect you physically, if you take care of yourself.

Andy: Oh, I guess if you're rich you can really go on it and really be very happy ...

BARB: *But won't it eventually take its physical toll?*

Paul: It really doesn't. You never get a cold – it cures colds ...

BARB: *Have you ever considered moving your headquarters to San Francisco?*

Paul: It would be easier to work here.

Andy: Yes, but since I'm not pushing anything I can work anywhere.

Paul: If you come here, you're going to get identified with The Cause or something. It's all right to be a degenerate or a drug addict, but here they make a thing of it, which is corny. I mean, if you're going to be a drug person, be an outcast. Like, a person who works for IBM isn't very interesting because he's part of a large organisation. A person who's part of this hippie garbage I don't think is very interesting.

Nico: How do you know you're not?

Paul: Not what? Part of a group?

Nico: How do you know you're not a hippie?

Paul: Get away.

Nico: Because you're not wearing flowers?

BARB: *Is there anything you'd like to say in parting?*

Paul: Yes, we want to know where the Salvation Army is so that we can go in our limousine Cadillac and buy some hippie clothes.

ANDY WARHOL WANTED NICO and Jim Morrison to make a feature-length film together. He was bucked by the commercial success of *The Chelsea Girls* and he knew that Nico had a lot to do with it. 'He wanted me to make a film with Jim Morrison, though he pretended that it was my idea. He wanted a pop star in his film. While I was at the Castle I looked after Edie who had joined me.

She was still beautiful, but she had a problem with heroin then. She told me to be careful of Andy because he would use me to get more famous and then forget me when he wanted. Well, I had already thought of that. I was not so dependent on Andy as Edie, I mean not for my career. So Edie said that I should do the film but with somebody else instead of Jim. So I did. Andy was expecting Jim and instead I took Jim's best friend, who was an actor called Tom Baker. Andy could not chastise me, but he was annoyed. This became the beginning of the end.'

That was how Nico told the story. However, Jim Morrison had no desire to make a film with Nico anyway, not even a photograph. Danny Fields recalled that 'I wanted him to do a photo session with Nico, but he refused to do it. He'd never say no, but he'd never turn up. Nico would be waiting at the location and Morrison was always nowhere to be seen. He didn't want to pose with a woman, and I don't blame him – his instincts were right. Posing with a woman would have diffused his image, and he wanted to remain aloof.' To save face, Nico took Tom Baker, a kind of 'next best thing' in her view, over to Warhol, though this handsome Hollywood actor was probably a better performer than Morrison. There is one other aspect to this that Nico confided at the time to Tina Aumont but never mentioned again. She spent some time with Edie and they had sex with each other. Nico's new film was called *I, a Man*.

The film was summarised by Warhol as 'a series of scenes of this guy, Tom, seeing these different women in one day in New York, having sex with some, talking with some, fighting with some'. The film was partly made in Los Angeles, to accommodate Nico. Ultra Violet flew there and remembered of Nico that 'although we shared the same room, I never had a conversation with her'. The other women included a sensational modelling colleague of Nico's from France, Ivy Nicholson, an American who was one of the first to become famous, and then notorious in Europe. She was joined by Ingrid Superstar, Cynthia May and Bettina Coffin. But there was another woman there who became linked to Warhol's fame more than anyone would have imagined. She was a feminist called Valerie Solanas, and in time she would be known worldwide as 'the woman who shot Andy Warhol'.

The film was meant to be 'really dirty', Warhol told a reporter. 'Dirtier than *The Chelsea Girls*?' he was asked. 'The new one has more close-ups,' he said. But it was neither dirtier nor better. Warhol and Morrissey had made it in response to a request from a New

York cinema that made its money from erotic films. The owner wanted something like *I, a Woman*, a new Swedish porn movie then in vogue. It spawned many imitations aside from Warhol's homage – *I, a Groupie*; *I, a Virgin*; *I, a Pussy*; finally *I, a Woman – Part 2*. 'It was supposed to be my film but I didn't do much in it,' grumbled Nico. 'I didn't like all these women in it, not at all. Can you imagine, though, to put your murderer in your film? There is a joke about *shooting* there, isn't there? What do I know, I have no sense of humour.'

At the start of the year Valerie Solanas had submitted a script titled *Up Your Ass* to the Warhol Factory. Warhol quite liked it, he said, but lost it somewhere. She started asking for money in recompense. As a settlement she was invited to take part in *I, a Man* and paid a fee of $25. 'She was not in it for long but she was funny, I have to admit. But she was a lesbian, and I don't like lesbians,' Nico lied. 'She had made a manifesto that Viva liked, I think, but I was not attracted to this woman and so I didn't read it. She had invented a society, the Society for Cutting Up Men. I thought this was really a joke. Or it is the sort of thing they did in concentration camps. If she had named it the Society for Cutting Up Jews, would she have been tolerated in New York? I don't think so.'

Nico would not have enjoyed a solitary page of the SCUM Manifesto, though she would have agreed with much of it. She certainly would not sign up for membership, but only because she never joined anything in her life, as a matter of principle ('they only take your money, these things'). In fact she could not join; there was but one member, and that was Valerie Solanas, who liked to keep things that way. Her leaflet starts with the notion that 'the male is a biological accident: the y (male) gene is an incomplete x (female) gene . . . the male is an incomplete female'. She writes that men are superior in one thing: public relations. 'He has done a brilliant job of convincing millions of women that men are women [emotional strength, vitality] and women are men [vanity, frivolity].' Nico knew plenty of men who were vain and frivolous; women, too. She could not make this bold alignment fit into her experience of life. She loved and hated people in turns, as she entered and left their lives (or their apartments). Nico was making a living out of ambiguity; she was the tall, powerful woman with the trousers and the deep, deep voice who hated men and women and desired them both. Valerie Solanas was too clear and categorical, she thought, though Nico was the one who would later write, 'Women are poison. If I wasn't so special, I could hate myself.'

For every cloudless thought that Solanas had, Nico would encounter a paradox. 'Traditionalists say the basic unit of "society" is the family; "hippies" say the tribe; no one says the individual,' wrote Solanas. 'He (the hippie) desires to get back to Nature, back to the wilderness, back to the home of the furry animals that he's one of . . . his time taken up with simple non-intellectual activities – farming, fucking, bead stringing. The most important part of the commune, the one on which it is based, is gangbanging.' Nico herself said, 'I was bored with the hippies I saw. They were supposed to stand for peace and love, but they were fighting about women or drugs. They had flowers in their hair but they looked at me like the men in clubs with drinks in their hands.' She was a resolute individual who couldn't live alone and detested the conventions of the home; yet she looked on communes with the same distaste she felt about shared dressing rooms. She revered her family as long as she could farm them out for care to other people, and she had attempted to erect for herself a phantom family of peers whom she forgot to notify. Yet she was alert to this derangement, and it gnawed at her heart.

Like the reverent Catholic he was, Warhol told Nico to seek solace in *The Imitation of Christ*. This treatise, five centuries old, by Thomas à Kempis, spoke of the Inner Life and, like a fifteenth-century agony aunt's column, gave council on 'inward consolation'. Nico read such advice as this:

> There is little light in us, and even this we easily lose through carelessness. Moreover, we often do not realise how blind we are. We often do evil, and we do worse in excusing ourselves. Sometimes we are moved by passion, and excuse it for zeal.
>
> Keep yourself free from all worldly entanglement, and you will make good progress; but if you set great value on any worldly things, it will prove a great obstacle. Let nothing be great, pleasant or desirable to you save God alone, and whatever comes of God.

On reflection, the SCUM Manifesto may have offered Nico wiser instruction. Warhol, however, loved the idea of Nico studying *The Imitation of Christ* so much that he made a film around it. He and Morrissey had been working on a structural sequel to *The Chelsea Girls*, something aside from *I, a Man*. They wanted to produce a film that lasted a whole day on two screens. They gave it a working title of 'the 24-hour movie', but later called the whole thing *FUCK* and then bowdlerised that to * * * * or, for the benefit of phone calls, *Four Stars*. By the time they had completed the project, in September 1967, it comprised 30 sections, of which *The Imitation of Christ* was the longest and the centrepiece. It lasts eight hours. There is a 100-minute version for existential tourists. The 'imitation of Christ' is literal; the storyline concerns the wayward son of Brigid Berlin and Ondine, who wants to wear a dress to school. Nico sits with the blessed boy (Patrick Tilden, the 'James Dean of the Underground') and reads out loud *The Imitation of Christ*. 'In the eight-hour version, the feeling and mood are established mostly through the silences and spaces,' says John Coplan's film guide. That makes it a very Nico kind of movie, and, indeed, she said that she liked it the best of her Warhol contributions.

A further three sections of * * * *, two of them set around San Francisco, use Nico. One, called *High Ashbury*, is with Ultra Violet and Ondine, and is 'all very flowery, with rock music and people smoking, sitting on the floor; there is little movement'. The other is *Sausalito*, a kind of alternative travelogue, showing the docks and streets of this gentrified suburb, while Nico intones odd lines, possibly from her dream-notebook:

A man is walking on the sea.

The sea is walking.

The sea is after me.

The night grows into the sky.

The light grows back into the earth.

One other section, number 21, is labelled *Nico – Katrina*. It has been viewed only once, alongside the others. * * * * was shown in a full-screen version at the New Cinema Playhouse in New York overnight on 15 and 16 December 1967. The images of the two projectors were superimposed on to one screen for the complete 24 hours (25, in fact). Warhol wrote that, 'At the time I didn't think of that screening as any kind of milestone, but looking back, I can see that it marked the end of the period when we made movies just to make them.' In the future Paul Morrissey and Warhol (no longer the 'producer' but the 'presenter') would make films to make money

– *Bike Boy*, *Nude Restaurant*, *Lonesome Cowboys* and, most successfully of all, *Flesh*. Nico was no use to them to make erotic films – her *Strip-Tease* had disabused her of her talent, and she'd even griped about *I, a Man*. They used instead Susan Hoffman, a sensually photogenic recruit with frizzy hair, 'though Andy preferred me to be called Viva, because my real name sounded Jewish'. Viva was crowned Superstar. She smoothly replaced Nico, who had lasted twice as long in the role as Edie. Yet Nico never considered Viva as a rival. Viva was Nico's opposite, just as Edie had been; Viva was swift-witted, avoided drugs, and she talked and talked – 'Well, she didn't talk, she *complained*,' said Morrissey. Yet Viva, bright as a button, enchanted Nico: 'Viva should have been my sister, she was intelligent which I always respect in women; we were so close in our outlooks.' ('What?' said Viva when she heard this. 'Never, never, never! Nico came from outer space. I came from Leadville, Colorado.')

Nico saw nothing more of her final films for Warhol. '*The Imitation of Christ* I prefer to *The Chelsea Girls* for personal reasons. There is one thing I would suggest when you see it – take a lot of beer, and sit near to the toilet.'

ALTHOUGH SHE HATED HIPPIES, who 'were always trying to sell you something', she finally bought from a San Francisco hippie a very hippie thing to buy: a little Indian harmonium. It was portable in the way a heavy suitcase is portable, but Nico considered it very portable indeed, because she always would find an unhired hand to drag it round for her. She would haul it out of a taxi, look lost and sweaty, and swiftly lure some good soul to lug it behind her. 'It is the kind of organ that Allen Ginsberg uses in his poetry readings. It is used for chanting by the Indians [those in India], and it means I do not have to rely on guitarists, who are unreliable people to work with,' she declared. The trouble was, she hadn't a clue how to play it. She bought the thing because she decided . . . she sometimes decided that Jim Morrison had discovered her, and sometimes that she had discovered herself through Jim Morrison. In whichever way, she chose to be a composer, because . . . he had opened the door, or he had watched her open the door. As she could not write music, and she did not have a band, she concluded that she must learn an instrument and compose directly on that. Then she could play her songs in public and not 'rely on guitarists'. Trust Nico to consider herself a model of reliability.

The choice of a harmonium is so terribly clever that it has been assumed John Cale or some other musical luminary must have suggested it. It was novel; it worked with a bellows; it sustained chords; it had a deep, reedy tone that fitted with Nico's voice; it was portable; it was ethnic and chic and had a religious source (Christian missionaries teaching hymns to Hindus). Above all, it was acoustic. She did not need electricity to play it, not in one of her cuckoo-nest apartments where she would rehearse to everyone's irritation, nor on stage, though the organ would be the despair of sound engineers who had to amplify the thing. Nico became increasingly interested in *natural* materials; candlelight instead of electrics, peyote instead of LSD, walking rather than cab rides. She even changed her diet, thanks to Leonard Cohen, who would watch her sing at the *Dom* and then invite her to meals just to be with her. He never seduced her, except to macrobiotic food, and for the rest of her life she would consider herself a vegetarian, 'except in France, where such a thing is impossible. But then I could provoke them by saying that vegetarianism is a good thing to do because Hitler was one.' Leonard Cohen, unrequited lover of Nico while Nico was a lover of his food, wrote a song about her called 'Take This Longing', with the allusive words:

> Hungry as an archway
> through which the troops have passed
> I stand in ruins behind you
> With your winter clothes
> your broken sandal-straps.

Nico – film star, composer and vegetarian – had returned to New York a deeply serious artist. After eighteen months of drifting, she felt she was in the driving seat for the first time in her life. All she needed now was somewhere to stay, to work. 'She kind of invited herself to move in with me,' Viva recollected. 'I was a new face at the Factory and she moved in – that's how she was. I had a garden apartment on 83rd Street, between Madison and Park Avenues. She thought she was the Queen of Sheba. Nico was a spicy combination of arrogance and insecurity. She tried to take over the house, take it over completely, you have no idea how she lorded herself about. She would get very angry if I had any boyfriends round that she didn't like. She would say, "You can't invite him round anymore." Can you imagine?! You are in your place and you get a house guest that turns into your mother. And then she had this fucking harmonium. She would practise it for hours, simple things, chords – really annoying stuff – for hours on end. She was very serious about it, dreadfully serious, like a Nazi organist. She'd pull the curtains across and light candles around her and do this funereal singing all day long. It was like I was living in a funeral parlour.'

Nico was overwhelmed once more by ambition. This time, she decided, she would not be dependent. She would do everything herself. She would compose the songs, write the lyrics, sing them and accompany herself on the harmonium. She would need to compose new songs, in any case, as much of her old repertoire was written with a guitar accompaniment in mind. Nico now knew, in a manner of speaking, how to work on songs, thanks to Jim Morrison's advice, but she could not play the organ's four-octave keyboard, not at all. That was why 'she would practise for hours, simple things, chords – really annoying stuff'. She was trying in a matter of months to compress the training youngsters were given over years. Nico wanted, as ever, to be perfect. She had learnt from Dylan, Jones, Reed, Cale, Browne, and Morrison that songs consisted of four distinct elements: the words that are set to music, the melody, the harmony that supports it and gives it direction, and eventually the arrangement or instrumentation by which the song is presented to the public. It seems that nobody dared talk to Nico about *rhythm*. She once told a journalist: 'I don't have a sense of time. Time is timeless to me, and I'm not in a hurry to get older. I mean, if I were worried about time, all the time, it would be terrible.'

She could not at first transfer all this knowledge into a practical way of working. There was all this structure, and then there was the notebook and the organ. Nico was too embarrassed to admit her confusion to her ex-lovers in The Velvet Underground. Instead she asked the young, brilliant black composer and 'jazz' improviser, Ornette Coleman, whom she said she'd met around town. Coleman was then devising an abstruse but fertile system of composition called Harmelodics, which has formed the basis of his work ever since. Apparently, he told her that the convention of the keyboard was that the left hand, in the bass half, played the supportive harmony. The right hand, in the treble, played the melody. However, there was nothing to stop this being reversed, and it made sense if the singer was singing low. So Nico used this way of rendering the song, the harmony in the treble and the melody in the bass. She did not explain to Ornette Coleman that the way she played the organ, everything came out low. Twenty years on, Coleman could recall nothing of the conversation: 'That's not to say it didn't happen!'

'HAVE YOU EVER been shot at? I have,' volunteered Nico to a journalist. 'It is not pleasant, especially if you knew my history,' she added, alluding to her father's death. Her claim was strictly true. One day in early November 1967, she was in the Factory with Warhol, Morrissey, her *Imitation of Christ* partner Patrick Tilden, Taylor Mead and others. Sammy the Italian, a friend of Ondine's, ran in with a gun. He made everyone, including Nico, sit in a line on the Factory's famous couch. Warhol's *Popism* continued the story: 'It seemed to me like he was auditioning for one of our movies . . . he started screaming that some guy who owed him five hundred dollars had told him to come to the Factory to collect it from us. Then he pointed the gun at Paul's head and pulled the trigger – and nothing happened.' Taylor Mead told him, 'You're just so absurd, you're not even good.' Nico got up to leave. Sammy the Italian aimed and pulled the trigger. This time there was a bullet.

It hit the ceiling. 'The shot seemed to surprise him too,' *Popism* added; 'he got all confused and handed the gun to Patrick – and Patrick, like a good nonviolent flower child said, "I don't want it, man," and handed it back to him. Then the guy took a woman's plastic rain bonnet out of his pocket and put it on my head.' Nico described what followed in this way: 'He made Andy kneel on the floor with this hat on. I could not believe it. It was like a play by Ionescu. I wanted to laugh, really I did. It was so absurd when he gave this gun to one of us and we gave it back! You see how crazy people act under tension? Taylor Mead finally jumped on his back and the man got out a knife. Taylor ran over to the window and smashed it and shouted for the police to come. The man ran away. It did not get on TV, this story, and I think Andy was most disappointed about that.'

NICO DID APPEAR on TV that month, however, though not on account of Sammy the Italian. A researcher dropped by a screening of *The Imitation of Christ*. He said he was 'hunting for talent', as researchers always do say; he worked for a popular evening magazine pro- gramme called *The Merv Griffin Show*. The researcher fell in love with Nico and found her a spot on the show. She sang one song with her portable organ, and then the urbane host Merv Griffin asked her some questions. Unfortunately, the first was 'Nico, where do you come from?' Nico sat there, mute. 'What exactly was the song about, Nico?' She could not answer. Merv Griffin laughed, uneasily. It was a live show and a few million people were sharing his embarrassment. 'Well, do you have anything to tell us, Nico, anything at all?' She did not. She sat there and stared into space like she so often did. In front of his audience, Merv Griffin called for someone from the production team to come on camera and explain who this Nico was and why she'd been booked. Nobody came. *The Imitation of Christ* – the original, not the imitation – states clearly: 'Avoid public gatherings as much as possible, for the discussion of worldly affairs becomes a great hindrance. Often I wish I had remained silent.' At least on the TV screens of respectable American homes, Nico was seen by all to be the very model of a bountiful, caring Christian. When Christmas, the time for caring Christians to reflect, came, Nico looked back on the past two years and decided that she had been 'discovered' as a Superstar and 'discovered' as a singer. Nevertheless, it was more important to her to recognise that she had discovered herself as a composer. Jim Morrison, she concluded, had led the way, just as Nico Papatakis had led the way to her lessons, and Tobias to her identity. However, she could not decide, she told a Dutch journalist, who it was who made the discovery of – 'my real self, or myself as Nico'. At least she knew the way ahead, as Nico the composer of songs that would 'tell the true stories in dreams'.

11 1968

No Nightingale did ever chant
More welcome notes to weary bands
Of travellers in some shady haunt,
Among Arabian sands:
A voice so thrilling ne'er was heard
In spring'time from the Cuckoo-bird,
Breaking the silence of the seas
Among the farthest Hebrides.

Will no-one tell me what she sings? –
Perhaps the plaintive numbers flow
For old, unhappy, far-off things,
And battles long ago:
Or is it some more humble lay,
Familiar matter of today?
Some natural sorrow, loss, or pain,
That has been and may be again?
            (WILLIAM WORDSWORTH, 1807)

CANDLES. The most profitable store in the world would be a candle shop near Nico, Andy Warhol figured. John Cale agreed: 'Candles. Yes, candles. Candles everywhere. I don't understand the fascination, but I can appreciate the practicality of having them around,' he hinted. The places where Nico lived – other people's places – had perfectly good electric lighting, but Nico insisted on buying batches of candles, planting them around the rooms and burning them instead of pressing a switch. 'It saves money,' she declared, unconvincingly. 'Candles make stars of light. A room is a universe. I can see the world from a distance, microscopically. The candles are my stars. Have you been inside a cathedral? The Notre Dame in Paris? There are thousands of candle lights, stars in the universe of the cathedral. It is so we can understand a feeling of the Holy Mother, Notre Dame. But I use Jewish candles when I can. The Jews have Hannukah, which is the lighting of candles. I will tell you what Andy told me . . . "They say the candle is the penis and the flame is the vagina." No, I told him. The candle is a star, and each star shines for a soul, even his. I would buy candles because they are stars and I am a Superstar. (That is meant to be a joke, you know.)'

The steady flame of a candle is prevailingly used by those devoted to hard drugs to melt the powder or to sterilise needles, and it was commonly assumed that Nico's passion for candles was tied to a more practical use than it really was. The candles were truly her shining stars, the room in which she stuffed them her universe, and she fantasised that the music she played on her harmonium was the music of the spheres ('really annoying stuff,' said Viva). A single candle-flame embodied glimmering images of religion and romance, heaven and hell, dungeons and dragons: 'I think of the church as something of the Middle Ages and candles are my association with that. I think that is my romantic nature. At least I don't think of dinner parties.' The more she was left to her own competence, the more she needed candles. Candles were the physical means of turning someone else's home into hers, into the Chapel of St Nico.

When she left Viva's place early in 1968, after a blistering argument about whose flat it really was, she took over the apartment of another new Factory face, Fred Hughes, and turned it into a shrine to herself, for herself. Frederick W. Hughes, seven years younger than Nico, was an engagingly handsome 22-year-old Texan who struck oil with the de Menil family, millionaires who bought art like Nico bought candles. Hughes toiled for them until he had acquired enough flamboyance to convince folk he was descended from Howard Hughes. He was certainly no fool and ran the art side of things for Warhol while Morrissey ran the films. The two were more like businessmen than bohemians, and they were keen to get rid of the flea-bitten characters that poked around the Factory like hungry dogs. They achieved this in a simple way during February 1968. They closed it down.

Searching for a serious environment, they took over a floor of an office block at 33 Union Square West. Out went the cosy sofas and the silver foil, and in came desks and files; out went the Factory and in came the firm. 'It was like going into a bank, but a bank without money – at least, I never saw any,' alleged Nico. 'What I found amusing was that they shared this building with the Communist Party. I think Andy quite liked this, because he was really socialist-minded. But Paul Morrissey hated communists more than he hated drug addicts. There is a joke there about Marx and marks, no? Well, what do I know, I'm German.' Fred Hughes leased an

apartment opposite the building on East 16th Street. Nico soon
moved in ('Fred doted on eccentrics', Warhol noted, 'and Nico was
a true specimen'). She would draw the curtains, light the candles,
peddle away at the organ and drill her hands to play the sombre
chords that passed for the music of the spheres. For a diversion she
would surround either end of Fred Hughes' bath with shimmering
candles and lie in the tub, allowing her lyrics to float through her
mind even as she floated in the progressively cooling water. She could
lie there for hours on end, beavering away in the bath. She disliked
the damp and generally avoided anything wet, but she was sacrificing
her aversions in order to endure the inspiration of water and fire, in
their union in a bathtub off Union Square. It was a very 1968 way
to compose. Warhol's *Popism* mentioned Nico's stay at the Hughes
address:

Fred was back and forth to Europe a lot. When he arrived at
the apartment one night with all his suitcases, he stumbled
into the living room and found that he couldn't switch the
lights on. He saw a candle flickering in another room around
a corner, and then Nico walked in holding a candelabra.

'Oh, Nico! I'm so sorry!' he said, suddenly realising that
Con Edison must have turned off the electricity. 'I just
remembered I forgot to pay the light bill, and here you've
been in the dark all this time!' 'Nooooo, it's fiiiiine,' she said,
positively beaming with joy. She'd had the happiest time of
her whole life, drifting around there in the dark for a whole
month.

Positively beaming with joy, in the bathtub all night, labouring away:
not normal Nico. If she was beaming more brightly than her candles,
it was because she had found something fertile for her mind. She
had finally become an artist. Up to now she was a celebrity because
some men had photographed her, some men had filmed her, some
men had written songs for her, and one man in particular had made
the others call her a Superstar. Yet now she was in charge. Not only
would she sing, she would control what she sang, and write
significant songs that would inspire the minds of an entire generation, just like Bob Dylan had done: that was how she saw her
mission. 'I did what I was told and I made two singles and two LPs
just as they told me. And nothing happened. Nico [Papatakis] and
Jim [Morrison] had not told me what to do, but I had stood in front

of a door and they had opened it like men are taught in the ceremony of *etiquette*. Then I made the steps myself, and no one was in front of me. Then I have my candle, to let me see inside the dark. Otherwise I am frightened there will be nothing left to see in my mind, and there will be only my body, like Edie. Edie was my warning. When there is nothing left inside for me to make, then I would have to die. I could be a poet or a songwriter, and I continue as this, in a seditious way. But what other way to do these things?'

She knew perfectly well: she considered that there was no other way. She had a guide in the matter, a poet whom Nico would talk about time and time again, yet she could never remember the poet's name. To a journalist in Holland in 1979 she said, 'I like the poems of a German poet who went to America and committed suicide. And there is a man from Boston who is good, but I forget his name now.' On a separate occasion in 1985 she told a writer, 'There is a poet in America who wrote about my childhood. Do you know this poem? I call it "Lazy Lady". Isn't that me?' The man from Boston was Robert Lowell. The poet from Germany who went to America and wrote 'Lazy Lady' was Sylvia Plath. In order to expel the Nicoist fog it is more correct to say that Plath's father came from Germany, and Sylvia Plath, who committed suicide in the London of 1963, wrote a poem – not about Nico, of course, not exactly – called 'Lady Lazarus' ('Out of the ash / I rise with my red hair / And I eat men like air'). This exceptional poem, centred on the Holocaust, informed the stories Nico told others about her childhood or put to paper for her songs, and shaped the style she adopted for her lyrics. In the poem we find everything from Nico's Nazi lampshade to 'the big strip-tease', and the close rhymes she used with her mixture of past and future tenses. She forgot the poem's title and she forgot the poet's name (even gender) because she never liked to reveal her true influences. Warhol said that Nico wanted to write songs like Dylan, but her songs were never remotely like Dylan's, not one; her intentions were similar, but not her style. Nico would never admit to the influence of women – especially Zarah Leander, Dietrich, Hildegard Knef – because women were not valued in the fraternity that surrounded her; that is, they were not valued as creative figures, but as contemplative icons. Nico renounced the good of women for the rest of her life from the moment, on the late afternoon of Monday, 3 June 1968, when Valerie Solanas, Nico's co-star in *I, a Man*, paid a visit to the serious office of Andy Warhol, with two serious guns in her paper bag.

*

SHE ENTERED THE BUILDING alongside Warhol when he arrived at Union Square for a day's work. He thought she was pestering him for some *I, a Man* money, or for the script she'd once left, but they made only small talk as she escorted him to the office. It was when he had sat down at Paul Morrissey's desk and taken over the phone from Morrissey to listen to Viva on the other end that Solanas pulled out her first gun and fired five bullets before it jammed. Viva, from her hairdresser's salon, thought she heard Gerard Malanga cracking his whip. Solanas shot Warhol in the chest, then shot a visitor in the leg, and finally aimed (but only aimed) at Fred Hughes before the gun jammed and the lift opened for her escape. Valerie Solanas gave herself up, far away in Times Square, and said that if anyone wanted to understand why she shot Warhol, they needed only to read the manifesto of the Society for Cutting Up Men:

> SCUM will always operate on a criminal as opposed to a civil disobedience basis . . . SCUM is against the entire system, the very idea of law and government. SCUM is out to destroy the system, not attain certain rights within it . . . SCUM will coolly, furtively, stalk its prey and quietly move in for the kill . . . that is, until enough women either unwork or quit work, start looting, leave men and refuse to obey all laws inappropriate to a truly civilised society. Many women will fall into line, but many others, who surrendered long ago to the enemy, who are so adapted to animalism, to maleness, that they like restrictions and restraints, don't know what to do with freedom, will continue to be toadies and doormats, just as peasants in paddies continue to be peasants in paddies as one regime topples another.

Half an hour after the shooting, Warhol was lying in Columbus Hospital, clinically dead. A surgeon's hard work ('and fate') let him live another nineteen years, 'but he was never Andy again, he was like a silkscreen of himself'.

Nico heard of the shooting from the TV in a flat where she was buying hashish. She ran round to the apartment of International Velvet and her boyfriend. According to Ultra Violet, Nico locked them in, 'drew the blinds, lit all the candles they could find, turned the place into a votive chapel, and stared into the candles, swinging back and forth like Moslem weepers until they heard his surgery was successful'.

Nico considered that account to be 'too dramatical. The candles are true, of course, and we meditated, but I didn't know the Catholic prayers. We meditated until we heard some news from the phone about the operation.' She lit fourteen candles: 'fourteen is my special number. It is just the way it is. Fourteen is half of a month of the moon. It is the number they use for hotels to avoid 13. I am someone who is divided; fourteen is twice seven, which is the number of the perfection of time. I am a Libra, you see, born in the middle of the month, and I am divided so that half of my fate grows like the moon while the remainder dies in a balance, as the moon [waxes and wanes].' Fourteen is the number of letters in the name Christa Päffgen, seven and seven. 'N' is the fourteenth letter of the alphabet; there are fourteen letters in the name she gave her son.

She added that 'Andy had been a real friend to me, and I cared more than some of the others. They dramatised my actions because they like to make fun of caring. They weren't too bothered about the incident. They were nasty. Paul Morrissey said things out of disrespect. Only Fred [Hughes] did not. That is how Catholics are; their confession redeems all their sins – it is too simple. Still, I am glad that Andy was a Catholic and not a Jehovah's Witness. He survived by a blood transfusion. Do you know something bizarre? Andy and Robert Kennedy were shot on the same day, two Catholics. It was like a competition, only I'm not sure who won or lost. Is dying to lose? Is coming back for twenty years of boredom to win?'

Warhol was placed under intensive care at Columbus Hospital, but Nico was afraid to go and visit him there – such places reminded her of Grete. 'Nobody had the right information, anyway. I got the feeling they were glad he was out of the way for a while. I did not dare go to his room. Later, Andy told me that I should have just forced my way in. I must confess that I cannot bear to be in hospitals. There is something unsavoury about them. It is people tempting fate. They are like casinos, these places. I avoid them. I do not like to have my body inspected.'

After Nico's fourteen candles had turned to a crusted pool of wax, she decided to write a song for Warhol. Her imagery came, not from 'the life outside, like Lou Reed's songs', but from 'the life inside'. She decided to write a song only for Warhol, not for public use, 'but then I let it be used in a film by Philippe Garrel which I thought was terrible of me to allow, but after Andy had seen Philippe's film, I recorded the song for my third album, with John Cale playing a piano the best he ever did for me. The song was called "The Falconer".'

The falconer is sitting on
His summer-scented dawn
unlocking flooded silver cages . . .

Father child
Angels of the night
Silver flame
my candle-light.

When she saw Warhol again she felt she was looking at a ghost, 'and I felt removed'. From that moment, she suggested, Warhol became manipulated by business people 'who made millions of dollars from the work we had done. There is not one girl known with the Warhol business now. No more Superstars! Well, there is Brigid Berlin who is now a receptionist – they gave her a job to keep her fat mouth shut. Andy made art, but now his organisation just makes money. This is the times we are in, of course. The money comes in now but it will disappear one day and they will have nothing, not even a reputation.' Nico believed that Andy Warhol was a good artist and much of his work important: 'Look at that series he did of the electric chairs. They are fantastic works, they have a lot to tell us about the sickness of our society. He never did anything like that after he had been shot. That fucking dyke destroyed everything. She let the businessmen in and she turned Andy into a zombie.'

Nico said the shooting was the start of society's vertigo, and that from that moment – the moment, too, of Robert Kennedy's murder – 'everything began to turn bad. It is like you are on a carousel and it starts to go round faster and faster until you are sick.' Her response, she claimed, was to jump off the carousel, but 'not into the outside but into the centre, where it is most controlled. You could see it quite wrong and say "I must leave the city and live in the desert". That is a mistake. They are the same place, that is one thing I know.' She stole the image of the world as a carousel from a Broadway show, *Stop the World, I Want to Get Off* ('It is a good title, anyway'). She continued, 'Timothy Leary said "Drop Out", and this was the solution in America. I didn't like this alternative, because it does not fight against totalitarianism. It lets others fight for you while you are asleep. In America Mr Leary had the students and the Blacks to fight against wrong. America was in Vietnam and making a joke of itself, but it did not change [leave

Vietnam] until the economy said it should change. Europe has better solutions. There is Situationism, which will overtake socialism in the future. And there is terrorism – Andreas Baader [Germany], the Red Brigade [Italy] and the Catholics in Ireland [the IRA], and there are others. That is the alternative that fights, not the alternative that says "Drop Out".'

It is frequently said that Nico was politically dim, but her opinions are never those of a congenital blockhead. She was consistently a nihilist who doted on the absurdity of everything, who supported the Situationists in the Paris of 1968 when they made a fool of society and a revolution out of comedy sketches. Her stand was defined simply by her opposition to convention and her desire to provoke. She preferred socialism to capitalism, communism to socialism, anarchy to communism, nihilism to anarchy – always selecting the alternative to whatever dominated; but nihilism saved her hours of relativist posturing. Pacificism she would follow, she claimed, if it was more aggressive; as she said in 1986, 'Pacificism is OK if you have money.' Money for what she never explained, and she said it when she supposed she had none herself. The trouble with Nico's life back in 1968 was that the finest alternative she found to society came from drugs.

It is unexceptional to claim that the Sixties turned sour when the drugs took hold. Drugs and rock joined armaments as the flourishing industries of the time, but Nico considered the development of a drugs culture to be a wonderful thing to 'liberate the locked minds of people'. Though she spoke in the plural, she really meant herself. By the spring of 1968 Nico was nearing thirty and quite alone. One set of relatives had her mother, another her son. Although she was relieved of her obligations, she was not relieved of her consuming guilt. She had implored friends to supply solutions to problems they could not even glimpse; they heard only half-truths, romantic tales and downright lies, and they failed her. Once they failed her they were discarded. Nico would find someone new, leaving in her wake a scattering of old friends she would remember solely in sentimental moments over a spliff and a bottle of wine. There was no one who'd been around long enough to offer an overview, to stand with Nico in her universe of candles and grasp her world 'microscopically'. She began to seek solace in loneliness. She began to count on new friends for their direct practical help: spare rooms, spartan sex and narcotics. For release from profound problems, she began to rely less on people and more on drugs: the mild hashish ('It helped me to relax, because then I did not smoke cigarettes') and then the hallucinogens: LSD, acid, peyote ('only in California where it is natural') and opium ('to help my dreams, which help my songs').

A lot of her LSD, the acid, came from Ibiza; her friends made it and she took it out of the country to sell it. She could go back to Ibiza as freely as she liked, now her mother was out of harm's way. But neither there nor in America, up to this time, did she taste the one drug with which her name has been eternally associated. Heroin was something she had seen, thanks first to Chet Baker, but not touched. 'It was all around. Once I realised what it was, I saw it so many times. When I started with the Velvets, I wanted to sing Lou's song 'I'm Waiting for the Man', but he wouldn't let me. I guess he thought I didn't understand its meaning, and he was right. And we had the song 'Heroin' which I thought was a provocation. I really took little notice about these things, because they wouldn't let me sing properly. But I have to say that Lou and John took heroin, and the songs were songs of realism. I first tasted heroin in 1968 or 1969, I believe, to test it. I took it by smoking, not injecting – smoking is not so strong. I threw up the first time I took it, but you get used to that. I thought it was too powerful. Heroin is a seduction. It is like loving someone you hate. But it can make you lethargic, and does not help concentration. I would prefer then opium, but I really had little of either then. I was first given heroin by . . . a woman who is a fashion designer. You see? After all, it was a woman who led me astray!'

What a shame that Valerie Solanas shot Nico's little friend; otherwise they might have got along quite well.

WHILE NICO SAT IN THE TUB composing, her first solo LP was released by Verve. The press gave *Chelsea Girl* a reception more tepid than her bathwater. The *Los Angeles Times* echoed everything Nico had feared: 'It is a wanly beautiful collection of nice songs by great writers. It would have been better if the songs were great and the writers nice. You get the feeling that there's a mysterious centre smothered in a sweet coating, but you just can't get deeper. Nico's a classy girl, but they'd sell more Nico if she were naked, if you'll pardon the word, and not hiding behind a string orchestra in a flowerprint dress.' The *New Musical Express* called it 'Joan Baez-like', which didn't annoy Nico as much as *Melody Maker*'s 'in the mould of Marianne Faithfull . . .'. The trouble was, Nico's own acquaintances had better things on offer at the same time, Bob Dylan with *John Wesley Harding* and Jimi Hendrix with *Are You*

Experienced? Worst of all, her debut was eclipsed by another – *The Songs of Leonard Cohen*. 'It's like Nico with whiskers,' observed Andy Warhol; he was not the only one to comment on the similarity between the glacial chanteuse and the young poet who sat there during her shows scribbling in his notebook before 'taking me out to eat macrobiotic food'. Cohen had not sung in public before he heard Nico, and now a year later he was acclaimed by *Melody Maker*'s John Peel for his fresh style, 'a very spare and simple voice. No embellishments'. Leonard Cohen the singer owed as much to Nico as Bob Dylan the singer owed to Woody Guthrie.

Nico blamed *Chelsea Girl*'s flute for her disappointments, but maybe she should have impeached the producer, Tom Wilson, the man on the phone. Little attention was paid to basics – the songs were in a lifeless order, the sequences of key were not considered (the first song in F sharp, the second a semitone lower), and the settings were hackneyed and monochrome. Nico's voice was plonked dryly in the centre without the aid of nourishing reverberation, and each microsecond of Nico's uncertain phrasing was flourished before the public, her head on a stick. The songs themselves were mostly fine. None were by Nico, as the LP was recorded before she'd turned to composing, but she sang some old favourites she knew inside out such as Dylan's song for her, 'I'll Keep It with Mine'. The most attractive of them were those, such as 'These Days', by the elfin Jackson Browne, all of eighteen years old:

> I had a lover
> I don't think I'll risk another
> These days, these days.
> And if I seem to be afraid
> To live the life that I have made in song,
> It's just that I've been losing out so long.

She nearly came a cropper on John Cale's contributions, sprinting round a musical racetrack littered with awkward words ('caricatures', 'recognised', 'rationalisation'), then jumping breathless over rickety hurdles of unsingable lines that appear to be bad translations of gladly forgotten operas: 'Primroses are the jewels that lurk among masks of pleasure that flicker with doubt'); Cale soon improved with age. The album held two unexpected treasures, however. The first came on the end of the opening side, a collaboration between Nico, Cale and Lou Reed ('Nico had the basic idea and we worked it up

– I think,' said Cale). 'It Was a Pleasure Then' carries an inventive arrangement in a modal D pattern that would be classed twenty years later as a 'Laurie Anderson'. It supports a Nico never caught on record before. She extends the words with sinuous melismas, and gracefully handles passages of pure vocalisation, probably remembering her singing lessons – La, la, la, la, la, la, la, la:

> It was a pleasure then
> When we could sit and stare again
> Until the stars fell through
> The cloudy trees unto the grass
> And start to smile with us
> Until they too have tears in their eyes
> And tell us this long tale
> Of how much we must not agree.
> La, la, la, la, la, la, la, la . . .

Nico's stars fell most strikingly to a phrase ascending through a seventh; the entire song demanded of her a range of an octave and a half, and she managed it with a deft conviction, for the song was rooted in the lowest key she had yet been challenged to sing. Her future lay in *low*; D had been a favourite key of Zarah Leander, the singer who made her mother cry, cry, cry.

Most unusual of all on *Chelsea Girl* was the final song, composed by Tim Hardin ('Poor Tim. We called him Tim Heroin'), his 'Eulogy to Lenny Bruce', a simple homage to the 'sick' Jewish comic who had just died. Bruce died of a heroin overdose in August 1966, though a friend argued he'd died of 'an overdose of police'. He'd been arrested at least three times on narcotics charges and five times for obscenity ('I attended the entire show of Lenny Bruce with Policewoman Schnell. During this time the following words were used repetitively: *shit*, bullshit, *motherfucker*, *fuck*, *asshole*. He had stories regarding unnatural acts with animals, including the Lone Ranger and Tonto', a policeman reported). Nico said she'd seen Lenny Bruce a few times in the early Sixties, and she acclaimed him as a 'nihilist philosopher who told good stories, not jokes, which are always cheap things. I can never remember jokes.' It is clear from the recording that Nico cherished the song and what it stood for (to support Bruce then was still a provocative act); this final track was the only one where the voice was awarded special attention in production. On the left channel a guitar plays a melancholy waltz, while entirely on the right Nico is set in half distance with a tight halo of reverberation, crooning with elegance:

> I've lost a friend
> And I don't know why
> But never again
> Will we get together to die
>
> And why after every last shot
> Was there always another?
> Why after all you hadn't got
> Did you leave your life to your mother?

Nico said that she couldn't bear to listen to the song after Warhol was wounded. She knew the dual meaning of 'shot', and she realised finally that 'the song was about my own fate, too'.

Nico's LP had the value of novelty on its side: a Warhol Superstar with a Dylan song. As a 'girl singer', she felt sure there weren't many new records in competition. The top women were consigned by racism to a separate 'Soul' chart, led by Aretha Franklin and Gladys Knight. But to Nico's annoyance, a new album was released the same month as hers by the top folk–pop singer of the day, Judy Collins. Like Nico, she sang a selection of other people's work – some Jacques Brel and Leonard Cohen's 'Sisters of Mercy'. Another young Canadian, Joni Mitchell, wrote a song for this album which Nico considered to be 'one of the most beautiful songs I have heard, though it is too complicated and full of artificial flavours' – 'Both Sides Now'. The combination of clever writing ('I've looked at clouds / love / life from both sides now') and Judy Collins's consummate technique was too much for Nico. From now on, she decided, she would record only her own songs, and they would come from 'somewhere else' inside her.

To write those songs for her next LP, she would have to live off the royalties of the first. Before *Chelsea Girl* was launched, in July 1968, she begged the record company publicists to bear in mind her independence. She insisted she was not merely the Warhol Superstar with a Dylan song, and in a manner of speaking they took her at her word. Verve ('The Sound of the Now Generation') took full-page ads in colour magazines, proclaiming:

NICO. You've seen her in Andy Warhol's Exploding Plastic Underground . . . starring in his 'Chelsea Girls'. They call her the Dietrich of the velvet underground. Nonsense. She's Nico. And you can hear her making the scene on Verve as NICO: CHELSEA GIRL.

Nico loved that subtle touch of 'velvet underground', lower case, but she didn't like to see the Dietrich tag in cold print. She was always flattered to hear the comparison, though she pretended otherwise as she never liked to be compared to other women. The exception was Garbo, who was too mythological to be considered merely human, and who in any case possessed a commendably similar build (it was no coincidence that Fellini and the others considered Nico to look as Swedish as Garbo; nor did the similarity of name miss their attention). But the cover of *Chelsea Girl* showed neither a Dietrich (all legs) nor a Garbo (all face), but the sensational, plaintive ash-blonde Nico of *The Chelsea Girls* (all hair and eyelashes), rather than the positively beaming, red-tinged Nico of 1968. The moody photographs were shot by Paul Morrissey as one more labour of love from her harried manager. It was this melancholy figure on the record cover that first caught the eye of thousands of future Nico fans, male and female. It is the image of Nico that is most readily remembered and most missed. 'It was a good cover,' said Nico. 'It hid the flute.'

The LP launched Nico on a career she was not yet prepared to develop. She was irritated that most people fell in love with her face on the cover and not with her voice on the record, and although she had worked for six months on her own songs, she had nothing on the disc to show for it. It was assumed she would capitalise on the release of *Chelsea Girl* – a few concerts, a TV show – but she disappeared to Europe to earn much-needed money by recording more Spanish cognac ads and doing odd print-model jobs in Paris: 'I missed my opportunity to become more famous than I was as a singer. I am always in the wrong place at the wrong time.' She accepted that *Chelsea Girl* was already something of the past, and her stock of new songs offered her a brighter future. By the end of the year she would compose twelve songs; not as fast as Schubert, but not as slow as Duparc. 'I felt that at last I was independent, and that I knew what independence was.'

Unhappily, the more she felt independent in spirit, the more she grew dependent on drugs.

*

Nico

NICO RETURNED TO NEW YORK in the early summer of 1969, no longer labelled a Superstar but an independent artist. The bouts of inspirational bathing had now palled, and the convalescence of Andy Warhol proved to be more tedious than she had expected. Nico was soon bored with Manhattan. She wandered over to the West Coast for a second Summer of Love. She stayed once again at The Castle, 2630 North Glendower Avenue, near the Griffith Observatory, site of *Rebel Without a Cause*. The owner Jack Simmons was her West Coast Morrissey, a benevolent aide and a phantom manager. From The Castle she phoned her social friend Mama Cass, the jumbo-sized singer of The Mamas and The Papas. 'Oh, Mama Cass, I heard Jim was in town. Do you know where he's staying?' she entreated in her plaintive, little-girl-lost voice. 'How the fuck do I know, Nico? Dammit, I'm not his fuckin' dating agency,' Mama Cass bellowed back.

Nico never saw Morrison again, she claimed, until the day of his death. She met plenty of alternative Morrisons at The Castle, but no one special enough to join her phantom family. 'She stayed a long time because she loved the atmosphere so much,' Jack Simmons recollected. 'She would stay in Bob Dylan's suite when he wasn't around; otherwise she had her own room at the top of a tower, a little place where she felt the most comfortable.' Nico recalled, 'When the sun rises in the tower it is especially beautiful, and at night I had cricket concerts.' She earned her keep mooning around, looking sultry and poetic, just as she had on the streets of Berlin, giving journalists guided tours. 'Jim Morrison once stayed in this room . . . but then, he stayed in a lot of rooms.' As autumn approached and Nico felt nomadic again, an enamoured writer for one of the American glossies slobbered to the world about his Nico-escorted visit in a full-colour spread. Not short of clichés, he called the place an 'electronic Olympus, the hip Versailles, the Taj Mahal of sound, the Rock Castle':

> Nico has run the gamut of all [the Castle's] twenty-two rooms, including the basement compartment which contains an imported Chinese opium den secreted in a wall. After walking out of the kitchen door, we arrive at a goldfish pond in the garden. 'There are five small deer who live down here near the fountain. It's just like living in a forest. And all the overgrown garden, it's like Gothic ruins,' she says wistfully.
>
> 'The Castle used to seem so happy to me,' Nico muses. 'But

now it seems sad. I had some wonderful times here, but I could never live in it again. It is a very unusual place in the world.' If you're planning to move in, bring plenty of friends. As Nico discovered: 'A twenty-two-room castle can be an awfully lonely place for just one person.'

According to Viva, 'Nico took a lot of LSD around this time; she was always a bit "spacey", but she was a *lot* "spacey" then. I remember meeting up with her in San Diego, probably on another of those Factory safaris. She and I decided to pay a visit to the zoo. We were both on some acid that Nico had got with her. First of all we spent ages, absolutely forever, inspecting the trunks of eucalyptus trees. We stood there mesmerised because, once you peeled at the bark you could see these breathtaking greens and rose colours underneath. We were entranced (you can imagine what we looked like, these two lanky Superstars, stoned out of our heads). Then we got to the apes.

'Do you know San Diego Zoo? It's an amazing place. It's a real Californian, liberal zoo. It doesn't have bars and cages. It has little moats. There's nothing but air between you and the animal. So Nico stood there for ages looking at an orang-utan. She's transfixed, just standing and staring because of this hallucinogenic drug. I have to physically move her along, like I'm heaving a block of marble. Then we get to a gorilla. We're staring at this gorilla. The gorilla's got real interested in us, and he starts doing this dancing about and scratching his armpits. Then he falls in love with us, he beats his chest and makes some noises, and moves towards us, right in front of the little trough. I move away, but Nico's glued to the spot. Then the gorilla starts shitting in his hand, and he starts to throw his shit at us. "C'mon Nico, let's move on," I yell at her – we're both getting splattered in this gorilla shit. "Oh no. It's so-oo wonderful. He's in lo-ove with us. He's giving us a token of his lo-ove." "Yeah, Nico, he's giving us the only thing he really owns – ape shit. Remind you of anyone?"

'We left San Diego, deodorised, and I drove Nico the long haul back to Los Angeles – that's the sort of thing you did for Nico, always. We got lost. We ended up in the Black section, Watts. We were really stupid back then, completely disorganised and constantly spaced out. As we used to say, we were *not there*. But, you see, we were two tall, long-haired, spaced-out white Martians. We escaped whatever indignities stupid whites could face in Watts simply because we looked *not there*. We looked somehow *invincible*. I phoned some relatives of mine in Santa Monica to get orientated. They were Danish. We met up with them. You should have seen Nico's face. She fled after one peek at these Nazi-looking Danes. She was so particular about who she met, especially Europeans. She did not hold with the American way: "Howdy pardner, how ya doin'?" Shucks, no, that wasn't Nico.'

Jack Simmons, king of The Castle, encountered Nico in her 'not there' moods. 'She was the most beautiful woman, and you could forgive almost anything she did. She had such a weird take on life. This is typical: I was once doing something in the kitchen, something ordinary like tossing a salad, or mixing some ingredients. Nico came in with her staring eyes, and she studied me doing this basic cookery. I thought she was going to ask me about what I was cooking, or some technical thing. But she just stared, then she finally said, "Oh Joooohn, your haaaands are sooo beau-ti-ful. They're like po-e-try in moooootion." She was so cute, I don't think anyone could say anything bad about Nico. You know, she even drove a car in LA, in this state. One day she knocked at my door. "Oh Joooohn, I was dri-ving my caaaar, and it sliii-thered off the rooooad." Well, where I lived was pretty mountainous, so I was a little worried when I heard this. I walked up around the road with her, and – I couldn't believe it – there was her car dangling over a cliff. The drop must have been two hundred feet. "It sliii-thered off the rooooad." You see, she was in another world. But whatever she did, whatever she smoked, whatever she shot, in every way, in every shape and form, she was a lady among ladies.'

The lady among ladies, drifting away all summer in an acid haze through zoos and kitchens (she called it 'collecting impressions'), had the bountiful comfort of fine patronage. There was Simmons in Los Angeles, Helma in Berlin looking after her mother, and Edith with Didi in Paris bringing up her son. Nico needed all the patronage she could get, because the money was no longer so plentiful as it had been. Record royalties came in lumbering batches, and she was starting to borrow a little money from friends or from the Factory to see her through the odd lean day. She would pay it back as she could, honourably, but the ready money for travel began to become a burden, and the ready money for drugs an irritation. Yet she was still the proud, independent artist with the Superstar face, and she was still constructing her own songs in the tower of The Castle, or wherever else her harmonium was hauled through the lonesome months of composition.

Finally the lady among ladies floated back to the Chelsea Hotel. Thanks to Morrison and Donald Lyons she had acquired a nodding acquaintance with Jac Holzman, who ran Elektra Records. Nico had enough songs of her own to record an LP for the company; Verve had not sold enough *Chelsea Girl* LPs to convince them she had a bright future. As Nico was petrified an Elektra staff arranger might book a flute player, she asked John Cale to orchestrate the songs. He agreed on the condition that he could produce. In effect, his arrangements constituted the production, while the company producer Frazier Mohawk was assigned to oversee the project. Cale had done nothing like that before: 'I was trying to advance my career as a producer because I'd left the Velvet Underground after a disagreement and was looking for a profession. Jac Holzman had Nico under contract and he simply said, "Let's see you go out there and do that album." On the basis of my work on that album, I got to produce The Stooges and never looked back.'

On 2 October, as Nico prepared for the studio sessions, she was shown a newspaper story that froze her to the marrow. Alain Delon's bodyguard had been found dead, dumped in a rubbish tip outside Paris, his body bound, gagged and wrapped in a plastic sack. It seemed to the pathologist that Stefan Markovic, a Serb, had been beaten to death in a fight. Nico phoned Delon's mother. Was Ari safe? Yes, he had been taken out of his regular, local school that very day and driven directly to an isolated private school near Versailles (where he would board until his teens). Nico asked why. 'Family security.' Three weeks later a second post-mortem was held. They found a bullet in the neck of Stefan Markovic. It took a full four months for the press to uncover Delon's real need for 'family security'. The Paris correspondent of *The Times* of London reported on 28 January 1969:

Attention in France centres on the threats to the life of M. Delon and his family. He said on Saturday, after he was released by the police, who had been holding him for questioning, that there had been an attempt to murder his wife Nathalie, who is also a film star. She had discovered while driving in Paris that one of the wheels of her car had been loosened and was about to come off.

The police state this incident occurred on December 19, but was kept secret at Mme Delon's request. The lives of M. Delon and his family have been threatened several times since the case was opened in October.

It seems that as early as mid-November the Yugoslav police warned the French police, through Interpol, that a friend and compatriot of Stefan Markovic was believed to have set off from Belgrade with the intention of killing M. Delon. M. Delon was warned of this and asked permission to carry a gun, but this was refused on the ground that the threat was too vague. He has been given a discreet police guard, however.

A few days later an anonymous letter, posted in Paris, arrived at the offices of Judge Patard and of two Paris newspapers. 'We are going to kill the eight people involved in the Delon affair,' it said, 'and you can tell them that nothing will save Alain Delon, Nathalie, and his child, whom naturally we shall not leave alive.'

None of this was known to Nico when she read of the bodyguard's murder back in October. But she followed the news as it developed through the months, and she couldn't help thinking: if the threats began no sooner than November, why was Ari hidden away so promptly after the body was found, and why was Ari so much in danger? She did not then know that it was the Boulognes who organised the swift transfer. When Alain Delon phoned his mother about Ari's displacement, he pointedly asked who was paying the school fees. Yet to Nico, 'it proved that Alain recognised his son. But it happened because I knew who the murderer was, I believe. It was not the first time it had happened.' Nico was right. In 1965, another bodyguard of Delon's, another Yugoslavian – Milosevic – was found dead in Hollywood. Nico confided to a friend, who remains silent on the subject to this day, that she knew who the murderer was. It was not Delon, she said. However, she was scared what might happen to Ari if she voiced her thoughts.

Nico was scared for the welfare of her son, but she felt avenged that Delon's disposition was so publicly and humiliatingly exposed through a major scandal – a scandal that remained a source of intrigue up to Nico's death and beyond. Nico maintained that she could not use the information she had while both Alain Delon and Ari were alive, but that, if one of them died, she would use it. She hadn't expected that she'd be the first among them to pass away.

The BBC World Service interviewed Delon after he had undergone 48 hours of interrogation by an examining magistrate. He

11 **1968**

denied a new development in the cancerous scandal, that the former Prime Minister of France, Pompidou, was implicated through a dinner party. He then agreed that he had a lot of 'toughs' among his friends. He liked weapons, he said, and had a collection of guns, 'because I think it's a man's object'.

WITH ALL THIS on her uneasy mind, Nico joined John Cale in the recording studio to record nine songs for her 'first real record'. They spent a couple of days with her and the harmonium. They simply recorded what she sang: no drums, no guiding pulse, nothing but a deep voice, her burning candles, the wheezing sound of wind through the organ reeds and the clatter of the foot pedals as she pumped air into the wooden box. The engineer wanted her to record the harmonium part first, so that he could play that back to her while she overdubbed her voice. She couldn't do it like that, nor could anybody else with her peculiar sense of rhythm. The timing of her songs was fixed by her personal sense of tempo; the producer discovered that Nico thought of phrases rather than beats, and there was a rhapsodic manner to her singing and playing that had little to do with rock, folk, country or soul, or even the supposed songs of old Mongolian peasants in Lübbenau.

'We had to record the whole thing first and try and separate the harmonium off later,' John Cale recollected. 'If you compare what she was doing then to other singer–songwriters like Judy Collins, Joni Mitchell or Carole King, Nico was like a European gargoyle. She really was unique. There was nobody doing that sort of gothic folk stuff. It was like something from another age, or another planet. And it wasn't a fashion or anything, she wasn't following some trend. It came from her own determination to create something individual; it came entirely from inside, from resilience. I knew what I wanted to do with the basic track, that wasn't a problem. The problem with Nico was her time-keeping. I was trying to control the session and have her come in at a particular time to do something, like any self-respecting producer will try and do, at least one with a budget to run. I'd say "two o'clock sharp" and she'd arrive at five. Or, she'd arrive at three and spend the next two hours in the bathroom adjusting her make-up. For a recording session! There were only two of us in the studio!

'I said to her once, "I want to start at two o'clock tomorrow. Do I have to go round to your place at ten to make sure? What's the problem? Haven't you got a watch?" She replied, "No. When I was

217

in The Actors Studio, Elia Kazan told me to do things in my own time. I took him at his word." She had this weird logic and you couldn't argue with it – it was just irritating. You might think that her awful time-keeping was offensively unprofessional or an egocentric indulgence. Not so. The timing of everything was immaculate. It was elegant, and everything that was done was done very beautifully – and very late.'

'She could spend hours in front of a mirror, playing with her make-up,' added Viva. 'It wasn't vanity, she wasn't admiring the length of her nose or anything, it was fear of being seen beyond the mirror less than perfect. She'd been perfect for years in front of the camera, and now there was no camera between her and the people. It was real life from now on.' Nico herself said that the reason she appeared to be late on the set of *La Dolce Vita* was because 'I was not correct for the camera. This was the problem of Marilyn Monroe, too. She told me this. It is a question of imperfection, having not everything in place.' Nico could not bear to be seen undressed, for dress was as much her disguise as her stories. Her face had to be dressed, too, even for the microphone.

'When she was ready to sing something, it was better to let her go her own way,' Cale considered. 'She had an internal clock. It was great for *The Marble Index*. This freedom allowed me *carte blanche* to bring in and develop all this European stuff that I was happy with. I was as surprised and shocked by the results of *The Marble Index* as anyone.' (*The Marble Index* – fourteen letters.)

Nico did not know what would happen to her songs once she had sung them; Cale did not allow her into the sessions of arrangement that succeeded her singing. As far as she was concerned, her songs were finished, enclosed and whole once she had left the studio, before he got to work. John Cale was amazed by her preparation: 'She'd written all the words down. They were clear on paper, in that spidery gothic script of hers. But I never saw a manuscript with a lot of corrections on it. I only saw – like, if she would be sitting down and writing something, I'd sneak a look (I think she would have hated that, had she caught me), and there was no crossing out. A lot of thought, an awful lot of thought, had been given to it before it went down on paper. That's remarkable, when you think of her working in an alien language. And once it was down there, it wasn't changed. She was very confident in her style.'

She had followed Jim Morrison's advice and made notes of her dreams, often opium-fed like those of Coleridge. The images nourished the words, but the words she chose came from the published poetry of old Romantic England and new-leaf New England: Coleridge and Lovell, Blake and Plath. The LP's name was stolen from William Blake, but some of the song titles – 'Facing the Wind', 'Roses in the Snow' – sound like those of Sylvia Plath ('Crossing the Water', 'Poppies in October'). Nico did not consciously copy this work, but phrases such as 'numberless reflections', 'crucial parody', 'master's voice cascades', 'dim and stale', 'titanic curses' did not tumble out of dreams or the Little Gem German–English Dictionary. Others did, however: 'thrown a joke on you', 'I mind not facing the wind', 'the game comes to a start', 'vanish from my glance'. John Cale didn't think they mattered that much anyway: 'I didn't pay close attention to her lyrics, they mostly addressed the *atmosphere* of the song.'

Paul Morrissey was more forthright. 'She'd play me her new records with her songs on, and I had to say, "Oh, Nico, these songs are so *hard* to listen to! I don't think anyone else can sing these songs, and I don't know that you can either." She was very diligent about the lyrics. She'd write them down carefully, these little lyrics in her beautiful handwriting, but I don't think her thoughts were ever clear in them, though they were never less than interesting. Her ideal was Bob Dylan, I guess, and there's a lot of impenetrable mush in *his* songs. When she started composing, Bob Dylan was considered the Greatest Talent That Ever Hit The Face Of The Earth. The line went: Shakespeare, Goethe, Tolstoy, Proust, Bob Dylan – and that was a kind of ascending evolution as far as the fans were concerned. He acted mysterious, he didn't go out in public, he was creepy. And that's why he fascinated people. By acting this way he caught people's attention and they idolised him for it. Nico probably thought, "Dylan is where it's at". She went into her drug cocoon, made sounds, wrote lyrics and sang them. In her mind she was Bob Dylan.'

That may explain the way she went about things, but not what she did, which was nothing like Dylan. He was then playing with the Country world of Nashville, but Nico's melodies came from a different country entirely. 'My melodies are from the Middle Ages,' Nico told a journalist. 'They are from my Russian soul. I do not mean this literally, but they are that in my imagination. John Cale said that they are not tonal. They do not come from our key system. They are too old in their arrangement.' Her melodies are modal, often aeolian, with flattened sixth and seventh degrees (that was what she meant by 'arrangement', the form of the scale). Plainchant is modal, as are many folk tunes and composed mediaeval pieces. When critics used the word 'gothic' to describe Nico's work, their choice was prompted by musical associations, had they but realised it.

In the year of Nico's birth, a Nazi composer called Carl Orff presented a huge work for chorus, soloists and orchestra that used fake mediaeval, modal tunes to set archaic texts on sex and sin titled *Carmina Burana*. It was probably the only piece of new music the Nazis ever acclaimed, because it 'reached back to the cultural roots of the nation'. This farrago, a cheap dilution of the style of Stravinsky, remains worldwide the most popular piece of modern concert music. Nico's melodies sound like the modal confections of Carl Orff, which were themselves styled out of rudimentary 'national' folk song material. They may have arrived in her mind from mediaeval Russia, but she picked them up at *volkslied* classes in the schoolrooms of Lübbenau. The beautiful, lucid, scale-driven tunes she composed are formed as much from her Nazi cultural heritage as the images of frozen borderlines and the Nibelungenland. It's a curious fact of cultural segregation that the type of melody that is consistently popular in a concert hall is considered chronically weird in a rock club.

The simplest song on the LP is the first, 'Lawns of Dawns' ('I cannot understand the way I feel / Until I rest on lawns of dawns'). It merely runs up and down the lower slopes of the modal scale, back and forth like a round dance: 'a *Ringelreihe*, *Reigentanz*, a round dance, one has an image of children dancing in a ring like a *blumenkranz*, a flower wreath,' she wrote in her notes. The most complex is the second, 'No One Is There' ('Some are calling, some are sad / Some are calling, mad'), but complex because the basic melody transforms its line and there is a middle section, contrasted not by mode or key but by metre – many of her songs use triple rhythms, which are uncommon for the period. It is the first glimpse of a sense of internal organisation. Once, at a concert some years later, Nico introduced this song to a baffled crowd with the comment, 'I wrote this for Richard Nixon.'

Two songs stand out from this singular album – songs as songs, rather than songs overhauled by John Cale. First there is 'Ari's Song', which is little less than a crib of William Blake's 'The Land of Dreams' (Awake awake my little boy / Thou wast thy mother's only joy . . . The land of dreams is better far / Above the light of the morning star):

Sail away, sail away my little boy
Let the wind fill your heart with light and joy
Sail away my little boy,
Let the rain wash away your cloudy day.
Sail away into a dream
Let the wind sing you a fantasy
Of the ancient silver sea.

Now you see that only dreams
Can send you where you want to be . . .

This unworldly lullaby to her son might be considered an indulgence, with its greeting-card sentiment, were it not for the circumstances at the time of its recording. 'You'd think she'd want him around, not to send him away,' remarked one of her Nico-teen fans. Quite.

The other song was singled out by Jackson Browne, among others, as an exceptional melody and an atmospheric ballad. 'Frozen Warnings' embraces the 'cloudy borderline' of her repeated dreams with an ominous image of Lübbenau ('Over railroad station tracks / Faintly flickers a modest cry'):

Into numberless reflections
Rises a smile from your lips into mine,
Frozen warnings close to mine,
Close to the frozen borderline.

These were the songs that Nico handed over to John Cale to 'arrange'. He started with their structure: 'All I had to do was shape them up a little, add punctuation, get an A-B-A form around them with introductions, endings, or interludes. Everything else for me was a matter of logic. The first problem to overcome was the harmonium. It was not exactly in tune with itself, or with anything else. Its notes were "in the cracks" – getting a guitar to play along with it was a bloody pain.

'Sometimes we had to varispeed it via the tape. The best solution was to ignore it or, rather, use instruments that were *consistently* out of tune with it. The guitar would be in and out of tune with it all the time – really annoying – so I used instruments that your ear could accommodate because of their consistency. The viola was useful in this way because of the long notes and drones I could play on it to set up the tuning right from the start, like in "Frozen

Warnings". Then I used "noises" to vary the texture. Each song needed fresh detail, and I had to present contrasts of pitch as well as timbre. I wanted to highlight an extreme of range – I just had to do something to leaven out the unrelieved low chords of the harmonium. Bells were best. That's where the glockenspiel and the piano came in at the head of the album, a little prelude to establish the extremes of texture. All the rest was assisted by the nature of the songs.'

Given the scant time in the Manhattan studio, John Cale's attention to detail was remarkable. He gave Nico's songs more than the kind of vapid orchestration that Stravinsky liked to call 'with colouring added'. The multiple violas on 'No One Is There' blur the harmonic field for the sudden switch into 'Ari's Song', dominant to tonic, and the same chord is transferred from violas to the highest, wheezing pitches of the harmonium, a mouth organ, and a bosun's pipe ('Sail away, sail away my little boy'). Then there is the magical choice of viola harmonics to encircle 'Frozen Warnings'. It is the album's only song in a mode (known as mixolydian) with a sole lowered seventh, which Nico centred on C – by chance, the bottom string of the viola. This gave Cale the opportunity to make full use of the natural harmonics of the strings he bowed.

'I was pretty much left alone for two days,' commented Cale, 'and I let her in at the end. I played her it song by song, and she'd burst into tears. "Oh! It's so beautiful!", "Oh! It's so beautiful" – you know, this is the same stuff that people tell me, "Oh! It's so suicidal!" We'd had some fights during the session, some nonsense about opium, for instance. We always had fights, physical at times. But at the end of all this, it was a wonderful moment of relief, and, for her, the realisation she had made something extraordinary. This crying–fighting business happened on every project we did together. Twenty years later, when I produced her final album, the first thing I said to Nico was, "OK, let's have the fight now, then the tears, get it over with while we're sober . . . and then get down to the music." '

NICO HAD MADE the music she had dreamt of. For the first time in her life, Nico the independent artist felt happy to talk to the press. The press was not too keen to talk to her, however – she was a she and not in a group. Nico was not Nice, nor The Grateful Dead, Blood, Sweat & Tears, Blind Faith, Steppenwolf ('That is a book by Herman

Hesse – it is a little better in German'), Pink Floyd, Led Zeppelin, Traffic, nor the New York Rock & Roll Ensemble. Events had overtaken her; everything was getting bigger, wider, louder – hair, flares, coats, heels, groups, planes, drugs, fury. Therefore, she welcomed the chance to talk to the German magazine *Twen* about her life to date. The interview remains a comprehensive source of her views at the time; the impressive interviewer must have compiled *Fragebögen* in her youth. Nico thought that her mother and Aunt Helma would see it and be proud of her. She especially liked the idea of talking to *Twen* because it was a magazine for women in their twenties and Nico had just turned 30:

Have you been in Germany since the Fifties?
I've just been only to visit my mother. She lived in Spain but then she became very ill. We are good friends. I have a son who is going to be eight in August. His name is Christian Aaron. I call him Ari: that means 'little lion'.

What is his family name?
He has my name because his father is too proud to accept him.

What is your family name, then?
Why should I tell you? It's not important. I have this or that name. I know it's illegal that way, but I don't care.

I'm sorry. But who is the father of your son?
Alain Delon. At that time he was at the zenith of his career. Now he is in such reduced circumstances that I'm almost ashamed that he is the father of my child. I don't think he knows what he's doing any more. When I was pregnant I was living in New York. I was very glad about the baby. It is a wonderful experience for a woman to have a child. It was very difficult to provide for Ari. I had to take him everywhere. This is not the life for a child. When he became ill two years ago I brought him to his grandmother, the mother of Alain Delon. She is a wonderful woman and she totally opposes the behaviour of her son. Ari is now living with her and goes to a school near Paris. He needs this kind of care, because he is a wild child. He would become a criminal if he didn't live with a sense of order.

Your songs seem to be torn from your soul.
Yes, I've already thought about that, too. My songs are not personal. But then I can't identify myself with anything at all, not even myself. I am nomadic, like in my song 'Frozen Warnings'. That's probably my favourite track on the record.

How did you get into music?
Through Bob Dylan, who I met in Paris six years ago. I started to sing all his songs – 'When the Ship Comes In', my favourite, and 'The Times They Are a'Changin' ', 'Mr Tambourine Man', of course, and 'It Ain't Me, Babe' . . .

Have you seen him recently?
He's retired. He's making a family. I can't blame him. What else can he do now? When you've spent your whole life as a tramp, it's going to get pretty cold outside after a while, and you get fed up with being outside. He can live a family life and still make enough money. So that's how he lives.

I believe you know Leonard Cohen, too?
Yes. I'm a little afraid of him. He always behaves in an odd way to me. Every time I see him I have to put him straight. He always imagines that I would be the ideal girlfriend for him, that I should become his wife or something. I don't like talking about it, but he makes no secret of the fact himself. I like him as a person, so long as he doesn't proposition me.

You've done so many things and collected so many experiences. How much is planned and how much unforeseen?
I never think about that. Things happen. Really. I have no motives. When I tell you I became a songwriter, I don't mean that I intended to do it. One day I had a song and that was the beginning. Everything happens somehow. There are no coincidences, it is all predestined. I am very fatalistic.

What do you hope for in the future?
Don't think I'm conceited, but I hope that I will succeed in expressing all my thoughts and myself either in music or in film. That through that, things will change.

Nico was probed about her notions of a career. She replied that she had no motives: things just happened, she said, there were no coincidences, only fate. With these words she escaped her responsibilities, just as she had escaped the funding of them. However, her strongest emotion was one of pride. She told the reporter she had survived ('I've often felt it was senseless to go on living'). She believed that now, at the age of 30, she could make no more bad decisions, because she'd done everything wrong already. She had decided to reconcile herself to her mother, and finally to make amends for the mistakes she had made. She would go to Berlin and do this . . . as soon as she found the time. Nevertheless, as John Cale pointed out about Nico's sense of timing, 'everything that was done was done beautifully – and very late.'

12 1969–1973

Full oft the riddle of the painful earth
Flash'd thro' her as she sat alone,
Yet not the less held she her solemn mirth,
And intellectual throne.

And so she throve and prosper'd: so three years
She prosper'd: on the fourth she fell,
Like Herod, when the shout was in his ears,
Struck thro' with pangs of hell.

Deep dread and loathing of her solitude
Fell on her, from which mood was born
Scorn of herself; again, from out that mood
Laughter at her self-scorn.

'What! is not this my place of strength,' she said,
'My spacious mansion built for me,
Whereof the strong foundation-stones were laid
Since my first memory?'

But in dark corners of her palace stood
Uncertain shapes; and unawares
On white-eyed phantasms weeping tears of blood,
And horrible nightmares,

And hollow shades enclosing hearts of flame,
And, with dim fretted foreheads all,
On corpses three-months-old at noon she came,
That stood against the wall.

(from 'The Palace of Art',
ALFRED TENNYSON, 1836)

B Y THE AGE OF 30 Nico had progressed in looks from a princess
to a peasant. It had been a sluggish journey, starting with hair
tinged a pale strawberry to please Jim Morrison, to the boots
of Spanish leather she continually wore, then working in from either

end to effect a seamless mood of rustic grace ('She'd smell like a pig farmer sometimes, she washed so little,' grumbled Viva). Nico was still obsessive about the *effect* of her appearance, and when she spoke to an American magazine in March 1969 she advised others to follow a simple rule: 'Simple means elegant, black means dramatic, simple and black means elegant and dramatic – this is a good foundation. I have even tried perverse combinations, such as black with brown leather which I created in my look. Because it was simple it worked, and you see it everywhere now.'

Nico had turned Tarot cards and tossed coins to find the answer to her overwhelming problem: 'How could I look mature without looking older?' The cards and coins gave her the perfect answer, she decided, one that, miraculously, fused with Dior's latest line in the season of late 1968 – the 'Pioneer' look. 'It is good to look to the East, but not to look fake. I like Indian clothes to look at. The sari is a combination of practicalness and sensuality, but if a European woman wears it, she looks as though she belongs to one of those religious sects that bother you for money on street corners. It is a big mistake to steal ideas from other races. It is not a *hommage*, it is imperialism. My solution is to underline my Russian-ness. I think it makes me look as though I am from another world or another time, which is quite true. I don't mind being a foreigner wherever I am. It means I don't have to pay taxes.'

The boots of Spanish leather truly came from Spain: 'She wore these big, thick, brown boots,' Viva recalled. 'I got a pair, too, when she showed me this place. It's a great shop. The boots are custom-made. The cobblers make a drawing of your feet onto paper, and they keep this line drawing of your foot on hand in case you want to write in for more boots. They've probably still got her feet marked out on a piece of paper somewhere, waiting for her call. She trudged around in these beautiful big boots into which she'd tuck long, loose pants, looking like a Dior cossack out of *Doctor Zhivago*. She wore capes, and she may have worn a shift over the pants, but not a skirt – there was still that masculine slant. Did Nico *ever* wear a dress? I doubt it – not since she was a child. That must be the only difference between Nico the kid and Nico the grown-up kid!'

Nico considered her new image to be a refreshing variation of the healthy, outdoor look that won her work and fame a decade earlier. It was not the look of a woman who actually spent her days and nights in funeral-parlour apartments or the back room of Max's Kansas City Bar, the Factory's favourite night-time haunt. She wanted to hide the hours spent in front of the organ pump and the mirror. If Nico wanted Manhattan to believe she'd breezed in fresh from another world, stark pastoral dress was just the thing, for the countryside was quite another world to New Yorkers. 'How I looked made an effect on how I was treated; this is a cliché which everyone knows. But I wanted to have respect, and that was why I chose to be independent in my look. It is hard to find a look that does not pander to expectation – I mean, that is the cheapest thing to do – but I wanted in some way to have allure and have dignity. I was no longer a mannequin but an artist. I wanted men to touch my records, not my bottom. (Ho, ho, ho, ho, ho.) And it was important to have a strong image, or an image that was confident, with all that was going on around me. I accept destruction, and there was everything destroyed everywhere. It was considered the end of a decade, and so it was predictable. But it was really the start of the fight against the death that was already in the society of convention. Did you notice that the violence is that of the cities? Paris, Los Angeles [Watts], Chicago, and also Berlin. I like cities best when they are burning and empty.'

A French journalist probed her sternly about the Paris revolution of May 1968, and all that followed: 'Of course, I was there and followed the events [this is not true]. It is not the unions I follow, because I am not in a union – what union could I be in? The Union of Models or the Union of Protest Singers? I follow the Situationists, which is only surrealism brought up to date. It is a good bohemian reaction. Jim Morrison tells me that people are looking at the streets while I am looking at the moon [this is a mutation of an Oscar Wilde saying]. I do not feel connected enough [with the issues] to throw stones at a policeman. I want to throw stones at the whole world.' She later said that Situationism pointed out the absurdity of life, and nihilism the absurdity of death. Everything else, she supposed – everything meaning Vietnam, Biafra, the Manson Family murders, the terrorist bombs, the protest marches, the assassinations of Warhol, Kennedy, Malcolm X, King – everything else was a sign of repressive authority thrashing around through the last days of its life. 'I will be happy if it ends,' she claimed, 'for the sake of my child. Otherwise, it means nothing to me. I have nothing to gain or lose. I wish to be independent and not make demands.' Aunt Helma and Mama Edith would have been relieved to hear that.

AS SOCIETY'S REBELLIONS passed her by, she waited for the moment – any moment now, she told John Cale – when *The Marble Index* would hit the shelves of the stores and ears of the music critics. She would then earn her dues as the equal of Dylan. In March 1969, it was released as planned and the critics were of one mind – she is *weird*. Wherever she was reviewed, Nico was placed in sections at the rear; in particular she was coupled with a new offering, *Born to Be*, from the fey Melanie. The remarks of Anne Marie Micklo of *Rolling Stone* were typical:

> Melanie reflects the confusion of an adolescent situation with much detail and little mercy . . . Somehow you can't really feel sorry for Melanie (she's 22, not 15) . . .
>
> How refreshing then, you feel, it will be to turn to Nico, whom you presume has been everywhere, seen it all, and is not about to react with grief-stricken pleas for help with any part of it. As a matter of fact, she doesn't react with anything. To anything.
>
> *The Marble Index* is hardly rock, though it exhibits sound trips that have found their way onto many a rock record – electronic chamber music, various sound effects, instrumental Gregorian chant. It's mood music, with an obscure and elusive text recited over it.
>
> Along about the next to the last song on the first side ('Ari's Song'), you begin to develop a faint suspicion that perhaps the words are not what's important after all. The harder you try to hold them (like the natural state of affairs with things in the universe), the more easily they escape. Once you're on to this, you're home free, and side two is a really worthwhile venture into musical infinity (or at least a try at it). It's mood, escape, consciousness, unconsciousness, vacuity, yes, Wonderland.
>
> . . . What remains to be seen is whether both Nico and Melanie can get beyond the fingering stage to a valid (for Melanie), consistent and believable (for Nico) realization of the moods that they've established. Nico seems to be running far ahead . . . unless, of course, you're one of those Who Think Young.

Nico despaired of reviewers whose views were as opaque as her own; the notion that a venture into 'musical infinity' could be made more 'believable' is an especially testing one. Nico's verses, however, proved to be an evident stumbling block everywhere ('I can't make out a single real word,' admitted *New Musical Express*). John Cale had persuaded her not to have the lyrics printed on the record sleeve, as 'it would take away her mystery', though he might have suspected they would not survive exposure in cold print. The strongest support came from *Melody Maker*'s Richard Williams, who presciently noted that '*The Marble Index* is one of those records which just might in ten or twenty years' time be regarded as some sort of milestone . . . the LP is a journey through a landscape not unlike Berlin, where she lived as a child: desolate and wind-blown, scarred yet futuristic.' Nico did not relish the thought of waiting ten or twenty years for milestone royalties. Despite the faint and flickering praise and the merely tolerable sales, the record's release decidedly turned her without delay into a cult figure far beyond the fringes of the 'happening' scenes. She was no longer Warhol's Superstar, she was the Lonely Chanteuse, the Ice Queen and, for the first time in print, the Moon Goddess. 'The problem was that Elektra had no idea how to sell the record. A lot of opportunities were missed. But I did not have a manager and I didn't know what to do.' She complained to John Cale, who simply retorted, 'Nico, how do you sell suicide?'

Nico's fellow artists promoted their records with concert tours, but Nico had neither manager nor agent to plan them. There was a demand she could not meet; promoters in faraway cities had no idea how she could be contacted, while a lingering fear of the Blue Angel 'hey baby' tone of their clubs discouraged her from trying. And now she had determined that there would be no guitarist by her side when she walked on the stage. A solo act, she could hide only waist down behind her Indian organ, and that was it. Nico knew she had to make an effort to perform but relied on local friends and friends of friends to give her work. Even then her insecurity took hold and she would dodge the opportunities. 'She was a big bag of nerves on these occasions,' Viva remembered. 'She could never rehearse enough, but she didn't have the rigor to do it with any method in mind. She didn't have what it took to go out there and perfect her art because she was too fucked up. But instead of saying "I'm fucked up", she made it a virtue. If something went wrong she'd say "I'm too good for this!"'

'She was supposed to do a show at The Scene, which I think the owner Steve Paul had arranged for her. At the time I had a column in *Downtown* magazine under my real name of Susan Hoffman (I would give myself rave notices). So, I went along to review the concert. She came on, played o-n-e note on her little organ, looked around and walked off. She didn't like the way someone looked; the audience wasn't worthy of her great art. So I had this review to do and like a dedicated journalist, ha ha, I did it. I reviewed the audience, just like Nico had: "We witnessed a young woman at the other table masturbating with a vibrator while Bishop Sheen walked by making eyes at Huey Newton . . ." I just made this stuff up. It shocked the readers, of course, but in those days we would just do anything. You have to remember this: we took nothing seriously. Not in those days. Not a thing, anything, not at all. Nico, on the other hand, started to take *everything* seriously.'

Aware now that the rocky road of music was steeper than she had supposed, Nico suddenly decided she had neglected the cinema too long. She had done nothing for eighteen months. She had made ten films to date and now it was time to make more. But Warhol was doing nothing while Morrissey was producing 'pornography' with Viva. Nico was a determined woman, however, and, as always under these circumstances, she hit lucky. Her old friend from the early Sixties, Tina Aumont, was working on a film in Paris, *Le Lit de la vierge* ('The Virgin's Bed') with Zouzou and a counter-culture matinée idol called Pierre Clémenti, a young man who had just made a name for himself as Catherine Deneuve's seedy devotee in Bunuel's *Belle de Jour*. The intriguing young director, Philippe Garrel, was hunting for a sound score and chose Nico in her *Marble Index* mode. It was for this film that she proposed, with misgivings, her 'Warhol' song, 'The Falconer'. From this overture she spent the next nine years with Garrel, for good or ill, and mostly ill.

Garrel was three years younger than Nico but no less *weird*. 'He looked like Laurence Olivier doing Richard the Third,' Paul Morrissey quipped. 'He was all hair with a pointed nose sticking through. You thought he should have been surrounded by snarling hounds and a raven on his shoulder. But he was terribly quiet and slightly pretentious – just the sort of person Nico would fall for then, of course.' Pauledith Soubrier remembered when Nico first brought him to meet Ari and Mama Edith: 'There was nothing to see above his neck but an immense mass of dark hair. My mother looked at this figure standing there, went right up and swept the hair from the centre across either side of his head. She tugged the hair aside like it was a pair of curtains, to look at the face. He was very bony.'

Philippe was the son of the distinguished screen actor Maurice Garrel; he made his first film when he was sixteen and by the time he was 25 had directed six feature films – none of them having had a public run, it must be said. Garrel's greatest moment came in 1968. His film *La Concentration* showed a young man and woman locked in a concrete room where a solitary tap drips blood. The young woman was Zouzou and the man Jean-Pierre Léaud, Truffaut's most regular regular. In the aftermath of the May revolution in 1968, the film summed up for many students the anguish of the time. 'If it is a claim to fame, Garrel was more *avant-garde* than Godard. By that I mean he could be even more boring,' one critic mocked.

With his talent for impelling others to shoulder his burdens, Garrel thrived as Nico had. He admitted that in the early days, 'I never had a producer. For *Le Revelateur* ['The Revealer'; 1968] a young woman friend of the painter Martial Raysse of the Nice school sold a portrait by Raysse to finance my film. *Marie pour Memoire* ['Marie, for the Record'; 1967] was financed by Claude Berri in return for the help I gave him during *Le vieil homme et l'enfant* ['The Old Man and the Child'] on which I was a trainee.' Soon after that he met a rich young woman who lusted to be a patron of the arts. Garrel wanted to do a project with Clémenti, he told her, and she jumped at the chance to pay for it: 'With *Le Lit de la vierge* I made my first normal shoot, three months with a modern camera, complete technical crew, location work, lighting, full cast. At the same time, I was shooting without a script, improvising – and it worked. My films weren't being distributed, but I didn't care. Henri Langlois liked my films and showed them once a year at the Cinématheque in Paris and I was happy with that.'

At the end of the shoot Garrel met Nico in Paris to talk about her music. They talked about more than that, and flirted. In return for using her music, Garrel recounted, 'she took me to New York and showed *Le Lit de la vierge* [with her 'Warhol' song] to Andy Warhol. He said it was very good, and in return showed me *The Imitation of Christ*.' As *The Virgin's Bed* lasts under two hours, and *The Imitation of Christ* lasts more than eight, it may have been more or less than a compliment that Warhol returned. Garrel considered the Warhol epic to be 'quite pretty'. He decided then and there that he would also make a big film about Nico, 'more ambitious than all the others'. Nico told him how Andy Warhol had presented *The Chelsea Girls* for a regular run in a New York commercial cinema. The public had come to see it, she claimed, and she advised Garrel to try the same thing in Paris: 'I had then to make a film with this objective in mind. I made this film for her, in four different locations: Death Valley in America, Egypt, Iceland and Italy. It took two years.'

NICO, STRIVING TO BE deadly serious and aesthetic when everyone around her was acting 'decadent and frivolous, like a party at the end of the world', sought a soulmate who would toil with her and contemplate the meaninglessness of existence, just as she'd seen wracked artists do in real films. Garrel was the very man she sought, she decided, an avant-gardist down to his boots of Spanish leather – imagine! A man even more boring than Jean-Luc Godard!

Viva was there at the start of the romance: 'First of all we're talking about a time which is very hard for anyone to remember anything about – the end of the Sixties, the start of the Seventies, there is general amnesia. As the saying goes, "If you can remember it, you weren't really there." So, I had finished doing *Midnight Cowboy* and I was due to do a film with Agnès Varda, when I had to go to Paris at the request of Pierre Clémenti, who was a hot shot. I went with Nico and when we got there, Pierre was already in a nuthouse in Italy. And Nico said she was going to Italy too in a week or so, so let's go together and visit Pierre. They were going to release him soon – he had another film or two to do [Bertolucci's *The Conformist* and Pasolini's *Pigsty*]. And then there was some other actors with us, like Jean-Pierre Kalphon, Valerie Lagrange, Babette Lamy. A gang of them seemed to have houses in Grottaferrata, just outside of Rome, so Nico and I went to stay there. I remember something about Tina Aumont throwing suitcases out of a window . . .

'Anyway, it was in Grottaferrata that Nico met up with Philippe Garrel, probably for the first *extended* time. I was being pursued by a photographer called Michel and I was kind of interested. Nico said to me one day, "Why aren't you with Philippe? Why Michel? Michel's a nobody. Philippe is an up and coming film director." It wasn't so much careerism on her part, because I don't think she was really that aggressive, though she was competitive. But it was a matter of status. He was supposed to give her intellectual prestige. She wanted to be with someone who was a serious artist, because she herself wanted to be known as a serious artist, too. I can't remember if he was free at that moment, or she had to get rid of someone else first – well, that wouldn't have been hard for Nico, she just had to stare at them. That's how and why she got her man. But why do I remember Tina throwing suitcases out of a window?

'Oh! Yes, Tina and Babette were having a feud and Tina decided she must follow Nico and I into Rome to see Pierre. So we ended up in a room at this hotel near Piazza Navona that was half lodging and half whorehouse – Pierre Clémenti has sent us there, the guy in the nuthouse. There was no electricity, only kerosene heaters with blue tongues of flame leaping out to burn the bed sheets. And there was my photographer, Michel, who followed us to Rome. He thundered down the street in his car and yelled to me "Get in!" so I did, I was so sheepish. I brought him back to the room, and like all men I ever brought back, Nico hated him, hated him, hated him. She was so moody around this time, the great artist with a permanent PMT – there was all this scorching aspiration, scorching away like the bed sheets. So Nico was affronted and moved across the hall. This was just as well, as I married Michel (who is now married to the artist Cindy Sherman). Michel and I stole back to Las Vegas together so I could do the Agnès Varda movie [*Lion's Love*] and he suggested we should go back to Italy to honeymoon, but keep away from Nico and Tina and all that, so he suggested Positano. Do you know about Positano? You should.'

John Steinbeck knew Positano: 'Positano bites deep. It is a dream place that isn't quite real when you are there and becomes beckoningly real after you have gone.' Round the corner of the coast south of Naples, its labyrinth of steep alleyways and steps has provided refuge to writers and artists for decades. The tourist guides call it a 'poor man's Capri'; the film director Franco Zeffirelli is the kind of poor man who owns a villa there. The town turned hippie at the end of the Sixties though the drugs scene was always as magnificent as its Mediterranean view. Nico knew many people who hung around the bars of the squeezed bay. One of her friends, the Australian artist Vali, still lives there for half the year, tending a nature reserve she lobbied to have designated so by the state, the other half of the year she spends in the Chelsea Hotel amongst animals of other kinds. But to Nico, Positano was 'Ibiza with spaghetti'.

'So we arrived at this chic little dropout village, and lo and behold, there was Nico and Tina and the fucking harmonium and Nico's luggage all strapped up because they'd had a fight and Nico was leaving *that very day*. But then she couldn't move in with us because she couldn't bear the thought of this respectable married couple swooning around the place, and she hated Michel. So every day in the middle of this paradise there was this scene between Nico and Tina, these two formidable amazons slugging it out, and the harmonium ready to heave-ho and the continually strapped-up luggage and Nico always on her way out but never quite going.'

Tina Aumont didn't remember it quite like that, though she said we must be thankful she could remember anything at all. She was another beautiful young film star (the daughter of Monsieur Dreamboat) who took a detour to drug heaven, and took a long time to find the way back again. She said she was just about to make, or had just made, or was making, Fellini's *Casanova*, in which she co-starred with Donald Sutherland, and her place at Grottaferrata 'was too full of people, as places always were in those days. Viva was in love with Michel Auder, a young photographer who also made movies, I was there with the painter Frederic Bardo, and Nico was in love with Philippe Garrel.' She wanted to get away from her work and the herd, and so she suggested the couples went down to her rented villa in Positano: 'It was a place to get away from working, and we had such fun, oh, a lot of fun. But Nico wanted to work. She was very serious about her composing. It was amusing to us.' Tina Aumont rented an island in the bay so that Nico could be alone and work. She would ferry her organ over to the island in a rowing boat and sit there, pumping out her sullen chords.

Aumont added, 'It seems funny to think about it now – everyone sunbathing or having fun, and Nico sat on her island singing her serious songs. I wanted to help her have a balance, though it could be difficult. She lived in her own *fantasma*. Reality was so far away from her (it's not in her favour to say that about her) and yet you could not bring reality to her, either. She thought that by being different she was overcoming the circumstances around her, which was rarely the case.' Nico had taken the sacred vow at the lap of Jim Morrison, no less, to be an artist. All around her she had seen intellectuals squandering their time; even Jim himself had neglected Nico and become fat and idle. She concluded she must take the opposite path. The Ice Queen would turn her back on lethargy. The Moon Goddess, waxing for a fortnight, waning for another, fourteen days and fourteen days, would have no time for earthly trivia any more. But Viva made it clear to Nico that she had little sympathy for this aesthetic posturing: 'I think the reason she acted so exotically was because she didn't know how you went about things. She'd missed all that out of her education and she picked it up from uncritical observation, off of the screen or out of books. She looked for excuses to appear unsocial.'

Tina Aumont saw Nico's odd behaviour as a reaction to her iconic status: 'I think when we were in Italy she was haunted by the beauty she still had. It's terribly hard to be a beauty. People want more and more and more. She wanted to be perfect, to appear always at the right moment. Music was her only release from this pressure to exist only for others, and I think she gave it all the serious attention one could give to it. Modelling is all "shut up and look good". Music was Nico's great escape from that.' The music was certainly a release from the pressures of the present. The folksong melodies she invented, like the peasant look she wore, evoked for her a transmuted childhood. It was a past she recognised but improved ('with colouring added') in order to hide the origin of her remorse. Above all it summoned for her a notion of *Heimat*, the phantom homeland she had covertly yearned. The music she worked on hour after hour did all of that: 'I start with the melody, and that is a question equally of creation and memory,' she told a French journalist. However, the words that went with the music were little less than a prison.

Nico discovered that while it was all very well to write down your dreams, after a while the same dreams kept coming back. 'It is like renting the same video. You say "Oh, I've seen this one." But you can't return it.' There must be other subjects which would kindle lyrics, she argued, but what could they be? She decided that other people could inspire her to write about them, just as Lou Reed had written a song about Edie Sedgwick and Bob Dylan had written a song about Edie Sedgwick, and both had written a song about Nico, too. She had already attempted a song about Warhol and another on Julius Caesar: 'Jim said I should write about heroes. He thought it would be a good discipline. I told this to Andy and he said "Gee, that's a good idea." So I did it. But I think it was not Julius Caesar that is the hero as much as Octavian. I wonder if people think about these things?' On reflection, she thought no, not at all.

WHEN BRIAN JONES's drugged body was found at the bottom of his Sussex swimming pool on 3 July 1969, Nico decided to write a song about him. When she learned that The Rolling Stones were to turn a free concert at London's Hyde Park into a memorial wake, she asked to sing it (though she had not actually bothered to compose it). 'I was told I could sing two songs. But I arrived too late anyway with my harmonium. It was an irony, in any case. Mick had thrown Brian out of the band a few weeks before this. He opened a box of butterflies for Brian which he thought was very poetic. Well, it was, because I saw a lot of dead butterflies stuck in the box afterwards. And the next day Marianne Faithfull tried to commit suicide.'

Nico added that backstage in Hyde Park she met a beautiful young man who made eyes at her. 'He was trying to sell his new record, which was the first thing of his I had heard . . . "Ground Control to Major Tom" ["Space Oddity"]. David Bowie looked like a pretty fairy, but he was a bit too effeminate and skinny to be truly *androgyne*. He was never equalled in that, though. He was the most perfect mirror of the times. Brian was his John the Baptist (did you know they really have the same family name? Bowie is really a Jones). I admit I was jealous of David for his looks, though he has bad teeth. But I was not jealous of his intelligence – he is entirely superficial, which is why he never knows what to look like. Or what music to make. Or whether to be a boy or a girl. At least I am consistent.'

Nico moved back to New York to pick up some royalties and work up some new songs. She wanted to compose her tribute to Brian Jones, and thought that a room in the Chelsea Hotel might be the very place to write it. She learned that John Cale had found more work as a producer following the artistic success of his *Marble Index* arrangements; Nico went along to the studio and sat beside him at the mixing desk. She was determined that she should not waste time in studios any more, and so she revived a pastime she'd learned as a child from her mother. Nico knitted. She wasn't too sure what to knit, but she resolved to knit something in black. The singer of the band Cale was producing looked through the window of the booth and saw John Cale in a big black cape, 'direct from a Hammer horror movie' and, next to him, an imposing Nico, knitting. The singer thought, 'Boy! what have I got involved with?!' As the singer in question was no less than Iggy Stooge of The Stooges, later notoriously known to the world at large as Iggy Pop, Cale and Nico might well have asked the same of him.

Iggy Pop's real name is James Osterberg, and Nico always called him Jimmy. Jimmy never forgot his first view of Nico: 'She was simply incredible. She had strawberry blonde hair like an *ingenue* with bangs long enough to sweep across her eyes if she didn't want to see something. Later, she told me to do the same – "You must keep your hair on your face, your face is not meant to be seen" – and it made good sense when you only wanted to see 10 degrees in front of you. I was real interested in her. I was a kid, basically, nineteen or so, and I'd never met anyone from Europe. I was like a boy who'd gotten a toy – "Hey, we've never had one like this before!" We started to have an affair for a few weeks, and it was a full education for me.'

Nico introduced Iggy Pop to three things: Dante's *Inferno*, Beaujolais, and oral sex. 'She'd just moved into someone else's apartment in September 1969 and they had this huge, illustrated version of Dante's *Inferno* in the centre of the lounge. "Jimmy, you must get into Dante, you really must." I said, OK, sure; I didn't really get the deal about this thing, but it was her pride and joy at the time. Then she acquainted me with wine. She drank a lot of red Beaujolais, and she loved to drink though a doctor had warned her that the drink was not helping to heal an abscess she had in her ear (she'd be taking ear drops about six times a day, and complaining to me, "I don't want to take these drops, but I can't give up drinking wine so I have no alternative"). I come from the Mid West and the only wine I'd ever heard of was called Ripple, 90 cents a bottle, very, very sweet. From Ripple to Beaujolais was quite a trip. But not such a trip as the moment Nico exposed me to oral sex. One day we were in bed together and she said, "Jimmy, you can do something for me . . ." '

Nico the educator is an improbable role, while Nico the aspirant mother is more credible, though not to Iggy Pop: 'She was ten years or so older than me, but I never would call her *responsible*. Nobody ever said, "Here comes Nico. Everything's gonna be alright now!" She didn't inspire confidence, but she was a great sport. She was very cute, charming, and a hell of a lot of fun. She was a little crazy, too. When I thought about her, I thought of The Katzenjammer Kids, Hans and Franz, a cartoon I used to read as a kid in the Mid West newspapers – kind of cheeky, and foreign. After we'd made our first LP, we had to move back to this farmhouse we had in the middle of a cornfield in Michigan. Nico came back with us, and we stayed together for another three weeks. By now all the guys in the band were walking around with fake German accents, but Nico wanted to act the farmer's wife, and she decided to cook for us: "You boys need feeding. I will make you a brown rice ratatouille." She made this thing, and it looked great. But we took one forkful and our mouths exploded. It turned out that instead of half a spoon of Tabasco sauce she'd put in half a bottle. I couldn't sing for a fortnight. Then she'd go into the nearest town with me. You can imagine the effect of this incredible woman walking into the general store and asking, "Dooo you hafff Beaujolais?" '

While the boys from *Bonanza* and Nico lived in the middle of a cornfield, they made a film. François de Menil was a young son of the oil family that had launched Fred Hughes in his fine-art career, and was infatuated with Nico. He wanted to make a film about her, and hung around New York until she told him 'I'm off to Michigan with Jimmy. If you want to make the film, you'll have to follow us.' He did. Iggy Pop kept looking at him, thinking, 'What's this gotta do with rock and roll, this goddam rich kid with his camera?' The rich kid got his revenge. He set up a scene for Nico and Iggy in a ploughed potato field. Clothing dummies were fixed into the earth, and Iggy's face was painted in the style of a white mime. They were instructed to frolic among the mannequins in the ploughed potato field, which they did, to their eternal embarrassment. The film footage has been mislaid, and today Iggy Pop might well pay good money to keep it that way.

During their time together, Nico advised Iggy on his appearance and his style – not only the hair, but also his manner: 'She would tell me edgy things – "I think you should be more poisoned as a performer. You are not yet totally poisoned". The more we were together the crazier she seemed, and the crazier I became. She wanted me to throw glasses into the audience, act mad, angry, violent. Eventually I had to say to her, "Hey, baby, that's enough." I couldn't handle this pressure, and we split. It's funny to mention it now, but I wrote a song about Nico for the first Stooges LP, a song called "We Will Fall". It was considered one of the worst Stooges cuts ever! The critics said, ". . . and when he fails he does so spectacularly, within 15 minutes of sheer boredom called 'We Will Fall' ". It ends the album, and at the heart of this very long track is me mumbling away about being in a room at the Chelsea Hotel waiting all night for Nico to come.'

Iggy Pop came to the Chelsea one day when Nico wanted to play him a new song. 'It stayed in my head for days. It was "Janitor of Lunacy", what an amazing song. It made me realise what a strength of character she had to write these songs. She'd had the opportunity to learn from The Velvet Underground and all the others – she told me that she'd hung around with the boys because she wanted to do it herself. But what she came out with was entirely unique. She had more to say than most people writing music, but she didn't have any of those mediocre tricks we often use to get our songs across to a wide audience. She was completely out on a limb, but she really had the guts to stay with it. She was a pioneer.'

The song she played Iggy Pop was her tribute to Brian Jones. When it was finished it was nothing like it had started out, and seemed to have little to do with the strawberry-blond sadist who slid a gun barrel up her vagina. As a diabolic incantation, 'Janitor of Lunacy' did, however, become her most famous song:

> Janitor of Lunacy
> Paralyse my infancy
> Petrify the empty cradle
> Bring hope to them and me.
>
> Janitor of Tyranny
> Testify my vanity . . .
>
> Janitor of Lunacy
> Identify my destiny . . .

It was the first of a chain of songs covertly centred on dead members of her phantom family: 'Some of my songs are like the poems on tombstones.' Her output from then on would fall into four genres – dream songs ('Frozen Warnings'), heroes ('Henry Hudson'), phantom family ('You Forget to Answer') and family ('My Only Child'). She did not have to rely on her dreams any more. She simply had to wait for someone else to die. Very few friends let her down. Yet she did not expect the next death to happen so swiftly. It was her mother's, and when it came, it shattered her life utterly.

AT THE START of a merciless, freezing February in 1970, her mother died. Grete had been 60 years old for eight days, and she died in the Berlin clinic, a cankered shell. 'My sister and I paid for the burial,' Helma Wolff admitted, '10,000 marks or more. We told Nico, "You must come now, you must come to Berlin and be there at your mother's funeral." She wouldn't have anything to do with it. She couldn't bear to come. She said, "If I go to my mother's grave, I will never leave it." ' Grete was buried in a cemetery in the heart of the Grünewald Forest, a graveyard protected through the bitter nights by wild boar. 'You might think that Nico didn't care about her mother,' said Helma, 'but of course she did. They were in love with each other. It was a terrible blow for her and I think everything changed from that moment into a nightmare that never concluded.' Nico visited the grave finally, many years later, and when she did she kept her word and never left it.

There had been no reconciliation between them. For seven years Nico had left her mother to wither away in solitude and die a terrible death. She had spent the money on herself rather than her mother out of spite. Nico avoided paying for the primitive medical treatment that offered her mother slender relief; Grete had not wanted Ari to come into the world, and in that case, Nico thought, Grete could leave it instead. But these kind of wishes are the vengeful sort that children commonly plot against their parents, and the bond that tied the Päffgens together was that of a child and a mother. The intimacy never matured. It was locked into a two-roomed tenement in Berlin, Christa in front of the mirror, the voice of Zarah Leander coming from the gramophone, Grete pedalling away at her sewing machine. When Grete died in the Berlin winter, Nico was nothing more than a little child who had lost her mother.

She was devastated by her mother's timing. Nico had managed to put together, by herself, a few touring dates: a night in Amsterdam, a concert in Paris, a booking in London and so on – a gig here and there, a middling fee, a cult following, a hangover. She was obliged to see it through. With her stock of self-penned songs, fifteen by the start of the Seventies, she attempted to acquire three things: a European tour, a manager, and a record deal. 'I got nowhere. It was a world in any case stagnant. I can only describe that time as starting with speed and ending with smack [heroin]. It was all society falling this way, and it became very difficult to get anything done.' The London concert, in March 1970, was booked by the Roundhouse, a converted train shed in Chalk Farm that used to harbour wrecked shunters and now housed wired hippies. 'I thought this was a rock and roll place,' she muttered to her audience, smiling gamely between songs. 'If anybody wants to give me a record deal, my name is easy to remember.' She was interviewed in the *Melody Maker* the following week, where she revealed, in typical Nico fashion, that her mother was dead:

NICO, THE LONELY CHANTEUSE

She is in London just now, attempting to make another LP, but has met only disillusionment and loneliness.

Her friends from the old days – Keith Richard and Anita Pallenberg [!], Paul McCartney and Linda Eastman – were too busy with their own lives to help her, and record company executives were uniformly uncooperative.

She played one gig, an Implosion night at the Roundhouse, but when I asked her if she had been invited to do any more she replied in that deep Wagnerian accent: 'No, who should ask me? I have a reputation for not turning up to sing. It's something I want very badly to get rid of.'

But back to the beginning, a brief history: Nico, born of a Polish mother and father who died in concentration camps . . .

'I don't want to play in any more clubs,' she says. 'I'd like to do concerts, and maybe colleges would be good. But I don't have a manager, and nobody knows me here. In New York all the young people know me . . . I have a lot of friends. But I hate New York.' She was planning to fly to New York later the day that I saw her, possibly to take up the option on her Elektra contract. But a couple of hours after we'd parted she rang to say that she'd changed her mind. 'I can't stand the thought of going to New York, so I'm flying to Ibiza. It's my favourite place, and I think I'll die there.'

Disillusionment . . . loneliness . . . Wagnerian . . . concentration camps . . . nobody knows me . . . Elektra . . . die. The planks of Nico's mythology, as opposed to Christa's, were in place at the start of the decade. It was at first her response to John Cale's question, 'Nico, how do you sell suicide?' It was her marketing strategy. 'There is a danger that you become a parody of your publicity, like Lou Reed,' she reasoned, 'but I try to keep above it, and at least I smile to the audience. I am not a witch exactly, but I might as well wear a skull and crossbones for the way the press writes about me.' She was upset she could not strike a management or record deal at the time she realised she needed them most. Above all, she was angry she no longer controlled her image. It was out of hand, she declared. Not what the press actually wrote – she could live with the Moon Goddess material – but the fact that they wrote next to nothing. She couldn't bear that.

Nico had already adjusted her image by degrees, and now, her mother dead, she moved drastically and passionately to sever her future from her past. 'What is white can be black,' she insisted. She chose from that day to endure ugliness. She decided that she must become unsightly in the eyes of those who loved her for her good looks. Philippe Garrel had already suggested she darken her hair with the red-brown pigment of henna, and this she did. Garrel also made his own clothes, in a manner of speaking. They can be seen quite clearly in his films – long white shirts and waistcoats. He decided to make clothes for Nico, and she wore them with a vengeance. She would look like a baleful parody of her publicity: Nico, the gothic vamp.

Carlos de Maldonado-Bostock met her by chance outside the post office off Boulevard Montparnasse: 'It was extraordinary. I had not seen her for some years and I was dismayed. She wore orange-red dyed hair, long but severely cut, and terrible clothes. When I first knew her she was uncontaminated but now she was contaminated beyond belief. I hardly knew what to say. In fact I didn't know what to say. I simply couldn't speak. It was as though some terrible tragedy had befallen her. I was appalled.'

'She came back to New York soon after with Garrel and she looked hideous,' Paul Morrissey affirmed. 'She had been one of the most famous blonde models there was, an icon to thousands of people whom she'd never meet, and here she was with this awful crimson hair and unshapely clothes and screaming to the world "I don't want to be beautiful any more". It was tragic to see this change. And this is the time when the drugs got heavy. This was the start of slide down to hell. It was this Garrel guy turned her round. She had become *artistic*, and she did what she thought artists do – go mad, get wired, go to hell.'

NICO BEGAN TO USE heroin frequently, 'because I had too many thoughts': remorseful thoughts of her lost mother, distrust of Ari's guardianship, suspicions about record royalties (to be chased from three separate companies), anxieties about her vocation as she lacked a manager or a record contract, worries of money, worries of repute, worries of age. The opiate powder 'made my good thoughts run slower and my bad thoughts go away'. She wrote to a friend that 'I have found the way to turn my shame about my mother into feelings of pleasure that I can dream I am in paradise with her. I have found a way to turn day into night.' The way she found was that of heroin. She smoked the powder, white or brown, on sheets of aluminium foil (for the first year at least, she claimed). Nico was soon shown how inefficient this was – wasted smoke, meagre impact – and she and Garrel joined the whole pack of 'artistic' couples, from John and Yoko to Pallenberg and Richards, who liquefied the powder and pumped it into their veins through a shared syringe. And then, just like Major Tom told Ground Control in that presumed hymn to heroin, she floated in a most peculiar way; Planet Earth looked blue but there was nothing she could do.

Time after time, in an endless circle, several warm hours of soaring narcosis ultimately plunged the couple into a prickly depression and the overpowering need for another shot. Anyone with a mind to it could outlive the craving for more, but few would wish to leave the padded paradise it offered, especially for a wilderness littered with 'too many thoughts'. Nico confided: 'Like everyone who starts, I did not expect to be addicted. I thought I was strong in these matters. Did you know that heroin is German? Isn't that ironic?' More so than she knew. When the German Heinrich Dreser christened his diamorphine compound in 1898, he took the name from the word *heroisch* – 'heroic'.

Her American friends wondered if Nico had led Garrel towards addiction, or if he had led her, and they wondered if they pooled their resources to pay for the drugs and the film, or was he paying for Nico, or she for him. Garrel himself declines to be drawn on the subject, but in 1991 he made a film, *Gentons plus la guitarre*, in which he drily portrayed his life with Nico. He tells the audience, through unhurried images, that the red-haired siren introduced him to heroin and led him through the tortures of addiction. The woman was to blame. He overcame his habit, she didn't. He survived, she didn't. That is his version, fixed on celluloid.

There is no denying, however, that like The Two Nicos a decade before, they became a couple, dressed identically in black and white, who went everywhere together. Their relationship was introvert, ascetic, and much tied up with their dual work. They had a film to finish – his feature film for Nico, a big movie set in fabulous landscapes. He had found his title – *La Cicatrice intérieure*, 'The Inner Scar' – a suitable title for a film starring Nico, though hardly a subtle one. He talked about the film to a critic who considered it technically impeccable. Garrel replied: 'Yes, films like *La Cicatrice* search for another way, the seventh art . . . At one point people called my films "underground", at another "revolutionary". I find love transformed into art to be the most impressive thing. In the last ten years people have got used to preferring a material investment rather than an emotional investment, but it's possible soon that people will realise that the material is not the only interesting thing.'

He then passed on to the making of *La Cicatrice*: 'In the USA we journeyed to New Mexico to film in Death Valley. At the same time I discovered American universities. I showed my other films there. Then we shot in Italy and Egypt. Then stopped. I showed [in Paris] what I'd done so far in order to get an advance against receipts. I got a grant to finish the film. We went to shoot in Iceland and made a film totalling one hour. Jacques Robert told me he'd like to distribute my films. He started with *La Cicatrice*. He showed it at The Pagoda [an exotic, prestigious cinema on the Left Bank]. One night he phoned me. "It's working! The cinema's full. There's 126 people sitting here." I was very happy. At that moment I thought [Nico was right] and my cinema could even make a bit of money and find an audience. I decided to carry on, with *La Cicatrice* the first in a trilogy.'

Like 'artists' do, they went to film in Egypt, oblivious to the fact that they had stumbled into the middle of the Israel–Egypt War. The critic who ingenuously enquired why they were all dressed in white had obviously forgotten that; Garrel replied: 'Because in Egypt there was a risk of being shot at. Who do you bump into in the middle of the desert? Soldiers. A liaison officer was always around during shooting. He was careful to point out what I could and couldn't film. He wouldn't let me film things that were not recognised by Egypt in the story of the Bible. We saw an Israeli jet get shot down. There was fighting all around Cairo. We were present when the sirens blew for an air raid. I'd just set up my location when all the Arabs dived into the trenches.' The trip must have cheered Nico up no end.

Nico not only acted in the film, but also wrote the dialogue. Garrel added: 'While I was preparing the shooting plan, Nico was inventing the dialogue. Then half an hour before the shoot she'd show me the dialogues and act them out. She functioned as a scriptwriter. Alone. There were even things she put in that I didn't understand, like dialogue in German. I sort of understood her English, but with a lot of contradictions. I let her get on with it because I knew that her view of the world was exactly like mine.' The dialogue, however, is not what one remembers from this extraordinary film. On its release, *La Cicatrice intérieure* was revered and derided in equal measure. It was acclaimed as the first truly *psychedelic* film, yet ridiculed for its pretensions and lifelessness – 'how to make Egypt boring', wrote one reviewer. The critic Alain Philippon wrote, in that terribly poetic French manner that rarely travels or translates:

One is elsewhere, very far away, in a cold, white desert (salt? ice?). A man and a woman are separated, torn apart. The man (Philippe Garrel) is silent and seems to carry all the troubles of the world on his shoulders. The woman (Nico) is in pain. She says – it's the first thing that we hear – 'Where are you taking me?'

This 'Where are you taking me?' is addressed also to you, dear viewer. If *La Cicatrice intérieure* recounts the delusions of a woman, two men and a boy on a distant, frozen planet, the film also invites us on a journey to the interior of oneself and to the very heart of cinema . . . At the same time it allows one to be swayed by a reflective cinema, a cinema where one is disconcerted, like a little child, by fear and pleasure, terror and seduction.

The word 'seduction' is used here in its strict sense: to captivate, deflect your attention – 'Where are you taking me?' . . . Take the sequence, shot at the middle distance (the double panorama at 360 degrees), a side shot of a boy guiding Nico on a white horse. Let yourself be calmed by the music, the rhythm of a soothed heart, the eyes relaxed and adjusted, a change of scale, and zoom slowly towards what you will, to the point of eternity which mainstream cinema refuses access. Philippe Garrel's cinema allows this, invites this, attracts condemnation for it, and offers terrifying perspectives to our sensory perception.

London's *Time Out*, then a weekly journal for the alternative folk, was more direct: 'You need a bloody big spliff to enjoy this. A miserable couple who you would not wish to meet at a party [Nico, Garrel] are joined by a naked weirdo [Pierre Clémenti] with a bow and arrow and a desire to set everything on fire. That's about it, frankly, unless I fell asleep, which is quite likely.' The film was tardily distributed around the independent cinemas and subsidised film theatres of Europe. At the Manchester Film Theatre in 1973, the manager noted that there were 30 people in the cinema when the film started and five when it finished. Nico thought it was 'an important film, a great film. It concerns the fragility of life. The film treats the story of a young lunatic who starts to kill all his sheep. It is not clear if he is a shepherd or a prince. He has no identity until I appear [of course!]. I am a queen on a journey. A queen finds a kingdom wherever she goes. There are more songs than dialogue in the film, which I think is a good idea [of course!].'

A journalist asked Nico if she was in love with her director, and wasn't this a hindrance to their work? She answered, 'I think that I am in love with Philippe Garrel. I come closer to myself when I am in love. Being in love brings problems along with it, not with the other person, but conflicts start to develop in my head. Even if our relationship creates problems of work, the film will be a masterpiece, because Philippe is a classical director in the traditional sense, but he has new ideas.' Another journalist asked Garrel if it was difficult working with Nico. He replied: 'Oh, yes! In comparison to my father [Maurice Garrel, who appeared in his son's films], we do not have a common background. The matters are more sensual, emotional, intuitive – it's more a matter of the senses. Immediately there are questions of aesthetics, a knowledge of speech patterns, phrasing, how she acts. The more you know someone, the more easy it is to work with him. It is a question of being in tune with each other.' It's intriguing to note he used the masculine – 'to work with *him*'.

WHEN THEY WERE NOT mooning around the world and traipsing into war zones, Nico and Garrel lived together in the heart of Paris. They set up in a Montparnasse hotel until family fortune smiled on them. On the narrow rue de Richelieu near the Stock Exchange, Garrel's father had a smart top-floor apartment he didn't use, so he gave it to his son. Philippe decided to get rid of everything surplus to his needs. He got rid of everything. There was no electricity, no gas, no hot water, no carpets, furniture, cooker, heat, lighting, decoration. 'But it wasn't exactly empty, either,' a musician friend observed. 'There were dead pigeons by the window, grime on the floor and the ledges, bird shit, stale grease, rubble, debris, dust. The most sensational feature was the fireplace. It had not been used in years, just a big black hole in the wall. But cascading from the grate was the most magnificent heap of cigarette packets I had ever seen. It was like a ski slope made of tiny cardboard boxes. Scattered amongst the packs were thousands of dog ends, crumbling cigarette tips flung from the four corners of the room. It took your breath away.'

Nico and Philippe decided to decorate the rooms. They chose the paint with the care of seasoned aesthetes – black enamel, two coats, everywhere. Viva recalled her visit to the place. 'I was invited to visit Paris for a break by the film actress Delphine Seyrig. During that time I started taping my dreams. I took a little tape recorder with me – I remember that I dreamt of a death the night before Delphine Seyrig's father died (Delphine's dead now, too). So: one night I'd met Nico, the new-look Nico, and she took me up to Philippe Garrel's family apartment way up in the top of this building; we had to walk all up the flight of stairs [Garrel and Nico had declined to pay the standard fee for the maintenance of the lift, so they had no access to it]. It was really late and we decided to sleep there. I hadn't paid much attention to my surroundings. They made a pallet for me on the floor of her freezing room. In the middle of the sleep I woke up and suddenly Philippe jumped in bed with me. We were like small animals in those days – you know, we weren't having sexual relationships, we were just fucking in bed. I looked around the room and it was all this spooky black enamel. I said, "My God, Philippe, listen to this tape!" I played him the tape of the previous night, where I'd dreamt of a room with black walls, floors, ceilings and doors. Bizarre, huh?'

Nico liked the place because 'it was not of this century and not of this world. I light candles, and my harmonium does not need electricity, so why should I?' She especially enjoyed a stroll across the street, past the statue of Molière (his books of plays supported by ripe, naked women), through a cool passage into the cloistered garden of the Palais Royale, where she would doze by the fountain. Nico had lived in Paris on and off for fifteen years, and she was starting to prefer it to New York, which she considered 'as claustrophobic as an empty desert'. She returned to New York one more time, however, as John Cale was about to acquire a deal with Reprise Records, through which he found a glint of an opening for Nico. Reprise, a subsidiary of Warner Communications, had built its solid reputation on solo artists, from Frank Sinatra to Joni Mitchell. But Nico was extreme, not solid.

Two days after she arrived at the Chelsea Hotel, the Electric Circus, her old Dom, was blown up; seventeen teenagers were injured. Then a 'bomb factory' in a Greenwich Village home exploded, killing three. Blasts in three downtown office buildings preceded a spate of scares, and a car carrying a bomb blew up in the middle of traffic. Nico was unnerved. It was fine to be a nihilist, but not to be the victim of someone else's nihilism. 'There is a difference between fighting the state and private genocide,' she decided. In addition, she was troubled by the business of the Black Panthers, a black militant faction, supported by several liberal whites, that aimed to confront white racism. She told the story in this way: 'Do you know Jean Seberg? She was a film actress who was very beautiful and intelligent with a very sad life. She played Saint Joan when she was eighteen in a big film which had terrible reviews and made her look a fool. Then Jean-Luc Godard made her a star and gave the world the look of the girl–boy with cropped blonde hair [*A Bout de Souffle* – 'Breathless'; 1960]. She worked in Hollywood [*Paint Your Wagon, Airport*] but lived in Paris, and she was a close friend of mine. We had an affair, if you like. She and Jane Fonda supported the Black Panthers, which was to do with black power. She thought it was a provocative act to speak for them at their meetings. So the FBI tried to kill her, and I knew this because she pointed for me to the agents who followed her around. Have you seen FBI men ever? They are exactly what you expect. Vulgar. Ask Alain Delon, he knows what they look like.'

Nico was right about Jean Seberg and the FBI. Twelve years after the event, in 1982, a Los Angeles FBI memorandum addressed to the FBI director, J. Edgar Hoover, was discovered and made public. An agent asked for permission to 'neutralise' Jean Seberg because she supported the Black Panthers. He had found an opportunity to do so, because she was pregnant. He wished to plant a story in the press that the baby's father was not her husband but a Black Panther activist. Permission was granted. The story was planted in the *Los Angeles Times* gossip column and spread nationwide from there. Jean Seberg was seven months' pregnant at the time. Traumatised, she gave birth prematurely to a still-born baby. A day later, she called a press conference. The journalists, to their astonishment, were confronted with the open coffin of the dead baby. The corpse was white. On each anniversary of the baby's death, Jean Seberg tried to kill herself. She succeeded finally in 1979 with an overdose of drugs on a Paris street.

'Can you imagine such a thing?' asked Nico. 'What I have seen and what tragedies I have lived by, next to nobody can equal. And they think I am just some name with nothing behind it. I cannot even be bothered to tell them everything true, because it is more frightening than anything they know themselves. You can't tell the truth when nobody will believe it.' Surrounded by explosions, Nico finally exploded. One night back in 1970, she was sitting at the Spanish restaurant, El Quixote, attached to the Chelsea Hotel. 'It's difficult to remember exactly what happened,' warned Viva. 'Nico was having a drink in the restaurant bar and there was this young black woman. Somebody said she was a friend of Germaine Greer's,

which brings an uncertain kind of feminist element into the story
that I don't know is valid. This black girl – if she *was* black – she
was moaning in a loud voice that life was tougher for blacks, and
whites didn't appreciate it . . . something like that? Look, doesn't
anyone else know the story better than me . . . ?'

Perhaps John Cale: 'She was a lesbian. She was a heavy diesel
dyke. They were at the Spanish bar and the woman was apparently
saying, "How I've suffered! How I've suffered!" Nico didn't have
time for Yanks who claimed to have a raw deal. Nico shouted back,
"Suffering? You don't know what suffering is!" Then – *wham!* –
she threw a glass of beer at the dyke. I can't remember whether Nico
told me she intended only to throw the drink and not the glass . . .
but anyway, she threw the glass with the drink in it and the glass
smashed against the woman's head and cut her face open. The
woman needed something like twenty stitches in her face. I can
believe it happened. Nico had paid more dues than this woman, but
she never spoke about it. That's what annoyed her. It kind of broke
the dam.'

Perhaps Vali, the Australian artist who spends half a year at the
Chelsea and the other half in Positano: 'It's so hard to remember,
because it was something that happened really quickly. But I think
the woman was black and had something to do with the Black
Panthers, or a friend of theirs. She said something stupid and so Nico
did something stupid, and I think the woman needed nineteen stitches
to her face.'

Perhaps Paul Morrissey: 'She was black, she was white – who
cares, frankly? The only fact you can glean from it is that Nico
smashed this glass in the girl's face. Because of it, Nico said she had
a contract out on her from the Black Panthers. Sure . . . !'

Perhaps Gerard Malanga: 'It was a black girl who was one of
the original cast members of the musical *Hair* . . . Nico actually
ground the broken glass in the girl's eye.'

Perhaps Nico: according to her the woman was black. The black
woman at the bar was looking across at whites like Nico and
proclaiming that whites didn't know anything about suffering. Nico
was infuriated. Not only could Nico tell her first-hand about Nazism,
she also had some knowledge of American imperialism – not only
the rape, but childhood privation, inner shame, misogyny, illness
and death, murder and deceit. Nico smashed a tumbler and ground
the broken glass around her eye. She meant at first to throw the
beer, but her hand slipped and the glass smashed against the counter.

Nico had the glass in her hand when she pushed it into the woman's face. Nico believed that the woman's friends were members of the Black Panthers, and they warned Nico to get out of town or they'd kill her. 'I had to leave, I couldn't bear this threat. They had a contract on me. I went back to Paris and I started my exile in Europe.' It would be five years before she returned to the States, and nine before she re-entered Manhattan. It was typical of Nico to turn herself into the victim of the affair.

In truth, it was not the Black Panthers who scared her, though they might have been justified in doing so given the savagery of her assault. Nico privately believed the woman had advised the police that Nico was mentally unstable and needed psychiatric attention. She once confided to Iggy Pop, 'They think I'm crazy.' She kept out of the way to avoid the attention of the police, and moved out of the country until the matter might have been forgotten. The idea that she was turning mad like her mother terrified her. It was men in white coats, not the Black Panthers, that she was evading.

SAFE IN HER FAVOURITE PARIS, in the black room, with the organ, the candles, and the sublime doses of heroin – she was still at the stage where she could enjoy it and not hate herself for it – Nico began work on a new album. 'I think John Cale had helped me to find a new deal eventually with Reprise in the States. I was supposed to re-sign with Elektra but I didn't want to because they made no effort to sell *The Marble Index* [Elektra re-released the album on CD after her death]. So, I was glad to have some money to make a new record.' She thought that the record would tie in with the release of *La Cicatrice intérieure*, and she chose a Joycean title to reflect that, *Desertshore*. She already had the 'Warhol' song and the 'Brian Jones' song. Nico added four songs for her real family: two for Ari and two for her mother. The songs for the eight-year-old Ari were placed back to back. 'My Only Child' was a warning to him to be wary of those who would condition him:

My only child be not so blind,
See what you hold –
There are no words, nor ears, nor eyes,
To show them what you know.

Their hands are old, their faces cold,
Their bodies close to freezing, their feelings find.

The second song was one she gave to him to sing, 'Le Petit Chevalier', in flawed French ('I am the little knight, with the sky above my eyes'). It was described by *Rolling Stone* magazine as 'a chilling little *chanson* reminiscent of "The Village of the Damned" '. John Cale added to the grand guignol ambience by playing a skinny harpsichord beneath Ari's sweet voice. The vocal tape was left to run full volume between verses, complete with coughs and unfledged breathing. The songs for Nico's mother were meant to contrast with each other – 'one for my living mother and one for my dead mother'. The living mother was assigned *Mütterlein*, Christa's affectionate diminutive:

> Liebes kleines Mütterlein
> Nun darf ich endlich bei Dir sein
> Die Sehnsucht und die Einsamkeit
> Erlösen sich in Seeligkeit

> *My dear little mummy*
> *At last I can be with you*
> *Longing and loneliness*
> *Are redressed through blessings.*

Nico, in a single audacious sweep, proposed to resolve fourteen years of nagging guilt through a simple, soft-hearted song. Cale surrounded it with chiming bells and death-knell fiddling, just to keep Nico in her place. The dead and buried mother was sent away with an *Abschied* ('Farewell Song'), its stern ceremonial message carried by a severe melody, strikingly close to the *chorale* style of Kurt Weill. Indeed, the entire album of songs employs the foreboding symbols of the German romantic tradition – dark forests, castles, falcons, bitter wine, cradles, tombs – and not only because there are two songs set to German lyrics. The songs were grouped in an order of allied keys, slipping song by song to the relative minor, in the manner of a classical composer writing a song cycle. Then Cale used the musical ciphers of the romantic vocabulary – military trumpet calls, drum rolls, tolling bells, choirs, falling basslines. These touches chiefly echoed the traits of Gustav Mahler, a turn-of-the-century composer 'rediscovered' in the Sixties (it must have galled Cale to hear at this time the crude renditions of 'classical masterworks' by pompous groups such as Emerson, Lake and Palmer). No wonder *Rolling Stone* called the album 'Gothick'.

Above all, Nico's technique, her writing, and singing, had improved. 'Her singing was more confident, and I was surprised to hear how her songs had become more musically coherent,' admitted Cale. 'The melodies became more adventurous, beautifully constructed, too. She focused much better on having subtle, simple lines and shorter phrases. And she started writing changes – contrasting sections, even.' 'Janitor of Lunacy' had a fake middle section, where a chain of bare fifths, like medieval plainchant, feigned a movement to the dominant ('Tolerate my jealousy / Recognise the desperate need'). But 'The Falconer' boasted a full-blown change to the major ('Father child / Angels of the night'). Her solitary days at the organ, pumping away off Positano, had not been wasted.

The album was released at the start of 1971. A photograph from *La Cicatrice intérieure*, Queen Nico on a white horse led by a boy (not Ari), was on the cover – evidence of how strongly Nico promoted Garrel. The most substantial review was published in America's *Rolling Stone*:

> Make no mistake, my friends, for this record is dark, dark. Its dominant mood is Gothick: guttering candles sputtering black wax on cold stone floors as the sound of Nico's harmonium drifts in from another room. It doesn't have a beat and you can't dance to it.
>
> I really don't know who to recommend this record to, but introverted adolescent girls, lovers of H. P. Lovecraft novels and Nico fans (whatever *they* might be like) will go for it, and, if you're in search of the unusual, you might too.

Introverted adolescent girls might not have been so grateful for the recommendation. The reviewer at the *New Musical Express* wrote that 'this is one of the most miserable records I've ever heard'. *Melody Maker* kindly called Nico a 'cool enigma', but still considered *Desertshore* 'a mediaeval ruin of a record'. At least Nico could not complain this time that the record company was lazy. Her third solo album would sell regularly in Europe, but not as well as her second, despite a genuine publicity drive and the link with the film. Reprise would not take up the option for a further record. 'People have decided in 1971 it is time for Nico to work regularly, to be known,' *Rolling Stone* reported. 'The publicity flow is cranking up and people from the trade papers have been in and out all day [of her London hotel].' The magazine carried a full-page feature on Nico and Cale, set around a photograph of Nico singing on stage at her harmonium, wearing a red Mexican suit elaborately embroidered in cream, her Spanish boots kneading the foot pedals of her harmonium. Slung around the chair is a woven shoulder bag, a precursor of the famous deep, black bag she would carry everywhere, within which her drugs would disappear from the grasp of police officers as though 'swallowed in a big black hole'.

The insightful *Rolling Stone* interview by Robert Greenfield mixed an account of a London concert with descriptions of her nomadic existence:

> Nico comes through a door. People who want to speak to her move towards her. They circle around. She remains standing still, perfectly secure, surrounded by talking people yet totally alone. She goes on stage first, before a large and noisy crowd packed in to see Pink Floyd, who will follow. 'I don't know what mood you're in,' Nico says to the audience in her unreproducible voice. 'I suppose you're in a very peace-loving mood.' She begins with 'Janitor of Lunacy'.
>
> The combination of her voice, syllables stretched to madness and dropped, and the cavernous repetition of the harmonium slow the Roundhouse crowd down. The stage goes all black except for soft purple and green spots high above her head. The light show flickers down to a single picture, all grainy and glowing. The people stop talking. A great hall becomes a mediaeval cathedral. . . .
>
> Another hotel room . . . Her speaking voice, like her singing voice, comes from the far side of death. 'If I had a back-up group now,' she says, 'I would do the old songs like "All Tomorrow's Parties" and "I'll Be Your Mirror", I don't think I would do "Femme Fatale". I haven't that much sense of humour. Back then it was all right. It was a part I was playing. My hair was blonde and I . . .' She turns and looks at the wall. 'It has changed. Now, I don't know what part I'm playing.'

She told the man from *Rolling Stone* that she would be in Rome tomorrow. She claimed she had a van there she would drive back to her 'hotel room' in Paris. Ibiza was on her mind, though, as it was the warmest place she could think to be in the middle of a European winter. In Ibiza she could relax alone and think what exactly she was doing. From 1966 she had drifted beautifully for two years; then she became an artist and pedalled more than drifted; now she felt she was drifting into blackness. California was certainly not on her mind.

THERE ARE TWO WAYS of regarding the Seventies – a sluggish, static Seventies, the rock press insisted. There is first the story of the Celebration of Life Festival in Louisiana in 1971: it opened when Yogi Bharjan stood on stage and asked for a minute's silence. 'Fuck you, let's boogie!' came the response. This is the Seventies of glam rock, funk, glitter and disco. In contrast, there is the conviction of Philippe Garrel: 'It was a sad period where, quickly, quickly, we went back to work in the aftermath of [the revolution of] 1968 and tried not to examine the impasse, nor to get our knuckles rapped.' Here stood Nico, though it was her heroin she wanted wrapped. She stood alongside everything visionary and morbid, from *The Dark Side of the Moon* to seditious Heavy Metal, though she noticed nothing but herself.

She once considered which decade she fitted best: 'I would say the time has not yet come. I rebel against the present, whenever it is, because I have not seen any change, other than oppositions grow stronger. I would be a communist if it was more anarchist. Otherwise, I see only everything as an absurdity, so I can laugh and cry. I have lived in a continuation, from birth and growing towards death in a chain that cannot end. I don't see this decade then that decade. The same things happen in different guises. I am a bohemian but at one time you would call me a hippie or a punk. I remain a bohemian whatever you call me. So maybe I am locked in the Fifties. But I have never desired to grow up from my world as a child, which is when things are most clear and utopian. They are clear because you are at the centre and you see all around you. When you get older you lose your sight . . . I lost something of my childishness when people around me started dying. Four of my family died within a year.'

The first was her mother. The second, Jimi Hendrix ('inhalation of vomit due to barbiturate intoxication'). The third, Edie Sedgwick, of a heroin overdose ('she was my warning'). The fourth was Jim Morrison, who had lately exiled himself to Paris in order to lead a quiet life as a poet and to blend in namelessly with the other junkie aesthetes. Nico did not know they now shared the same city (and possibly the same heroin dealers). On 3 July 1971, Nico was walking down the avenue de l'Opéra when a black car slowly passed. She saw Jim Morrison in the back seat, bearded and bloated. 'I signalled but he didn't see me. He was looking straight ahead, facing death. It was the anniversary of the death of Brian Jones. I am destined to die at the same time [she did indeed die in July]. I knew it was Jim. They said he died that night in his bath, of heroin. But I knew his spirit entered me, and it was an unbearable load. It meant nothing but pain. Thoughts were flying round my head, male and female. And then you can say that heroin became my lover.' They had exchanged blood exactly four years before (Nico would claim it was to the very day, though the dates don't tally). Nico believed that was why she felt his spirit. She could not bear to attend the funeral, nor his grave at the Père Lachaise cemetery. 'It was the wrong place. His ashes should have been scattered in the desert, or pickled in mescal.'

Now Nico was acting the mysterious diva to the hilt. She was increasingly erratic – not an hour late for meetings but a day overdue – and she was dogmatic beyond belief, telling people what to do and how to do it. It was assumed that the 'aesthetic' life had gone to her head. Yet there is another view her friends put forward: surely Nico suffered a breakdown, or schizophrenia following the death of her mother. It would be understandable for her to assume the presence of the 'spirit of Morrison' in such a condition. The heroin she increasingly relied on would have cushioned the symptoms, or fed them; disorientation was now a part of her daily life. She found a doctor who prescribed her Valium. She also smoked cannabis, 'to help my inspiration'. Over the next months, while Garrel edited *La Cicatrice intérieure* for final exhibition, Nico floated around Paris, a celebrity, a fake recluse, and she could get away with almost any behaviour at all short of grinding glasses into women's faces. She especially liked to steal money out of people's coats and bags.

When *La Cicatrice intérieure* was first shown complete in 1972, the 'underground' fame she accrued from it made her untouchable. It gave her the respect she sought but also left her sequestered on occasion. She had new songs to write, but instead of sitting at her organ to work she would find an excuse to 'walk the streets of Paris which I love to do so much, seeking the inspiration of the chance event. I preferred the night. The day is full of troublesome distractions.' Now and again she thought of her son and would wander into the calm suburbs to the home of Pauledith Soubrier. 'She came over once because she said she had a few days with nothing to do,' Madame Soubrier recalled. 'But Ari was on holiday with Anne-Marie Quazza and her children in Morocco. So Nico spent a week in our house. It was so strange because she came in and never once asked me, "Where is my son?" She asked nothing about him. At the end of the week it became impossible because she treated me as her maid. She invited friends to join her in my house, and I had to cook for them and organise the hospitality. After three days my husband left the house because he couldn't bear her behaviour, she acted so disturbingly. At one meal she had a friend, a Frenchman, but I remember that they spoke in English, and the man said to Nico, "Perhaps you can help Paula, she has had to do everything so far this evening." And Nico replied, "Oh no, she's used to it." I was furious.'

One night in a friend's apartment Nico was caught stealing money from a wallet. She promptly returned the money to the wallet, pretending it was simply a joke. 'I was completely without any money. So I started stealing. I started ripping people off. It was very embarrassing. And the amounts of money that I was ripping off were the kind of amounts that I would make anyway if I were successful [in my career].' Money was a problem, but money for heroin was a greater one. During 1972 she claimed that she bought a gram of heroin for Garrel and herself twice a week. That was not the demand of a dependent, which is more like a gram a day. But she was perilously close to addiction, though she had too small, and too irregular, an income to sustain the habit. (Warhol had warned her in 1967: 'Oh, I guess if you're rich you can really go on it and really be very happy . . .') She was not rich now and anything but happy.

She justified her binges of theft by pointing out that she had given thousands and thousands of francs away to her friends when she made money from modelling. Now she was collecting it back. 'I consider it like a bank. You put money into a bank and the bank makes some money out of your money. At some time you can go to the bank and take your own money back. That was all I was doing. What is so wrong about that?' A friend saw her pocket a tip left for the waiter in a restaurant. The waiter saw her too, and remonstrated. 'I put that tip there,' she lied, 'but now I've taken it back because you are rude to me.' She found a money-saving use for her cape. One day she went to a smart boutique on rue du Four and shop-lifted a chic jacket into her cape. Unfortunately, she returned to the store a few days later wearing their jacket. She got away with the gaffe by her usual escape route: 'Don't you know who I am? Do I look like the kind of person who would steal your cheap clothes?' Unfortunately, by now, she did.

It must not be thought, as all America thought, that Nico flew to Paris to retire. 'It annoyed me so much to be told that Nico disappeared from music in the Seventies,' complained Tina Aumont. 'Music was a part of her daily life, and she made a lot of concerts. It just shows how cut off America is from Europe. Nico's problem always was that she didn't have a manager. There was no one to plan her musical life. There was no co-ordination or publicity.' The nearest Nico came to a manager was Hassad Debs, a Lebanese who earned his keep as a rock-concert promoter and a partner in Paris rock clubs such as La Cigale. He offered her, as a friend, the occasional prestige concert, fully aware that she could accomplish such a thing only once or twice a year. He also introduced her to a new lover who was to become her most faithful guardian – he still tends the grave – since the time she first stared at him in 1973.

Lutz Ulbrich is a notably attractive, affable, blond guitarist who has lived in Berlin all his life and plays in the respected group Ashra. 'I have played guitar in a band since the age of twelve,' he recounted. 'In the early Seventies I played in a group called Agitation Free, which was a German *avant-garde* band making free-style "underground" music (God, these clichés now!) a little like Pink Floyd. We played on tour in the Near East during 1972, and we met Hassad Debs who was on holiday. He liked us so much that he promised to arrange a tour for us when he returned to Paris. In 1973 we got an invitation to play a small club tour in France. It was a success, so he asked us to take part in a special concert at the Opéra Comique, which is truly a fine, old opera house in the centre of Paris. It was a festival of different bands such as a French band popular at the time called Crium Delerium. Nico was headlining.

'There was a party at Hassad Debs' place. Nico was there, completely magnetic and quite intimidating – the most famous person in the room. We were introduced to her because we spoke German, which was a kind of novelty for her there. I was sitting around with the guys, when suddenly she stared at me and walked over quickly and said, "Come with me, let's go outside and talk." I thought, why me? She was this star and I was, well . . . a guitarist. We got outside and she dramatically said, "I feel like a robot. There are so many thoughts in my mind." I was completely overawed by this. How was I supposed to react? I was 22 and she was 34. It was certainly a seduction, but more a *hint* of seduction. I was given the distinct impression she was preoccupied but not uninterested. I went back with the group to Berlin. Then some time later Agitation Free was invited to play in Clermont Ferrand alongside Nico and Kevin Coyne. I was waiting in the hospitality tent and one of those hippie groups that were always on the bill in those days offered me some tea. They hadn't told me it was laced with acid. I got totally stoned on a cup of tea. I was trying to concentrate, desperate before the gig to keep the slightest hold on reality. I played my guitar with my eyes shut. When I opened them, there was Nico sitting next to me like she'd always been there. We flirted.

'She was living at this time with Philippe Garrel. I thought he was an extraordinary man. He could have made a fortune filming for the TV, but he was entirely independent and singular by choice, making curious films for the big screen. They lived together in a . . . I can only describe it as a garret. It was rotten. There was no heat, the windows were broken – they seemed to be terribly poor. She invited me there. It was grim. Philippe was in bed, which consisted of his coat and a blanket. There was the smell of a burnt-out candle and the stench of the menthol cigarettes he continually smoked. There were the signs of heroin. I was very uncomfortable because I was kind of a guest, flirting with his girlfriend. But she was not having a full affair with him. It was more the affair of lovers of heroin – they were in love together with smack. I didn't stay there. I returned to Berlin.'

Alone together, Garrel and Nico made a second film. It was called *Athanor* (*Athanasius contra mundum*: Athanor is the melting pot of the alchemists). A continuation of *La Cicatrice intérieure*, and the centre of Garrel's trilogy, this film of two women (Nico and a beautiful actress called Musky), a mirror and a mediaeval window is in colour but silent and lasts just twenty minutes. 'It is a perfect film,' Nico claimed, 'though I am naked and my body was not flawless then. It is a film you should see at the Odeon, Leicester Square on a very big screen. Well, it is more interesting than advertisements for hot dogs.'

By the time *Athanor* was premiered in Paris, Nico noted that she had made twelve films, three singles, and four albums, 'and I had nothing to show but my fame'. It was frequently said of Nico that she was 'famous but not popular'. And now, as the 'sluggish, static Seventies' ground on, she had found a way to accommodate her pace of living to the times. But the heroin had retarded her: she was no longer childlike, but childish. 'I was invited to parties still and people would look at me and point at me and say, "Look, that's Nico!" But I would be slipping the cutlery into my pockets and making sure I got a lot of drink and a free lift home. I was like a little child at their party. I was like a little child everywhere I went, being spoilt by grown-ups.' A little child who lost her mother.

13 1974–1981

O soothest Sleep! If so it please thee, close
In midst of this thine hymn my willing eyes,
Or wait the 'Amen', ere thy poppy throws
Around my bed its lulling charities.
Then save me, or the passed day will shine
Upon my pillow, breeding many woes, –
Save me from curious Conscience, that still lords
Its strength for darkness, burrowing like a mole;
Turn the key deftly in the oilèd wards,
And seal the hushèd Casket of my Soul.
(JOHN KEATS, 1848)

NICO KNEW ANDREAS BAADER, of course. When the terrorist escaped from Germany, she sheltered him in Paris. He stayed at the barren flat before she drove him down to Positano for a holiday. One day in that hippie refuge, while a tourist couple were frying on the beach, he stole their car and raced to Germany where he was arrested for speeding. 'The trouble with him was he thought he was God's gift to women. He wasn't. But I liked him because he blew up the KaDeWe, where I had been discovered. That's why he split from Germany. He put a bomb in the fashion department. I would like to have seen it the morning after – all those fur coats in shreds. I must say I preferred Ulrike Meinhof, who was not as arrogant. But then, Andreas was better-looking.'

She didn't know Andreas Baader, of course. He bombed the department store in April 1968 when Nico was lying in a New York tub. He bombed it, by the way, 'to protest about the Vietnam War'. Baader escaped to Paris with his girlfriend Gudrun Ensslin, but rather than doss in an 'aesthetic' hovel they stayed at the clean, furnished, lit, heated, pigeon-free apartment of the writer Régis Debray. They did indeed drive to Naples; it's possible they sunned in Positano – while Nico mooned around LA. Furthermore, those shredded fur coats lay in the Kaufhof, not the KaDeWe. In Frankfurt, not Berlin. Andreas Baader may not have been God's gift to women, but Nico would never find out if she were God's gift to him.

'If I were not Nico I would be a terrorist,' she confided to a

London journalist ('Leave it out!' spluttered one of her musicians from the next room). The rise of urban guerrillas was the best thing to happen to Germany since the death of Hitler, she announced. Violent subversion appealed to her sense of romance – the shattered store, the charred fur coats, the insurance-company boss smudging the cheque with his tears, her dark-haired and blue-eyed hero zooming down the autobahn to the fraternal arms of Nico, *chanteuse* to the Resistance. The Kaufhof blitz preceded many more bombings and killings in Germany, mainly of the American forces (Nico rather liked to hear of that). Through these actions they intended to shake the Raspberry Reich, as they called federal Germany, and shatter the 'myth of the omnipresence of the system and its invulnerability'. By the start of 1974, Baader, Meinhof, Ensslin and their associate Raspe were detained in prison, awaiting the building of a sturdy court to house their murder trial. Nico swore it was being built by the same people who built Auschwitz: 'I am not so stupid to think terrorism is only a spectacle to annoy rich people,' she continued. 'It is important to fight the deceit of society. It is a question of a deeper grievance. It shows the country that it is not invulnerable to proper justice.'

As she was nothing less than Nico the Moon Goddess and novice junkie, she decided (with the advice of cards and coins) that she would make a momentous contribution to the cause, in her own special way. She would write terrorist songs. They would inspire rebellion for sure. Moreover, she had a splendid outlet for them. In early 1974 John Cale had signed a new contract with the British label Island; on the back of it he gave Nico a chance to record another album. It was ratified in a curious deal with the entrepreneur Jo Lustig ('He thinks I owe him money. But he owes me money and he hasn't paid me a penny, ever. I signed with Island because I was absolutely broke'). She resolved to make the album a memorial to her soul brother Jim Morrison. It was her first chance to pay public respect to him since his death soon after the release of her last album. She would sing his favourite song and call her record by its name, 'The End', a very terrorist kind of title. 'Nico, are you sure you're not tempting fate?' quizzed her Island contact. 'Oh, no. I don't tempt fate. Fate tempts me.'

She yearned to make a provocative act through her music, and she claimed she found the solution in a dream: Nico was Christa once again. She was standing by the railway singing the national anthem when a train passed full of soldiers who told her to be silent or they would kill her with a special drug. She ran to a cemetery and saw the name of her mother on a tombstone. A flag was mounted by the grave. She sang the national anthem and the flag melted. The soldiers were chasing her and as they ran closer she woke up. 'The national anthem I sang was the one I knew as a child. It is now forbidden to sing it as it was then, but the one they sing today has exactly the same melody. It is the same thing with softened words. I realised that I should sing the forbidden words to expose the old sentiment behind the new one.' Nico decided then to use the anthem's melody for all of her songs on the album. She worked hard – at least, as hard as heroin allowed – to write three songs and to rework three old songs to fit her new plan. Eventually five of her songs carried variants of Haydn's tune, each opening with the same three notes, while the sixth mixed the tune with that of 'The End'. 'I don't think anyone cares about these things,' she sighed.

Nico wrote songs for two heroes, Jim Morrison and Andreas Baader. To Morrison, her soul brother, she recalled the moment she last saw him, in a black car facing death. She uses solely the present and future tenses:

> When I remember what to say,
> When I remember what to say,
> You will know me again,
> And you forget to answer all.
>
> You seem not to be listening,
> You seem not to be listening,
> The high tide is taking everything,
> And you forget to answer all.

The line that runs, 'You seem not *to* be lis-te-*ning*' was cited more than once as Nico's inability to cope with the stresses and accents of the English language. 'I don't care,' she retorted, which is exactly what Stravinsky said when he was accused of the same violation. Nico would have done well to memorise Stravinsky's subsequent remark, that Handel, a composer revered above all others by the English, often got it wrong ('*For* unto us a child is born'); Handel had once been as German as Nico. And while Judy Collins could squeeze the words 'oranges' into two syllables, Nico fattened into three words like 'car-ri-age' and 'flo-w(u)-ers'.

As for Baader, she wrote 'We've Got the Gold', with its recurring final line, in his honour:

> Very proud and very poor,
> I'm waiting at your prison door;
> *But it does not bear a single flo-w(u)-er.*

With these images, Nico led the listeners to her wilderness. From its misted centre rose her magic palace peopled with kings and warriors. She evoked from these the most compassionless and brutal vista she had yet created: 'To feast our naked eyes upon the open blade, the hungry beast', 'The battle bracelets do not fit my favourite gladiator', 'I am a savage violator', and, set to an elegant melody, the most outlandish of all:

> Without a guide, without a hand,
> Unwed virgins in the land,
> Unwed virgins in the land,
> Tied up on the sand.

SHE WAS ONCE ASKED why she didn't use images of contemporary life, like Lou Reed had done: 'Because he does it very well. If I use words of modernistic images, you would be bothered about whether I got everything right. You would not concern yourself with the deeper reality. William Blake wrote about men in the Bible and we read him today. But we do not read the newspapers he read. They are forgotten. What was news then is now only history. I want to go beyond history. My songs are visionary. They are ceremonial.' Are they ceremonies of death? 'Everything is a ceremony of death, in the end.' This was the kind of glib remark she enjoyed making, because rock journalists often wrote such things down most reverently, and she swore they recorded it in gothic script, by the light of one of her candles.

When they came to recording the album in London, Cale chose to work with two old members of Roxy Music who had contracts with Island, Phil Manzanera and Brian Eno (the sound engineer's two children were recruited, too). But Nico had decided that she didn't like Cale any more: 'He's such a married person.' She'd tried to lure Lou Reed in the hope he would provide new songs, but 'Lou's got bad problems. He wants to be black.' She was stuck with Cale – a good job, too, because her albums without him were never as good as her albums with him. Cale used the same schedule he'd used twice before: Nico in first, then out of the way, everyone else in for the arrangements, then Nico back for the final mix. He was surprised at Nico's prospering confidence: 'She'd be there with her candles and headphones, singing the melody and playing the organ. There were no markers on the track, no flags. It might have been ten minutes' worth of a song, like "The End". But, say, she was a little out of tune. So we went back to the beginning, which seemed like standing at the bottom of a mountain you'd just crossed only to cross it again, a ten-minute journey into the unknown, and tried once more.

'It was uncanny. Nico'd sing in exactly the same spot, without anything to guide her. Remarkable. It was so precise I could have double-tracked her voice. The pitch was right, the timing was right. I don't know where it came from, but it was unique. This happened after eight years of me trying to figure out how to accommodate her! I realised making this record that there was another thing going on in her head, which I've yet to explain.' But he exploited it to the hilt. The opening song was propped up with pulsing bells and a stately triplet rhythm on Eno's synthesiser set in counterpoint. The same trick was tried on 'You Forget to Answer', where the block chords of Cale's piano and the fiery, baroque decorations of Manzanera's guitar managed to fix on to Nico's elusive tempo with milliseconds to spare. Other features lent finesse to the album: on the first side the range of colours is reduced song by song until all that remains is Nico and her organ, and the keys descend in a chain of thirds – E minor, C minor, A minor – to the veiled F minor (the key of 'The End') that governs the second side. Nico, too, phrased her singing with more care and used the arabic decorations she threw into lines with advanced subtlety. 'I was really trying to build on *The Marble Index* and make something more commercial,' reckoned John Cale. 'I wanted to add some percussion to her voice. Drum kits were clearly not the answer. But exotic percussion such as boobams and the cabaça suited her voice very well.' Of the production in general he said fondly, 'It just drips . . .'

When the record was released in the autumn of 1974, the reviews reached rock bottom. *Melody Maker* led its evaluation with a marvellous headline:

NICO: AS MISERABLE AS EVER

Weirdness for weirdness sake can only go so far, and though there is a certain 'gothic' beauty about *You Forget to Answer*, that seems like a John Cale production achievement rather than a victory for Nico.

This one's recommended only to those who get satisfaction out of knowing that somebody else is more incoherent and screwed up than they are.

The writers were especially confused by Nico's dramatic version of 'The End', which they regarded as male territory ('she certainly concocts a bitch's brew,' claimed *Crawdaddy*). There was just one exuberant review to be had, from Richard Cromelin of America's *Creem* magazine. Nico kept a copy of the piece in her bag for some time, as she considered the comparison with Morrison's voice to be wonderfully 'valid' (not to say flattering):

Her *The End* is the soundtrack for the free-fall to the bottom. It's a totally mesmerizing performance by this lady hidden in musical mists, yet at the same time all too clear. If Morrison sang it as a lizard, Nico is a sightless bird, lost but ever-so-calm, somehow knowing the right direction. She is the pure, dead marble of a ruined Acropolis, a crumbling column on the subterranean bank of Morrison's River Styx.

'It's rubbish, but it's good, romantic rubbish,' she remarked. Nobody, though, had a good word to say about '*Das Lied Der Deutschen*' ('The Song of the German People'). It was the most provocative thing she had ever done, so she should not have been surprised. But she was annoyed that Jimi Hendrix could play 'The Stars and Stripes' and be acclaimed a hero of the counterculture, while she was vilified a Nazi for what seemed to her the same thing. Beyond the German borders the song signified nothing less than the sound of marching Nazi feet. It did not help that she would introduce it at concerts with an impudent preface: 'This is a German song, but lots of foreigners seem to like it':

Deutschland, Deutschland, über alles,
Über alles in der welt.

Germany, Germany, above all others,
Above all others in the world.

These words had been forbidden since 1945. They were established, however, not by the Nazis but in the nice, liberal Weimar republic of 1922. Nico was playing with ironies lost on her 'foreign' audiences. She sang the full three verses of which the anodyne third verse alone survives as the anthem's text ('*Einigkeit und Recht und Freiheit für das deutsche Vaterland!*' Unity, justice and freedom for the German fatherland). Nico liked to emphasise 'Fatherland'. Her provocatively clear singing of the forbidden text was rendered utterly surreal by the straight-laced but dopey harmonies she devised. For the seven years she had been playing the organ, she had kept faith with Ornette Coleman's advice to play the melody in the bass and the harmonies in the treble. Yet here was something that was supposed to have a separate bass line. So she kind of played the tune and she kind of played a bassline at one and the same time. It managed to sound simultaneously right and wrong. She was dreadfully proud.

She was even prouder of the hoop-la that surrounded the album. Island Records had prepared a publicity scam to launch a group of LPs by Cale, Eno, Nico and Kevin Ayers, a cute-looking intellectual hippie who started Soft Machine. On 1 June 1974, the company ran a concert at the major Rainbow Hall near London's Finsbury Park. It was tagged, rather unfortunately, as the *ACNE* concert after the performers' initials, and it was given massive publicity. Nico was touted as the *femme fatale* of the ultimate supergroup. 'It was really the last days of the dinosaurs, only no one could see that Punk would jump on their necks,' said *Rolling Stone*, much later. A live recording was made and released three weeks later, which in those days was considered a miracle of technology and hyped as such. In the event, Nico had one substantial track on the ACNE album (which is still sold on CD), her version of 'The End', accompanied by the ACE of ACNE supported by Robert Wyatt and Mike Oldfield, whose *Tubular Bells* had just gone gold. She detested the whole thing.

She said afterwards: 'It was not four people working together, it was four people fighting for the spotlight. I don't know who was more arrogant. Not me, this time, I promise. I had the impression that nobody cared. It was a sign of the time. A kind of death wish.' Brian Eno agreed: 'I think it was made to seem more important than it actually was. There wasn't really much else happening and, since there are a lot of people who are professionally committed to discovering novelty, this was seized upon and blown up beyond its real significance ... 1 June 1974 suffered from the lack of close scrutiny – not to mention the personality problems involved, which I shan't mention. Generally speaking, people weren't willing to surrender their own positions for the greater good. It was a depressing experience.' Nico brawled with Kevin Ayers' manager over something trivial and pulled a knife on him. It was *that* kind of depressing experience.

If it achieved little else, *ACNE* brought A and N together. 'I had met Kevin Ayers before in France. He knew Ibiza, too. He had been touring in France with one of his groups – he could never keep people together for more than a few days without trouble, I think – and he wanted me to mother him. He said he would write a song for me, and then he asked me to sing for his next LP [*Confessions of Dr Dream*]. It was a difficult song to sing and he decided that we must do it lying on the floor. I couldn't work out if he was making fun of me or not. I think I got drunk because it was all too stupid. It was a misconception. It should have been just straightforward, like two children singing together.' The song was called 'Irreversible Neural Damage'; it was only stupid and difficult because she was supposed to keep in time. The engineer played with a pre-echo and her separate takes to disguise Nico's grogginess. 'I decided not to appear in future on other people's records,' Nico concluded. She wasn't asked anyway, not for many years. She did, however, appear at an 'impromptu' concert in Paris with the man who was too married and the man who wanted to be black. Nico, Reed and Cale were filmed (not by Garrel) and it is believed that the tape languishes for no good reason in a vault at the Paris Cinématheque. 'Has anyone seen it? I can't remember if I have or I haven't,' she told one of her musicians. 'I bet Lou looks terrible. Do you remember he wore a lot of make-up then, and tried to look like David Bowie? He looked more like David's grandmother.'

They played another ACNE in Germany before Nico was induced to give solo concerts around Britain. It was a dispiriting mistake. She couldn't handle the marathon by herself, and neither could the audience. She thought back to her Dom days, and hit on a wonderful solution. She would take along a copy of *La Cicatrice intérieure* and show it in the middle, for a full hour. At the Sallis Benney Theatre in Brighton, the sound equipment was provided by the redoubtable Binky Baker, a local performer and personality who remains haunted by the occasion: 'She sang some songs with her wheezy organ, and then suddenly she strode off. I was running the sound but she hadn't told me what she was playing at. Then the lights went out in this silent hall. Suddenly there was an ominous sound from the back: ka-chug-ka-chug-ka-chug. All we could see were these flickering scratches on the stage. Ka-chug-ka-chug-ka – rrrip. After a very long moment of painful silence we heard a deep voice from the back. "Oh dear. The film seems to have brooooooooooken." '

Nevertheless, 1974 was a busy and fruitful year, for Nico also made a film with Jean Seberg. Directed by Garrel, *Les Hautes Solitudes* ('The Outer Reaches of Solitude') was a study of the film actress 'who was very beautiful and intelligent with a very sad life'. Tina Aumont was there too: 'Jean Seberg produced the film. I think she knew nothing about this world of new cinema. I was used to moving from Fellini and so on, but I don't think it's so easy from *Paint Your Wagon* to Garrel.' The director had this to say: 'I had an idea for a film in black and white because I wanted to quit colour. I wanted to make films that were closer to reality, and I wanted them to intersect with Freudian psychoanalysis. In the days when I'd distanced myself from Freud I fell into symbolism, and even further. As the composer Pierre Schaeffer said, after seeing *La Cicatrice intérieure*, my work was hieroglyphic, like picture-language. I pulled my camera toward day-to-day psychology. I made a portrait of Jean Seberg with very little money. I financed it myself by borrowing 50 francs here and there. The film is silent.' Nico thought this was all a bit silly. She had little time for psychiatrists and psychoanalysis. 'They are too rude with people's lives. They can't change anything anyway. I'd rather take drugs. That's what Jean did in the end, anyway, isn't it?'

When the film was premiered in Paris at a repertory cinema, Nico invited Lutz Ulbrich to see it with her and Garrel. 'We went together to this little cinema. It was all very serious, with an audience acting profound and all that. This film with Jean Seberg and Nico opens with Jean Seberg in bed, sleeping. You are told it is a portrait of Jean Seberg and suddenly that's exactly what you get. For half an hour, Jean Seberg sleeping, just like a Warhol movie. The audience would be nodding and murmuring respectful things. Well, Nico was sitting there, and I could see she was trying not to laugh. Then she couldn't control herself and she was giggling. It got embarrassing. She had to get up and go outside, she was cracking up so much. You could hear her in the corridor, laughing. And she was actually in the film!'

Nico found little opportunity to laugh in those days. Her life was absurd but not funny. She'd assumed that Ari would come to live with Philippe and her, and she was peeved by the suspicious looks from Mama Edith and the others. Nico presented herself to them as a caring mother, but all they could see was a bohemian junkie, unstable and perverse. She would show them her home in the centre of the city, but all they would see was a squalid, barren flat occupied by two aesthetic men younger than Nico. She could show them her records, her films, evidence of income. But they could say, 'You have no proper manager, no bookkeeper, no bank account, no savings, no property, just some cash you've probably stolen to waste on drugs.' To make matters worse, she didn't dare tell them that she'd just been dumped by her record company for racism.

Nico was dropped by Island when the press picked up on a racist comment she made: 'I said something that was misinterpreted. I said to some interviewer that I didn't like negroes. That's all. They took it so personally, although it's a whole different race. I mean Bob Marley doesn't resemble a negro, does he? He's the archetype of a Jamaican, but with the features like white people. I don't like the features. They're so much like animals ... it's cannibals, no?' Island Records made its money out of 'cannibals'. Bob Marley was an Island artist, and reggae was the company's major line. Short of Tamla Motown, Nico could not have picked a firm less tolerant of white racism. She said later: 'I am not a racist. My opinion was meant as a matter of fact, not a provocation. I was not attacking anyone. The press had not explained the circumstances of why I said it.' Neither had she. Two sources of her bigotry were clear but apocryphal: the childhood rape and the Black Panther contract on her life. The more credible reason was heroin. Lutz Ulbrich admitted, 'I was advised by Nico, "Never buy from black men." She'd been ripped off several times and it made her hostile. Anyway, people say all kinds of strange things when they're drugged.' It was Nico's lowest moment in the eyes of the discerning public. She would not land a record contract for another ten years.

At the time she hardly cared. Nico was still on her honeymoon with heroin; she was cosy and calm so long as she had some of it swimming in her veins or sitting in her bag. But the honeymoon ended like a journey in a juddering car, a stop-start lurch whenever she ran out of money, or had to wait too long for a new supply, or was conned into buying salt. For the first time in her life she saw the benefits of giving concerts. She would travel and she would meet new people to spoil her rotten, and they would pay her and find her a failsafe dealer in town. No waiting for the man for Nico, she thought. The man would stand backstage, waiting for her. From now on her husband was heroin, and Ari was not his child. Ari did not hear from his mother now for four years – not a word, not a sign of life.

Her career as a concert junkie started most grandly in Rheims Cathedral on 13 December 1974. She was sandwiched between two sets by the German band Tangerine Dream, a group she vaguely knew because she'd worked in their studio with Lutz Ulbrich. Eight thousand fans watched Nico surrounded by candles in the gothic gloom, staring for ages at the floor around her organ, looking for something crucial, then banging her fist. 'Somebody forgot to buy me a drink,' she muttered down the microphone. Under the heading 'The High Priestess of Weird', the *Melody Maker* critic noted only how 'that chillingly savage voice intones those crazy words'. It was the kind of phrase that Nico rebuked as 'irresponsible. I sing the words very clearly and they are considered, not crazy. Have you ever seen these journalists? They are usually drunk and always ugly.' The critic spent more time reviewing Nico backstage:

> Nico is there surrounded by male admirers and barrels and barrels of France's exquisitely good alcohol. She still doesn't look as though she's having any fun.

Ulbrich, whose benign romance with Nico had flowered in the same way it had with so many others, remembered the concert because it was there, in Rheims Cathedral, that Nico introduced him to heroin: 'She was telling me, "Go on, take it, it's so nice, it's good, really, try it, there's no danger, it's fine . . ." I didn't want to take hard drugs, but when you are in love with a girl you want to be on the same level. For social reasons you become obliged. Afterwards I became addicted, too. And from then on there is a period when we played together and my memories are only tales about drugs!' It is all too easy to defame the evangelical passion of addicts. They are simply in love and they want the world to join them, like born-again zealots. Economic self-interest is low on their list, though they reach it in time. The most missionary-minded of dependants become dealers to sustain their own habit, and Nico's problem was that she would not follow the consequences of her dependency. She was far too lazy. From this point on her entourage would include someone to set up the organ, someone to run the sound, and someone to stand on the street corner in the cold, waiting for the man, when the man hadn't called backstage.

*

NICO LIKED TO PLAY in Amsterdam. She had a good following in that liberal city, and the promoters knew how to look after her. Above all, it was a great place to buy heroin. 'We were going to Amsterdam all the time, even when she didn't have a gig,' admitted Ulbrich. 'Whether we were staying in Paris or Berlin, we had to cross the border, and we were certainly smuggling. Our dealer lived on a houseboat. He was a cocaine addict. We called in once and he gave us our heroin powder, which was a large deal, an ounce or more. But he decided he wanted to introduce his girlfriend to a cocaine injection. He was so excited about the prospect that he was completely preoccupied. We wanted to leave, but we hung around out of sociability (these things are never simple business transactions). Nico said to him, "Here's our money, we have to go now." He looked at it vaguely and replied, "Oh, it's German money. Go change it somewhere. It's 1,500 marks an ounce, sort it out yourselves." He was just dying to get the needle into his girlfriend. We already had the dope! And we had the money! We were waved outside with the money and the dope in our hands. Well, what does one do in a situation like that? We hit the road!'

The epilogue to this story is a profoundly moral one, to show that there is such a thing as instant karma, even in the life of a Moon Goddess. They hit the road and took the greatest care to cross into Germany at the quietest border at the quietest time, the heroin hidden in the bottom of the guitar case. It was 5 a.m. when they passed the little crossing that was never manned so early in the morning. Wham! Five guards jumped into the road ahead and stopped the car. They searched everything. Nico sat there, cool, detached, very 'elsewhere', as though she was above all such inconveniences. They saw that Nico was holding a black bag. When they searched it, the bag appeared to hold the whole world inside and seem as deep. Out came the valium, some other pills ('for sea sickness') and they knew they would find something better if they searched her. They asked her to stand in the road. But Nico said in an innocent voice, 'Excuse me asking, but if you want to search me, shouldn't there be a lady officer present?' She was right. They hadn't brought one. They were foiled by their own procedures. Then they found the guitar case in the boot. It was still dark outside and one of the officers shone his torch down into the case. Lutz was sweating, at 5 a.m. Nico suddenly coughed and asked for a sweet out of her bag. The diversion worked and the officer failed to spot the pouch of heroin. Finally the five men ganged up on Nico and tried to intimidate her: 'Are you *certain* there's nothing we should know about?' Nico stared right back at them. 'Do I look like that sort of person? You can see I'm far too wise for that sort of caper.' Nico and Lutz drove on, rather surprised that they had got away with it.

Lutz Ulbrich became her lover and friend. To Nico, these were very special words. They meant to her: butler, go-fer, actuary, cleaner, engineer, manager, fixer, heavy, brother. Ulbrich was assigned any and all of these in order to feed her habit. They were caught in a chain of obligations. She needed to work in order to buy heroin, she needed heroin in order to work, she needed money in order to do the concert, but she needed money to buy the heroin that would get her through the concert in order to get the money. Ulbrich followed Nico through this labyrinth day after day: 'Once we were short of money in Berlin. We had to plan a concert in order to make some money, in turn to allow us to go to Amsterdam and buy heroin which we needed in order to be fit to fly to Madrid and play a festival in nearby León. So I organised the concert at the Kampkino – we showed one of the films of Philippe, who had joined us. We got our money from the concert and I drove them all the way from Berlin to Amsterdam as fast as possible, because we had to get the final flight from there at 7 p.m.

'It was a boiling hot day, and just twenty kilometres short of Amsterdam Nico was going cold turkey [withdrawal pains from lack of heroin]. I tore along with no concern for speed limits when, suddenly, *ka-blam!*, we were slithering around the road, completely out of control. A wheel had blown. It was 5.30 p.m. and we had not yet been to the heroin dealer. I fixed the wheel, raced to the dealer, threw the money at him and grabbed whatever heroin he had, drove like hell to the airport, and we were just allowed on as it was leaving. Well, the heroin was good but we hadn't got enough of it to last. Nico wanted to go from León to Ibiza for a few days' rest. By the time we got there, we hadn't any heroin left, and Ibiza was not a good place for heroin – about the only drug it wasn't good for! I said, "No problem; I'll fly back to Amsterdam, now that I know your dealers, and I'll be back within 48 hours." ' Lutz Ulbrich boarded the plane with a list of three addresses. Over in Amsterdam he had three hours to get back to the airport. First address, nobody home; second address, gone out; third, nobody. He had to do something – Nico and Philippe were going cold turkey on Ibiza.

Ulbrich went to the Amsterdam railway station to check the scene – there are always dealers. A black guy approached him. Nico had warned her lover, go-fer, butler, 'Never buy from black men.' Ulbrich had no other choice. The man took Ulbrich to a café where he was the only white. Then four men showed him upstairs where the deal could be done in private. They gave him a little of the smack. It was fantastic, certainly worth the money; he was stoned the whole day on the sample. Then they showed him the entire deal of Chinese rocks – sublime. 'Have you got the money?' they asked. 'Show us it.' Ulbrich's heart pounded: 'I thought that this would be the end – they'd steal the money and maybe do me in. But no, they took the money and gave me the wrap, and it was over so fast. I was out of the café in seconds. I got back to Ibiza the next day. Nico and Philippe were surprised and I was so proud. Nico took the wrap: "But it's so heavy!" I told her, "It's the best we've ever had. I tried some." Philippe took some: "Yeah! It's good! It's heroin OK." A big relief. The next day, Philippe's eyes were out on stalks. He was so ill. I felt like a stupid, little boy. They'd switched wraps. I went down into Ibiza town – everyone says you can't get heroin in Ibiza – and I tried everywhere only to prove it. Three days later, Nico herself flew to Amsterdam to buy what we needed. You see how it is? The money (think of all that money – the drugs, the flights), the time, the crazy things you do for this stuff.'

Nico shuttled between Lutz's home in Berlin and Paris, Ulbrich and Garrel. She had concerts to play through Hassad Debs, four more films to make through Garrel, and an overwhelming desire to be taken seriously. Nico despaired, however, that she was no longer in command of her life. She was dependent on drink, drugs, deceit, and – worst of all – money. She had changed her looks again. Her very long hair was no longer any shade of red, now that Morrison was dead, but brown. Nico wore black ('in mourning for ever'), though she hung on to her brown boots ('Brown at the top and brown at the bottom, and brown comes out in the middle – ho, ho, ho'). Her reliance on public concerts had led her to theatricise her make-up. She was no longer 'ugly', she was 'autumnal'. Nico toiled to give her face a sheer pallor ('It looked like someone had thrown a packet of flour in her face,' a journalist noted) and she often wore sunglasses indoors to hide her heroin-pinny eyeballs. One Italian promoter stood at the airport waiting for Nico to arrive for a concert. He held in his hand a picture of Nico, so he would recognise her. She strolled over to him. He looked on. She said, 'Ciao, I'm Nico.' He stared at her, then at the picture, the cover shot from *Chelsea Girl*, the blonde of ten years ago. He sighed, generously.

In Berlin, which had become a *chic* city to visit due to its mythic air of decadence and its dramatically young population, Nico was excited to discover that David Bowie was living there with Iggy Pop. It was a strange alliance to Nico's mind, and she never quite understood why Bowie had taken to patronising her old lover just because Pop had become a junkie: 'It was like an old *roué* had taken an orphan from the streets to *improve* him.' But as she was desperately short of money, she considered it rather good news. She tried to find out where they were living. Ulbrich took her to a police station to look up the address. They couldn't find it, until the police confided that the address could be found under Osterberg, Iggy Pop's real surname. Nobody was there when they visited the apartment, so Nico left Bowie a note: 'I want to see you.' He sent a note back: 'I don't want to see you.'

Nico's days and nights in Berlin were spent in a haze of drugs and drink. 'She once called me, out of the blue,' Aunt Helma recollected. 'It seemed to be urgent: "I must see you at such-and-such an address, but I'm busy with appointments right now." Her tone was so odd that I decided to go anyway. It was an apartment. It smelt sweet, very sweet, and I found the atmosphere very uncomfortable. Christa was not exactly in good shape for conversation. She was on a sofa in a small room. I called to her, "Christa, we've made a date. What do you want?" A man came in and said in English, "She is sleeping, she is tired." I went back home, puzzled. I learned later that it was an opium den. Then I recall another occasion when she was with some friends in a car. It was the night, or rather it was early morning, and they were cruising round looking for alcohol. Christa remembered that my son, her cousin Ulli, had a wine cellar at his home! They rushed over there and Christa started banging on the door, "Ulli! Ulli! Open your wine cellar! I'd like a drink! Open up!" You can imagine the noise in this sedate suburb, everyone asleep. Ulli had to get rid of them as calmly as he could. You certainly paid to be part of Christa's family.'

In wild contrast, Nico's days and nights in Paris were spent in a haze of drugs and drink, and filming. Garrel followed his silent portrait of Jean Seberg with a silent portrait of his father, the actor Maurice, in *Un Ange passe* ('There Was a Silence' – literally, 'An Angel Passes By'; 1975). 'I made it so it didn't cost too much. I made it very quickly. It turned out to be a film that looked exactly like it cost – it was *industrially* just right. But it was also useful to do [to show] I love my father.' He resorted to Nico's songs again, and she acted in the film with the beautiful Bulle Ogier, who went on to make a mainstream film career. He followed it with *Le Berceau de cristal* ('The Crystal Cradle'; 1976), where Garrel asserted a private independence by engaging Anita Pallenberg to take part alongside Nico. It is a shame he didn't use Zouzou as well – the thought of three of Brian Jones's partners in the same film is intriguing. This time Garrel used the music of Lutz's group Ashra. He didn't seem to mind that his partner Nico was having an affair with somebody else, though Ulbrich felt dreadfully uneasy. When a writer asked Garrel why, out of all the bands in the world, he chose Ashra, he evasively replied: 'Half of their pieces were conceived for the film. The other half were things they already played at that time. They're my age. There was a kind of (how can I put it?) . . . complicity between us.' These films, hermetic in style, are rarely seen anywhere. Garrel rather likes that. His most popular film, the one about his life with Nico, was shown in a suburban cinema at 10.30 on Sunday mornings. He rather likes that, too.

NICO THE NOMAD flew to California. She was bored stiff with her active and aesthetic but aimless life. She wanted a record contract. It was her first trip to America since her exile five years ago. There had been talk of The Doors reforming with Nico as the new Jim Morrison ('we have the same voice'). It was talk and little else. She sought advice from Paul Morrissey, who was now scriptwriting in Hollywood. She called a few contacts, but nothing useful happened. Pierre Cottrell, the film producer and translator, paid a visit to Morrissey's place by Crescent Heights and Sunset Boulevard: 'Nico would spend all day, eight hours or so, playing her portable harmonium. At night she would go out to get smack. She'd hang out in a little bar filled with gangsters and prostitutes, near the old Trubb's drugstore – the one where people sat waiting to be discovered. The place was called Boogie's; in its day it had been James Dean's hangout, but now it was just dangerous. Many times she'd been ripped off in there. Her cheques were stolen . . . she must have liked the down-at-heel ambience. There was little else to like.'

Disheartened, Nico returned to Paris to learn that she was no longer Ari's legal mother. In August 1976, at the age of fourteen, he had reached his majority. Nico had left him stateless. Mama Edith realised the simple solution was to adopt him, to make him a Boulogne and a French citizen. His grandmother became his mother, making his father his new half-brother. 'My grandparents explained to me that my mother was a drug addict,' Ari contended, 'and they tried to turn me against her, to hate my mother. I accepted their offer of adoption, of course, because I was an innocent boy and didn't really understand the consequences. So my grandmother became also my mother, and my father closed the door on my actual mother. That is what happened in return for my legality. I was living as a straight French boy who had glimpsed an alternative life – you can imagine how split I was about this.' He later accused Mama Edith of 'spoon-feeding' him, that she had protected him too much from the truth. She thought this was *strictly* accurate, but that she was not exactly swimming in options, given the extraordinary circumstances of both his mother, Nico, and his father, Delon. Madame Boulogne had not received a sou from Nico for Ari when Nico was rich, and Nico was not now in a position to change the habit of a lifetime. 'I sold my jewels,' said Mama Edith, 'my diamond, other things, whatever I could sell to get us through.' A little later on, when he was sixteen, she sent Ari to military academy. With his short hair, she claimed, he looked just like her son Alain 'when once he came out of prison'.

Nico was now mainlining her heroin daily and was wholly dependent on the drug. She considered suicide. It would be easy and cruel to add 'but she was too lazy'. She was held back by the conviction that she would have to die for a reason, and though she could see no reason to live, she could find no reason to die. Her work also helped her to live. She had composed yet more music and she was determined to leave the world a legacy of awkward, insightful songs about resistance. She needed only a record contract, a publishing deal, a real manager, an accountant, an attorney, an address, some money, oh . . . and a little smack, 'just for today, you understand'.

Suddenly, for a fleeting moment, something made her smile. Punk. 'It was like a change of atmosphere. The music was heavy metal – it was the same thing we had heard for nearly ten years, but it was like heavy metal played by The Velvet Underground, kind of amateur. What surprised me most was the situationism of it. Here was a new generation thinking like me. I was like a proud mother!' That is how punk used her; the romantics among them would cry on her shoulder while the thugs threw cans in her face. She first discovered punk in Berlin. On 16 May 1977, she had joined 4,000 others in the Protestant cemetery for the funeral of the terrorist Ulrike Meinhof ('I think you mean liberator, don't you?'), who had committed suicide in her prison cell ('Yes, it was suicide, but Andreas and the others were later murdered'). From now on whenever she sang 'Das Lied der deutschen' she would dedicate it to the memory of Ulrike Meinhof. In a further homage, she acquired a pair of little round glasses of the kind Meinhof wore at her trial. Nico would wear these at frontiers, so she looked more like a librarian than a junkie (Meinhof would hardly have been touched by this practical gesture of remembrance). After the uneasy funeral, Nico went on a personal wake to a new club on the 24-hour circuit of hedonism in Berlin. She saw 'a wonderful look of striped jumpers in mohair with real rats on the shoulder. The make-up was extreme like in a silent movie, and there was a new kind of *androgyne* look that was robotic. It was totally rebellious. I felt I was returning to earth.'

Before she landed with a bump, however, she had two films to finish with Garrel. *Voyage au jardin des morts* ('Journey to the Garden of Death') featured Nico with two established film stars, Maria Schneider and Laurent Terzieff, in Garrel's version of a famous short story by D'Annunzio, 'The Triumph of Death'. Then came the final panel of the trilogy on Nico, *Le Bleu des origines* ('Original Blue'). Black and white and silent, Garrel wanted to evoke a title like John Ford's film *How Green Was My Valley*, a monochrome movie with a colour to its name. Only Nico and Zouzou appeared throughout its 50-minute length. 'He shot us separately,' stressed Zouzou. 'There was nothing we would wish to say to each other, anyway. He was our only connection, and by then it was the end of his relationship with her. They were bored with each other.' Nico was filmed on the roof of the Paris Opéra, crouching by the carved muses, utterly alone. 'I set up the film with an old-fashioned hand-cranked camera,' recalled Garrel. 'It was truly the end of the trilogy, for in the film the young girl dies.' Pierre Cottrell reckoned that there was a more resonant evocation in the film: 'He used the old camera in the manner of Von Sternberg. He was Sternberg and Nico was his Dietrich.' They had got tired of each other and drifted their separate ways, and – according to his film account of their liaison – he needed to escape the dependency of drugs. But when Nico died, Garrel flew to the funeral, one of the few to bother.

Nico was now an international icon once more. She had been acclaimed as a punk paradigm by two new singers who led the field: Siouxsie Sioux of Siouxsie and the Banshees, and the American Patti Smith. 'I had met Patti in New York, when she was a young poet on the scene. She was a female Leonard Cohen, when she moved from writing to singing, and I liked her because she was thin but strong. John Cale produced her first album, which was about heroin [*Horses*; 1975]. Then I met her in Paris, and got to know her better. I felt like she could be a sister, because anyway she was the double of Philippe Garrel, and I liked to be together with her. But she has become boring now and married. She should have married John Cale and they could live in a gingerbread house and make gingerbread children. Patti was very kind to me. Early in 1978 my harmonium was stolen from me. I was without any money and now I couldn't even earn a living playing without my organ. A friend of mine saw one with green bellows in an obscure shop, the only one in Paris. Patti bought it for me. I was so happy and ashamed. I said, "I'll give you back the money when I get it", but she insisted the organ was a present and I should forget about the money. I cried. I was ashamed she saw me without money.'

Edith Cottrell, married to Pierre and an agent for film actors, knew both Nico and Garrel, as Garrel used many of her clients. She watched the couple's addiction drive them close to destruction, and flinched at their induced poverty: 'I remember one night when Nico called round looking like a gothic peasant in heavy, large robes, imposing and not at all what the public would call "feminine". She coyly asked me if I could lend her some cash (she seemed to think I was in the money because my apartment was large!). She brought out her passport and offered it against the money. She asked for something like 600 francs. It was to buy a gram of heroin, of course. I think I had something like 300 francs I could lend her, but she tried to force me to take the passport, as though the exchange made her less of a borrower. But then, a little while later, she was a different woman in my eyes. She had got a little concert in a club in Montparnasse – the place was owned by Jean Bouquin, who had catered to all the beautiful people in the Sixties and Seventies. She was excited and asked me to go (maybe she thought it made up for the favours, though it wasn't necessary). I went and I was completely surprised, because she was excellent. I didn't think she had it in her. She was supported by Didier Lockwood, the young jazz violinist, who was starting his career. I think it was an astonishment to everyone there to realise how good a performer she really was.'

She called on Nico Papatakis too, who had not seen her for fifteen years: 'She suddenly appeared in my apartment and said, "I'm going to sing. You started me up and never saw me. I have arranged a concert in a club nearby, so you don't have to walk very far." I was fearing the encounter. I thought I would be embarrassed. But I was completely surprised. She not only sang, she composed the songs and accompanied herself. Finally, you see, she had it in her.' The concert gave her the confidence to take to the road once more. The Rough Trade agency in London had found her dates on the budding punk circuit around Britain. Nico was energised by the prospect. Here was a new generation, the daughters and sons of adults her age, the very people she detested for their petty conformities. The children were taking revenge. They were the new generation of Situationists, sticking safety pins through the noses of queens. She would supply the moral ammunition and they would supply the mohair. Nico was their palpable link with bohemianism, a *chaper-onner* to their inheritance, a survivor who had the key ('somewhere, just wait a moment') in her bag. The High Priestess of Weird expected to face shining young nihilists of Ari's age, gazing reverently into her pinned eyes; she had not expected the mass gobbing of drunk punks yelling 'Fuck off, you old cunt!' Time after time she retired from the stage covered in lager and phlegm: 'They would not do this to a man.'

On 29 April 1978, between The Killjoys and The Adverts, she ran to the wings of London's Music Machine, near to the end of 'The End', ducking the flying beer cans as she went. Her romance with British punk finished one autumn night on the stage of the Top Rank, Cardiff. Siouxsie and the Banshees were euphoric that Nico – goddess of prehistory – was opening the concerts on their first big British tour. But the initial date had gone badly for Nico. She was drowned out by a massed chorus of 'Piss off'. Now, in Cardiff, close to the birthplace of John Cale, she felt more assured of a sympathetic response. Regrettably, at the third song she was hit on the cheek by a beer can, only this time the can was full. Pelted by tins and gob, she stood up and shouted into the microphone, 'If I had a machine gun, I would shoot you all.' She was taken off the tour at her own request.

The group's singer, Siouxsie Sioux, was embarrassed and annoyed about the incident. She had listened to Nico's records ever since her fellow Banshee Steven Severin had played her the LP of the *ACNE* concert in 1974, which he had attended. 'I was struck by the pictures on the records, how beautiful she was. It was the first time I'd heard such a deep voice, and that made an impression on me. Nico had an other worldly character, which was enhanced by the choral quality of the organ she used. She was like a mature dark angel.' Sioux saw Nico perform at The Adverts concert at the Music Machine: 'It was so horrible. The audience didn't give her a chance. Punk had generally changed for the worse once the media got hold of it at the time. It encouraged the mob element to turn up. They were just a bunch of hostile drunks. It was very ironic that these people supposedly representing the punk scene were so narrow-minded. Nico bore the brunt of their hostility because she was like nothing they'd experienced before.'

Steven Severin added, 'Nico was like a demigod to bands like us. Her LP *The Marble Index* was a revelation – it remains my favourite, and it was the Velvet Underground sound that we were attempting to develop, especially the starkness of the music, which Nico and John Cale always held to. They were our models, as opposed to the West Coast groups like The Doors and the hippies. Therefore you would have thought that Nico might have played to an appreciative audience, but they just didn't grasp where she came from or what she was doing. We were obviously drawing a lot of people who had never been to a punk concert before (the national tour was the first since our hit "Hong Kong Garden"), and Nico was the last thing they expected to hear. I was upset about the reaction she was forced to face; the audience got a good tongue-lashing from us when we got on. But she came over here a bit too early. Two years later the bands like Echo and The Bunnymen in Liverpool and Orange Juice in Glasgow went on about their debt to The Velvet Underground and made Nico, Lou Reed and John Cale more in vogue again.' Siouxsie Sioux wasn't even sure if Nico knew what she was doing there: 'She seemed confused, confused about everything. She didn't seem to know why she was there with us. In a better world, it would have been the ideal bill – us and Nico.'

It was said of Nico that any concert she did would sort out the 'new wave' from the punks. 'The punks were nice kids playing louts, mixed in with louts playing real louts, while the "new wave" were nice kids playing dead,' a promoter alleged. 'Nico always looked like she was deader than the rest. She was an icon to a whole generation of raincoated zombies. You felt you should have booked her into cemeteries rather than clubs. Her tours should have been sponsored by the Co-op Funeral Service. I used to tell the promoters to stick a poster outside: "Free razorblade with the first 100 tickets". She looked like that Morticia out of the Addams Family, and – do you know how miserable she was? – I'll tell you. She was more miserable than Joy Division, and their singer hung himself – that's how miserable she was. I used to have a hearse standing by at her gigs, just in case.' Ho, ho, ho, ho, ho.

She wrote a letter to Ari to say that she felt finally she must kill herself (she never got round to it, of course). Garrel was right to kill her off in her final film, she thought. She was alone, a junkie, no prospects, on top form and nobody wanted to know. She was lurching in limbo towards the end of the Seventies, just like she'd ended the Sixties. Nico could see no way forward. Not for the first time, however, her luck ('my fate') quickly changed. After a concert in Paris with The Rollmops in 1978, she met with two Corsican brothers who weren't really brothers. Philippe Quilichini was reggae's premier white bassist. His pretend brother Antoine Giacomoni was a young, good-looking and charming gay photographer who fell in love with Nico 'as my godmother, like a fairytale character. I was intimidated by her and shy. But she went into the kitchen and said, "I will make a soup for you." She was like no one I'd ever met before. I told her an idea I had. I wanted to remake *Death in Venice* but to transpose it to today, not in colour but in black & white, not perfect but rough, not in Venice but Bangkok, not with Mahler's music but hers, not with a boy but a girl who looks like a boy, and not with Dirk Bogarde but with Nico. She said OK. But I went to Jamaica instead with my brother Philippe.'

When he returned to Paris on business, Giacomoni asked Nico if he could photograph her. She told him she never wanted to see another camera in her life. That's OK, he said, you won't have to see it. He used a mirror. She sat in front of the mirror and studied her reflection. He photographed her from behind, so that she saw the image exactly as it would be to the viewer of the photo, and not in reverse, which is normally the case: 'I did not know then that she sang this Velvet Underground song, "I'll Be Your Mirror". It worked, and she loved the photograph I made, and I then made more with other rock stars in the mirror. So we became friends, and she taught me many things, simple things. She was a poet, with an acoustic personality. We would walk everywhere – no metro, no taxi – and we would stare at a window or a detail of architecture for, say, ten minutes. I saw things I never would have noticed in life without Nico.'

Philippe Quilichini had moved to London with his fiancée Nadett' Duget and Giacomoni. They took a flat at the corner of Cambridge Gardens and Ladbroke Grove, just above the noisy Westway, and

Nico moved in with them, for they had decided to create an album for her, with Nadett' as the executive producer, Quilichini as the producer and, instead of John Cale's scratchings and jinglings, a real rock band. Nico would outpace Patti Smith. It would be Nico's fifth solo album, and she chose to call it *Drama of Exile*, 'because my life has been a drama of exile. I've been disappearing from myself. I've become a total stranger to myself.' Giacomoni admitted that 'It was tough to get this record out. Nico was on some sort of black list. She had a bad reputation. And there was a big campaign against drug users. Nico wasn't the only one to suffer from this – you may remember that Marianne Faithfull, who was on heroin longer than Nico, tried to make a comeback then with *Broken English*, and she had a terrible time. But once we got into the studio and started work with Andy Clark from David Bowie's *Ashes to Ashes*, it was terrific.' Nadett' Duget took some rough mixes to CBS Records; 'Nico with a rock band, what an idea,' the production men responded. They were willing to take on promotion and distribution and line it up with a band tour, so long as Nico signed a paper to say she'd clean herself up and get 'healthy'.

Then came the disaster. According to Giacomoni, 'This guy turned up from a little company called Aura Records. He called in the studio and he was also interested in the project. He had this extraordinary name, Aaron Sixx; he was sweet-talking Nico and being pleasant.' One day, according to the Corsican, when the tapes were nearly finished, Sixx gave the studio engineer £2,000 in return for the tapes. Later he gave Nico another £2,000: 'she was like a child in these things, and took the money because she could certainly find a use for it!' The French team were furious and acquired a music lawyer to stop the man. But Aaron Sixx apparently told them that 'the tapes are on my side, you'll have to sign with me now'. Giacomoni continued: 'We argued that wasn't how British law worked. So he took the tapes to Amsterdam and did what I prefer to call a "bootleg" with my photos on the cover. As the LP was imported back into Britain, we couldn't stop him through the courts because the record was no longer made in the country. This was real bandit stuff, and it held up the record's release by two years. You can imagine how much this hurt poor Nico.

'In the meantime we had invested in the record and so we had no option but to re-record it. Philippe went back into the studio and did the whole thing again! This was printed in France by Invisible Records and distributed by Virgin. It is the same project as the Dutch record, *Drama of Exile*, but it has a different cover, re-recorded songs that are the same. If this is not crazy enough, there is more. The very month that the record came out in France, my brother Philippe and Nadett' were driving to Paris from London when they crashed. Philippe was killed. Nadett' went into a coma and died three years later. Nico was already in hospital with some drug problem [septicaemia], and was told of the disaster there. You felt Nico was always surrounded by tragedy.'

'Nico was surrounded by them, that was the tragedy,' retorted Aaron Sixx. 'They came to me with some demos they'd made with Nico (which were eventually used for *Hanging Gardens*) and I put up a portion of the money to enable them to proceed with the LP at Gooseberry Studios, Tulse Hill. Nadett' said she'd sign a contract, but she stalled (she was too busy drug trafficking between Paris and London). I learned from the studio that Nadett' was removing the nearly finished tapes, so I scuppered her plan – the law was on my side, which they soon discovered. Nico did a deal with me behind their backs. I gave her a thousand dollars straight up. She didn't give a shit what happened to the LP, she just wanted the money for drugs.' Giacomoni concluded, 'In six years I lost three of my family, Nico the last. They are dead, they cannot defend themselves; let them rest in peace.'

'I RAN A CLUB called Rafter's in the middle of Manchester,' Alan Wise began. He is an imposingly large man, intelligent and genial, who is not keen on drugs but rather drawn to food; he parodies the image of the Jewish manager he is, surviving years of creditors and dodgy deals in order to help musicians get on stage. 'We did really well then because there was this new scene of punk and "new wave", and Manchester was quite a centre for it with The Buzzcocks, Joy Division and The Fall and all that. The Rough Trade agency in London phoned me up and said, "I've got a great act for your club – Nico." I made the classic mistake, "Who's he?" So one night Nico turned up. I'd never seen anyone look so forlorn. She was a sad sight. She was followed by this rather gormless boyfriend she'd picked up, Robert King, the singer with The Scars, a Scottish punk band. He was half her age and the sort that latched on to Nico for the rock and roll life. She called him her "artistic adviser". She told me she needed drugs right away in order to do the gig. It was the kind of blackmail you learned to accommodate in the rock business. Somehow we got hold of this Iranian guy who sold her some heroin. She must have thought we were terribly clever, because the next day we got this message from Eric's club in Liverpool, "Can you come and 'help her out'?" So we went over and "helped her out" again. I remember watching the gig at the back and laughing for some reason, when Nico suddenly stopped singing and called out, "Will that idiot at the back stop laughing? Will somebody throw him out?!" '

Wise soon established she had nowhere to stay – she was dossing on the floors of anyone who'd have her. The French gang were getting on her nerves, she would tell anyone who listened, because they were always checking her for drugs ('They look at my eyes all the time') and they were junkies themselves avid for her stash, she reckoned. Four men shared a flat further down Cambridge Gardens, and Nico, who had met one of them at a pub, would often call round and fall asleep in their kitchen. One of the four, Barry Tyler, remembered her visits: 'She would sit in the kitchen, shot to fuck, stringy hair, pasty face. She looked like a fat, bloated old broad; if she were in a movie, she'd be played by Shelley Winters. It was only when she spoke that you could tell it was the great Nico. She complained about the French people down the street as though we knew them, though we'd never even met them.' Nico would sit in the kitchen and wait for another of the flatmates to appear – the one who was addicted to heroin. They would jack up, and then, claimed Tyler, 'she'd be bright and alive for a while, dropping names of her famous friends *apropos* of nothing – "David's a funny boy. He's very nice but he's fucked up" – then she'd fall asleep.'

Alan Wise was shocked to learn that Nico the Moon Goddess was reduced to the state of a 40-year-old junkie without a penny to her name, sleeping on other people's shabby floors. He decided to deal with her problems one by one: 'I put her up at my expense at a Polish hotel in Manchester called the Polex, a fiver a night, dead grotty, full of old Poles, but a step up from grubby carpets. Nico quickly discovered my father owned a chain of chemist shops around town. Admitting that to a drug addict is like telling a little girl your father's Santa Claus! Suddenly I was the Doctor who could do anything, Nico's Mr Fixit.' She soon moved into his flat in the smart suburb of Didsbury, but her harmonium was back in London and she needed to see Nadett' about work, and so she shuffled back south. 'I suspected that Nico and Nadett' were having an affair, the way she talked about her,' considered Wise. 'Nico was rapaciously fond of certain women (Nico easily frightened women away because they thought she'd devour them), and Nadett' was a very attractive half-Vietnamese type. But in order to get her hands on their drugs again, Nico told them she'd been taken for a ride up North: "They're cheating me, robbing me of earnings in Manchester."

'I went down to see her about some gigs I could find and I took Yankie Bill with me, a nice guy but a "heavy". The Corsicans insulted us – typical French, I thought, no sense of humour, and blindly possessive of Nico. I was their opponent, because they were junkies and I've never taken drugs in my life; they thought anyone who wasn't on drugs couldn't be trusted! But Nico was very impressed that I'd got a strong man, so she decided to carry on with the show with us: "Oh, Alan, I'll stay with you. I don't want to go back to them, they're dragging me down." Basically she'd dragged herself down to their level; she was just a desperate junkie. So she ambled back up to Manchester and I told her we would do three things: get her off heroin and on to methadone so she could move legally between countries with medical authorisation; get her regular tours to pay off her drug debts and get her saving her earnings; and finally find her somewhere secure and decent to live. I was in love with her, if the truth be told, unrequited love as it happens – and I wanted to wash away all the crap and filth that had tainted her life and get the Moon Goddess glowing again. I didn't recognise how *fucking* hard it could be to bathe a junkie clean – but we nearly made it, with a lot of mad adventures on the way.'

Nico, sweetened by the promise of management, decided that here was a chance to pick herself up. First, she thought, she must see old friends again to get her bearings. She started with the ever-reliable Lutz Ulbrich in Berlin (she borrowed the money for her ticket from future concerts). 'She never announced a visit, she just appeared,' observed Ulbrich. 'At the time my girlfriend was living with me, and I'd been working late. I came into the apartment to find my girlfriend crashed out on the sofa. I went to my bedroom, and there she was again, fast asleep. I had to pinch myself before I realised it was Nico, who'd arrived expecting shelter, which we always gave her. It was 1979 and I decided to go and work as a guitarist in New York. "I want to go there, too," insisted Nico. "I'll go with you." I winced because that meant I'd have to pay for her ticket as usual. She said, "Don't worry. After two weeks there I'll have a gig and everything will be alright." I didn't believe her, but anyway . . . when we arrived in New York she phoned up Jane Friedman who was Cale's manager, and she phoned CBGB's, a good club to play, and it was interested. It was booked for two weeks' time, just enough time to get an announcement in *The Village Voice*, which also said that John Cale would appear. Two shows. Nico's hunch paid off!'

Ulbrich was fascinated by the relationship between Nico and John Cale. They had two rehearsals with Cale in the Chelsea Hotel where they stayed, and Ulbrich was amazed by Cale's consideration of Nico's musical shortcomings: 'She couldn't read music, she just remembered where her hands went on the keyboard – that's why she rehearsed so much on the same material. I remember that she suddenly forgot the placing of her hands. She panicked. It had been five years since Cale had worked with Nico, but he just went over and said, "I think it's like this," and showed her. He played it correct first time, because to him it was a matter of logic. But then, end of the night, and they would beat each other up because of some argument about heroin. The whole scene was unnerving her due to this big reappearance in New York, and then because of Sid Vicious who had killed himself a few days before right there. Nico was friends with him, because he had been in Siouxsie and the Banshees before The Sex Pistols, and they talked about him playing bass for her on a record, but then his suicide . . .'

The concerts at CBGB's are recorded on a bootleg tape. It not only captures Nico singing to Ulbrich's guitar, but also her elegant debate with a drunk heckler – a man, of course:

Nico: This is a song from my album that has not been released.
Heckler: Yeah!
Nico: Some of you people seem to be pretty drunk. Well, so am I.
Heckler: We wanna hear some rock'n'roll!
Nico: You shouldn't have come to see me then.
Heckler: Funky. Get funky, baby. Yer funky but chic!
Nico: I don't think I want to continue unless some people shut up.
Heckler: Why don't you get off?
Nico: Oh shut up, will you? If you have anything to say go out of here, get out of here, will you?
Heckler: Can't we talk?
Nico: No you can't, damn it!

A member of the Velvet Underground Appreciation Society tried to interview Nico between concerts for the house magazine *What Goes On*. He loyally recorded Nico's chain of tetchy retorts:

WGO: I thought your first set tonight was gorgeous.

Nico: It was dreadful.

WGO: Do you know if today is John Cale's birthday?

Nico: Oh, don't ask me questions like that! I don't even know when my own birthday is. (A man walks in)

Man: David Bowie is here, Nico.

Nico: When did he come in?

Man: Just now.

Nico: Good, then he missed the first set.

Ulbrich continued: 'We had other gigs in America, organised very quickly, attracting a crowd who came out of idle curiosity – Isn't she dead? – because she hadn't played America for over ten years. It was an ugly time. The tour was hell for Nico because it is terribly hard to find heroin in that country. She had to make do with the medical substitute methadone. Methadone is a very boring drug. You don't get a hit from it. Nico would drink beer and wine to get a buzz; it was this combination of methadone and alcohol that made her fatter.' The writer Philip Milstein noted her looks at the time: 'Her face was not much more lined than that on the cover of *The End*, but the jowls, once sallow, were puffy, somewhat of a double chin was beginning to show, and the fingers were downright chubby. But those glamorous, glorious cheekbones were still glamorous, glorious. Her hair was the same as it's been for years, brown and in straight bangs. She was still beautiful, but reminded me of a sort of New Age Elizabeth Taylor – the beauty remains, but it is more a memory than a present reality.'

'Nico didn't care any more what happened to her appearance,' recalled Ulbrich. 'I think the lowest point of her concert life came at San Francisco. Just a minute before the concert started Nico told me, "I must have a piss." There was no toilet backstage, you had to go through the audience to find one. I told her this while the announcer was already on stage, "And now the Goddess of . . ." Nico insisted, "I've got to piss. I'm desperate." She just pulled down her trousers and pissed right on the side of the stage. But she also managed to piss on her trousers. She went on stage with this awful stain on her pants. She sang the first song, and the footlights by her were hot and making the piss steam from her legs. The Moon Goddess they had all come to see stopped, looked down, and said right into the mike for the benefit of the audience, "Oh, look. I've pissed on my trousers." '

For five years Nico was a junkie. She lost her son, her money, her record contract, her audiences, friends, her dignity, and any sense of direction. She was no longer even in her palace; she was 'lost in the land'. From the moment her mother died she had descended to the point of suicide, and ended the decade in a narcotic daze on the floors of strangers. She was even a stranger to herself, she claimed, and she was no longer Christa or Nico or anyone she recognised. She decided that she could no longer bear to be Morticia from the Addams Family or Shelley Winters. She wanted to be Nico once more. All she needed to do now was to try and remember who Nico really was. She thought it would be simple enough . . . wouldn't it?

14 1981–1988

When I have fears that I may cease to be
Before my pen has glean'd my teeming brain,
Before high-piled books, in charactery,
Hold like rich garners the full ripen'd grain;
When I behold, upon the night's starr'd face,
Huge cloudy symbols of a high romance,
And think that I may never live to trace
Their shadows, with the magic hand of chance;
And when I feel, fair creature of an hour,
That I shall never look upon thee more,
Never have relish in the faery power
Of unreflecting love; – then on the shore
Of the wide world I stand alone, and think
Till love and fame to nothingness do sink.

(JOHN KEATS, 1848)

'NOW I UNDERSTAND this difference between a biograph and an autobiograph. But I do not read biographs. They are full of lies, in fact, because they say a life has a beginning, a middle and an end. I do not believe in the middle. Such a book pretends to be true but it is really artificial. And the end leads on to another end; that is what Jim's song is about, "The End". I prefer novels because they have more imagination in their truth. Do you know what Oscar Wilde wrote? He wrote that "In fiction the good end happily and the bad unhappily – that is what fiction means". You can only say one thing at the end – Nico has survived these indignities. Biographs tell you that somebody moves through life. I am saying that my life moves after me. Do you follow me?'

The writer admitted that he did not truly understand. Some sentences made sense, certainly. 'Well, I would like a novel about me because it will come from the imagination and so it will explain my mind, not my life. My mind and my life are two different things. My mind is called Christa. My life is Nico. Christa had made Nico, and now she is bored with Nico because Nico is bored with herself. Nico has been to the top of life and to the bottom. Both places are empty; she has discovered this. But Nico does not want to be in the middle either, where people turn their back on each other. To avoid these places of unhappiness it is better to be nowhere, and drift. That is the conclusion I have come to.' The writer enquired if she meant Nico or Christa had come to that conclusion. 'Oh, are you making fun of me, now?' Did Christa want to be a woman? 'No, she wanted to be a Nico.' Nico had lovers. 'No! Nico never wanted lovers. She wanted friends! Ho, ho, ho . . .' Does Christa want to be a *femme fatale* like Nico? 'I guess I cannot think this game any more. Do you have by any chance a little hash?'

WHEN ALAN WISE took hold of Nico's life, 'it was like he'd lifted her out of a dustbin, cleaned her up, got her breathing, walking, drinking, moaning, playing and travelling and living for better days; but she fucked it up by dying on him, which was very rude of her,' a fellow agent claimed. 'He must have gone through hell to get her all those gigs. Mind you, there's a lot of folk think he deserves to be dragged through hell – Nico, too. When Alan managed Nico he had to put her on a vicious spiral in order to get her straight again. It was like she'd wound herself into a big hole, and he had to unwind her out again. So that meant hundreds of gigs, anywhere in the world that would take her, so she could earn her money – which she spent straight off on smack; then he had to control the smack, get her on to methadone so you could control the dosage; then save the money she was saving off smack for her retirement (because when he picked her up she was already 40 years old); then get her off the methadone; then get her songs done by other people so she gets her royalties, I suppose . . . well, whatever, it was a ridiculously tough job. You have to hand it to him, he nearly managed it. As far as I'm concerned, though, I think it's a shame he saddled her with all those crap musicians from Manchester. He was doing too many pals favours.'

Although 'someone's lost the paperwork' (a favourite Manchester expression, it seems), it has been calculated that Nico performed over 1,200 concerts between 1980 and 1988. Aside from two major LPs released in that time, there were nine recordings of concerts officially made from which she would have accrued royalties, and countless 'bootlegs' from which she wouldn't. 'In those years,' Alan Wise considered, 'Nico earned at least £12,000 a year from concerts and £8,000 a year from record royalties. That was £20,000 nett, because she never paid taxes!' The trouble was the heroin. At £60 a gram, bought hand to mouth a gram a night, her heroin bill alone was

£22,000 a year. That figure doesn't include locating the drug dealer, delivery, or disasters.

Wise mockingly proposed a Michelin Guide for Junkies, because, 'there were so many bad deals and rip-offs in so many varieties in so many places, I think between me and the musicians we could write a good book'. Typical of his experience was in Copenhagen: 'You know how heroin's bought? In a little, folded paper wrap. Well, we were a bit short of money, but Nico wanted some heroin. We paid some of the last money to the roadie who had to go and stand in the main square trying to score. The concert was due to start in two hours. Just as Nico was supposed to go on, he turned up in the dressing room with the little wrap of smack. Nico was beside herself with excitement – every time a junkie sees a wrap, it's like it's Christmas Day.' The wrap was carefully covered in opaque cellophane. She unwound it, and unwound it. The audience was restless; 'Come on, Neek, it's time to get on stage,' Wise shouted. She was uncoiling, uncoiling, uncoiling . . . that's all there was to the wrap, a reel of cellophane. Nothing in the middle. She was furious. 'You idiot! I can't trust you fools with anything! I've got to do everything myself. I'm going out there to get my smack. You'll just have to wait.' The audience was impatient, it was way over starting time, but they were not to know their star was standing around town squares, waiting for her man. Half an hour later she came back to the dressing room, triumphant, with a wrap of heroin. She sat down, unwrapped it, unwrapped it . . . She'd gone to the same dealer. She'd been cheated twice in two hours, by the same man. Then she had to do the gig. 'She was in tears, inconsolable,' Wise recalls. 'That's how it went.'

In Paris she bought crushed Polos, in Milan salt, in Leiden sugar, in London scouring powder. Alan Wise continued: 'One time in the early Eighties she wanted to go for a break to India. She went entirely alone to Calcutta. When she came back she was stopped by Customs, but they didn't find anything. As usual, she'd hidden her drugs in a condom she'd shoved up her bum. She came back very pleased with herself – she'd bought a load of virtually pure heroin in India. She pulled it out of her bum, unwrapped it . . . concrete mix. She'd smuggled in two ounces of concrete mix up her arse! That proved to be a horrible occasion; she spent the next few days going cold turkey while everyone rustled up a few quid to get a quarter of a gram so she could have an hour or two of comfort. If Nico suffered, everyone suffered.'

When she stayed in Manchester her heroin from London occasionally came by the train's Red Star service, collected by a contact at the neighbouring BBC. The wrap was hidden in the corner of record sleeves. The shuttle service stopped when the courier got embarrassed by the record covers he had to lug around the BBC – *Russ Conway's Greatest Hits*, or most appropriately, *Germany Calling – The Speeches of Lord Haw Haw*. Nico would often send parcels, sheltering heroin and addressed to herself, to foreign hotels in advance of visits. Once in Helsinki, the street-wise porter fathomed what was happening and blackmailed Nico's tour manager into handing over the entire earnings of the concert. She would often perform in a state of withdrawal which would end in tears on stage – 'Why am I doing this shit? I can't carry on . . .'

Phil Jones managed two of her foreign tours and recalls the drug disasters, of which his most traumatic memory was this: 'In spring 1982 she toured Holland with The Blue Orchids as her backing band. We did twelve concerts in thirteen days. The audience levels were high because Nico had been rediscovered then by the "new wave". The money was good and the band was banging stuff up their noses and smoking marijuana like it was going out of fashion. Before we knew it we had to come home. Nico had gone on the streets of Amsterdam early in the morning to buy some smack. We drove onto the ferry and Nico went to rest in a cabin. I had something like £5,000 in guilders on me from the gigs and I arranged to leave it with the purser. I should have known better. He started asking me funny questions about the money, and I told him it was the earnings of a singer resting in her cabin. I was sitting in the ship's cinema when Martin and Oonagh from the band tapped me on the shoulder. "Nico's looking for you and she's not very well." I followed them out to the deck and there was Nico walking slowly up and down. Everyone was staring at her – she was six foot tall and weird-looking anyway – but she'd turned purple. The purser saw me next to Nico and put two and two together.' The purser made a radio call to Harwich Customs shed.

As Jones helped Nico down to her cabin, she collapsed in the stairwell. Her face had turned blue. He jostled the slumped body into the cabin and on to the thin bed. 'I believed she was going to die. I didn't know what to expect next. I discovered that the band had been bringing her those little cartons of orange juice when she first felt ill – orange juice always seems to help with overdoses and such – and her blue pallor was slowly turning red. But she looked beyond redemption.' The cause of the grief was the bad deal of heroin she had bought that morning in Amsterdam – first the poison of it, and then the withdrawal from the previous binge. Nico, however, had the constitution of an ox. When they docked she was alive enough to be lifted into the van, from where Jones hoped he could get her home fast: 'I'd forgotten about Customs. They called us into the vehicle search area. They went through everything – thirteen days of soiled socks, dirty mags, the lot. They pulled the van apart. Nico was leant against the wall, groggy and obviously ill. Needless to say, they took a special interest in her.'

The Customs officials yanked everything out of her huge bag, tore through her diaries, her notebook and her make-up; it wasn't long before they found a syringe ('for my Vitamin B12 shots'), traces of marijuana ('I'm a Rastafarian, it is part of my religion') and a methadone pill ('They are legal – don't you know that?'). They split the band up and interviewed them one by one. What do you know about heroin? Nothing. Can you roll up your sleeves, please, let me see your arms? OK. 'The bass player had a wrap of amphetamine on him while he was being strip-searched,' Jones recalled, 'but he'd learned magic tricks and he kept the speed out of sight by turning it round in his hands. They kept going back to this notebook that Nico carried because it had some scribblings from William Burroughs about heroin that Nico had copied. I happened to know that Nico had a wrap of cocaine secreted in a corner of the book cover.' The book was as much a dilapidated mess as Nico, and the pages were stuck together with the cotton buds she used when she mainlined. It was a gift to the Customs officers, and they worked through it page by page, hunting for heroin. 'In the end we all started giggling,' continued Jones, 'it was all so absurd. The band looked exactly like the archetypal rock druggies that Customs officers pray will step their way, and everyone had a stash of something or other about them. But these dunces couldn't find a thing! They had to let us go.' The officers had warned the police. There were no less than three police cars following the van as it entered Ipswich.

Jones stopped at a pub: 'Nico was slowly coming back to earth, and I wanted to get her sorted out before the police searched us (they needed a warrant to raid the pub). She snorted a little of her cocaine and she was somewhat less purple after a drink, but she was completely severed by the day's drama. Luckily the police cars had got bored waiting for us, so there was just one behind when we left the pub.' He took Nico to a local hotel and placed a pile of banknotes in her hand. 'I'll be back tomorrow to pick you up,' he promised. The band carried on to London, watching the police car turn back at the town boundary ('They just wanted to see us off the premises'), but they decided in the end to continue the last 150 miles back to the band's base in Manchester: 'We simply forgot about Nico. Sometimes, after you'd been through some harrowing nonsense because of her foolishness, you just felt "sod it". The next day she took the train back to London. It didn't mean a thing to her in the end. She was watching a film, and we were the actors – that's how she handled her life.'

Nico's habit, rooted in remorse for her absent son, was doubled the moment she was reunited with him. The fit young god sought her out and found his *maman* in England, sharing a bed and needles with a 'gormless' lad his age. Ari insisted Robert King left; Nico obliged, booted him out, and her son took his place. Her darling Ari was as perfect in looks as she could have desired, almost a replica of the stunning 22-year-old Delon. 'There was a devotional bond between Nico and Ari,' considered Wise, 'but it was a bit too sugary for some of the musicians who worked with her. There was also an erotic charge in their intimacy that led to unwholesome gossip amongst the band – the usual rubbish that musicians indulge in. They shared beds together, mother and son, and I assure you that was it. She tried to make up for the years she neglected him, but all she could do was shroud him in affection. Then again, there was a lot of fighting and tantrums. You can imagine what caused them.' Ari had not yet encountered the absolute heaven that was grade-A heroin. Nico was keen to take him there. 'My mother helped me to inject heroin and we shared needles. I became addicted like my mother, and since her death I have tried on and off to get myself straight,' Ari admitted.

He knew all about drugs, of course, before their reconciliation. It was said he left school a well-behaved young man and worked for a time in a traditional restaurant ('I said, "Listen man, your customers I spit in their faces" '), then had a year of army conscription ('I spent most of the time in the infirmary – I was playing safe, you know'). Back in Paris he lived a routine Parisian life ('I was hanging around, chasing girls and stuff; I look a lot of drugs'). He found work as a male model, and his slim body could be found for a time on poster sites around France advertising Laura jeans. Paul Morrissey met up with Ari and introduced him to Edith Cottrell, the film agent: 'Paul thought Ari could find some respectable work in films or TV, and I took him on for a year. But he was not the most reliable of people, and eventually I passed on him. If I remember rightly, he worked in an impressionistic TV serial about the rebel poet Rimbaud, which seems in retrospect to be good casting!'

When mother and son met up, 'it was another mouth to feed,' hinted Wise. 'We'd managed to get rid of the "artistic adviser" and now we'd got *le kid* in exchange. Ari considered I wasn't serving his mother too well by booking her in small clubs, in hired vans on bum-numbing tours. He had this vision of her stepping out of a silver limousine into the Carnegie Hall – Nico Minnelli with the New York Philharmonic Orchestra, rather than Nico the Valhalla Vamp and her Seven Dwarves sitting in a cupboard at the back of the Scunthorpe Trades Club. I can appreciate his frustration, but he hadn't seen where his mother had been since the punks spat her off the stage. I think he presumed a lot about his mother before he met her again, and the disillusion must have been dreadful. He never recovered from that, and Nico hadn't a clue how to address it, apart from heroin, her answer to everything. She kept saying to me, tears in her eyes, "What can I do about Ari? It's all my fault." Now I love Ari like a son. What happened to him is a tragedy.'

Ari joined the tours now and again as a 'roadie', an assistant who normally gets the equipment on and off stage, but who, when working for Nico, stood on street corners waiting for the man. Ari maintained: 'We would have fights because I wanted her to stop the heroin, and it was difficult because I was drawn to it too, but it had to be resisted. She was also very critical of my girlfriends – there would always be some fight about who I was seeing. I remember in Stuttgart there was a guy came backstage offering her some opium, and I told her, "I don't want you to take that crap, or you'll never see me again!" But she was stubborn and she left with him. The next morning she was sick, withdrawing. I was firm with her: "See what I told you yesterday? You're stupid!" She turned round, "Ho, ho, ho. I bet I had a better night than you!" ' The other members of the road crew would remember the fights: 'Chairs were a favourite weapon – bang, crash, smash – in the clubs, hotel rooms, people's homes . . . It was all very passionate and garlicky.'

Nico, six feet tall, stout and strong, turned aggressive with beer inside her. Ari, too. She said that Ari had an untempered streak because he was a Leo, 'a little lion' – and 'you only had to look at his father's reputation'. But it wasn't always a matter of the son shaming the mother. They once stayed a while together at the London home of a married couple who were friends of Alan Wise. The couple heard a terrible fight one night in Nico's room, but they were too polite to enquire what the hell Nico and Ari were doing to their furniture. The next day the husband came home to find Nico sitting alone, crying. He tried to comfort her, but her weeping grew worse. He asked what the matter was. 'Oh, I have something terrible to tell you, and I don't know how.' He said it was OK, he wouldn't be offended. 'My son is fucking your wife.' He was offended.

NICO HAD DECIDED she didn't want to be a musician any more ('It can be too boring; all those dressing rooms'). She had heard of the perfect job: 'Alan, I would like to be the person they test drugs on. I think I have the qualifications, and certainly the experience. It will help me to become a robot, which I would like to be because I have too many thoughts to cope with. Can't you arrange this? After all, your father the chemist must know the right people. I have always found you can rely on a family for support.' Alan Wise advised Nico that her time would be best spent in writing new songs and earning the money that would help her, and her son, survive. In the meantime, he indicated, he was very interested to learn that CBS had been keen on the idea of Nico with a band, before the Frenchies and Aura messed it up. He would organise a band to back Nico on her tours.

In the event, he organised more than one band. 'Nico became an employment agency for Manchester musicians tapping into trips round Europe, America, Australia, Japan – anywhere who'd have her and a bunch of raincoated Mancunians,' an agent alleged. The musicians themselves couldn't work out who went on what: 'There were basically three bands: The Blue Orchids, The Bedlamites, The Faction. To Alan, however, there were only two bands: the Old Band and the New Band. Or was it the Old Band and the Young Band? No, it wasn't that because there was often a keyboard player called Jim Young, yet he was in the Old Band. Actually, if you took a photo of any of the bands at any one of the 1,000 or more gigs they did, you would find some of the same players alongside people you'd never seen before or since, because they were deputising for someone who could get better money working at the end of a pier. Nico got 50 per cent of the fee, and we got between £30–£50 a night each. It was better than nothing, but not much.'

The Old Band comprised keyboards, bass guitar and drums. Even this classic set-up caused Nico problems: 'The bass guitar was a mistake, for a start. Nico didn't understand bass lines, because of this weird way she had of playing the harmonium with the melody in the bass. She liked to have freedom around her, but the drums and bass just imposed a straitjacket. It would be good with Jim Young on the piano and synthesiser, because he could just float around Nico and her organ. Eventually they dumped the bass and put Graham Dids in on percussion, which gave Jim a lot of space. The New Band was a way of addressing that problem, because there was more percussion and melody instruments to improvise aside her. Andy Diagram (the long-coated trumpeter of James) played the trumpet, Henry Laycock (now with Primal Scream) was on guitar, and Graham Dids or Eric Random played ethnic percussion. Though there'd be sometimes too many instruments on stage, it essentially put less pressure on Nico to, erm . . . get it right!'

Martin Hennin (bass) and Dick Harrison (drums) were faithful members of the New Band who suffered for their art backstage and front: 'She never spoke much and when she did she seemed to come from a different planet. We were all in awe of her. Alan called her Neek and we called her Mam,' recalled Martin. She called Dick Bill because she could never remember his name. She never appreciated the work they did to pull her concerts together: 'I remember once we were stuck in a stifling back room of some Italian club one morning getting a backing tape together for the concert that night,' recalled Hennin. 'Alan hadn't booked a drummer and there were no backing tapes done. We worked out a drum pattern for the opening number. We taped it and decided to play safe and put down ten minutes of it for a four-minute song. On the night, the tape started up and we vamped along. It took Nico six minutes to walk on to the stage! She mucked about and then she started singing. Halfway through, the tape ran out! Nico was mortified. She couldn't work it out. We'd spent all morning in a sweaty room doing something for Nico and we ended up looking a fool on stage and Nico screaming at us in the dressing room.'

Dick Harrison was struck by Nico's off-key memory: 'She could never remember the order of the songs, and often she couldn't even remember the songs. She'd get confused and sing a different song to the one we were playing, the one she was supposed to sing. She just carried on, in her own little world. One night we started to play the introduction to "I'll Be Your Mirror", a Velvets song. We played this four-bar intro at least four times, round and round. Nico just sat there staring at the audience. We carried on playing, round and round. Eventually she turned to us and she shouted, "What's this song called?" She'd only been singing it for twenty years! Basically, she was bored out of her head on methadone and beer. She started to enjoy any kind of diversion. It got a bit pathetic really. Jim Young and the "old band" used to squirt water pistols at her when she did her solo spot with the harmonium – that was generally the best bit of the evening, to tell the truth.'

Martin added: 'We'd just played in Athens which had gone really well, and Nico was full of herself. We went straight on to a little club in Edinburgh. Nothing went right. The sound was awful. Nico decided to put on a bit of a show about it. She picked up a chair and started swinging it round and shouting that the sound engineer was sabotaging her gig. She could see the audience was loving it – they were seeing the actress in Nico – so she started to throw chairs around, "You idiot, you've ruined the gig . . ." The next night we played Glasgow. She started doing it again, the drama with the chair and the swearing, for no reason at all. I'll never forget the wink she gave us before she threw the chairs. "Why do you make me do shit like this, Alan?!" It was all a sham because she was bored singing.'

Geoff Muir, one of her tour managers, had a different impression: 'She never had the idea she was putting on a show. She was incapable of thinking, "I've come to entertain them." She saw it like this – these people wandered into her room, and if she wanted to say, "I'm going off for a smoke," that was alright because it was her room. Sometimes, in private, she'd say, "I hope it will be good tonight," but you didn't know whether she meant the gig or the smack! It was no good trying to plan the gig with Nico, or rehearse something different. You just had to work out the basics and go for it every night. There were little things in each song that were regular, but everything had to be as loose as possible because Nico went her own sweet way.'

'She was touring so much (and she was over 40 years old) that nobody should be surprised if a little boredom crept into her performance,' Dick Harrison observed. 'Martin and I were always asking to rehearse more, but it wasn't encouraged by the management. I think that's why she was fed up, too. There was too little musically to get involved in because we were scratching the surface night after night.' To make matters worse, the tours weren't planned with a map of Europe in mind. On one trip up and down Germany, the van seating Nico and the band crossed Frankfurt every day but they never played there. The schedule for a tour in 1986 was typical:

30 Nov Zürich	11 Dec Frankfurt
1 Dec Basel	12 Dec Düsseldorf
3 Dec Geneva	13 Dec Hamburg
4 Dec Turin	14 Dec Hanover
5 Dec Milan	15 Dec Berlin
7 Dec Nuremberg	17 Dec Utrecht
8 Dec Saarbrucken	18 Dec Tilburg
9 Dec Stuttgart	19 Dec Haarlem
10 Dec Munich	

Nico didn't like her bands at all. In her notes she grumbled, 'Doesn't Eric Ransom [sic] look great, but, frankly, he can't play . . . Should I ask Jim Young again to go on tour with me, he is such a Prima Donna. He likes to be me. But he can't be me. He can't sing . . . The band should adapt themselves to my singing not the other way around. I don't know who the hell they think they are . . . My management doesn't do me justice at all . . . The end of the month my tour is starting again, the mere thought of it is already wearing me out. This time I will not travel with my group, they have to play their damned music nonstop and loud.' She did travel with her group, of course, the sole woman among a posse of northern gentlemen. 'They are so immature. They keep falling for these little girls. I won't have these groupies backstage because they are too stupid. I like the new boys . . . They follow me around, write me letters, they are very beautiful boys, but, of course, I'm not interested. It's a solitary life,' she lied.

Martin Hennin remembered the nightly parade of Nico-teens: 'There were a lot of look-alikes, or "image-alikes" who saw her as a dark gothic figure. They were a lot of drips, really. I had people that ended up writing to me as a way of getting in touch with Nico, and you'd get these awful poems and phone calls in the middle of the night. There was one guy phoned me from Italy about 4 a.m., asking about a postcard he'd seen with a bizarre poem on it that I'd thrown in the bin. We were just musicians doing a gig, but they saw us as a secret society. Nico wouldn't talk to them – in a way, you can't blame her. She hated seeing girls flirting with us, she never liked them around.' Nico told a journalist: 'These kids look to me as role model. What kind of role model can I be? I can only be a role model to people that are already my age. And they don't want to know. Why would they give up their secure lives to take an adventure into the unknown? To a different city every night? For a life on the road? Not for the money, certainly!' Unlike Nico.

THEY HAD TO GET NICO off heroin. If addiction to the drug was not self-destructive, the economics of it certainly were. She had toured the USA with one of the Wise bands in 1980 and it was a disaster from start to finish. She had insisted on heroin when the best thing available was methadone. They lost money hand over fist to meet her craving, and she was still paying off the debts after she returned to Britain. To make matters worse, she nearly killed herself from a filthy injection and ended up in hospital. 'She terrorised the other women in the ward by dictating the TV programmes they could watch,' claimed Wise. 'She told me "The woman in the next bed to me has three children, the other woman over there was a musician, and the third woman sleeps with a tiger. She sleeps with a tiger – or am I dreaming?" '

Alan Wise took her down to a private doctor on Harley Street (he would often spend his own money on her in this way). 'I'd been to the licensing place for addicts and they recommended Dr Anne Dally, well known for her mature and *pragmatic* attitude to dependency. Addicts were supposed to go on a reduction programme of the heroin substitute methadone. Many doctors had this naive idea that you could cure every heroin addict by putting them on something like a diet! Dr Dally declined to put her on a reductive programme, but instead saw the wisdom of a maintenance programme of methadone. She gave Nico a formal letter which allowed her to apply for a licence.' The licence didn't entitle her to take the methadone out of the country but she could use it at Customs sheds to declare the drug coming in and leaving. The Customs officers were compliant because methadone was considered a *cure* for heroin addiction. In fact it was just like taking heroin in another form, a very boring form, as Nico often took pains to point out.

'When Nico and I moved back to Manchester again around 1983,' continued Wise, 'she registered as an outpatient at the local nuthouse, the Prestwich Hospital. She'd go there and queue up for her methadone pills or the sugared-up liquid version they doled out. I was with her there one day in the queue. A poor-looking guy came up to her, wizened, wretched, a junkie. He stared at her and said, "You. You. Everything that I am now is because of you." I thought he was going to belt her. Instead, he offered her his last bit of methadone!' Nico took all the methadone that was going but mainlined heroin when she could get it. She would use other members of the touring entourage to help her behind the boss's back. Wise retaliated by picking them off one by one. She nevertheless made strides to curb her dependency, and Wise became rather proud of his student in the art of abstinence. He invited her round to his parents' house for Christmas dinner in 1983. She arrived late. The turkey was burned. 'I'm sorry I'm late,' she apologised as she strutted in, 'but I couldn't find a vein.'

She started to ride a bicycle round Prestwich Village, a Jewish suburb in the north of Manchester. She would ride it from 22 Prestwich Park Road South to the Forester's Arms to play pool, which she did badly. Her days were otherwise spent asleep, watching the TV soaps and old films (it's claimed she was a fan of George Formby) or writing. When they moved down to London in 1985, she rode her bike around Brixton, where she unwisely shared a flat with another of Wise's acts, John Cooper Clarke, 'the punk poet'. If Alan Wise thought that two dogmatic junkies could share the TV and 'cooking' facilities, he was soon disabused. 'You see, Clarkie was off heroin when he joined,' Wise contended. 'CBS had paid £18,000 at a private clinic to get him and his girlfriend off the stuff. It worked, too, for a few days.' Wise put it about that Nico and Clarke were lovers ('yes, lovers of heroin'), a dim idea that nevertheless kept Nico's name in the gossip sections of the music papers for some time.

Nico did not like London any more: 'I don't know why I moved. Brixton is *interesting*. But I prefer quiet days and the idea of the countryside. The trees are darker in Manchester. It is more decadent. It reminds me of Berlin after the war. Everything was broken and falling down. That is what happened in Manchester, because of Mrs Thatcher's war against it. The north is socialist, I believe. So am I, then. I like to ride on my bike to see the strange, big houses that the Jews built in Prestwich. I'm glad I have a bike because it is good for my legs and my heart and my fatness. Also, Alan would take me in his car to the countryside. I liked it across the moors of Yorkshire. Or is it the dales? I like the wildness. I could die there very happily – isn't that what you say in England?' Quite.

During 1984 Nico had escaped England to live for some months in New York. She had taken money from Illuminated Records to write an LP, but couldn't manage it. She kept the money, though. She hung around the Squat Theater, a radical workshop from the

Seventies close by the Chelsea Hotel that had bloomed into a major institution. She had friends there that had looked after her many times when she was low or broke. Ari was there too, and he had found work making photographic backdrops for sets ('and doing a lot of coke and smoking bush'). 'I saw Nico for the last time then,' recalled Viva. 'She came to see me and she was wearing the same sort of clothes she'd worn at Positano – black capes and boots – and she was so depressed. She told me she wanted to make a dish of cauliflower cheese: "Could you get me a cauliflower, do you think?" I had to go across the street to buy her one from the store. She could have done it herself. A five-year-old could have done it herself. She was still the helpless adult kid I'd known all these years. I think she was trying to write some songs. And then she went back to England to sort herself out. Ha!'

Back in England she did kind of sort herself out. She told a journalist then that she didn't feel in exile any more since she had been to Manchester and seen the Yorkshire Moors. 'It's only that and English poetry that keeps me sane,' she declared. 'She'd had this awful trek out of the private hell she'd been in,' reckoned Wise, 'and now with the methadone and the bicycle she felt more alive – funny what it takes, isn't it?' Wise had a surprise for her. He had gained Nico a record deal with Beggars Banquet in London. The company paid off the debt to Illuminated, and she was now free of obligations to Aura. She'd already known Peter Murphy, the singer from Bauhaus who were signed to Beggars, and she sang a version of 'I'm Waiting for the Man' with them for a Beggars Banquet single. Now she had the chance to record her own LP. 'There was a lot of other stuff floating around that I'd organised to get a bit of money in, mainly concert tapes,' claimed Wise. 'They helped to keep the wolf from the door.' Most notorious of these was *Nico – Live Behind the Iron Curtain* which was recorded in Rotterdam ('Yes, but it was the same set she took with her to Hungary, Czechoslovakia and Poland') and for which they were paid £4,000. Less notorious, but certainly the best in quality, was *Nico in Tokyo*, which was not taped off the sound desk but recorded from a mobile studio. She would receive fulsome reviews from these tapes in *Sounds*, *Record Mirror*, *New Musical Express* and the *Melody Maker*, probably because they seemed so 'underground':

> Her lost-in-the-cloisters overtones, the sturm-und-drang wail from the catacombs, plus that harmonium, a great wash of aural ennui . . .

a bleak erotic mystery . . .

her voice like some fragile lifeline through an inexpressible, plague-ridden past . . .

What a voice! Extraordinary is hardly the word for it. A voice born in the depths, raised in the dark, cavernous, echoing the tragedy of generations . . .

To beat these accolades with a studio album would take some doing. Alan Wise acted boldly: 'We got John Cale over as producer for a fee and a percentage. Nico tried to get some songs ready, but it really was hard for her to concentrate. She managed five for the LP, a couple of new ones and some old unrecorded stuff. Jim Young and Graham Dids played the arrangements, then Jim went and wrote a little book [*Songs They Never Play on the Radio*] about the experience. It was curious to see Cale with Nico. He bullied her. They'd sit in the Brixton flat watching the TV and she'd say, "John, turn it down." He'd turn it up. "Why are you teasing me?" And he'd suddenly jump on her back, shouting, "And it's Nico coming round the bend, it's Nico on the final stretch, Nico by a nose . . ." It was the oddest thing to see.'

In the Shoreditch studio Cale wouldn't let her smoke, which drove her crazy because by now she was chain-smoking Marlboros. When she was trying to sing her songs, he'd say to her, 'You're deaf in one ear and you're tone-deaf in the other. Why d'ya bother?' He galvanised her, to fire the spark he knew she had once had and had now mislaid. It was their fourth album together as composer and producer, and they had both tired of the game. Wise was happy to see Nico creating something, and Nico was happy to see her picture in the shops once again. 'The album came in on time and on budget,' Wise claimed. 'It did OK, nothing special. It was no great shakes, it wasn't bad, but it was to be Nico's last studio LP, and she should have done better songs. She considered it a new start, but certainly a starting point, not the end, not to say *The End*.'

It's stimulating to see now that the reviews for the 'Corsican' *Drama of Exile* outclass those for her final *Camera Obscura*. 'A tiny miracle . . . The album sounds like it cost a million dollars, when it obviously didn't,' wrote the reviewer of *Sounds*, while the *New Musical Express* considered *Drama of Exile* 'probably the most accessible of her romantic tales of gloom . . . The songs, as ever, are about a kind of tragic individual splendor, failure coupled with fame, or the romantic self-destruction of the drug addict.' The rock arrangements gave her dark songs a bright veneer, and hid the fact that a song like 'Genghis Khan' was a dull reworking of 'Janitor of Lunacy'. The song that worked least well was the intriguing 'Henry Hudson':

> White light lays above
> Henry Hudson's river bank
> And you will see a lady standing
> Stealing past a happy ending.

Its melody was phrased in sixes, but the crude arrangement tried to force it into four-square box. The song that worked best was '60/40' (the number of a cell door) which takes a disciplined melody of Lou Reed simplicity:

> New York Lower East Side fame
> In a golden circle game
> New York Lower East Side frame.

Camera Obscura, on the other hand, was routine in both its songs and its overdrawn arrangements. There was one song, mischievously classed as a Nico composition, that she had known as a girl in Berlin in a recording made in 1952 by Hildegard Knef, the Fifties film star she said she couldn't bear because her mother hadn't liked her. It is a Thirties song with a beautiful melody, 'Das Lied vom einsamen Mädchen' ('The Song of the Lonely Girl') and it tells of a girl with blonde hair who is taken into heaven to end her loneliness:

> weil sie einsam war
> und so blond ihr Haar
> und ihr Herz so tot wie Stein
> dann rief er 'armes Kind, komm
> sollst nie mehr einsam sein.'

> *because she was lonely*
> *and so blonde her hair*
> *and her heart as dead as stone*
> *he called, 'poor child, come*
> *you'll never be lonely again.'*

She placed next to it 'My Funny Valentine', a song from her Blue Angel days, and recorded it in Chet Baker's key of C minor, the lowest she ever sang (in both songs she sounds remarkably like Hildegard Knef). It has a cute lyric about character and ugliness:

> Your looks are laughable,
> Unphotographable,
> But you're my favourite work of art.

In finding material to fill her album, she had followed Paul Morrissey's advice to sing other people's songs, just like she'd done when starting out. She discovered in doing so that her own songs would have to be as good. She decided to start again. She borrowed some tapes of the baritone singer Paul Hillier, a concert artist who specialised in mediaeval songs. She fell in love with the simplicity and the form of the songs, their spontaneity and the Arabic embellishments. 'The songs are so beautiful, and the decorations like Arab music. They will be an inspiration.' Where the words would come from was another matter.

NICO WANTED to rebuild her life, she maintained. 'Aesthetic life has been reduced to ashes.' She started with a bank account. In 1987 she opened one for the first time in her life: 'Opening a new bank account has been easier than I thought . . . The convenience is staggering.' She oiled her bike and read her horoscope whenever she came across the predictions of Patric Walker ('it is good for reference') in the London *Evening Standard* and the *Manchester Evening News*. She asked to move her concerts away from clubs and into theatres. She especially asked this once she had done one of the worst concerts of her life at The Fridge in Brixton as a memorial to Andy Warhol, who had died on 22 February. She came on two hours late, thanks to inept support acts, and started her tribute with the information that she hadn't sung a note in two months and 'we didn't even have a soundcheck'. When she introduced 'The End' as 'Jim's favourite song', someone shouted out, 'Wrong fucking corpse.'

The life she wanted to rebuild most of all was that of her son. Nico wanted to help Ari overcome the emotional problems she had increasingly noticed: 'I am responsible for them. I must lay the ghost.' She did not know how strong the ghost had grown. Ari used to go on holiday as a child with Anne-Marie Quazza, the Chanel model, and her family, and now they took the adult Ari on holiday again to Morocco. 'A friend of my children invited him. He went to the beach with them but after one day he disappeared. Six days later they came to me for help – they'd been searching all that time. We found him and I can't tell you what had happened. He was terrible, a mess, a mental destruction. One day soon after, my younger son went to the bathroom when Ari ran out with a large knife, "I'm going to kill myself." He was taken to a psychiatric hospital. It was a tragedy.' Ari recalls: 'I spent two months in a mental hospital, and that was the beginning of the Inferno, because, since then, I've been in psychiatric hospitals so many times that I don't remember how many times, how many pills, electroshock . . . I have been in a coma, I had a brain lesion . . .'

Nico went to Paris to see Ari's supervisor, Dr Dahoud ('He must have thought that you have a funny mother, asking him for methadone'). She agreed to undergo a session of psychoanalysis as Ari's mother, which *she* found to be a waste of time. Yet the guilt gnawed at her and she could only think that Ari would be better living with her in eternally autumnal Prestwich, with the good mother who gave him to her mad mother, brought him a present of a Camembert, who watched him drinking liquor dregs and developing jaundice then sent him packing, who forgot about him, wrote suicide notes to him, chased away his girlfriends, brawled and scrapped with him, shared needles and fine and bad heroin with him ('promises that I can't keep and feeling like a traitor, an unloyal mother'). Dr Dahoud did not think the idea of Ari leaving Paris was sound. Ari left anyway. Prestwich, after all, had its own hospital.

Nico continued her 60/40 life as a Prestwich recluse and a touring terrorist singer. To supplement her earnings she accepted a few hundred pounds to sing with Marc Almond on 'a dreadful song by an idiotic man'. She was photographed with him playing pool. Nico was convinced she could write better things herself, but she couldn't imagine how to write her songs now her methadone dreams were so dreary. Nico felt she had lost the grasp of composing. 'I still think that I am rather apt to taking heroin again,' she noted. 'My mind does not function like it should, but as soon as a change of scenery will refresh my imagination [sic]. If only time would stand still. The more it moves forward the more I will turn the clock backwards.'

Lutz Ulbrich had contacted her from Berlin. The Ashra guitarist had organised a festival at the Berlin Planetarium called *Fata Morgana*. He commissioned Nico to compose a sequence of through-composed songs and to perform them. Instead of going through Wise this time, Nico booked the musicians herself – Henry Laycock, Jim Young, Graham Dids. When it came to the event in June 1988, she'd written next to nothing. One song comprised two lines:

> I, I will be seven
> When we meet in heaven.

The musicians put everything together as best they could, and created something passable for the occasion. A tape of the concert was spliced with some early 1980s sessions and exploitatively sold to an innocent public under the title *Hanging Gardens* by a Dutch company in 1990. 'I went to the concert and met Christa backstage in the interval,' recounted Aunt Helma. 'She was rolling a cigarette and said, "I need this for the second half." I asked her what was in the cigarette. She replied, "Oh, Tante Helma, don't be so naive." I cried a little, she could see my tears. Then she gave me a beautiful ring that she had once bought in Spain for her mother – a surreal butterfly design. Christa put the ring on my finger and said, "From now on this is yours." I wear it to this day. In retrospect I can say it was like a final gift, I don't know. It was as though fate was allowing me to see her a last time.' The last song she sang was her song to Jim Morrison about the moment she saw him before his death.

Nico returned to Manchester to confront Alan Wise, who was angry that she'd arranged a concert privately. 'Oh, please don't be angry with me, Alan. I needed the money so that I can go to Ibiza to work on some new songs and be with Ari.' Nico and Ari flew to Ibiza, where Nico had rented a cottage up in the hills behind Ibiza town. 'Late one morning, on 17 July, my mother told me that she had to go into town to buy some marijuana,' said Ari. 'She sat at the mirror and wound a black scarf around her head. My mother stared at the mirror and took great care to wind the scarf properly. She rode down the hill on her bicycle. "I won't be long." By the time she left it was the start of the afternoon, say 1 p.m., and the hottest day of the year, 35 degrees centigrade.'

A taxi driver found her slumped on the side of the steep road down Figueretas hill, her bicycle on the dusty ground nearby. The wheels had stopped spinning. He settled her in the back of his car and sped to the nearest hospital. The cab driver was obliged to call at four hospitals before he could unload. At the first two Nico was ranked a foreigner, and not admissible. At the third she wasn't considered an emergency – she looked like an old beatnik, possibly too long in the sun. After the driver nagged, the fourth hospital admitted her. She was conscious but couldn't speak. Nico saw the hospital entrance and tried to say 'No, no.' They put her on a trolley and the nurse diagnosed sunstroke; a doctor examined her the next morning. She had had a cerebral haemorrhage. The doctor thought he could save her with injections, but he couldn't find a vein. Nico died officially at 8 p.m. on 18 July 1988.

Lutz Ulbrich, Alan Wise and Ulrich Wolff made the funeral arrangements. They tried to get Nico cremated in Ibiza, but this was not possible, they were told, as she was a foreigner. The undertakers placed her body in a crate for shipping to Barcelona, where she could be cremated – but this was not possible, they were told in Barcelona, there's a two-week waiting list. The crate was finally flown to Berlin, where the body was burned and her ashes placed in an urn. On 6 August a memorial service was held at the Protestant church in Holmfirth, Yorkshire, where she once told Alan Wise she wished to be buried. On 16 August the urn of her ashes was buried in the grave of her mother. Nico's prediction had come true: 'If I go to my mother's grave I will never leave it.'

'THE FINAL WORDS she printed on my typewriter were *The last days of a singer*,' noted Ari, 'and I had the feeling she was preparing for death. In three months she would have been 50. She spent nearly an hour winding the black headscarf around her head, staring at herself in the mirror. I did not know for two days what had happened to her. The authorities didn't care. They thought she was just an old beatnik.'

'I think Ari and the family have a tendency to romanticise her death,' reflected Wise. 'She didn't consider she was about to die. Nico had a lot to live for – she'd survived a living hell, she was starting to reduce her methadone and I believe that she would have discarded it finally in five years' time. She had more songs she wanted to compose, and she had Ari to care for. Frankly, you could take any of her lyrics from the past twenty years, thirty-eight songs in all, and point out a premonition of death. In truth her death was a tragic blunder. Three of the hospitals wouldn't have anything to do with her because she looked to them like a beatnik, simple as that. She lived the bohemian life and died because of it. Then at the fourth hospital there was no doctor on duty when she arrived and the nurse misdiagnosed it as sunstroke; the doctor who diagnosed the haemorrhage told me that later. By the time he got round to her the next morning, a lot of blood had leaked into her brain. I'm appalled to say that she had a slow death. If you want a moral, the only moral you can drag out of Nico's life is this: *Don't get ill in Spain.* Her death's nothing less than an indictment of the Spanish health system.'

'It was those awful clothes killed her,' suggested Paul Morrissey. 'The most beautiful woman in the world wanted to look ugly and she wore those horrible black clothes to hide herself. There she was, on the hottest day of the year, cycling in those heavy black clothes with a black headscarf tied around her – I would say she tempted fate if I didn't know better than to say it.' Viva added: 'To survive all those years and then fall off a bike to your death seems a little cruel. When I heard the story I said, "I bet she was stoned." She outlived most of the others – Edie, Jim Morrison, Tim Hardin, a lot of the Factory people, even Andy himself. It's kind of hopeful news for junkies. She's their Saint Nico now.'

'Was it an accident or was she killed?' asked one of the Parisians, rather too avid for intrigue. 'It's ironic, given her inclination for romance, that her death was already mythic,' observed Victor Brox. 'Her final story mirrors that of Bessie Smith. The Empress of the Blues was spurned by the hospitals after a car accident because she was "a nigger". She also died because of medical bigotry and neglect. For outsiders like Bessie Smith and Nico, it seems that things never change.'

'In the end,' suggested Nico Papatakis, 'you can only think back on this breathtaking woman, and say, "She deserved better." But what about her son? What will happen to him?'

Ari concluded his story: 'When my mother died, Alan Wise took me to the probate registry in order to inherit the royalties (and the debts). When I got my mum's royalties for the first time I spent the money on smack. I was hooked. I was taking a gram a day. So I called my psychiatric doctor in Paris and I spent two weeks in the hospital. I got off heroin. Then I got a cheque from The Velvet Underground and bought a ticket for Raroïa, Tahiti. I was taking Valium, pot and beer and I got beaten up, then arrested and someone tried to kill me with a harpoon.

'Back in New York I went out of my mind. I spent winter out on the streets; rescuers found me in the River Hudson. Then on Staten Island I fell down a chute, fifteen metres, in an old flour mill. I now have steel pins in my feet. Workmen found me and said, "Are you crazy?!" and maybe I was – I had no money, no passport, nothing. Someone called the cops who took me to a psychiatric hospital. They gave me five brain electric shocks. A friend got me out and took me back to Paris. I had two months of treatment in psychiatric hospitals there and then in the south of France. Now I'm trying to get back into myself. I'm not yet strong enough, but one day, when I am, I will confront my father and I will do it for the sake of my mother.'

Nico – The Covergirl Queen, Nico – Mr Warhol's silent Super-star, Nico – Miss Pop 1966, Nico – the Dietrich of the velvet underground, Nico – The Moon Goddess, Nico – the Garbo of Punk, Nico – The Last Bohemian, Nico – As Miserable as Ever, Nico the lover of numbers would have wanted to die at the age of 196 not 49, 14×14, not 7×7. She had contemplated death many times, whether in the childhood cemetery or by the railway tracks of Lübbenau, through her friends, through her veins, and in her exceptional songs. She may have thought of suicide but she was pleased to tell the press, 'I am a survivor.' If the curve of her life had dipped off the chart by 1979, it was visible and rising again when she died a decade later. She had once told a journalist that Nico might die, 'but I could live on as someone else'. She meant Christa. Close to her death, she told Alan Wise that she was fed up with being Nico, and she wondered if it would be possible to perform in future as Christa Päffgen. 'Then I won't have to lie so much.'

Nico was a born liar. She lied in part to save herself but uppermost to shield her mad mother and her wild son. 'I didn't want them to be lost in the land, like me,' she alleged. Nico may have been a born liar, but not a true one.

> Yet pull not down my palace towers, that are
> So lightly, beautifully built:
> Perchance I may return with others there
> When I have purged my guilt.
>
> (from 'The Palace of Art',
> ALFRED TENNYSON, 1836)

Discography and Filmography

DISCOGRAPHY

First left-hand column numbers the songs in Nico's repertoire. Second column numbers Nico's compositions, though not necessarily in chronological order (this cannot currently be determined). Composers and lyricists of the other songs are named in the right-hand column.

The release date and recording company refer to the original pressing. Subsequent pressings, including re-releases on CD, may have been the responsibility of succeeding companies, which may vary in different countries.

Studio LPs

I The Velvet Underground & Nico   March 1967: Verve

1	Femme Fatale	(Lou Reed)
2	All Tomorrow's Parties	(Lou Reed)
3	I'll Be Your Mirror	(Lou Reed)

II Chelsea Girl   July 1968: Verve

4	The Fairest of the Seasons	(Copeland/Browne)
5	These Days	(Jackson Browne)
6	Little Sister	(Cale/Reed)
7	Winter Song	(John Cale)
8	It Was a Pleasure Then	(Nico/Cale/Reed)
9	Chelsea Girls	(Reed/Morrison)
10	I'll Keep It with Mine	(Bob Dylan)
11	Somewhere There's a Feather	(Jackson Browne)

Nico

42	27	Henry Hudson	
43		I'm Waiting for the Man	(Lou Reed)
44	28	Sixty Forty	
45	29	The Sphinx	
46	30	Orly Flight	
47		Heroes	(Bowie/Eno)

VII Camera Obscura   August 1985: Beggars Banquet

48	31	Tananore	
49	32	Win A Few	
50		My Funny Valentine	(Rodgers/Hart)
51		Das Lied vom einsamen Mädchen	(Heymann/Gilbert)
52	33	Fearfully in Danger	
53	34	My Heart Is Empty	
54	35	Into the Arena	

Singles

55		I'm Not Sayin'	(Gordon Lightfoot)
			September 1965: Immediate
56		The Last Mile	(Oldham/Page) [re-released May 1982]
		[Sunday Morning]	March 1967: Verve
		Femme Fatale	
		All Tomorrow's Parties	June 1967: Verve
		I'll Be Your Mirror	
57	36	Vegas	1981: Flicknife
58	37	Saeta	
59	38	Procession	1982: One over Two
		All Tomorrow's Parties	
		Secret Side	
		Femme Fatale	
		Heroes	June 1983: Aura
		One More Chance	
		My Funny Valentine	June 1985: Beggars Banquet
		My Heart Is Empty	
		I'm Waiting for the Man	1985: Aura
		Purple Lips	

Concert LPs

I ACNE Concert, 1 June 1974   June 1974: Island

II Nico en personne en Europe   1983: One over Two
       Frozen Warnings
       Saeta
       Purple Lips
       These Days
       I'll Keep It with Mine
       Heroes
       Procession
       60/40
       The Sphinx
       Femme Fatale
       I'm Waiting For My Man [sic]
       Orly Flight

III Nico: Live in Denmark   1983: VU Records
       Saeta
       Vegas
       Sixty Forty
       Valley of the Kings
       Janitor of Lunacy
       I'll Keep It with Mine
       Femme Fatale
       I'm Waiting For My Man [sic]
       Heroes

IV Do or Die   1983: Reach Out International
       Janitor of Lunacy
       Saeta
       All Tomorrow's Parties
       No One Is There
       Femme Fatale
       The End

V The Blue Angel   August 1985: Aura
       Femme Fatale
       All Tomorrow's Parties
       Heroes

Waiting for the Man
The End
I'll Keep It with Mine
Chelsea Girls

VI Nico: Behind the Iron Curtain April 1986: Castle

All Saint's Night from a Polish Motorway
One More Chance
Frozen Warnings
The song of the lonely girl [Das Lied vom einsamen Mädchen]
Win a Few
König
Purple Lips
All Tomorrow's Parties
Fearfully in Danger
The End
My Funny Valentine
60/40
Tananori
Janitor of Lunacy
My Heart Is Empty
Femme Fatale

VII Live Heroes 1986: Performance Records (USA)

Heroes
Procession
My Funny Valentine
All Tomorrow's Parties
Secret Side
Femme Fatale
The End

VIII Nico: Live in Tokyo February 1987: Castle

My Heart Is Empty
Purple Lips
Tananore
Janitor of Lunacy
You Forget to Answer
60/40
My Funny Valentine

Nico

All Tomorrow's Parties
Das Lied Einsanen Mädchens [sic]
Femme Fatale
The End

IX Nico: The Peel Sessions   November 1988: Strange Fruit/BBC
Secret Side
No One Is There
Janitor of Lunacy
Frozen Warnings

X Nico at the Chelsea Town Hall   August 1992: Great Expectations
(recorded June 1986)
Tananore
One More Chance
Procession
My Heart Is Empty
Janitor of Lunacy
The Sphinx
You Forget To Answer
Fearfully In Danger
60/40
All Tomorrow's Parties
Purple Lips
Femme Fatale
Saeta
The End

Other Recordings

I Hanging Gardens   1990: Restless Records (Netherlands)
Hanging Gardens
The Sound
You Forget to Answer
Vegas
I'm Waiting for the Man
Your Voice
Your Word Against Mine
I Will Be Seven
The Line [actually Saeta]

II Kevin Ayers: The Confessions of Dr Dream 1974: Island
   Irreversible Neural Damage

III Bauhaus: Beggars Banquet
   I'm Waiting For The Man [single]

IV Marc Almond: The Stars We Are 1988: Parlophone
   Your Kisses Burn

FILMOGRAPHY

The release date refers to the country of origin only.

1 La Dolce Vita (Italy, 1960)
   Dir: Federico Fellini
      35 mm, black and white; 190 mins.

2 Strip-Tease (France, 1963)
   Dir: Jacques Poitrenaud
      35 mm, black and white; 95 mins.

3 The Closet (USA, 1965)
   Dir: Andy Warhol
      16 mm, black and white; 70 mins.

4 The Velvet Underground and Nico (USA, 1966)
   Dir: Warhol/Morrissey
      16 mm, black and white; 70 mins.

5 The Chelsea Girls (USA, 1966)
   Dir: Warhol/Morrissey
      16 mm, black and white/clr; 195 mins.

6 Imitation of Christ (****) (USA, 1967)
   Dir: Warhol/Morrissey
      16 mm, colour; 8 hours.

7 Sausolito (****) (USA, 1967)
   Dir: Warhol/Morrissey
      16 mm, colour; 30 mins.

8 **High Ashbury (****) (USA, 1967)**
   Dir: Warhol/Morrissey
      16 mm, colour; 30 mins.

9 **Nico–Katrina (****) (USA, 1967)**
   Dir: Warhol/Morrissey
      16 mm, colour; 30 mins.

10 **I, a Man (USA, 1967)**
   Dir: Warhol/Morrissey
      16 mm, black and white; 100 mins.

11 **La Cicatrice intérieure (France, 1970/1972)**
   Dir: Philippe Garrel
      35 mm, colour; 60 mins.

12 **Athanor (France, 1973)**
   Dir: Philippe Garrel
      35 mm, colour, silent; 20 mins.

13 **Les Hautes Solitudes (France, 1974)**
   Dir: Philippe Garrel
      35 mm, black and white, silent; 75 mins.

14 **Un Ange Passe (France, 1975)**
   Dir: Philippe Garrel
      35 mm, black and white; 80 mins.

15 **Le Berceau de Cristal (France, 1976)**
   Dir: Philippe Garrel
      35 mm, colour; 80 mins.

16 **Voyage au jardin des morts (France, 1977)**
   Dir: Philippe Garrel
      35 mm, colour; 55 mins.

17 **Le Bleu des Origines (France, 1978)**
   Dir: Philippe Garrel
      35 mm, black and white, silent; 50 mins.

18 Ballhaus Barmbek: Let's Kiss and Say Goodbye
     (Germany, 1988)
     Dir: Christel Buschmann
       35 mm, colour; 80 mins.

(****): Separately screened sections of the '24-hour movie' titled
****, otherwise known as FOUR STARS.

Sources

Translations from the German were made by Natascha Scharmberg, from the French by the author and Ben Goold.

Baudrillard, Jean: *Seduction*. Macmillan, London, 1990 (French: Ed. Galilée, Paris, 1979).

Chapter 1
Hirszowicz, Lukasz: *The Third Reich and the Arab Past*. Routledge, London, 1966 (orig. Warsaw, 1963).

Rauschning, Herman: *Die Revolution des Nihilismus*. Europa Verlag, Zürich, 1938 (English: trans EW Dickes, Windmill Press, Surrey, 1939).

Grunberger, Richard: *A Social History of the Third Reich*. Wiedenfeld & Nicolson, London, 1971.

Worch, Thomas: *Spree Wald*. Statbuch Verlag, Germany, 1991.

Brauereien und Malzereien in Europa. Happenstedt, Germany, 1976.

Niesieckiego, Wolnosci (ed): *Korona Polska*, Lwow, Poland, 1740.

Grosser Atlas zum II Weltkrieg, vol 3. Südwestverlag, Munich, 1975.

Chapter 2
Gruber, Frank & Richter, Gerhard: *Die Grunderjahre der Bundesrepublik 1946–1955*.

The Annual Register (Allied Occupation) vol 189. Longmans, London, 1947.

Berger, Joachim: *Berlin, freihietlich & rebellisch*. Goebel Verlag, Berlin (1991?).

Westdeutschlands Weg zur Bundesrepublik 1945–1949. Verlag CH Beck, Munich, Germany, 1976.

Becker, Howard: *German Youth, Bound or Free?* Kegan, Paul, Trench, Trubner & Co., London, 1946.

Zink, Harold: *The United States in Germany, 1944–1955*. D. Van Nostrand Co., Princeton, USA, 1974.

Obituary of Zara Leander, *The Times* (London) 8.7.81.

Chapter 3

Sieff, Jeanloup: *Sieff photographs 1950–1990*, Contrejour, 1990.

Kezich, Tullio: *La dolce vita di Federico Fellini* (film transcript). Cappelli, Rome, 1960.

Maywald, Wilhelm: *Die Splitter des Spiegels*. Schirmer/Mosel, Munich, 1985.

Hemingway, Ernest: *A Moveable Feast*. Grafton, London, 1966.

Chapter 4

Strasberg, Lee: *A Drama of Passion – the development of the Method*. Bloomsbury Press, London, 1988.

Miller, Arthur: *Timebends – a Life*. Minerva, USA, 1987.

Shelton, Robert: *No Direction Home* (Dylan biography). Hodder & Stoughton, London, 1980.

Heylin, C: *Dylan, Behind the Shades*. Viking, London, 1991.

Chapter 5

Booker, Christopher: *The Neophiliacs – a study in the revolution on English life in the Fifties and Sixties*. Collins, London, 1969.

Hewison, Robert: *Too Much*. Methuen, London, 1986.

Marshall, Cherry: *The Cat-Walk*. Hutchinson, London, 1978.

Aftel, Mandy: *Death of a Rolling Stone*. Sidgwick & Jackson, London, 1982.

Booth, Stanley: *The True Adventures of The Rolling Stones*. Heinemann, London, 1985.

Baez, Joan: *And a Voice to Sing With*. Summit (USA), 1987.

Chapter 6
Warhol, Andy, with Pat Hackett: *Popism – The Warhol 60s*. Harcourt Brace Jovanovich, New York, 1980.

Warhol, Andy, with Gerard Malanga: *Screen Tests: A Diary*. Kulchur Press, New York, 1967.

Ultra Violet: *Famous For 15 Minutes – My Years with Andy Warhol*. Methuen, London, 1989.

Turner, Florence: *At the Chelsea*. Harvest/HBJ, New York, 1987.

Stein, Jean, and Plimpton, George: *Edie – An American Biography*. Knopf, New York, 1982.

Reed, Lou: *Between Thought and Expression – selected lyrics of Lou Reed*. Viking, London, 1992.

Chapter 7
Bockris, Victor: *Warhol*. Penguin, London, 1989.

Manzano, Alberto: *Reinas del Rock Canciones*. Espiral, Spain, 1987.

Chapter 8
What Goes On (editor: MC Kosek), magazine of The Velvet Underground Appreciation Society, Stuart, Florida, USA.

Chapter 9
Albin, Michel: *Jim Morrison au delà des doors*. Paris, 1973.

Densmore, John: *Riders on the Storm*. Bloomsbury Press, London, 1991.

Coplans, John: *Andy Warhol* (with catalogue of films). New York Graphic Society, New York, 1970.
Jones, Dylan: *Dark Star*. Bloomsbury, London, 1991.

Chapter 10
Dorman, L, and Rawlins, C: *Leonard Cohen, prophet of the heart*. Omnibus Press, London, 1990.
Morrison, Jim: *Wilderness, the lost writings of Jim Morrison*. Villard Books, New York, 1988.
Berkeley BARB (USA), interview conducted by Richard A. Ogar, 1.9.67.

Chapter 11
Solanas, Valerie: *The SCUM Manifesto*. Phoenix Press, London, 1991.

Chapter 12
Courant, Gerard: *Philippe Garrel* (retrospective programme, pamphlet). Studio 43, Paris, 1983.

Chapter 13
Giacomoni, Antoine: *Photographs*, pub. La Sirène, Geneva, 1991.
Adrien, Yves: *NovoVision (Les Confessions d'un Cobaye du Siècle)*. Les Humanoïdes Associés, Paris, 1980.
Pacadis, Alain: *Une Jeune Homme Chic*. Le Sagittaire, Paris, 1978.
Becker, Jillian: *Hitler's Children – the story of the Baader–Meinhof group*. Lippincott & Co., USA, 1977.
Raubell, R: *Die Baader-Meinhof-Gruppe*. De Gruyte, Berlin, 1973.

Chapter 14
Obituaries: *The Times* (London) 22.7.88, *Guardian* 23.7.88,
Chicago Tribune 23.7.88, *Los Angeles Times* 23.7.88, *New
York Times* 23.7.88, *Libération* (Paris) 23.7.88, *die tages*
(Berlin) 23.7.88, *Independent* (London) 25.7.88, *Bild*
(Germany) 27.7.88, *Variety* (USA) 27.7.88, *Melody Maker*
30.7.88, *New Musical Express* 30.7.88, *Billboard* 6.8.88,
Rolling Stone 8.8.88, *Village Voice* 16.8.88, *Creem* (USA)
Oct 1988; *Das Orchester* (Germany) Oct 1988, *Downbeat*
(USA) 12.11.88, *Spin* Dec 1988.

Other
Magazines, other than those specifically cited in text:
Melody Maker 3.10.87, 21.3.87, 24.5.86, 17.8.85, 2.11.85,
14.9.85, 27.7.85, 23.3.85, 26.1.85, 28.5.83, 29.1.83,
1.1.83, 25.9.82, 30.1.82, 17.10.81, 12.9.81, 29.8.81,
29.4.78, 21.12.74, 16.11.74, 15.6.74, 25.5.74, 18.9.71,
30.1.71, 23.1.71, 28.3.70, 21.3.70, 27.8.65, 13.8.65,
28.5.65. (*New Musical Express*, corresponding coverage
1965–1988; *Sounds*, equivalent coverage 1980s.)
Creem Nov. 1987, Sep. 1980, May 1975, Dec. 1974; *Variety*
(USA) 15.9.82, 23.7.80, 13.6.79; *Rolling Stone* 15.12.88,
17.8.87, 14.3.85, 12.9.74, 4.2.71; *Crawdaddy* May 1975,
March 1972, Aug. 1968, June 1968, Sep. 1967; *Jazz & Pop*
vol 8, Aug. 1968.
Films & Filming Oct. 1960, Dec. 1963, Feb. 1965, Jun. 1970;
Le Canard Enchainé June 1963; *Fiches du Cinéma* June
1963; *Cinémonde* Dec. 1962; *Le Film Français* June 1963;
Ciné Revue Jan. 1963; *Image et Son* April 1972; *Cinéma*
April 1972.

Lyrics:
'Birds of St Mark's' (pp. 171–2) by Jackson Browne.
Copyright 1970 Open Window Music and Atlantic Music
Corporation, USA. Used by permission.

'Chelsea Girls' published by Sunbury Music Limited, USA, 1967, reproduced by permission of Metal Machine Music, Inc, through Viking Books (Penguin Group, UK), 1992.

'Das Lied vom einsamen Mädchen' published by Meridian, Munich.

'Eulogy to Lenny Bruce' published by T. M. Music, USA, 1968.

'I'll Keep It With Mine' published by Warner Bros, USA © 1965, 1968.

'I'm Not Sayin'' by Gordon Lightfoot, published by Warner Chappell Music Limited and reproduced by permission of International Music Publishers Limited.

'It Was a Pleasure' originally published by Sunbury Music Limited, USA, 1968.

'Janitor of Lunacy' published by Warlock Music Limited.

'The Kids' published by Metal Machine Music, Inc, and reproduced by permission of Viking Books (Penguin Group, UK).

'My Funny Valentine' published by Chappell Music Limited.

'My Only Child' and 'Mütterlein' published by UFO Music.

'Take This Longing' published by Stronger Music, Inc, 1969.

'You Forget to Answer' published by Bee Bee Music.

The author has made every reasonable effort to contact holders of copyright in all quoted material. Any omission of copyright acknowledgement is unintentional, and the publishers will, if notified, correct any such omission in subsequent editions.

Index